Filmmaking

3rd Edition

by Bryan Michael Stoller

for dummies®

A Wiley Brand

Filmmaking For Dummies®, 3rd Edition

Published by: **John Wiley & Sons, Inc.**, 111 River Street, Hoboken, NJ 07030-5774, www.wiley.com

Copyright © 2020 by John Wiley & Sons, Inc., Hoboken, New Jersey

Published simultaneously in Canada

For general information on our other products and services, please contact our Customer Care Department within the U.S. at 877-762-2974, outside the U.S. at 317-572-3993, or fax 317-572-4002. For technical support, please visit https://hub.wiley.com/community/support/dummies.

Wiley publishes in a variety of print and electronic formats and by print-on-demand. Some material included with standard print versions of this book may not be included in e-books or in print-on-demand. If this book refers to media such as a CD or DVD that is not included in the version you purchased, you may download this material at http://booksupport.wiley.com. For more information about Wiley products, visit www.wiley.com.

Library of Congress Control Number: 2019952445

ISBN 978-1-119-61785-3 (pbk); ISBN 978-1-119-61786-0 (ebk); ISBN 978-1-119-61789-1 (ebk)

10 9 8 7 6 5 4 3 2 1

Contents at a Glance

Table of Contents

Introduction

Welcome to the wonderful world of filmmaking — or as many now call it, *moviemaking or digital filmmaking*. Whether you love the escape of watching movies or the excitement, challenge, and magic of making a movie yourself, this book is an informative, entertaining guide to help you realize your dream. For the beginner, this book is your primer and reference guide to making a movie, whether it be an independent film, a short narrative, an insightful documentary, entertaining YouTube video, or just slick home movies. For the seasoned professional, this is a perfect refresher course (with many new ideas and tons of advanced technology) to review before starting your next big flick. My holiday release, *Santa Stole Our Dog*, was distributed by Universal Home Entertainment. Before I signed the contract with the studio, I reviewed the second edition of my book *Filmmaking for Dummies*, which reminded me of some great ideas and techniques and recapped some smart negotiating points when it came to signing contracts.

This book will inspire you to reach for your filmmaking goals — and it will be a great adventure along the way! *Filmmaking For Dummies,* 3rd Edition, comes out of my moviemaking experiences — both my successes and my mistakes — and is bursting with helpful information and secret tips to assist you in making your own successful movie.

This book has been completely updated from the second edition of *Filmmaking For Dummies,* which was written almost 11 years ago. The advancements in technology have really gone further than anyone could imagine. I'm actually writing this introduction from my spaceship quarters right now (okay, maybe not that advanced)! Movie cameras that used physical film stock are almost obsolete (at least in the independent filmmaking world). New technologies have made it affordable for almost anyone to shoot a movie now — even with your smartphone! Dollies, flying drones, and camera-stabilizing systems that used to cost tens of thousands of dollars are now at the disposal of the independent filmmaker for only a few hundred dollars or even less.

The first television show I directed was an episode of *Tales from the Darkside* entitled "The Bitterest Pill." The show was about a crazy inventor who created a pill that gave him total recall. The premise of the episode was that knowledge is power. With *Filmmaking For Dummies,* 3rd Edition, you gain the knowledge and thus the power to make movies. Whether you're a great filmmaker depends on how you apply the information and secrets you'll find in this book. This third edition is jam-packed with all the information, techniques, and advancements in gadgets and software to help make your movie, along with tips and secrets — including how to tell a great story and working with actors — that you need to get started. This book that you hold in your hands (or are viewing on an electronic screen or in a futuristic hologram format) is your prescription for making your own movies — so read it and call your distributor in the morning!

About This Book

I've written this book with over 40 years of hands-on experience (I started young, eager and naïve at the age of 10), so I have the experience and knowledge of everything I talk about in this book through trial and error. I can save you a lot of time, trouble, and money because I've been there before — this book helps make your first time on the set seem more like you've been there before, too.

This book contains valuable information on:

>> Writing or finding a great screenplay

>> Raising financing for your production

>> Budgeting and scheduling your movie

>> Finding and hiring the right actors and crew

>> Choosing the right camera and medium (digital or motion picture film stock)

>> Planning, shooting, and directing your movie

>> Putting your movie together in the editing room

>> Finding a distributor to get your masterpiece in front of an audience

>> Entering (and maybe even winning) film festivals

The new age of filmmaking includes the advent of high definition (HD) digital technology, so throughout this book, all creative elements apply, whether you're shooting with film stock or with a digital camera that records onto digital files. Technically, shooting on film stock or recording to digital files is different, but the methods in creatively constructing a movie remain the same. As an independent filmmaker, digital has become the norm, because shooting on film stock is costly and because with film, the post-production stage is more involved and expensive. These days, it is now looked at as almost archaic to shoot film.

Foolish Assumptions

In writing this book, I made some assumptions about you:

>> You have some knowledge of the Internet and have access to the websites I list. I direct you to some pretty nifty sites to get free downloads, special software deals, and fun stuff to look at. Keep in mind, however, that web addresses can change or become obsolete, so be prepared to find a few that may lead to a black hole in cyberspace.

>> You also like to watch movies and are interested in how they're made so that you can make some of your own, whether feature length, or YouTube shorts. This book can even help you make slick and watchable home movies.

>> You may be a beginner with a consumer digital camera or smartphone, or a seasoned professional who wants to make an independent film.

>> If you don't want to actually make movies, you're a film buff who wants to know what goes on behind the scenes.

This book can't possibly cover every aspect of running a camera and putting together a movie. So if you don't know the difference between a camera's eyepiece and the lens, and which end to look through, pick up other books that are more specific to the technical aspects of filmmaking. You may also want to pick up other *For Dummies* books that complement this one, such as *Digital Video For Dummies*, by Keith Underdahl; *Screenwriting For Dummies*, by Laura Schellhardt; *Breaking into Acting For Dummies* (Garrison and Wang), and *YouTube For Dummies* (all published by Wiley). After you start making your own films, you may need to read these books: *Stress Management For Dummies* (Elkin) and *High Blood Pressure For Dummies* (Rubin). If you do really well, then check out, *Retirement For Dummies!*

Icons Used in This Book

This book uses icons to bring attention to things that you may find helpful or important.

This icon shares tips that can save you a lot of time and trouble.

This icon is a friendly reminder of things that you don't want to forget about when making a movie.

WARNING

This icon makes you aware of things that can negatively impact your movie, so be sure to heed the advice here.

TECHNICAL STUFF

Information that appears beside this icon is interesting, but nonessential. It shares filmmaking esoterica that, as a budding filmmaker or film buff, you'll find interesting but don't need to know. Consider these fun-but-skippable nuggets.

Beyond the Book

In addition to the material in the print or e-book you're reading right now, this product also comes with some access-anywhere goodies on the web. No matter how well you understand filmmaking concepts, you'll likely come across a few questions where you don't have a clue. To get this material, simply go to www.dummies.com and search for "*Filmmaking For Dummies* Cheat Sheet" in the Search box.

Where to Go from Here

Unlike watching a film from beginning to end, you can open this book in the middle and dive right in to making your movie. *Filmmaking For Dummies,* 3rd Edition, is written in a nonlinear format, meaning you can start anywhere and read what you want to know in the order you want to know it. This means that you can start on any chapter in this book and move around from chapter to chapter in no particular order — and still understand how to make a movie. You can even read from back to front if you're so inclined.

1

Getting Started with Filmmaking

I help you put the world of filmmaking into perspective and set you on track for a cinematic adventure.

I introduce you to the different film genres so you can decide what kind of story you want to share with an audience.

I guide you through a crash course on the process of writing an original screenplay — or finding a commercial script and getting the rights to produce it.

Chapter **1**

So You Want to Be a Filmmaker

M otion pictures are a powerful medium. With the right script under your arm and a staff of eager team players, you're about to begin an exciting ride. The single most important thing that goes into making a successful movie is the passion to tell a story. And the best way to tell your stories is with pictures. Moviemaking is visual storytelling in the form of shots that make up scenes and scenes that eventually make up a complete movie.

As a filmmaker, you have the power to affect people's emotions, make them see things differently, help them discover new ideas, inspire them, or just create an escape for them. In a darkened movie theater, you have an audience's undivided attention. They're yours — entertain them, move them, make them laugh, make them cry. You can't find a more powerful medium to express yourself.

Independents Day versus the Hollywood Way

There are three main types of full-length films made to be distributed (hopefully) for a paying audience:

>> **Studio films:** A studio film is usually greenlit by the head of a major studio, has a healthy budget averaging $60 million and up (some go as high as $150 million or more), and has major star names intended to guarantee some kind of box office success (as if such a guarantee were possible). Nowadays many studio movies are based on franchises, brands, best-selling books, and sequels to successful properties. Examples include comic book superheroes (*Superman, Batman, Spider-Man*), popular TV shows (*Mission Impossible, Star Trek*), best-selling books (the *Harry Potter* franchise), high concept (unique ideas that have commercial appeal like *Jurassic Park*, or *The Avengers*) that end up becoming their own franchise, and/or big name stars (Brad Pitt, Tom Cruise, Hugh Jackman, Emma Stone, Jennifer Lawrence). If a major film studio puts up the money for a movie, the studio — not the filmmaker (unless you're Steven Spielberg) — ultimately ends up calling the shots.

>> **Independent films:** A true independent film is often a low-budget movie (costing anywhere from $5,000 to $3 million) because the filmmaker has to raise money to make the movie on his or her own, independent of a studio for the financing. A true independent film has no studio influence. One major advantage is that the filmmaker doesn't have to report to anyone or to be limited creatively by a studio. Many films circulating the film-festival circuit are independent films, produced independently of the studios (with some exceptions at Sundance and Toronto International Film Festival). Kevin Smith started his career with his small independent film *Clerks*. Robert Rodriguez started his career with an original budget under $10,000 for his film *El Mariachi*. *The Blair Witch Project* is one of the most profitable independent films, grossing close to $250 million on a $60,000 budget.

>> **Independent studio films:** A studio's independent division is really a smaller "boutique" division of the big company, with smaller budgets and possibly fewer black suits deciding how to make and distribute the films that come from these divisions. Some films are acquisitions and then distributed by the big studios. *Get Out, A Quiet Place,* and *The Big Sick* are perfect examples of independent films released by major studios — and all received the exposure that a big studio picture expects, including studio marketing dollars in the millions, when they were nominated during the major awards season.

REMEMBER

The term *independent studio films* is actually oxymoronic because a film produced by a studio is not truly independent. A film produced by a studio's "independent" division is a studio film in disguise.

You can find both advantages and disadvantages to making a studio picture or an independent film. On an independent production, your movie ends up on the screen the way you envisioned it, but you are restricted by your budget. A studio picture has larger financial backing and can afford to pay the astronomical salaries that actors demand as well as for seamless special effects and longer shooting schedules, but the movie ends up the way the studio envisions it — and in the most commercial way. The studio looks at commercial viability first and creativity second. Many independent filmmakers discover that, although having and making money is nice, being independent allows them to tell their story in the most creative way.

An independent film doesn't always have to be a low-budget or no-budget film, however. George Lucas will always be known as the ultimate independent filmmaker. He was independent of the studios and made his own decisions on his films without the politics or red tape of a studio looking over his shoulder. The original *Star Wars* may not seem like an independent film, but that's exactly what it is — even though you may have difficulty seeing yourself as one of Lucas's peers. Eventually, Disney bought out the *Star Wars* brand from Lucas for a few billion dollars, and now the franchise is definitely major studio fare.

Filmmaking: Celluloid Film Stock or Digital?

Today, you can shoot your movie in several different formats. You can choose digital — high definition (HD) using a digital camera or even your smartphone — or a traditional film camera using Super-8, 16mm, or 35mm motion-picture film stock. However, the majority of studio films are now shot on digital.

REMEMBER

The medium on which you set your story — whether it be actual film celluloid or digital (high definition) media with a film-style look — engenders specific feelings and reactions from your audience. A movie shot on actual film stock tends to have a nostalgic feeling, like you're watching something that has already happened. Something shot on digital elicits more the feeling that it's happening right now — unfolding before your eyes, like the evening news. You can use this knowledge to enhance the emotional response your audience has to your movie. As technology continues to develop, digital cameras are coming closer and closer to emulating the look of film. Arri, for example, has been very successful with this look with their Alexa digital camera. Currently there is a myriad of software applications that helps you play with the grain, colors, and other elements to better emulate the look of film in post-production.

TIP

Another style you can give your film is to finish it in black and white. Steven Spielberg delivered *Schindler's List* in black and white, as did Alfonso Cuarón for his film *Roma*, to help convey the film as a long-past event and to express the dreariness of the era. Black and white can be effective for a vampire or zombie movie as well. As an independent filmmaker, you would shoot your movie in color (just in case) and turn it black and white during post-production.

REMEMBER

Why do we still call it *film*making when hardly anyone uses film anymore? When we go to the movies, we often say, *Want to go see that film?* or *they're filming a movie at the local mall.* When we enter our movie masterpiece, we submit it to a *film festival,* not a digital festival.

The word *film* as a noun refers to a thin flimsy strip of celluloid with sprocket holes evenly lined on one side (to accommodate the projector registration pins). As a verb, the word *film* means to record or capture something through a lens — that is, to create moving images or motion pictures, whether it be through the use of a film camera, a digital camera, or even your convenient smartphone — *Hey, I'm filming you!* So when I use the word *film* throughout the book, remember that it refers to the same thing whether you are shooting on digital or with actual film stock.

All digital: The new age of technology

The professional format of choice for most television shows, including TV movies and streaming films (Netflix, Amazon Prime, and so on) is shooting digital. It's less expensive and much more convenient than shooting with film, and it's perfect for the fast schedules of television productions and mini-series.

In this age of digital technology, anyone with a computer and digital camera (or smartphone) can make a movie. You can purchase a digital camera (like the Panasonic Lumix GH5 or the Black Magic Pocket Camera) that emulates the look of motion picture film without incurring the cost of expensive film stock and a pricey motion-picture camera. You can also purchase computer software such as Magic Bullet Frames (www.redgiantsoftware.com) that can take a harsh video image shot with an inexpensive home camera and give it the look of a motion-picture film camera.

Most digital cameras use SD (Secure Digital) flash memory cards to store your footage, which can be downloaded to your computer or a separate hard drive, and then the SD card can be erased and used over and over again.

If you can't afford a professional digital camera, you can shoot your movie on your smartphone. The quality is almost as good — or even fully as good — as many consumer digital cameras. The main disadvantage of using your smartphone is that it has a fixed lens.

Many new computers come preloaded with free editing software. In Chapter 16, I give you tips on starting your very own digital-editing studio. You can also find out more information on the technical aspects of capturing digital footage to your computer and then editing and sharing your work in *Digital Video For Dummies* by Keith Underdahl (published by Wiley). You can uncover more camera information in Chapter 10.

High definition (HD) is the new-age technology that has replaced standard definition, taking the camera image one step further. The picture is much sharper, richer, and closer to what the human eye sees as opposed to what an old standard definition (SD) video camera shows you. Watching HD is like looking through a window — the picture seems to breathe. The new HD digital cinema cameras combine HD technology with 24-frame progressive technology to emulate a unique film-like picture quality in an electronic digital file format, without the use of physical film. 2K HD has been the norm for years now, but 4K and 8K will soon come into their own.

Thanks for the memories: Memory cards

Now that 90 percent of filmmakers shoot in digital, SD memory cards and external hard drives are the norm. Those small, thin, delicate SD cards slip into the memory card slot of most digital cameras. You can then transfer the SD card onto an external hard drive. Or, if you prefer, you can run a cable from your camera to an external hard drive and record directly into the drive. There are also external solid-state flash drives (SSD) that have no moving parts and thus have less chance of losing your footage to glitches, drop-outs, or worse — a dead drive — and they are much faster than standard hard drives.

Developing Your Sense of Story

Because you can't possibly make a great movie without having a great story, choosing the right material is more important than anything else. Successful film careers are more often built on making the right decisions about a story than on having the right talent and skills. So where do you find good ideas to turn into a movie? An idea starts in your head like a tiny seed; it has a gestation period, and then it sprouts and begins to grow, eventually blossoming into an original screenplay.

Don't have that tiny seed of an idea just yet? Turn to Chapter 3, where I tell you how to find ideas and give you tips on turning your idea into a feature-length script. In that chapter, I also show you how to *option* (have temporary ownership of) existing material, whether it's someone's personal story or a published novel.

Financing Your Production: Where's the Money?

To get your movie made, you have to have financing. Raising money isn't as difficult as it sounds if you have a great story and an organized business plan. You can find investors who are looking to put their money into a movie for the excitement of being involved with a movie and/or the possibility of making a profit. Even friends and family are potential investors for your film — especially if your budget is very low.

SURFING SITES FOR FILMMAKERS

Becoming a filmmaker includes plugging yourself into informative outlets that help you be more aware of the filmmaker's world. Here I list websites that may be helpful to you as a low-budget filmmaker:

- **The Internet Movie Database (www.imdb.com and www.imdbPro.com)** lists the credits of film and TV professionals and anyone who has made any type of mark in the entertainment industry. It's helpful for doing research or a background check on an actor, writer, or filmmaker. The difference between the two? Imdb.com is free, and imdbPro.com costs around $20.00 a month at the time of this publication, but lists contact information and pertinent details not found on the free version.

- **The Independent Feature Project (www.ifp.org)** is an effective way to get connected right away to the world of independent filmmaking.

- **Film Independent (www.filmindependent.org)** offers assistance to its members in helping get their movies made and seen. They also produce the Los Angeles Film Festival and the Independent Spirit Awards.

- **The Independent (www.aivf.org)** is an organization that supports independent filmmakers. At the website, you can find festival updates, along with what's happening in the Independent scene.

- **IndieTalk (www.indietalk.com)** is a discussion forum for filmmakers where you can post and read messages about screenwriting, finding distribution, financing, and lots of other topics. It's a great site for communicating with other independent filmmakers.

- **Filmmaker IQ (www.filmmakeriq.com)** is one of my favorite sites for independent filmmakers with fun graphics and visuals to explain all about the process of making movies.

In Chapter 5, I give you some great tips on how to find investors and how to put together a *prospectus* to attract them to fund your production. Crowdfunding is a whole new ball game — and I'll tell you all about that too! You also find out about other money-saving ideas like bartering and product placement. I even show you how to set up your own website (or crowdfunding site) to help raise awareness for your movie, attract investors, and eventually serve as a promotional site for your completed film.

On a Budget: Scheduling Your Shoot

Budgeting your movie is a delicate process. Often, you budget your production first (this is usually the case with independent low-budget films) by breaking down elements into categories, such as crew, props, equipment, and so on — the total amount you have to spend. Your costs are determined by how long you need to shoot your movie (scheduling determines how many shoot days you have) because the length of your shoot tells you how long you need to have people on salary, how long you need to rent equipment (if you're not using your own camera and lights), and locations, and so on.

When you know you can only afford to pay salaries for a three-week shoot, you then have to schedule your production so that it can be shot in three weeks. You schedule your shoot by breaking down the script into separate elements (see Chapter 4) and deciding how many scenes and shots you can shoot each day, so that everything is completed in the three weeks you have to work with. An independent filmmaker doesn't usually have the luxury of scheduling the logistics first (breaking it down into how many days it will take to shoot) and then seeing how much it will cost.

TIP

Have a budget (and even a possible schedule) ready when you talk to a potential investor, including whether you are doing *crowdfunding*. It serves as ammunition to show that you didn't just draw a number out of a hat and that you did your homework and know where every dollar will go and to which category.

Planning Your Shoot, Shooting Your Plan

Planning your production includes envisioning your shots through *storyboarding*, the technique of sketching out rough diagrams of what your shots and angles will look like (see Chapter 9). You can storyboard your movie even if you don't consider yourself an artist: Draw stick characters or use storyboard software, like Storyboard Quick (www.powerproduction.com) or Frame Forge (www.frameforge.com).

Each comes with an eclectic cast of characters along with libraries of props and locations.

REMEMBER

You also need to plan where you shoot your movie. You research where you're going to shoot much as you would planning a trip, and then you make all the appropriate arrangements, like figuring out how you're going to get there and the type of accommodations, if your shoot is out of town. As you plan where to shoot your movie, keep these points in mind (and head to Chapter 6 for more detailed information):

>> You have to choose whether to shoot at a real location, on a sound stage, or in a virtual location that you conjure up inside your computer.

>> Regardless of where you're shooting, you need to sign agreements with the location owners to make sure you have all your location settings reserved for your shoot dates.

Hiring Your Cast and Crewing Up

Your production crew becomes your extended family (although maybe a dysfunctional one). You spend many days and nights together — through good and bad times — so hiring people who are passionate about your project and willing to put their all into it is important. You may have to defer salary to your crew if you're working on a tight budget. (Find out how to do that and more in Chapter 7.)

Acting is not as difficult as you may think. People are born natural actors and play many parts on the stage of life. Everyone is constantly in front of an audience — or performing monologues when alone. In Chapter 8, I lead you step by step through the process of finding a great cast to bring your screenplay to life. I also fill you in on acting secrets so that you can direct your actors to get the best performances.

Shooting in the Right Direction

Making a movie requires special equipment, like *cranes* (tall apparatuses on which you place the camera for high shots), *dollies* (which are like oversized skateboards that you put the camera on for movement), camera systems, and so on. In today's day and age, affordable advances in moving the camera have arrived: from camera drones to sophisticated camera stabilizers. Getting it right also involves lighting, sound, performances, and more, as explained in the following sections.

Seeing the light

Lighting, which can set a mood and enhance the entire look of your film, is important. Without it, you'll leave your actors in the dark — literally.

The eye of the camera needs adequate light to "see" a proper image. What's adequate light? Whatever produces appropriate exposure for the camera and lens. Many digital cameras today have advanced significantly — to use very little light to capture a good quality image. Low-wattage LED lighting has changed the trajectory of movie set lighting and is becoming the medium of choice over expensive halogen and old fluorescent and incandescent bulbs. Chapter 11 gives you the lowdown on lighting.

REMEMBER

Lighting can be very powerful and can affect the mood and tone of every scene in your film. A great cinematographer combined with an efficient gaffer (see Chapter 7) will ensure that your movie has a great look.

Being heard and scene

In addition to seeing your actors, you need to be able to hear them. This is where the art of sound comes in. You need to place microphones close enough to the actor to get a good sound recording, but not so close that the microphone creeps into the shot. The skill of recording great sound comes from the production sound mixer. New advances in wireless microphones using Bluetooth and Wi-Fi are introduced in Chapter 12.

REMEMBER

Production sound is extremely important because your actors must be heard correctly. Your sound mixer, who's primarily in charge of recording your actors' dialogue on set, needs to know which microphones and sound-mixing equipment to use. Chapter 12 shares all the necessary details.

Actors taking your direction

If you're taking on the task of directing, you'll become a leader to your actors and crew. You'll need to know how to give your actors direction, because it's the director's job to help the actors create believable performances that lure the audience into your story and make them care about your characters. Directing also involves guiding your actors to move effectively within the confines of the camera frame. It's almost like choreographing a dance. Chapter 13 guides you in the right direction with some great secrets on how to warm up your actors and prepare them to give their best performance on set.

Directing through the camera

In terms of telling your story visually, you'll need to understand a little about the camera (whether it's a film camera or a digital one). Much like driving a car, you don't need to understand how it works, but you do need to know how to drive it (your cinematographer should be the expert with the camera and its internal operations).

Directing the camera requires some technical knowledge of how the camera works (film or digital) and what each lens and filter does, which I explain in Chapter 10. Chapter 14 addresses how to frame your shots and when and how to move the camera. In that chapter, you also discover the skills that make a successful director and how to run a smooth, organized set.

Cut It Out! Editing Your Movie

During the editing phase, the scenes are finally assembled. Editing your movie gives you a chance to step back and look at the sequence of events, to review all the available shot angles in order to shape and mold them to tell the most effective story. You can even work to repair a bad film (or at least make it better) during the editing process. During editing, you really see your movie coming together.

Nonlinear editing software is now available for virtually any computer at affordable prices (many computers come with free editing software). With it, you can edit anything from a home movie to a professional theatrical-length piece (90 to 120 minutes). The technology of nonlinear editing allows you to cut your shots together in virtually any order. You can easily and quickly see different variations, cutting different shots together, rearranging them, and moving or deleting in between scenes in a concise and easy-to-understand manner. Chapter 15 tells you what the new-age digital technology and software makes available to you for editing your movie on your desktop.

Listening to your movie

Contrary to what most people think — that the sound they hear in the movie is the natural sound from the set — the entire soundtrack must be built just as the visual elements of the film are built. At the editing stage, you add and create the audio, dialogue, sound effects, and music (Chapter 16 has the details). Titles and credits are important, too, and I discuss them in Chapter 18.

Simulating a film-look with software

Most digital cameras today provide more of a film-look than they used to. The old days of harsh video are gone. If you want to enhance that film-look, post-production secrets and special software can help you. These software programs emulate grain, softness, subtle shutter flutter, and so on. Magic Bullet Frames software, available at www.redgiant.com, can convert any footage and soften it to look more like it was shot on motion picture film stock.

TECHNICAL STUFF

The natural frame rate of video is equivalent to 30 frames per second (technically 29.97). Motion picture film operates at 24 frames or images, per second. As a start, converting digital footage to mimic 24 frames (technically 23.97 in video) makes the image feel and look more film-like.

Distributing Your Movie and Finding an Audience

The final, and probably most important, stage of making a movie is distribution. Without the proper distribution, your film may sit on a shelf and never be experienced by an audience. Distribution can make the difference between your movie making $10 (the ticket your mother buys) or $100 million at the box office. *The Blair Witch Project* or *RGB* (the story of Justice Ruth Bader Ginsburg) may never have generated a dime if they hadn't been discovered at the Sundance Film Festival by a distributor. Even mediocre films have done well commercially because of successful distribution tactics. And great movies have flopped at the box office because the distributor didn't carry out a successful distribution plan. Chapter 19 offers a slew of tips and secrets for finding a distributor, as well as some tips on how to become your own distributor, including using the Internet and social networking.

GEARING UP FOR CINE GEAR

Cine Gear is one of my favorite expos. Every June in Los Angeles, thousands of people flock to the outdoor Cine Gear Expo held on the backlot of Paramount Studios to schmooze with fellow filmmakers, network, and see the latest developments in equipment technology (and, in many cases, to even experiment with the equipment, hands-on). It's like a giant toy store for filmmakers. Cine Gear has also started a film series with a call for entries. The expo runs for two days of exhibits, seminars, and screenings, and you can get a free pass by pre-registering at the expo website (or pay $20 at the entrance). Cine Gear also operates an annual expo in Atlanta, Georgia in early October. For information on all Cine Gear expos, go to www.cinegearexpo.com.

AN INTERVIEW WITH A STUDIO HEAD

I sat down with Alan Horn, former president and chief operating officer at Warner Bros. Studios, for an interview. Alan is one of the nicest guys, very down-to-earth, and also one of the most influential people in Hollywood. We still keep in touch regularly via email and often run into each other at industry and black-tie events where he always takes the time to chat with me. With a myriad of major hits behind him like *The Dark Knight*, the *Ocean's Eleven* trilogy, *The Lord of the Rings*, and the *Harry Potter* franchise, Alan left Warner Bros. in 2012 — but instead of retiring, he took a lucrative offer to become chief creative officer and co-chairman of The Walt Disney Company. He also oversees the Marvel Studios empire, a division under the Walt Disney banner. The Walt Disney Company also owns Lucasfilm, the *Muppets* franchise, and as of recently, 20th Century Fox.

A chess enthusiast, Horn makes use of his skills — savvy calculation and strategic planning — to run a studio and release theatrical feature films successfully.

Horn has been in the industry for many years, having co-founded Castle Rock Entertainment with his friend director Rob Reiner in 1987 (which produced many successful films like *When Harry Met Sally . . .*, *City Slickers*, and *A Few Good Men*, as well as the hit TV series *Seinfeld*). I asked him how the industry has changed over the years.

Without hesitation Horn said, "Technology — the technology that manifests itself in the production process — in the making of the movies and in the completion of the movies. The special effects technology now is stunningly good and it's seamless; the audience has come to expect first-class technology. They expect to see a tiger and not be able to tell if the tiger's real or not" (and he was right about that — he oversaw the all-computer-generated *The Lion King*). To make his point, he told me about a "little movie" the studio did when he was at Warner Bros.: *The Bucket List*, starring Jack Nicholson and Morgan Freeman and directed by Rob Reiner. "In the movie, these two characters travel all over the world, but the actors actually never went anywhere. So when we tell people, no, they didn't go to the Pyramids — it's such a shock. It's all green screen." Horn laughingly recalled being on the set of *300* and seeing "twenty buffed-out guys charging each other in an empty warehouse with a bunch of fake rocks! It really is amazing what they can do nowadays." Since this interview, special effects and CGI, including motion-capture, have only continued to evolve to amazing heights. The computer-generated *The Lion King* is opening this weekend (as I write this), and Disney is destined for a record-breaking weekend and a huge commercial success.

I asked Horn what he looked for in a screenplay. "The most important thing is a good story," Horn said. "I'd like to see a screenplay that is about something. It doesn't have to have a message in it, but it needs to have a good story. It's easy to get sidetracked by the spectacularity that exists in special effects and technology and lose the story to that," Horn continued. "It's always about the story. If it's supposed to be a comedy, then it ought to be funny; if it's a horror movie, it ought to be scary; if it's a dramatic movie, it ought to be dramatically compelling. If it isn't, you wind up with what I call a 'feathered fish,' which is just a little bit funny and a little bit dramatic and a little bit this and a little bit that — and I think you have a problem."

When asked about the advice he'd give filmmakers just starting out, Horn said, "Filmmakers need to understand and have a comfort with technology, but it's always back to basics. A filmmaker should find something about which he or she is passionate. Everything flows from passion. Mr. Shakespeare said many years ago, 'The play's the thing.' Filmmakers have to find something that interests them, and they should build on their strengths." He went on to say that the filmmaker should strengthen his or her weaknesses and make his or her strengths "super strengths."

I agreed with Horn, especially that it takes passion to be successful. I could have asked him many more questions, but even though Horn seemed in no hurry to end the interview, I didn't want to overstay my welcome. After all, in addition to being one of the most powerful people in Hollywood, an adroit chess player, and gracious interview subject, Horn also holds a third-degree black belt in *tae kwon do* (although that was back in the day)!

Chapter **2**

Genres in General

I n the mood for a quiet romantic comedy or an action-packed adventure? Feel like a good scare with a suspense or horror movie? How about a sci-fi epic or a fantasy adventure to take you to new worlds? Next time you go online, think about what genre interests you — not only to watch, but also what film genre you want to make. If you want to make people laugh and feel good, obviously a comedy is the way to go. If you want the audience to escape from everyday troubles and tribulations, a magical fantasy makes a great getaway. If you just want to excite your audience and take them on a whirlwind ride, then produce an action picture that plays like a never-ending roller coaster. Pick a genre that you enjoy watching, or combine genres as many films do.

In this chapter, I introduce you to the various genres and tell you which ones have been the most popular at the box office and which ones are best to avoid. Understanding the various genres and what characteristics make up each one helps you decide on the best story for you as a filmmaker to produce. I also introduce you to the *media categories* of filmmaking — commercials, music videos, shorts, industrials, documentaries, and feature-length films — and address the benefits of each. After all, not everyone can start out successfully by making feature films; these other categories give you a chance to get your feet wet before you make the leap to full-length features.

Exploring Film Genres

A *genre* is a category characterized by a particular style or form of content. In filmmaking, each genre has its own set of rules and characteristics. Commonly recognized genres include comedy, drama, horror, romance, action, and several others, all explained in the following sections.

Genres can be combined to create a variation in genres. A romance can be crossed with a comedy to become a romantic comedy like *Crazy Rich Asians.* A comedy crossed with a crime genre gives you *Ocean's Eleven (Ocean's Twelve, Thirteen, and Eight). Robocop,* which crosses multiple genre categories, is a science-fiction/action/crime drama.

REMEMBER

The time period of your story is not a genre but a setting that can fit with virtually any genre. A *period piece* is a story set in the days of yesterday (a story set in the future is considered fantasy or science fiction). *Sherlock Holmes* (Robert Downey, Jr.), for example, is film noir but also a period piece. *The Green Mile* (in the sci-fi, horror, and suspense genres) is a period piece, too, as is *Catch Me If You Can.* Tarantino's *Once Upon a Time in Hollywood* is a comedy/drama/period piece set in the '60s. Unless you're doing a studio-financed picture with a healthy budget, avoid period pieces, period. They require special art direction, wardrobe, and props dealing with that specific time period.

FROM ZERO TO HERO: COMIC BOOK SUPERHEROES

From the colorful pages of comic books, superheroes have claimed their own type of story. Not traditionally classified as a genre, the comic-book–hero film can be classified as an adaptation from comic book to the big screen. These stories usually fall into the fantasy and science-fiction genres, and almost always the action genre as well. That's why the toy replicas you buy of your favorite superheroes are called *action figures.* The Hulk is classified as a science fiction character because a scientific explanation accounts for how scientist Bruce Banner (Mark Ruffalo) became the Hulk (as extraordinary as this science may be). Sometimes superhero movies are classified as a combination of both sci-fi and fantasy, when they are facing off against powerful villains from other worlds. Since the original *Iron Man* movie in 2008, approximately twenty-six Marvel superhero movies have been released through 2019. Other popular heroes successfully pulled from the pages of comics and placed on the silver screen include *Spider-Man, Batman, Superman, X-Men,* and of course the phenomenal box-office–breaking *Avengers* movies. *Avengers: Endgame* is currently the highest-grossing movie of all time.

John Truby, a prominent screenwriting consultant in Hollywood, developed a unique writers' software called Truby's Blockbuster. You can also purchase and download additional software packages for Blockbuster that guide you through specific tips and examples that help make up each separate genre (www.truby.com).

Making 'em laugh with comedy

Comedy can be dry humor, slapstick, or just plain silly fun. Comedy works with other genres, including romance, science fiction, fantasy, western, and even drama. Many comedies branch out into a series of films based on the success of the original concept, such as the Zucker brothers' classic *Airplane*, *The Naked Gun*, and the *Austin Powers* films. Here are some other comedies to laugh about:

>> *Pitch Perfect*

>> *Ted*

>> *The Hangover*

>> *Deadpool*

Scary Movie is a perfect example of a film *parody* — a subgenre that pokes fun at other movies. My parody film *Miss Cast Away & the Island Girls* (a.k.a. *Silly Movie 2*) crosses *Cast Away* with *Miss Congeniality* — what happens when a planeload of beauty contestants crash-land on a deserted island? Other popular parodies include the *Austin Powers* movies (spoofing *James Bond* movies), *Superhero Movie*, spoofing superhero films), and many of Mel Brooks's zany movies, including *Young Frankenstein* (parodying horror films) and *Blazing Saddles* (parodying westerns).

Dark subject matter mixed with comedy is known as *black comedy*. A black comedy includes dark elements, combining pathos, pain, sickness, and death with comedic undertones. Often a black comedy has twisted humor in the characters and situations, as exemplified in films like *The Dead Don't Die*, *Birdman*, and Tarantino's groundbreaking *Pulp Fiction*.

REMEMBER

Comedy is difficult for some filmmakers to conceptualize, whereas it comes naturally to others. Comedy requires proper structure, comedic timing, gimmicks, and unique setup and situations. Choose this genre only if comedy is something that is natural for you. You don't want the audience laughing *at* you; you want them laughing *with* you.

If your movie is a true comedy, make sure that you establish it as one as soon as possible so the audience knows right away that it's okay to laugh. Don't wait until the narrative has rolled for five or ten minutes before introducing a comic gag or a humorous piece.

Getting dramatic about it

Drama is one of the broadest genres. A dramatic story has serious issues that usually deal with a character's struggle that could put him or her into a life-or-death situation. Drama is often combined with other genres: horror, crime, thriller, science fiction, western, and even fantasy genres. Many dramas successfully include romance, such as *Titanic* or Lady Gaga and Bradley Cooper's version of *A Star is Born*. Examples of other dramatic films include:

>> *Bohemian Rhapsody*

>> *Green Book*

>> *Roma*

>> *Black Panther*

Drama combined with comedy becomes a *dramedy*. Dramedy is different from black comedy in that it is much lighter and the characters are more logical and realistic in their actions. *The Secret Life of Walter Mitty* (Ben Stiller) made for a great dramedy as Walter escapes his mundane life by moving out of his comfort zone and going on a journey he never imagined. Tina Fey's *Whiskey Tango Foxtrot* also made for a great dramedy with the underlying story during turmoil in Afghanistan. *The Truman Show* and *The Intern* (Robert De Niro) are other prime examples.

Even in times of tragedy, dramas need humor. No audience would sit through a drama and come out of the theater unscathed unless the film provided some comic relief. Even Shakespeare had comic relief in his serious plays. Audiences want that relief; they need to breathe between the tragic moments. The movie *Rain Man* had a touch of comic relief in Dustin Hoffman's character, Raymond; the comic relief broke the tension at times when the story became too serious.

Horrifying horror films

Alfred Hitchcock pulled out all the stops in horror with his film *Psycho*. Steven Spielberg scared people out of the water for years with *Jaws*. Actor/director John Krasinski successfully spooked audiences, starring with his wife Emily Blunt in *A Quiet Place*. Audiences love being terrified and on the edge of their seats — in the safety of a movie theater. Horror uses the element of shock value that works by surprising the audience. When I was a kid, I hid under my little sister Nancy's bed and waited until she was tucked in for the night; then I jumped out and scared her — she was horrified. Here are a few titles that'll bring some chills to your bones:

>> *The Exorcist*

>> *Get Out*

>> *Silence of the Lambs*

>> Stephen King's *It*

A *slasher* film is a subcategory of the horror genre that often includes shots showing the killer's point of view, vulnerable teenage girls (usually virgins at the beginning of the picture who get murdered as soon as they lose their virginity), and very naïve victims. Slasher films also tend to be very graphic. *Friday the 13th, Halloween, The Texas Chain Saw Massacre,* and *Child's Play* are great examples of slasher films.

Horror films do well overseas, mainly because their graphic images translate well in any language. Domestic audiences often like the sight of blood too, as long as it's not their own.

TIP

Less is more when it comes to shooting horror films. The robot shark that kept breaking down during production of the film *Jaws* worked to Steven Spielberg's advantage, because the less we saw of the shark, the more suspenseful and frightening the threat became. Barely seeing the creatures in *A Quiet Place* fueled the terrifying suspense and kept audiences on the edge of their seats. If you want your horror film to be more effective, don't overexpose the villain or spine-chilling monster.

Romancing the romantic

For the sensitive (myself included), a good romance makes for a great date movie and fills the bill when you're in the mood to be romanced. Romance stories focus on the love story and how it develops, regardless of whether it ends happily ever after. Romance mixes well with comedy, too, as in *The Big Sick* or *There's Something About Mary.* Romantic comedies are now known as *romcoms.* Others meld romance with fantasy to create fantasy romances, like *Ghost, Beauty and the Beast, Somewhere in Time,* and *The Princess Bride.* You'll be swept away by these titles:

>> *Casablanca*

>> *Silver Linings Playbook*

>> *The Shape of Water*

>> *The Theory of Everything*

There's always an audience for a good romance. If you cry at the movies when the guy finally gets the girl, that means you're sensitive, and a romance may be the perfect genre for you to undertake.

Getting physical: No talk and all action

Action movies like *San Andreas* (starring The Rock) are a treat for the eyes with the energy of a sporting event. With a good action picture, you can turn off the sound and enjoy the visuals without having to follow the dialogue. Audiences with a competitive nature enjoy action films with a lot of physical conflict. Action-packed examples include:

>> *John Wick*

>> *Taken*

>> *Mission Impossible*

>> *Skyfall*

Action does extremely well internationally. Everyone likes a good action piece, especially when it doesn't rely on a detailed story with heavy dialogue that can get lost in translation.

REMEMBER

Shooting action scenes can be dangerous. Always have a trained stunt coordinator and a pyrotechnician on set if your film involves any explosions or gunfire. Even better, stay safe by adding your magnificent explosions and loud penetrating gunshots in post-production — which can be done easily with visual effects software or layover graphics (such as those at www.footagecrate.com) — and then adding booming sound effects to seal the deal.

Separating fact from (science) fiction

Audiences appreciate an escape and the opportunity to ask, "What if . . .?" So science fiction has always been popular at the box office. If a film's subject stems from a scientific explanation (even if it's a rather fantastic explanation), it falls into this genre. Time travel in *Back to the Future* makes for great science fiction, as does interplanetary worlds with aliens and monsters like in *Arrival*, which plays on the idea that we may not be alone in the universe. Here are some titles that are considered science fiction even though you probably didn't study them in science class:

>> *Close Encounters of the Third Kind*

>> *Jurassic Park*

>> *Iron Man*

>> *Star Wars*

REMEMBER

Science fiction stories can be very expensive to produce if they require a lot of effects, and are normally out of reach for a low-budget independent film. However, the leaps and bounds in the technology to generate creatures and effects with software are making it easier and more affordable.

Indulging your fantasy

The fantasy genre combines fantasy worlds and magical elements that could never exist in today's world (this is what separates this genre from science fiction). *Game of Thrones* is set in a fantasy medieval world, putting it clearly into this genre. Many fantasy stories, such as *Toy Story* and *How to Train Your Dragon,* are told through CGI animation. For a fantastical adventure, take a look at these titles:

>> *The Wizard of Oz*

>> *Harry Potter*

>> *Fantastic Beasts*

>> *Lord of the Rings*

REMEMBER

A fantasy story doesn't always require special effects — consider *It's a Wonderful Life,* which sets up a fantastical situation without visuals weighed down with special effects — but making a movie in the fantasy genre can be expensive if you have to create worlds that don't exist. Some effects (with some ingenuity) can be done inexpensively, as I show you in Chapter 17.

Go west, young man: Westerns

Westerns were popular years ago (they even ruled at the box office) but seem to have gone west over the years. Clint Eastwood can still make a western that audiences will flock to see, though, and John Wayne westerns will always be popular on TV and Netflix, especially late at night and on rainy Sunday afternoons. Find a ghost town, some horses, and a couple of cowboy hats, grab a sarsaparilla, and you've got yourself a western, like

>> *The Good, the Bad, and the Ugly*

>> *The Magnificent Seven*

>> *Unforgiven*

>> *The Hateful Eight*

REMEMBER

A western may be inexpensive to shoot if you have a couple of horses and a ghost town at your disposal, but westerns aren't the most commercial of film genres today and are considered more of a risk. And for that reason, many distributors steer away from acquiring them.

Going to war

War movies have always been popular. It's the good team versus the bad team with lots of gunfire and explosions (which can be expensive for an independent filmmaker). War is a global theme; no matter what country or language, audiences are intrigued and get caught up in the heart-pumping action of a good war movie. For this reason, war movies do well internationally as well as at home.

War movies are categorized as action films on most streaming platforms. Mel Gibson's films *Hacksaw Ridge* and *Braveheart* are classified under the war/action genre. Here are some other movies worth fighting for:

>> *Apocalypse Now*

>> *Saving Private Ryan*

>> *American Sniper*

>> *Platoon*

REMEMBER

War movies seem to do better at the box office when the world isn't dealing with an actual war or with pending warfare issues. When there's talk of battle between countries, the studios tend to saturate the market with combat stories, which makes the films less successful at the box office. Plus, these pictures come too close to reality; people dealing with war issues in the real world typically don't want to see more of it in the theater.

Thrilling audiences with suspense

Suspense thrillers keep you on the edge of your seat. A good suspense movie is like a ball rolling downhill, picking up speed — the audience doesn't know where and when it's going to stop. Alfred Hitchcock was the master of suspense with such films as *Rear Window* and *North by Northwest.* Horror and crime films incorporate the suspense genre effectively as well. A suspense/thriller can also mix in science fiction, as in *A Quiet Place* and *Minority Report.* Other titles that'll keep you in suspense include:

>> *Fatal Attraction*

>> *Jaws*

>> *Get Out*

>> *Gone Girl*

A good suspense thriller relies on a great script, not on special effects or even fast-paced action. This genre can be done on a low budget — you just need to intrigue your audience with a story that they'd love to see unfold. The mechanical shark in *Jaws* kept breaking down. This actually helped fuel the suspense by only getting quick glimpses of the man-eating monster.

Stealing the audience's attention: Crime pays

Audiences have always been intrigued by police dramas, detective tales, and mobster stories because an audience likes to piece the clues together and doesn't want to know all the answers right away. Many crime dramas fall into a subgenre known as *film noir* (which conjures up images of darkness and shadows in the 1940s, along with exaggerated high and low angles and often unique composition of shots to tell the story). The movie *Dick Tracy* is a prime example of the crime genre and film noir. *Batman* (the series of theatrical films) is a science-fiction comic-book action story in the film-noir style. Other crime drama titles include

>> *Chinatown*

>> *The Maltese Falcon*

>> *The Untouchables*

>> *L.A. Confidential*

As an independent filmmaker on a limited budget avoid this genre, especially if it's a film-noir period piece. Crime genres usually contain visual elements — guns, explosions, expensive wardrobe, and blood effects (which ruin the expensive wardrobe) — that can contribute to a higher-cost production.

Making music with musicals

A musical film is like a real stage show combined with the magic of moviemaking — without the intermission. Classic musicals include *The Sound of Music, My Fair Lady,* and *The Wizard of Oz* (which is also a great film in the family genre). Many of Disney's animated movies, like *Fantasia, Frozen,* and *Aladdin,* are also considered musicals.

Musicals seem to be making a comeback, with *The Greatest Showman* and *Mamma Mia! Here We Go Again* earning high praise and doing well at the box office. Here are some other full-length musicals that will have you shouting "Bravo!":

>> *La La Land*

>> *Grease*

>> *Pitch Perfect*

>> *Mary Poppins Returns*

REMEMBER

A full-length musical film would be difficult and expensive for an independent film but could work more effectively as a short (twenty minutes or less). A short three-minute musical is what helped filmmaker Adam Stein move to the next round on the Steven Spielberg TV series *On the Lot.*

TIP

Movie soundtracks are big business. Sometimes the soundtrack does better financially than the film from which it came. The soundtrack for Lady Gaga's *A Star is Born* topped the charts worldwide, fueled by Lady Gaga and Bradley Cooper singing the Oscar-winning song, "Shallow." The music video to "Shallow" has over a half-billion (yes, I said *billion*) views on YouTube! Selecting the right music for your movie, including original songs, can make your film sing. Check out Chapter 16 for more information on movie music, songs, and soundtracks.

Kidding around: Family-friendly films

A family picture often contains positive family values that both children and adults can enjoy. Family movies encompass many genres, except for war, crime, and graphic horror. The *Muppet* movies are classified as family entertainment but also fall into the fantasy genre. Disney/Pixar's *Toy Story* films are examples of the family genre at its best. Other great movies to watch with your family include

» *Paddington*

» *Despicable Me*

» *E.T. the Extra-Terrestrial*

» *The Wizard of Oz*

The family genre lends itself well to the technical category of animation (drawings, stop-motion, or computer-generated). Animation is a style that young people immediately accept as friendly, safe, and inviting.

ANIMATING ANIMATION

Animation is a technique that works with most genres (and combinations of genres), especially family films. Often, though, animation is more fitting for comedy or light humor. Fantasy and science fiction stories are also good candidates for animation, because drawing fantastic worlds or outer-space environments is easier (and cheaper) than creating them in a convincing setting. Filmmakers have the following animation techniques to choose from:

- **Traditional cel animation:** Individual drawings (up to 24 images for 24 frames a second — or 12 drawings shot two frames at a time) are inked onto clear acetate cels and photographed against painted backgrounds. Animated flipbooks use the same principles as cel animation. Disney's movies in this style, from *Snow White and the Seven Dwarfs* to *The Lion King,* are popular examples of traditional cel animation. This technique has pretty much been replaced by computer animation.

- **Stop-motion animation:** Gumby, shown below, and Pokey are two of my favorite stop-motion characters. I started my filmmaking career emulating Gumby movies on Super-8 film when I was 10 years old. Tim Burton's *Corpse Bride, Shaun the Sheep,* and *Isle of Dogs* are stop-motion feature films that use three dimensional models often molded in clay and placed in miniature hand-built sets. An animator moves the characters slightly into different positions between single frames taken by the motion-picture camera. Stop-motion is a fairly inexpensive technique and a good way to learn about animation. An affordable and fun software program called *iStopMotion* lets you make your own stop-motion films using your computer or digital camera (www.boinx.com).

(continued)

(continued)

Courtesy of Arthur Clokey

- **CGI Computer animation:** Computer animation has become more the norm than the traditional three-dimensional stop-motion techniques and 2D cartoon animation used in the past years. CGI (computer-generated images) creates virtual three-dimensional characters in a digital environment. These images can then be articulated within the computer as if they were actual three-dimensional creations outside the computer. Successful computer-generated image (CGI) films include *The Peanuts Movie, How to Train Your Dragon, Toy Story, The Incredibles,* and the reimagined CGI remakes from Disney that include *The Lion King* and *The Jungle Book* (mixed in with live action elements). This technique often uses *motion-capture*, which uses an actual actor covered in strategically placed dots that the camera recognizes to emulate the actor's movements and translate them to a CGI-created character. Many smartphones have built-in animated avatars that use this technique to turn your face into an animated character.

- **Flash animation:** Flash animation is a computer 2D technique that uses limited animation over the Internet or on TV shows like *South Park*. Flash animation has a staccato and sometimes jerky motion and uses simplified drawings that often look like cutouts, with solid, clean lines and prime colors (as Dodo the bird, below, illustrates). It's an inexpensive and fun way to animate a short film and have it viewed by a large audience via the Internet.

©Mr.Dodo, courtesy B.M.Stoller

Categorizing Your Genres

Your production not only is part of a particular genre or combination of genres, as explained in the preceding sections, but also falls under one of several media categories: feature film, documentary, short film, television program, TV commercial, and more. Read on for details of the different media categories.

Featuring films

Most filmmakers dream of making a feature film that will be projected in a movie theater to a captive audience. Getting your movie into the theaters is much more difficult than getting it onto DVD, streaming or TV. In addition to the actual cost to produce the picture, a major studio spends millions of dollars to get a movie into theaters. The costs include 35mm prints, or more commonly now DCP (digital cinema package) hard drives that have to be delivered to sometimes up to 3,000 theaters, along with the expense of advertising on television, radio, newspapers, and the Internet. Advertising costs of thirty million dollars and up are often the norm for a studio picture. Without a major advertising campaign, a theatrical film has a hard time recouping its picture costs plus the marketing and distribution expenses.

A major distributor such as Paramount Pictures or Universal tends to distribute big movies with big stars. These pictures are often referred to as tent-pole movies (they help hold up the studio financially). A theatrically released picture often has to have an event feel to it to get the wide theatrical release, along with name stars that an audience is familiar with; otherwise, it's considered a risk, and few studios nowadays are willing to take that risk.

The hardest thing about making a feature film is that it has to be feature-film length (meaning at least 90 minutes long), and it's not easy to get enough money to pull it off. However, with the advent of digital high definition, shooting at feature-film length is becoming more affordable. You don't have to budget for raw film stock and lab costs, which include developing, color timing, along with a negative cutter, and answer print (see Chapter 15). Also, be prepared to spend a lot more time making a feature film than you would if you were making a TV commercial, short film, or documentary.

Made-for-TV movie

A made-for-TV movie is a cross between a feature film and a television production. It is usually shot on a tight television schedule (two to three weeks, as opposed to a feature schedule of several weeks to several months) and casts recognized television names from popular TV series, as opposed to big screen actors. Budgets are much smaller and on scale with a TV series budget (between $1.5 and $3 million).

A made-for-TV movie is often developed in-house by the TV networks, or by streaming companies like Netflix, and hiring is usually internal, using producers, directors, and crew that have worked with the network or streamer before. Many independent films have found their way onto a TV syndication schedule or streaming platform — I was fortunate to license my independent movie *Undercover Angel* starring Yasmine Bleeth, James Earl Jones, Dean Winters, Casey Kasem, and Emily Mae Young to Lifetime Television, PAX, UPN, and Bravo. Additionally, my movies *First Dog* and *The Amazing Wizard of Paws* sold to TV syndication, and both films also streamed on Netflix.

Documenting documentaries

Documentaries feature actual people and factual events as opposed to the fictional characters and stories used in feature filmmaking. In rare situations, a documentary may receive a wide theatrical release, such as Academy Award winner *Free Solo* about professional rock climber Alex Honnold, and the Fred Rogers documentary, *Won't You Be My Neighbor?* The feature documentary by Al Gore, *An Inconvenient Truth*, entailing the concerns of global warming, received rave reviews from many film critics in addition to two Academy Awards.

If a documentary puts a fictional, humorous spin on its subjects, it can be categorized as a *mockumentary*, like *This Is Spinal Tap* and *Best in Show.* If you put a serious spin on a fictional documentary, you end up with the chilling *Blair Witch Project*. I did a mockumentary called *Hollywood Goes to Las Vegas* about a filmmaker (I hired myself) who wants to meet Sandra Bullock at a film convention and who encounters Russell Crowe, George Carlin, Nicolas Cage, Haley Joel Osment, and John Travolta along the way.

Shooting digital shorts: Keep it brief!

Producing a short film is a good way to get your foot in the door. A short film lasts, on average, 3–20 minutes, during which time it has to include an entire story arc, from beginning to end. Because of the short time in which to tell a story, the film-maker often tells a controversial, funny or unique story that would normally not work as well in a feature length production. I've made over 50 comedy short movies called *Undershorts* that have appeared on *TV's Bloopers and Practical Jokes* with Dick Clark and Ed McMahon and *Foul-Ups, Bleeps, and Blunders* with Don Rickles and Steve Lawrence. You can check out my *Undershorts* at www.bryanmichaelstoller.com. Most short films are more of a "calling card" than feature films; they're difficult to sell but are ideal for showcasing your talents online and for garnering awards and exposure at film festivals.

Shorts can also be used as interstitials on television. *Interstitials* are short movies that fill in the gaps between regular programming — usually on pay channels that don't run commercials, like Starz or Showtime. My comedy shorts have appeared as interstitials on HBO and various other pay and cable channels.

Short films that are between 1–4 minutes lend themselves well to streaming over the Internet, using such sites as www.youtube.com and www.vimeo.com. These short films can be quickly streamed or downloaded for immediate viewing. You can set up your YouTube page to get paid for views if you allow commercials during your presentation. You can see my short parody film *The Linda Blair Witch Project* (starring Linda Blair), at www.youtube.com/watch?v=ftqEhTpZtQs. Uploading your own movie into cyberspace is free at YouTube — hurry up, the world is waiting!

Directing television programs

Television directing consists of working under tight schedules (which means less time to do numerous takes, as compared to a feature film) and working under the pressure of a network and many television executives looking over your shoulder and making the final decisions. Directing a television series also consists of studying and emulating the style of the show, knowing the characters and their idiosyncrasies, and keeping the direction consistent with past episodes. Breaking into producing or directing television shows is a lot harder than making an independent feature film. With television, you have network executives and a lot of red tape to deal with. Developing a new concept for a TV show is the best way to get in the door.

Directing commercials

A 30-second commercial is quick to produce, and the pay can be very lucrative. Many big-time feature directors have come from a commercial background, such as Michael Bay, who directed *Bad Boys, Armageddon,* and *Transformers.* When I was 16, I was producing, directing, and writing several TV commercials a month out of my basement studio. Check with the TV stations and advertising agencies in your city to see whether you can produce some local commercials for them. For several years now, Doritos has produced the *Crash the Super Bowl* contest. Anyone can submit a funny homemade commercial featuring Doritos to compete for a million dollars in cash and other great prizes.

Minding your PSAs: Public service announcements

TV networks have an obligation to air *public service announcements,* also referred to as *PSAs,* for campaigns dealing with health and safety issues. PSAs include anti-smoking and antidrug commercials, don't-drink-and-drive or don't-text-and-drive campaigns, and environmental messages. The FCC requires TV stations to run public service announcements that are usually commissioned by various government agencies. Try making an inexpensive PSA on a subject that you're passionate about — this is your chance to make a statement. You can upload it to YouTube and gather an audience. If it's well made, your local TV station may air it.

Feel like dancing? Music videos

Music videos are another great way to break into filmmaking. Find a local band and offer to shoot their first music video. Music videos can be shot inexpensively, even on your smartphone, and are a fun way to experiment and play with visuals — and they're a great way to tell a story without dialogue.

Industrials: Industrial strength

An *industrial* is usually a production commissioned by a corporation showing how its products are manufactured and how they function. Industrial films can also be shot as training films for employees to find out more about the company and the products they represent. Industrials are often very technical and instructional in nature. Check out local corporations in your area to see whether they may be interested in having you produce an industrial video for them.

A word about branding and sequels

Movies are a risky business, even for the major Hollywood studios. A safer bet for the studios is to make a sequel on a successful movie. This makes the financial risk less risky because the audience already is familiar with the brand. Examples of this are many of the Marvel movies, such as *The Avengers* and *X-Men*. *Toy Story* is a popular brand and has been successful with its sequels, and so has *The Incredibles*. *Star Wars* is a mega-brand that instantly has a proven audience. Brands are also successful by their worldwide recognition; that's why some video games like *Angry Birds* have had their own movies.

Chapter **3**

Penning and Pitching a Great Story

n order to make a movie, you must first find an interesting *screenplay* (a properly formatted manuscript that follows industry guidelines) or at least a great story idea. And where do screenplays come from, you ask? Well, anywhere actually. You can put out feelers in the industry to let writers know you're in the market for a screenplay, or you can write one of your own. You can find fascinating articles in your local newspaper and online, funny stories in magazines, and intriguing biographies that are just begging to be made into screenplays.

In this chapter, I show you the secrets to structuring the elements of your screenplay and developing characters that your audience will care about. You also see how easy it is to acquire stories or even the rights to a published book, if that's the route you want to take. Finally, you discover how to pitch your story ideas to a studio executive or potential investor in the hopes of getting your story made into a movie.

Screening for the Perfect Screenplay

Finding a screenplay isn't difficult, but finding a good one is. If you look carefully, you can find many talented, up-and-coming writers who have good or maybe even great scripts under their arms just waiting to be made into a great movie. Or, if you find an intriguing story from a published book, you can adapt it into a screenplay.

REMEMBER

If you're a beginning filmmaker, you should select or write a story that is realistic to shoot as a first-time movie. Don't choose material that's too ambitious. Keep the locations and characters to a minimum and keep away from special effects (they can be costly and time consuming and worse, look cheap and distract from your story).

The "write" way to find a writer

How do you find screenplay writers? Here are some ideas:

>> **Put an ad on one of the entertainment networking sites** such as *InfoList* (www.infolist.com) or Stage 32 (www.stage32.com) to let writers know that you're seeking an original screenplay for production. You can also peruse the site *Simply Scripts* (www.simplyscripts.com) to find unproduced screenplays.

>> **Read online screenplay magazines** such as *Creative Screenwriting* (www.creativescreenwriting.com) and *Script Magazine* (www.scriptmag.com) and look for articles on writers. Check the classified sections and request available screenplays being advertised by writers.

>> **Attend film festivals** to meet screenwriters. Usually attendees at film festivals have future scripts ready to produce. Also, the American Film Market (www.americanfilmmarket.com) in November in Santa Monica, California, is a great networking avenue to meet writers looking to get their script(s) produced.

TIP

Screenplay magazines usually list writers' newsletters and writers' groups that you can join in order to find writers who have a screenplay ready to turn into a movie. Also check out www.writerswrite.com for a one-stop website with resources on writers for writers, including a place to post your job listing looking for a writer.

>> **Attend writing seminars.** You can find these advertised in the various writers' magazines or in the classified sections of trade papers both in print and online. Join InfoList to be notified of any industry seminars (www.infolist.com). You can also find out about seminars from a writers' group, then network with the people in attendance, in addition to the speaker. Many attendees probably have a script they're peddling. Check out www.fwmedia.com and www.scriptwritersnetwork.org to network with writers through blogs and discussions and in-person seminars.

>> **Send an email to everyone you know.** We all have a screenplay in us. Tell friends, family, anyone you can that you're looking for a great screenplay or idea for a great movie. This can include posting on your Facebook page to all your online friends that you're actively searching for a commercial screenplay. After the word spreads, especially through the Internet, you'll start getting submissions.

>> **Contact agencies that represent writers.** Send a query letter or call, and tell the agency that you're looking for scripts. Be sure to give them an idea of your budget range — how much money you have to make your movie (a little or a lot); go to Chapter 4 for budgeting your production. You can request a list of agencies from the Writer's Guild of America at www.wga.org.

INKING FOR A SCRIPT

InkTip is a great website that brings new and even seasoned writers (and their unproduced screenplays) together with filmmakers and producers. Searching for a script doesn't cost the producer or filmmaker anything, but you do have to qualify for free membership. You can apply for membership at its website (www.Inktip.com). You can also subscribe to InkTip's free email newsletter and its bi-monthly *InkTip* magazine.

As a member, you gain access to writers' contact information and can contact writers directly with no agent or middleman. You can even download screenplays (as PDF files, a format that most computers accept — if yours doesn't, go to www.get.adobe.com/reader to download Adobe Acrobat Reader, free of charge). The InkTip network has a robust search engine that can find very specific types of screenplays. If you're looking for a sci-fi script with a female lead that takes place on another planet and has some comedy undertones for a low to medium budget, click a few buttons, and away the search goes. The site also has listings of short screenplays available for production if you don't have the funds to do a full-length film.

Adapting: A novel idea

One of the best ways to get a studio deal in Hollywood is to find a great book and option the rights to it. When you *option* a book, you're temporarily leasing the rights to it, giving you exclusive permission to adapt it to a screenplay and to shop it around as if you owned it. In a sense, you *do* own it — for a limited amount of time. An option can be as short as four months or as long as two years or more.

Literally hundreds of thousands of books are out there. Go to the library or a secondhand bookstore. You're sure to stumble across a little gem that somebody has missed. Scan the racks for something that could work as a movie. Surf online and see if you can find an obscure book that Hollywood has overlooked. You could even take a short story and adapt it into a full-length feature film. *Total Recall* came from an 18-page short story by Philip K. Dick. Ted Chiang's short story "Story of Your Life" became the feature film, *Arrival.* Many of Stephen King's short stories were adapted into full-length films: His short story "Children of the Corn" and "The Lawnmower Man," were turned into full-length feature films, and his novella *The Body* was released as the theatrical film *Stand by Me.*

The popularity of the book will determine whether you can get an inexpensive option. The chances of getting an inexpensive option are very good for an older book that few have heard of — especially if you can contact the author directly.

When you option the rights to a novel, you draw up an agreement (preferably have an attorney do it) and you name a purchase price to be paid if and when you sell the novel to a studio or produce it yourself. You can offer an option for $1 and set a purchase price that is paid only if and when the movie is produced. Often the purchase price of a script is 10 to 15 percent of the budget on an independent production, plus any agreed-upon royalties on the picture's profits. You're probably saying to yourself, "Why even pay a dollar?" Any monetary amount makes it a legal agreement. Plus, I once optioned a story from a writer for $1 and he was able to treat himself to a no-frills fast-food burger — I felt good that I helped a starving artist!

Writing Your Own Original Screenplay

If you can't seem to find the perfect screenplay, then why not try writing your own? "Because I'm not a writer," you say. To that I say, "Just try." In Los Angeles, everyone, no matter what he or she does for a living, seems to be writing a screenplay. When you pass people on the street, you don't say "Hello." You say, "How's your screenplay going?" Usually people answer, "Great! Thanks for asking. How's yours?"

If you can converse with people and relate incidents and stories verbally, you can probably put your words on paper, so give it a try. Do you have a friend who you can collaborate with on a script? Maybe they're good at dialogue, and you're good at ideas and description. I highly recommend the book *Screenwriting For Dummies* (for which I was technical editor) by Laura Schellhardt (published by Wiley). Start by perusing newspapers and the Internet to trigger ideas for your story, or think about subjects that interest you and that you want to see on the big screen. Choose a story that keeps the reader glued to the page because they need to know what happens next.

Before you start writing your screenplay, familiarize yourself with the basics of what makes up good story structure. You also need to decide if you're ready to tackle a feature-length screenplay or ease your way in by doing a short treatment first (go to Chapter 2 for a discussion of media categories). Regardless of whether your screenplay is a 10-page script or a feature-length one (90 pages), similar story principals apply with regards to structuring your screenplay.

Note: A *spec script* is a speculative screenplay that a writer has written without being commissioned by someone in the hopes that it may be considered for production. It's usually a story the writer is extremely passionate about.

Structuring your screenplay

Feature films are usually structured into three acts. Each act is characterized by certain elements that move the story forward. In a nutshell, Act One introduces the characters and starts the problem or conflict in motion. In Act Two, the adventure begins and the conflict intensifies. In Act Three, the problem comes to a head and is finally resolved. Here's a very simple example: In Act One, the dog chases the cat up the tree. In Act Two, the cat is stuck in the tree, and an attempt is made to get it down safely. In Act Three, the cat gets rescued. The following sections go into more detail.

Act One

Act One is the beginning of your story — you've got one chance to grab your audience and pull them in. In Act One, you introduce your main character (the *protagonist*). You also introduce the *inciting incident* — the element that sets your story into motion. In my movie *First Dog,* the story is set into motion when an attempt on the president's life is diverted by the First Dog, Teddy, trying to warn him — and when the shots ring out, the president is protectively thrown into the presidential limo by the Secret Service and whisked away. In the pandemonium, Teddy is left behind. After sneaking into the back of a truck and being transported a thousand miles away, Teddy meets a lonely foster boy, Danny Milbright (the protagonist). Danny, realizing the dog belongs to the president of the United States, vows to return the dog to the White House. So begins the journey that leads into Act Two.

Act Two

In Act Two, the conflict intensifies and the enemy (the *antagonist*) is introduced, if he or she is not introduced already by the end of Act One. The antagonist can be things like

>> **A person:** Terrorists in *Air Force One*, zombies in *World War Z*, Thanos in *Avengers: Endgame*

>> **Nature:** Any of the elements Mother Nature can throw at us: bizarre repercussions of global warming in *The Day After Tomorrow*, earthquakes in *San Andreas*, the challenges of outer space in *The Martian*, Steven Spielberg's shark in *Jaws*, or a meteor racing toward Earth in *Armageddon*

>> **A disaster:** The sinking ship in *Titanic*, or the mechanical failure in *Apollo 13*

The antagonist can also be any combination of these and other challenges.

In *First Dog*, as Danny and Teddy venture across the country determined to make it to the White House, the two journey through a lot of conflict and encounter challenges and adventures. There are several antagonists in this film: the Secret Service agents who are after the pair, Animal Control workers who try to separate them, and more. By the end of Act Two, Danny is taken to a detention center as a runaway, awaiting transport back to the foster home, and Teddy ends up at an animal shelter. It looks like the end for both Danny and Teddy.

Act Three

In Act Three, the conflict comes to a climax and the problems are finally (hopefully) resolved. In *First Dog*, for example, Teddy's life is spared when the scanning of his chip (imbedded in his shoulder) identifies his home address as 1600 Pennsylvania Avenue, and Danny goes to the White House to meet the president and to be reunited with Teddy. The story's resolution continues when Danny finds out that he is to be adopted by the president and First Lady, and Teddy, First Dog, is now his dog too!

Creating conflict

Conflict is what propels a story into motion. Without conflict, you have no action. Every day you deal with conflict, good or bad. Paying bills, getting stuck in traffic, having an argument with your spouse, missing your plane, getting a flat tire, being too rich — these are conflicts. Conflict usually starts when your protagonist, the lead character, encounters friction, a problem. Your character then deals with and tries to solve this problem. If the story is a good one, the protagonist grows from his or her experiences, whether they eventually solve their problem or not. A good story has your protagonist a changed person at the end of the movie.

Conflict can also be an opposing character, the *antagonist*, like Thanos in the *Avengers* movies, whose beliefs and self–indulgence lead him to snap his fingers and destroy half of humanity. Or it can be the elements of nature, such as the storm that strands Tom Hanks's character in *Cast Away* on a deserted island or the island itself, or it can be the elements of life and nature that try to pull apart Sandra Bullock and Ben Affleck's characters in *Forces of Nature*. In *Titanic*, a historic and tragic event takes the lives of many innocent passengers; the film also has a human antagonist in the form of Rose's fiancé. Conflict can also occur when the antagonist and protagonist want the same thing — money, custody of their child, the same woman, and so on.

When creating conflict in your screenplay, keep the following ideas in mind:

>> **You don't want your story to be predictable.** What fun would that be for your audience?

>> **Your story should be believable.** A story loses credibility if the answer to the hero's problem conveniently falls out of the sky. (This is called *deus ex machina,* a convention from Greek stage plays where a god is lowered in a chair from above, conveniently solves the situation, and then is cranked back up to the heavens. It works in cartoons and silly comedies, but not in most genres, especially dramatic pieces.) You don't want people saying your story was contrived.

>> **Think outside the box.** Once a truck got stuck under a low bridge. The whole town came out to push and pull, but to no avail. The truck seemed permanently wedged under the bridge. Then a little girl, who was watching the firemen and townspeople pushing and pulling, stepped forward and quietly said, "Why not let the air out of the tires?" She was thinking outside the box. People want to be surprised. *Gone Girl* surprises the audience with unexpected turn of events. I loved the twist in *The Sixth Sense* when Bruce Willis turns out to be a ghost. (I hope you've seen the film. If not, I apologize now for ruining it for you.)

>> **Studios like high-concept ideas.** *High concept* means something out of the ordinary, unique, something that is fascinating. *Jurassic Park* with dinosaurs being brought back to life in a theme park is a high-concept idea. *Ted* is high concept with an adult man's teddy bear coming to life — and with a foul mouth at that. *Spider-Man* is a high concept — a man is bitten by a scientifically altered spider and becomes a super human spider. Another high concept is when Jeff Goldblum in *The Fly* accidentally merges with a fly to become a six-foot insect with horrifying results. Hey, what a great idea for a sequel, *The Fly Meets Spider-Man* — and it's high concept!

Developing characters

You're taking a drive out to the country. Who do you want to ride with you? Call up some of your favorite people and have them go along for the drive. Make it an enjoyable journey, not just a destination. The same is true with the characters in your story. Make them interesting enough that the reader will want to go with them on a ride, no matter what the destination is. Make them good company! Give your characters personality.

REMEMBER

Your characters should be real and well-rounded outside the scope of your screenplay as well. Does the audience care about these characters? The audience can then see them as no one else in the story sees them — their true selves and quirks are revealed by what they do when they're alone. Follow them around in your head and see what they do.

In a motion picture, visuals are very powerful. In *As Good As It Gets*, we aren't told Jack Nicholson's character is OCD — we're shown it! He opens his bathroom cabinet, and it's stocked to the brim with anti-bacterial soap. He uses a full bar each time he washes his hands under scalding hot water. He can barely stop from flinching as he tries to sterilize his hands. Not a word is said, but now we know more of his character, and we didn't need for him to tell someone he's OCD. When someone is a drunk, it's much more powerful to see that person as a drunk than it would be to have another character tell someone, "Tim's a drunk!"

TIP

When I'm driving, I often try to come up with names for my characters. I pay attention to street names to see which ones have a good sound for my characters' last names, such as Danny Ventura, named after Ventura Blvd., or Susan Riverside, named after Riverside Drive.

TIP

Follow the Law of Threes. If you want to establish a developing relationship in your story, you need at least three situations where your characters interact. If a relationship builds too fast, your audience will think it's contrived (too convenient). A great example of the Law of Threes is the three brief encounters between Elliott and E.T. in *E.T. the Extra-Terrestrial* before they befriend each other. First, Elliott hears something in the shed; then Elliott goes to the forest; and, finally, Elliott sits outside on a lawn chair in front of the shed and is approached by E.T. This gradual lead-up to their bond makes it more acceptable, believable, and effective for the audience. This element of three also works well in romance films.

Drafting your screenplay: Scene by scene

The process of writing a screenplay includes writing a first draft. You need to remember that it's only a first writing session, and there will be changes. Writing is rewriting. Knowing this helps your ideas flow from your thoughts to the page, and you should not be too concerned about editing your words at this point. You're free to put any and all of your ideas on paper at this first-draft stage.

TIP

If you have trouble getting a first draft down on paper, pick up some index cards. Cards are an excellent way to put your story together, and they can make writing a first draft much easier. Here's how it works:

1. **Write on an index card a scene that you envision in your film.**

   You only have to write the location and a brief summary of what the scene is about. If it takes place at the exterior of the diner, you would write: *Ext. Diner — Tim finds out that Sheila works at the diner outside of town.*

2. **After you've written all the scenes you've thought of, lay the cards out on the floor.**

   Spreading out the cards helps you stand back and look at the whole picture, much like a traffic helicopter — you can see where your story moves and where it gets stuck.

3. **Fill in the missing pieces.**

   This part of the process is like doing a jigsaw puzzle — you have to find the perfect pieces to fill in the holes. When you get a brilliant idea for a missing scene, write it on an index card and slip it in where it belongs.

4. **Translate the final order of the scenes into a screenplay format.**

The advantage of using index cards is that they create a nonlinear environment for experimenting with your story and the order of events. You can rearrange each scene in any order until the story begins to fall into place. Some software programs, like *Story O* by Jungle Software (www.JungleSoftware.com), let you work with virtual index cards and easily shuffle them around or add and delete them right on your computer screen.

Using cards can also be useful in adapting a book into a screenplay. When I adapted a memoir for Mel Gibson's Icon Productions, the task of turning a 293-page book into a 100-page screenplay was overwhelming. I broke the book down into separate incidents or events and turned them into individual scenes on over 400 index cards. I arranged the cards and then decided which scenes to keep and which scenes to discard. I rearranged the order of some cards and saw which scenes needed to be consolidated. It helped organize the adapting process and made it much easier to end up with a completed screenplay.

TIP

When you're finished with your first draft of your new screenplay, put it down and walk away. That's right — just walk away. You're too close to it when you've just finished it to start considering rewrites. You need a break: Get away from your screenplay, take a vacation for a few days, or even a few weeks, before you begin rewriting. When you return, you have fresh eyes and can see things more objectively. If you revise too soon, you won't want to change a word — even though you probably need to.

Keeping focused

Writing is fun, but it also requires discipline if you want to turn out a commercial screenplay to produce yourself or sell to a studio. In order to accomplish your dream of writing a screenplay, certain things will help you reach your goals:

>> **Set a deadline and stick to it.** Tell everyone that you're writing a screenplay, and tell them the date you plan on finishing it. Give yourself a reasonable time (at least a couple months, if not more) to write a solid first draft. If you beat your deadline, people will be more impressed. Broadcasting your deadline forces you to sit down and write because everyone will be asking you how your screenplay is going, and you don't want to let everyone down now, do you?

>> **Force yourself to sit down and write within a reasonable schedule.** If you set a goal of writing three pages a day, you'll make your deadline of a first draft in a little over one month. The worst thing you write down on paper (or type on your computer) is always better than the best thing you didn't write down. I'm often amazed at how much better my writing is than I thought it would be, even when I feel that I'm forcing it.

>> **Get over writer's block.** Writer's block is a familiar condition, but it's really nothing more than procrastination. Don't convince yourself that you have this symptom called writer's block; you'll only make yourself feel intimidated. Instead think of *writer's block* as a term referring to a neighborhood of successful writers (and you're one of the writers who lives on that block).

>> **Always know that writing is rewriting.** Rarely does a person write a letter, story, or screenplay that is ready on first draft to be read by all. Knowing that you can rewrite what you wrote is a comfort — even the most brilliant of writers rewrite, often more than beginning writers do! You can, and often will, go back and edit what you've written.

>> **Just start writing.** Look at it as crossing the bridge. Just cross halfway. Now that you're in the middle, it's the same distance to go back where you started — so why not go the same distance but at least finish crossing the bridge?

WATCHING WORDS: CLOSED CAPTIONS

Want to watch a movie and see the script at the same time? Most TVs (and streaming apps) nowadays have a closed-caption function that allows you to read along with a movie or TV show. Closed captioning was established for the hearing impaired, but it's also a great way to study the actual written words while you watch the actors and scenes play out. It lets you compare what you see written on the bottom of the screen with what is delivered in dialogue by the actor onscreen. It makes you realize that everything the actor says is scripted and how the written word is delivered in a natural way following the script verbatim.

Registering your script via the Internet

The main reason for registering your screenplay is to show that you had the idea first — that it is original with you on a certain date. This way, if someone steals your idea or has a similar idea *after* the date that you registered it, you have proof that you had the idea first.

The Writer's Guild of America now has online registration. You can submit your screenplay via an email attachment to the WGA. You pay by credit card and immediately get an online receipt, which you can print to show that your story is registered with the guild. This is the quickest and easiest way to register your script. The cost is $20 for non-WGA members ($10 for members). Go to the WGA website at www.wgawregistry.org and click Online Registration Service.

I also highly recommend you copyright your screenplay through the U.S. Copyright Office (for around $55, but the cost could change so check online). Treatments and screenplays can be registered online. Go to www.copyright.gov.

TIP

You can also do a poor man's copyright. Seal your script or story idea in a manila envelope, address it to yourself, and take it to the post office to be stamped for registered mail. The U.S. Postal Service is considered a legal entity and can mark your package with its USPS stamp at all the corners and sealed edges. A USPS stamp can be used in a court of law to prove you had the idea first. You don't have to mail it — unless you love getting letters. The post office can hand it right back to you. File it away in a safe place. If you want to be protected by statutory laws, then it's best to copyright your work officially with the Copyright Office. This gives you legal rights under copyright law and can reward you financially with statutory damages that you wouldn't be entitled to if you didn't register with the Copyright Office.

Collaborating with writer's software

You can find some great software programs that help you concentrate solely on the creative aspects of your screenplay (leave the formatting for later). Most of the software is very easy to use. Some of these programs offer free trial downloads so you can check them out. Most work for both PCs and Macs. Some of these programs are a little pricey, but the organization and inspiration you'll gain from the software will save you time and trouble in the long run.

>> **Outline 4D** by Write Brothers tracks your story with charts, cards, and color-coding, and literally creates a map of your story that you can stand back and study. Currently Outline 4D only works with PC. The program retails for around $75, and you can find it at www.screenplay.com.

>> **Dramatica Pro** by Write Brothers helps you design your story by asking you questions, giving examples, and guiding you through the creative process of writing a screenplay. I like it because it makes you think about your story from every angle, leaving no stone unturned. It's also a lot of fun to use. Dramatica Pro retails for around $129 (Academic version). Go to www.screenplay.com to order.

>> **Truby's Blockbuster** software, priced at $179, makes for a great writing companion. The program lets you interact with actual examples from many well-known films. It includes Truby's Story Structure Course along with a list of the 22 building blocks of every great story. Add-ons are available that help you write for specific genres such as romance, sci-fi, thriller, action, and so on. Take a look at www.truby.com.

>> **Power Structure,** at about $99, is a powerful program that encourages you to ask yourself questions and brainstorm ideas to develop a strong structure for your screenplay. Check it out at www.powerstructure.com.

>> **Save the Cat** lets you work with index cards and a beat sheet to help structure your screenplay. The program has a *litter box* section for brainstorming and lots of other helpful steps. The software includes tips and a tutorial from screenwriter Blake Snyder at www.savethecat.com, starting at an annual subscription of $99 per year.

>> **Story O** from Jungle Software (www.junglesoftware.com), whose virtual index cards I mention earlier, also helps you organize your story, develop your characters, and write your story. There's even an iOS app version for the iPhone and iPad.

You can also find most of these software programs and others by visiting The Writer's Store at www.writersstore.com. Many software products have lower-priced Academic versions for students, and sometimes discount specials.

TIP

Another great idea to get your creative juices flowing is to check out a card game called *The Storymatic* (www.thestorymatic.com). It's a fun non-virtual card game that comes with over 500 cards that powers your thinking cap, and triggers you to come up with almost unlimited concepts and story ideas. It's also great for unlocking writer's block, or just to play as a game with your family and friends.

Formatting your screenplay

You'll be submitting your screenplay to people who get them every day, so not only does your screenplay idea need to be creative and unique to stand out, but you also need to know the basics of proper screenplay formatting so that when your screenplay comes across the desk of an executive, buyer, or distributor, it looks like the real thing. Take a look at *Screenwriting For Dummies* by Laura Schellhardt (published by Wiley) for the lowdown on formatting as well as writing. Also consider investing in one of the following software programs, which do all the script formatting for you automatically:

>> **Movie Magic Screenwriter** is a formatting program that includes a setting that lets you view your scripts in outline (card) form. I especially like this software because it allows you to export script information, such as location settings, characters, props, and scenes, so that you can begin scheduling your shoot days. The software includes iPartner, which lets you collaborate on a script over the Internet with your writing partner whether that partner is across town or across the world. I've written most of my scripts using this great software, which costs $169. Free technical support and customer service is great! Check it out at www.screenplay.com.

>> **Final Draft** is similar to Screenwriter. The software also includes a collaborative streamlined option to work with writing partners anywhere in the world in real-time. In addition there's an app version for your smartphone and iPad called *Final Draft Mobile* for under $10. The program retails for $249. ($129 for Academic and Military versions). Go to www.finaldraft.com.

>> **Writer Duet** is similar to Screenwriter and Final Draft — but it's free for your first three screenplays! You can download the program at www.writerduet.com.

WARNING

Regardless of what software you use to write your screenplay (Word, Screenwriter, Final Draft, and so on), always convert it into a PDF file before emailing it to someone. Do *not* send it in the software format that you wrote it in — many recipients may not have the same software you do (and if they do, it's an invitation to edit and manipulate your words) and thus will not be able to open your screenplay file. Of course, if you're printing your screenplay out and snail-mailing it or handing it to them in person, you can disregard the PDF warning.

Selling Your Screenplay to a Studio, Distributor, or Investor

You can sell your screenplay physically to a studio or distributor, and they will make the picture on their own. Or you can sell a distributor on the idea of your screenplay and story, and the distributor could give you a written commitment to distribute the picture when it's completed (this is called a *negative pickup*). If you get a commitment from a distributor, finding investors willing to take a chance with your movie, knowing it already has distribution interest, will be a lot easier.

Selling a production studio or distributor on your idea consists of setting up a meeting to verbally pitch your story. If your idea is well received, the next step is to follow up with either the story in the form of a short one- to two-page synopsis, a *treatment* or *outline* (a detailed synopsis 10 to 20 pages in length), or a copy of the actual screenplay.

Getting your foot (and screenplay) in the door

Some companies receive hundreds of screenplays a month, in addition to one-page summaries from eager screenwriters. The head of the studio or the producer can't possibly read every script that comes in, so the studio hires a script reader to sit all day reading and evaluating screenplays that are submitted to the company. This means you only get one chance at a good first impression. If the reader doesn't like it, your screenplay never goes any further.

The script reader usually reads your script and then fills out an evaluation page or pages grading your screenplay — similar to what your elementary-school teacher used to do with your assignments. In addition to grading your script, the reader also writes a short synopsis of your story so that the studio executives, producer, or potential buyer can know what your script is about. It's kind of like the *CliffsNotes* of your story. These are some of the things a reader evaluates:

>> Is it an interesting story that holds the reader's attention?

>> Is it well written?

>> Are the characters engaging?

>> Does it have commercial potential?

>> Is it a "pass" or a "consider for further evaluation"?

If your script does get a thumbs-up from a script reader, you now have to prepare for the rest of the battle. Sharpen your selling skills by warming up for your meeting with an effective pitch that you can deliver in person to close the deal on your great screenplay idea.

Pitching a home run

When you're trying to sell your screenplay to a studio or distributor, you need to throw a powerful *pitch*. A pitch is a verbal sales tool that explains your story and tries to convince the receiver to accept your idea so you can land a distribution deal, a financing commitment from an investor, or a production deal with a studio to produce your movie. Oftentimes you will be initially asked what is the *logline*. A logline is often a brief one or two sentence describing your story, presented to intrigue the listener into wanting to know more.

REMEMBER

Who you make your pitch to is as important as the quality of your pitch. If you pitch to the wrong person, you're wasting your time (and his or hers as well). Many executives in Hollywood are hired just to say "no." You want to give your pitch to someone who can say "yes" or at least to someone who likes your screenplay and has the clout to take it to the person who says "yes." A development executive at a studio or an acquisition person at a production company is usually the person you need to get a meeting with.

Keep the following tips in mind as you prepare and give your pitch:

TIP

>> **Identify your film with other successful films.** Hollywood executives need a quick reference point to decide whether your story is something they want to know more about. The quickest way to identify the genre and commercial viability of your screenplay is to cross it with at least two other well-known films.

Always cross your movie with *successful* films. If your concept is the same genre as a movie that just bombed at the box office, the executive you're pitching to won't want anything to do with it. My comedy parody *Miss Cast Away & the Island Girls* crosses *Cast Away* with *Miss Congeniality* along with the crazy humor of *Scary Movie* and *Austin Powers,* which paints its possible success as a commercial vehicle.

>> **Keep pitching until you get a home run.** Babe Ruth was known for his home run record (over 700 throughout his career), but he could have set a record for the most strikeouts, too. You have to keep trying pitches to get a hit. Selling your screenplay is very similar. You wind up for the swing, you pitch, and maybe your pitch creates a home run — or at least gets you to first, second, or third base. And then again, maybe you strike out. So you wait for a new game and start all over again. Each time you strike out, go back and work on your pitch so that it's better the next time around.

>> **Intrigue the listener so that he or she will want to hear more.** A way to do this is to begin your pitch with a question (for example, "What would happen if the sun suddenly burned out?"), and then tell them what happens in your story.

>> **Practice your elevator pitch.** The *elevator pitch* is a quick, intriguing pitch of your story (usually only a few sentences) that can be told between elevator floors. You never know when you're going to accidentally enter an elevator and find Steven Spielberg standing there. You have his full attention until he gets off on his floor!

I heard a story once about a frustrated writer who took a famous award-winning film, changed the names, updated the time and locations, and sent it out. It was turned down by every agent and studio in town. *The Wizard of Oz* was turned down by every publisher who didn't have the courage — some had no heart — but L. Frank Baum had the brains to self-publish his stories, which then attracted a publisher to pick up the sequels — and the rest is history. So use a little creativity and keep trying.

PEN NAMES

Want to use a different name on your script? Stephen King and many writers have used *pen names* for one reason or another. Maybe you're submitting the same script again with rewrites and you don't want your real name to cross-reference with the new script. Or maybe you have several projects out for consideration and you don't want them to all have your real name on them. Maybe you're not thrilled about the script and don't want to associate with it at all. Here's a suggestion for finding a pen name: Take your middle name, or your best friend's middle name, and then the street you grew up on. For example, my middle name is Michael, and I grew up on Westbrook Drive. So my pen name is Michael Westbrook.

2

Gearing Up to Make Your Movie

You discover how to successfully budget and schedule your movie and also find secrets for financing your production.

You learn how to find the right locations for setting your story and how to get the best cast and crew you can find.

Planning your film with a visual eye before ever stepping on set is important. In this part, I help you visualize your movie through shot-by-shot sketches called *storyboards.*

Chapter **4**

Scheduling and Budgeting Your Movie

B efore you begin filming your movie, you have to budget and schedule what you're going to shoot. The schedule helps you figure out what scenes you need to shoot first and the most economical way to get your movie completed. The schedule and budget go hand in hand. Often, you don't have much choice: When you have a set amount to make your movie, you have to make your schedule fit your budget and your budget fit your schedule.

In this chapter, you discover how to accurately budget and schedule your independent film, whether you have no budget, a low budget, or a budget in the millions. You can also find out how to outline your whole shooting schedule on a production board so that you know who's shooting what, where, and when. Finally, I let you in on secrets to shooting your movie on a tight budget.

WHAT COMES FIRST — THE SCHEDULE OR THE BUDGET?

Which you tackle first — scheduling your shoot or doing the budget — depends on your situation. It would be nice if you could schedule your movie and then see how much money you need, but filmmakers often have only so much money and have to make their films fit the budgets, not their budgets fit their films. It's like trying to pack too many clothes into a small suitcase — you push them in as tight as you can and hope you can still close it. Whatever you can't fit in the case, you have to manage without.

Scheduling your movie lets you know where to direct the money and to which budget categories. You usually have a set amount of money, and it's the distribution of that amount that is determined by the scheduling — what will be spent where.

By breaking down your script and sorting out cast, crew, props, locations, and shooting days before doing your detailed budget, you leave nothing to chance — this at least lets you know if you have enough money to make your movie. You're able to know that what you've scheduled fits within the budget, and so present a more accurate and detailed budget to satisfy your investor, if you're lucky enough to find one.

The Art of Scheduling a Production

Even if you have a definitive budget, you need to break down all the elements of your production to determine how to distribute the money you have. These breakdowns also help you figure out how many days it will take to shoot your movie. You have to make your budget fit your schedule, so be prepared to do some juggling. If you're on a tight budget, you won't have the luxury of shooting your movie over a period of several months. Your budget may only allow you to schedule a 12-day shoot (every additional day is going to cost you money). Juggling includes consolidating scenes. If you can shoot the scene in the cave in two days instead of three, and the breaking-up scene in the car, instead of in the shopping mall, you'll be able to shorten your schedule, thus saving time and money.

Scheduling a production is like playing with a Rubik's Cube, where you keep turning and adjusting and twisting and tweaking until the elements fall into place. And scheduling your movie efficiently is essential to saving time and money. Scheduling your movie includes:

>> *Lining* the script by going through and marking items such as actors, props, wardrobe, and special effects

>> Putting those items on individual *breakdown sheets,* each representing one scene from the movie

>> Transferring the elements on the breakdown sheets to *production board strips*

>> Rearranging the order of production strips to find the best shooting schedule

The director and the first assistant director (A.D.) usually work on the schedule together. The process includes figuring out what scenes and locations can be shot together in the same day, scheduling actors to work consecutive days, and deciding how to tighten the schedule so the movie can be shot in fewer days. If you don't have an assistant director to help schedule and be on the set to keep things organized, then you have to do the schedule all by yourself.

TIP

A calendar is your best friend when scheduling your shoot. You choose the date to start principal photography and the date the production will wrap. By looking at a calendar, you see what days the weekends fall on and whether any statutory holidays (like Christmas and Memorial Day) occur that the cast and crew should have off. Calendar programs are also great for reminders and scheduling appointments. Here are two smartphone apps to make a date with: PocketLife Calendar and Tiny Calendar. Scheduling software usually includes a calendar. Most computers come with calendar software installed; that might just be all you need.

Lining your script

You break down, or *line,* your script by marking elements that affect your budget and schedule. With different-colored highlighters in hand, start combing through your script (or have the assistant director do it, if you have one), highlighting important items with a different color for each category. You end up with a very colorful script after the process is complete. This process is intended to flag the script so accurate breakdowns can be made. The categories to highlight include:

>> Actors

>> Extras (background people)

>> Props

>> Wardrobe or special costumes

>> Sets and locations

>> Special effects

>> Vehicles

>> Animals

>> Special equipment

>> Special makeup

Breaking into breakdown sheets

After you highlight the various categories of items, transfer the highlighted elements to individual *breakdown sheets* — one for each scene in your script. A breakdown sheet contains separate category boxes to add the elements you've highlighted in the script. You enter each element in the appropriate category box, such as a hammer in the props area, either by hand or by using one of the available software programs (see the section "Scheduling software to make your life easier" later in this chapter).

Number each breakdown sheet so that you can go back and reference it if you need to. Every character in the script is also given a reference number, usually starting with the number 1 for your lead actor. You transfer these numbers to the breakdown sheets and eventually to the individual strips on the production board (more on this in the section "Creating production strips"). Numbering saves space so that you don't have to keep writing the characters' names (plus there wouldn't be enough space on a strip).

A breakdown sheet also has a *header* that includes the following details:

>> Scene number

>> Script page

>> Page count (length of scene divided into eighths — for example, a 1/2 page would be counted as 4/8 of a page)

>> Location/setting

>> Scene description (one sentence)

>> Exterior or interior

>> Day or night

>> Script day (for example, the third day in the story when Mary arrives at the plantation — this is helpful for knowing wardrobe changes)

>> Breakdown sheet page number

Figure 4-1 shows a sample breakdown sheet from my film *The Dragon's Candle*. Scene 106 has Ghandlin the wizard driving a borrowed police car and zapping traffic out of his way with his magic wand. The breakdown sheet provides separate boxes listing the elements that are needed for this scene.

Scene # 106	THE DRAGON'S CANDLE	Date: 10/5/2002
Script Page: 94		Sheet: 102
Page Count: 2 2/8 pgs.	**BREAKDOWN SHEET**	Int/Ext. EXT
		Day/Night: Day

Scene Description: <u>The Wizard steers the policecar into oncoming traffic</u>   *Page 1*
Setting: <u>Freeway</u>
Location: <u>(Ottawa Queensway)</u>
Sequence: _____ Script Day: <u>8</u>

Cast Members 1. GHANDLIN 2. RICK	**Stunts** stunt car drivers	**Vehicles** Police car
	Props magic wand	**Special Effects** cars zapped out of the way
Extras drivers x 9		
Wardrobe wizards robe	**Makeup**	**Livestock**
Animal Handler	**Music**	**Sound**

Courtesy of Gorilla ™ Jungle Software ©2002

FIGURE 4-1: A breakdown sheet created with Gorilla production software.

TIP

If you can't afford scheduling software, you can create your own breakdown sheets. A yellow lined note pad works well. Just create categories for each element and enter them into the correct category. You can also go online and download an empty template breakdown sheet from www.studiobinder.com and make as many copies as you need.

Propping up your prop list

Every prop that will appear in your movie must be pulled from the script and added to the props category in your breakdown sheets. A *prop* is defined as anything your characters interact with, such as guns, cellphones, brooms, and so on. On a low-budget film, try to borrow your props — especially if they're contemporary items. For hard-to-find props, you can usually rent them from a prop house or rental house — or you may find them listed online at the 411 directory in New York (www.ny411.com) and Los Angeles (www.la411.com) as well as the Creative Handbook (www.creativehandbook.com). In Los Angeles, California, you can actually rent props from Warner Bros. Studios (www.property.WarnerBros.com), which has over 200,000 square feet of storage that houses thousands of props from productions throughout the last 80 years. For my feature film *First Dog,* I was able to rent furniture used in the TV show *The West Wing* to dress my Oval Office set, including the oval rug — making my set look very presidential.

REMEMBER

Often, props are confused with set dressing, but the difference is that actors don't interact with set dressing. Set dressing includes a picture frame on a mantle or flowers in a vase on a table (the vase becomes a prop only if someone picks it up and smashes it over the head of another). The baseball bat in Mel Gibson's film *Signs* would normally have been categorized as set dressing, but because the actors actually interacted with the bat (which was displayed on a wall), it is categorized as a prop. You address set dressing in your breakdown sheets only if it's crucial to the story.

Dressing up your wardrobe list

You add certain wardrobe elements to your breakdown sheets, such as costumes, uniforms, or clothes that have to be rented or sewn from scratch. A character's jeans and T-shirt don't need to be entered in the wardrobe box, but a gangster's zoot suit or a Santa Claus outfit does. Because scenes aren't usually shot in chronological order, each outfit is given a script day number to ensure that the actor wears the correct wardrobe in each scene. Script days (the timeline of your story) will be part of the breakdown sheets, and if the story takes place over five days, you'll sit down with the wardrobe person and decide what clothing your actors will wear each day if it's not addressed in the script.

Locating locations

You can list your location settings in the heading of each breakdown sheet. Locations dictate a lot regarding scheduling and budget. Moving your production team from one location to another takes precious time — so you want to shoot all your scenes that take place in that one location first (even if one scene is at the beginning of the movie and the other scene at that location is at the end) before moving to the next location. If you're using software like Entertainment Partners Scheduling (see the section "Scheduling software to make your life easier," later in this chapter), you can group all the same locations together. You should also make notes — are your locations private or public property? Do you need to secure permits or pay location fees, and how much do they cost? Keep your locations to a minimum; otherwise, you may end up going over budget.

TIP

Many states offer incentives to encourage filmmakers to shoot in their cities. See Chapter 6 for more information about location deals.

A "special" on special effects

Scheduling special effects on your breakdown sheets helps you determine what kind of effects you can afford. Keep effects to a minimum if you're working with a lower budget. You may find that designing special effects on a computer fits within your budget better than shooting effects in the camera — such as, for example, adding a floating element in post-production instead of filming it floating on a wire while shooting. (This saves you time on set.) If you can get away without special effects and concentrate on a good story, though, I recommend that route. See Chapter 17 for much more on creating special effects for your movie.

Creating production strips

After you've copied all the category elements from your screenplay onto your breakdown sheets, you're ready to start transferring these elements to the individual strips that go onto your production board. *Production strips* are about 1/4-inch wide and contain the information from your breakdown sheets. Each strip represents an individual scene and contains all the elements featured in that particular scene, such as location, actors, props, and wardrobe. The header contains the names of your characters in the script with a number assigned to each character. These numbers are added to the strips and line up with the header, so you can see at a glance which scenes each actor appears in.

By having the scenes of your script on individual strips, you can move them around to find the most economical and effective shooting schedule. Movies are rarely shot in continuity. Rather, you want to group the same locations together in your shooting schedule so that you don't have to jump back and forth. Shooting the scene at the airport, wrapping up, and then later in the story going back to the airport to shoot more scenes would be silly.

You also want to color-code your strips so that you can step back and see how many interior and exterior scenes you have, making arranging shooting times easier. If the schedule shows you there are more interior scenes, then you know you don't have to worry about weather as much. If the schedule shows you that you have a lot of daytime exterior scenes, then you know you don't have to rent movie lights and a generator — but you do have to be aware of what time the sun sets and when you'll be losing the light. You can choose the color code that works best for you. I usually color-code my strips as follows:

Exterior Day = yellow

Exterior Night = blue

Interior Day = white

Interior Night = green

You schedule as many scenes as you feel you can shoot in one day and group locations, rooms, and so on together. The number of days you shoot has an impact on your budget, so try to fit as much into each shooting day that you feel you can realistically cover without sacrificing the quality of your production. Always allow yourself more time than you think it will take to shoot a scene. Remember, time is your biggest enemy. Time is the one thing I wish I had more of when shooting my movies. Shooting a dialogue scene may be quicker and easier to cover than an action scene that needs to be choreographed and covered from several different angles. An experienced assistant director can help you determine whether your shooting schedule is realistic.

After you've selected the scenes (strips) for each day's shoot, you separate them in your production board with a black strip and then begin the next day's schedule of scenes. You should complete your production board well in advance of shooting (during the preproduction stage) so that everyone on your crew knows ahead of time what is shooting and when.

Scheduling software to make your life easier

A physical production board is a heavy cardboard or plastic compartment board that allows you to fit your strips into it and see your entire schedule at a glance. Because physical production boards aren't as practical as software that does the same thing only better and faster, it doesn't make sense to use them anymore.

One of the advantages of scheduling your film with a software program as opposed to taping strips of paper onto a piece of poster board is that the software allows you to easily group locations and actors and the software's algorithms can present you with a series of alternative shooting sequences. The other nice thing about scheduling software is that it enables you to generate various lists and customized breakdown sheets. The software automatically transfers the items on your breakdown sheets to your production strips.

There are a variety of software programs that work to help you schedule your production like EP Scheduling (www.entertainmentpartners.com) or Gorilla's Scheduling software (www.junglesoftware.com). Jungle Software also makes a powerful and affordable program for smaller productions called Chimpanzee that not only does scheduling and budgeting, but crew and shot lists as well. You organize your scheduling in the computer and then you can print or email to the appropriate crew members. Breakdown sheets and category lists can be easily generated using the appropriate scheduling software as well.

TIP

If you can't afford a professional scheduling program, you can put all your scenes on 3 x 5 index cards and then organize the index cards in the order you are going to shoot your scenes, grouping the same locations together to minimize the time and cost of moving to each location.

Stripping down your schedule

Two main factors determine the order in which you shoot your scenes: characters and locations. Start organizing your production strips by grouping the characters that appear in the same scenes together. Then arrange the strips with the same locations as close together as possible. Most of the scheduling software programs will let you feed the elements into the program and then automatically arrange the best schedule keeping the same locations and actors in mind.

Actors

Try to schedule your actors so that they work as many consecutive days as possible. Otherwise, you have to drop and then pick up the actors again. In some union agreements, you still have to pay actors who are *on hold* for days they don't work. With non-union agreements, you don't have to worry about this. However, if a union actor is on hold, he or she has to be available at a moment's notice should your schedule change. If you're doing a union production with union actors, special weekly rates will save some money in the budget if you're working an actor more than two or three days at a time.

After you have your production strips in place, you can generate a *day-out-of-days* chart that shows when your actors work during the shooting schedule. You can do this by hand or generate it from the software program you use to produce your production board and strips.

Locations

Grouping the same rooms, buildings, and locations together helps the schedule. Picking up and moving your cast and crew from one location to the next takes time and money. Most films are shot out of continuity for this reason.

TIP

Schedule outdoor scenes first. That way, if it rains or the weather isn't appropriate for your shot, you can move indoors and use the time to shoot interior scenes under safe cover. If you start shooting indoors and then go outside, you aren't giving yourself a security blanket for a *cover-set* (backup location). By having a backup interior location when it rains on a day you've scheduled a sunny outdoor scene, you can go into the indoor location without shutting down production, and then go outside again when the weather has cleared up.

Figure 4-2 shows a production board created with EP Scheduling. The Academic version (student) is $185. You can even check out the software by downloading the free demo off its site.

Balancing Your Budget

If you're doing a low-budget production, you have a finite amount of money to work with. Therefore, creating a budget and sticking to it is critical; you aren't likely to have a big studio (or a filthy rich Aunt Sally) provide you with extra cash if you overspend and come up short. Creating a budget involves allotting the proper amount to each area. Adding at least a 10-percent contingency to your budget to allow for overages is also important; otherwise, you could end up with an unfinished movie.

Everything has a price. If you pay full price for everything, your independent budget could end up at $100,000. But if you're a good dealmaker, you may be able to shoot the same film for $50,000. If you *barter*, you might be able to do it for $25,000. Hollywood spends money and often doesn't have time to work the deals. You, on the other hand, probably have no choice.

REMEMBER

If you've already found people to finance your movie, they're going to want to see a detailed budget. They'll want to know how you intend to spend their money. So even if the money isn't coming out of your own pocket, you can't escape doing a budget for your production.

Tightrope walking above the line

First, you need to determine what your *above-the-line* numbers are going to be. Above-the-line items include negotiable and influential salaries, such as those paid to the writer, director, producer, and star actors. Your cast is usually found above-the-line because they drive the commercial viability of your movie, and their salaries have to be negotiated. If you're doing a studio picture, a star can demand up to $20 million or more these days. On an independent low-budget movie, your actors (especially if they're union) are going to up the cost to make your film. The other above-the-line positions like the producer, director, and writer (unless they're all you) are also negotiable, but may be controlled by a union (Director's Guild DGA or Writer's Guild WGA) or agent wanting mucho bucks for his client.

On a non-union film, you can save a lot of money if your cast works for deferred pay, meaning that they don't receive salaries until, and if, the movie makes a profit. Getting actors to work deferred is easier than getting crew members to do so, because actors often need the exposure and experience and can add the role to their acting reel and resume.

STARRING CAMEOS

If you're creative, you may be able to slip a recognized actor into your film and not have to pay a $20 million salary. If you hire an actor for one day, or even a couple of hours, you can shoot several scenes and insert them throughout the movie. I had Dan Aykroyd do the voice of Dexter the computer in my movie *The Random Factor*. I spent a little over an hour with him and was able to use about 15 minutes of his voice-over throughout the film. James Earl Jones played a judge in two scenes for my movie *Undercover Angel*. I shot with him for a whole day so I only had to pay him a one-day salary. George Carlin performed a cameo in my American Film Institute student project many years ago. I had the camera set up and ready to go. He came in, did his scene, and we wrapped in less than 45 minutes.

I had a 20-year friendship with Michael Jackson, and as a favor, he did a cameo as Agent MJ in my movie *Miss Castaway & the Island Girls*. I was able to shoot all his scenes at his Neverland Ranch in less than an hour.

The best way to approach actors is through referrals, or meeting them happenchance in a store or restaurant. I found Yasmine Bleeth's (from *Baywatch*) purse after she left it in a restaurant, and then I asked her to star in my movie *Undercover Angel,* and she did! You can also write a letter to an actor's agent or manager to see if you can convince him or her to be in your movie.

TIP

If your cast is union, you can't defer pay (unless it's classified as a short or student production), but you may qualify to do your movie under a special agreement with the Screen Actors Guild – American Federation of Television and Radio Artists (SAG–AFTRA) called the SAG Indie Program. This program works closely with independent filmmakers so that they can afford to use union actors in their films. The agreements that SAG–AFTRA offers to independent filmmakers include:

>> **Student Film Agreement:** You don't have to pay the actors to be in your film as long as the production is done under an accredited college or university and you are a student. The film's budget has to be less than $35,000 and the movie can't be longer than 35 minutes. The movie cannot be sold or distributed (you can use it to showcase your filmmaking skills and help get a paid position in the future).

>> **Short Film Agreement:** The budget must be under $50,000 and 40 minutes in length or less. You can negotiate the actors' salaries. The bonus is that you can use union (SAG-AFTRA) and non-union actors.

ACTORS WILL WORK FOR FOOD

Whether or not your budget allows for your actors to receive salaries, you have to budget to feed them (don't forget to feed your crew too!). Feeding your actors is one of the most important things — don't skimp in this category. People can get very irritable when they haven't eaten properly, and you don't want to fill everyone up on burgers and pizza every day. Budget for not only a great caterer, but for *craft services* (snacks) as well. There are also new online delivery services like DoorDash and Grubhub, that deliver from any restaurant on-demand for any amount of food orders. Being generous when it comes to feeding your actors can make all the difference in the world. Make sure to find out whether anyone requires a special diet, such as vegetarians or those with food allergies or lactose intolerance. You don't want anyone starving on your shoot.

>> **Ultra Low Budget:** The total film budget must be $250,000 or less. You can mix union and non-union actors, and you pay a $125 daily flat rate to your talent. This is the agreement I recommend if your budget is under $250,000 and you're planning on having it distributed.

>> **Modified Low Budget:** The budget must be between $250,000 and $700,000. $335 day rates apply for actors, or weekly rate is $1166. You must use all union players. Requires an initial theatrical release to qualify.

>> **Low Budget:** The budget for the film must be between $700,000 but under $2.5 million. You pay your actors reduced union rates of $630 a day, or weekly rate of $2,190, and you must use all union players.

>> **New Media:** For projects with budgets over $50,000 and intended for the Internet or any form of new media outlets. Requires initial release through the Internet or a new media platform. This is a fairly new agreement, and it is recommended to contact SAG-AFTRA's new media department that handles these contracts at sagindie@sagaftra.org.

These agreements pertain to the actors only, not the filmmaker and crew members. For more details on each SAG indie agreement, go to www.sagindie.org. Always check the SAG–AFTRA website because actor's salaries are always changing, as well as contract stipulations.

Hanging below the line

Below-the-line items include your more definitive numbers — flat fees and fixed salaries. These usually include your staff and crew, film stock (if you're going that route), memory cards or hard drives for shooting digitally, and other categories in which the dollar amounts aren't astronomical and in which you have choices of where to purchase, barter, or rent things to fit your budget. On a feature film for which the stars are getting paid millions, the above-the-line numbers can dwarf the below-the-line numbers.

Staffing and crewing

You can find many ways to enlist staff and crew to work on your production. You can pay them something, or you can get them to work for free and defer their pay. The best of both worlds is to pay your crew a little something up front and defer the rest. Getting a staff member or crew person to work deferred is more difficult than getting an actor to work deferred because, unlike the actor, the crew member's work is not as visible on screen. The only advantage for a crew member to work for deferred salary is if they are new to the business and are willing to learn and even apprentice on your production. A crew member may work for less if he or she is looking to graduate to a higher position and receive a better credit for their resume (for example, moving up from gaffer to cinematographer on the shoot). See Chapter 7 for more about crew members.

REMEMBER

You need to negotiate with each crew member and put in writing (a *deal memo*) whether he or she is working by the hour or being paid a flat fee. You can find all kinds of production forms, including actor and crew agreements from Film Daily (www.filmdaily.tv/production/film-contracts). They average about $15 per template. If you go to No Film School (www.nofilmschool.com) and search *99 free templates,* you'll find tons of agreement templates for free. If you're working with a non-union crew, you have a lot more flexibility in negotiating salaries. Minimum-wage laws will help you set a limited hourly payment (check the minimums in your state) for your crew so they don't feel you're exploiting them. For more information, go to U.S. Department of Labor (www.dol.gov) and click on "Wages."

Equipment costs — yes it does!

Equipment costs are also part of the below-the-line expenses. Equipment includes things like sound equipment, cameras, tripod, dolly, and lighting equipment (stands, lights, cables, and so on).

There are lots of camera rental houses that will negotiate with you. Check out rental houses in the Creative Handbook (www.creativehandbook.com) and of course search online for rental houses in your area. You can make deals on renting or borrowing props, and getting locations to use in your movie through friends and family.

TIP

Nowadays, sometimes it's cheaper and easier to buy all your own equipment instead of renting. If you're doing a low-budget production, look for crew with their own equipment. You may find a cinematographer who has his own camera — most do as digital cameras are much more affordable these days. Some cinematographers even own 16mm and 35mm cameras if you still want to shoot with old-fashioned film stock. Some crew may have lights and grip equipment, too. Your sound mixer will probably own their sound equipment, including a recorder and microphones, as these have become more affordable, especially if they are part of the crew's livelihood. (See Chapters 10, 11, and 12 for more on equipment.)

Film stock or digital hard driving

The medium on which you choose to shoot your story affects your budget, whether you shoot Super-8, 16mm, 35mm, or digital (see Chapter 10). Your *shooting ratio,* or the number of takes in relation to the number of shots you end up using, is also going to determine what you spend on film stock and developing or on digital memory cards and hard drive space if shooting in HD — and ultimately your budget. Do you plan on shooting 1:1 (one take per usable shot) or 3:1 (three takes to get the shot)? Whether this is your first movie or last (just kidding), determine whether you need to do three takes to get the shot or ten takes to get the shot (even many seasoned directors like to do multiple takes). This is also another reason why shooting on digital makes more sense. Film stock is expensive. With digital, you can do as many takes as you want because you are always downloading the digital footage and reusing the memory cards.

Memory cards are used in digital HD cameras. They're like mini hard drives that your camera's high definition footage is recorded and stored on. The content on the memory card can then be transferred to a computer or external hard drive and the card reused. Memory cards come in various sizes starting at 8GB and going all the way up to 512GB (from SanDisk).

Topping your budget

The budget *top sheet* is a summary of your budget that lists the main budget categories and the totals of each. You can reference each department by its budget category number assigned on the budget top sheet for a detailed breakdown in the long-form budget. Usually, the top sheet is enough for an investor to see how your production breaks down in terms of cost. Eventually, an investor will want to see the detailed budget and how the categories are broken down.

Each budget item on the top sheet is assigned a category number that helps you reference the details of that category within the long-form detailed budget. It's like a table of contents. For example, Production Staff is category 07-00 and can be found on page 3 of the long-form detailed budget breakdown. On page 3 of the budget detail page, category 07-00 will be broken down listing the individual staff positions and the duration of employment and salary of each.

Budgeting for budget software

Like scheduling software, budgeting software can take a lot of the hard work out of creating a budget for a movie. The following are some of the programs available:

>> **Microsoft Excel** enables you to create your own budget template. Apple has a version called Numbers that works similar to Excel.

>> **BBP Software** makes a film/TV budgeting template that runs on Microsoft Excel, and works with both Mac and Windows. It sells for $49. You can download it at www.boilerplate.net.

>> **Studio Binder** offers a free budget template download. The program features standard categories and automatically totals columns (www.studiobinder.com).

>> **Gorilla** has a budgeting template included in its complete production software package and is available at www.junglesoftware.com for $249. Jungle Software also offers a more affordable budgeting template for smaller productions that is included in its program Chimpanzee for $179.

>> **EP Budgeting** by Entertainment Partners is the budget software of choice in Hollywood. The academic version starts around $185, and $489 for the non-academic version. It can be expensive for the low-budget film-maker, but it's the top of the line if you can afford it. Check it out at www.entertainmentpartners.com or www.writersstore.com. If you're a student (and can prove it), go for the more affordable academic version.

The different budgeting software programs are similar, but some are easier to use than others and some have additional applications. Which program you use is usually a matter of personal preference and also depends on how much you want to spend. Entertainment Partners budgeting software has all the categories that you can use or modify — and most studio pictures use this software. If you use Microsoft Excel, you'll have to design a budgeting template and set up the tables to give you the proper calculations. Some software like BBP Software, mentioned earlier, uses Excel and turns it into a film–budgeting program.

Factoring in a contingency amount

One concern is to make sure you don't go over budget. It happens all the time with studio pictures, but it's not as much a problem for studio pictures as it is for independent films. If a studio picture at $30 million goes over $5 million, the studio usually covers it. If your independent $50,000 movie goes over budget by $10,000, getting that additional funding and completing your movie could become a serious problem. Films often go over budget; rarely do they come in under budget.

Make sure that you allow for a contingency in your budget (usually 5 to 15 percent of the total budget). This will be helpful if and when emergencies come up and things end up costing more than expected, or the schedule changes because of an actor, weather, or some unplanned event. An additional $15,000 contingency on a $150,000 movie could make the difference between having a finished or unfinished movie in the end.

Insurance Is Your Best Policy

An important budget item is insurance for your cast, crew, and equipment. In the long run, insurance *saves* you money, not costs you! It's kind of like wearing your seatbelt: You may not need it, but if you do, you'll be glad that you buckled up for your journey. Better safe than sorry.

Purchasing insurance for a film production is a mix-and-match situation. You need to decide what type of coverage you need and how much of each type of coverage you want. You also need to decide how much of a deductible you're willing to pay (just like with your car or health insurance) if you ever have to activate the policy. You should consider the following types of coverage:

>> **Cast insurance:** Getting cast insurance usually requires physicals for your actors to make sure that they're starting on your production in a healthy state. If a cast member gets sick (and cannot continue on with production) or dies, cast insurance covers any additional costs that can arise to finish the picture — even if it has to be recast. This coverage can be extremely expensive and should be purchased on an independent film only if a cast member cannot be replaced.

>> **General liability insurance:** This is required insurance that protects you and your production from claims against you for property damage and claims against you from the public or a third party for injury or accidents incurred on the set. Your insurance company, upon request, will issue you *certificates of insurance* (proof of insurance) for each property you shoot at.

Make sure that your general liability policy covers any interior locations you shoot at. If you're filming at the art museum and one of your movie lights ignites a priceless painting and ends up burning down the museum, you don't want to be stuck without insurance to cover the disaster. No one will let you shoot on their property until you hand them a certificate of insurance, anyway. An average liability policy covers up to $1 million.

>> **Negative film and faulty stock coverage:** Though it's still called film and stock coverage, this includes all digital, hard drives, and equipment used to

record and download your camera footage. It also covers original faulty film stock and processing disasters. This includes coverage for damage to film and hard drives. A policy can also cover faulty lab work, ruined negatives, bad stock if you shoot on film, defective memory cards or hard drives, footage lost during shipping, and so on. Also known as *negative insurance,* it pays for the cost to reshoot footage that was lost or damaged. This is not as crucial for shoots when you're using digital and hard drives — *if* you make backups of your footage. (If you shoot digital and use external hard drives, always back up — just in case — because this is your insurance, literally.)

» **Props, wardrobe, and sets coverage:** This covers damage, loss, or theft of important props, wardrobe, and sets. If your movie doesn't require expensive props and costumes, you can go without this insurance, or take out a low coverage policy (only insure for the total value of all props, wardrobe, and sets). Don't insure for more than the value — it will cost you more, and it's not necessary (you can only be reimbursed the total value of what you lost, not beyond that).

» **Production equipment coverage:** This covers any equipment used on the production. Many rental companies won't rent equipment to you if you don't insure their equipment under a property coverage policy. Most companies request an *insurance certificate,* which is issued from the insurance company showing proof that you have insurance and what your coverage is. On most low-budget productions, a $250,000 minimum coverage should suffice. If you're using your own equipment, it may be covered by your home or renter's insurance (if you have those policies).

» **Errors and omissions (E&O) insurance:** Before a distributor or network will present your movie, it needs to be protected with errors & omissions insurance, also referred to as E&O insurance. E&O insurance covers lawsuits resulting from copyright infringement and using products or names without permission (usually in bad taste). An E&O policy can run you anywhere between $3,000 and $7,000 depending on the subject material of your movie and the possible liabilities as determined by an attorney's legal opinion.

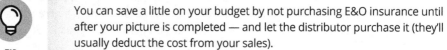

You can save a little on your budget by not purchasing E&O insurance until after your picture is completed — and let the distributor purchase it (they'll usually deduct the cost from your sales).

TIP

» **Worker's compensation:** As an employer, you're required to cover your employees under worker's compensation. This protects you and the employees should they have an accident while in your employment. You can buy worker's comp coverage through an insurance agency or payroll company at between 3 to 4 percent of your payroll (the percentage differs in each state). Worker's comp covers people who work as volunteers on your set as well as those who work for pay.

TIP

When you take out an insurance policy, you need it only for the dates of your actual production (although for cast and crew insurance, you may want to overlap the weeks or months during pre-production and right through the end of shooting your movie). Taking out insurance for a period of a month instead of a year is much more affordable, especially if you're on a tight budget.

When you take out production insurance, you'll have a *deductible* (the amount you have to pay should you have damages and have to activate the policy). Depending on your coverage, a deductible is generally between $2,500 and $5,000. After you pay the deductible, your damages are covered up to the amount of the policy coverage amount. For example, if your camera and tripod fall off a cliff (it happens all the time), the price of the equipment ($35,000) that went over the cliff would be covered, minus the $2,500 deductible. If your cameraman went with the equipment, that's a more serious issue!

Finding an insurance broker

Specific insurance companies specialize in production insurance for your film. (*Note:* Your homeowner's or renter's policy is not appropriate for a movie shoot, though it may cover some of your personal items or consumer equipment if they're lost, damaged, or stolen while you're on a shoot — including stolen from your car.)

>> **Truman Van Dyke** offers independent feature film production insurance for around $3,500 to $4,500 depending on the budget and production requirements (www.tvdco.com). I've bought policies from them on almost all my productions and they have been fantastic to work with — ask for JonPaul!

>> **ProductionInsurance.com** (a service of Supple-Merrill & Driscoll) is another great place for insurance information and like most insurers, they offer different types of insurance packages: (www.productioninsurance.com).

>> **Film Emporium** also provides insurance to independent productions. You can fill out an insurance application form, choose the type of insurance you want, and submit for a quote. Go to their website (www.filmemporium.com) and click on "Insurance" for more information.

TIP

If you find that production insurance is too costly, see if you can go on a *rider*. A rider is what it sounds like: You ride along on someone else's insurance policy. If you're doing the production for a company, chances are you can ride on its insurance policy. Check with the insurance company to make sure that you're covered if you decide to go this route.

Before you go on another company's insurance policy via a rider, make sure that company is legitimately affiliated with you and your production. If you end up having to make an insurance claim, the insurance company will *not* honor the policy if it finds out that a company not associated with your production was just letting you use its insurance.

Bond, completion bond

A *completion bond* is an insurance policy that guarantees to the investor or financing source that if your movie goes over budget, the completion bond company will finance the difference to complete the picture. The catch is that the completion bond company charges a percentage to do this (usually between 3 and 5 percent of the total budget), whether you need them in the end or not. And if you do go over budget and they have to step in, they can take over your movie — and you're history. Usually, productions with budgets of less than $1 million are not bonded, so if you're working on a low-budget production, this is not something you need to worry about.

A completion bond company conducts an extensive survey with you and all the production elements. They want to make sure that your budget is realistic. They don't want to have to finance the movie — they just want their percentage fee. If you have an underwater fantasy that ends with resurrecting the *Titanic* on a $30,000 budget, they're not going to bond your movie.

One of the leading completion bond companies is Film Finances — they've bonded some of the biggest studio pictures. You can get more information about completion bonds and the services of Film Finances by going to www.ffi.com.

Chapter **5**

Financing Your Movie

You can write a script with virtually no money, but to make a movie you need dollars to put it all together. So how do you go about financing your dream? Maxing out your credit cards or mortgaging the house is not the smartest or safest way to get the money to make your movie. A better idea is to find an investor or investors who are prepared and can afford to take the risk of financing a movie. Before you even start looking for the production dollars, you need to prepare a professional presentation to show to your potential investors. After you've hooked the money people, you need to offer them a good incentive to believe in you and your project.

In this chapter, I introduce the various ways and places you can find funding for your movie. And after you have the funding, I show you how to get started so you can turn the dream of making your film into a reality.

Creating an Enticing Prospectus

Making a movie takes money, and that's where the almighty investor comes into the picture. An investor is the person or group that believes in you and your film and has faith in its commercial potential to make money for them. The investor is the one who makes it possible for you to actually produce your movie. Without the investor's money, your idea would remain on paper and might never see the light of the projector.

I use the term *investor*, but that doesn't necessarily mean just one investor. Getting people to invest in your film is like selling stock in your movie. It's easier to find ten people with $5,000 each than it is to find one with $50,000.

Before you can start looking for investors, you need some ammunition. In order to entice investors, you need to put together a formal written presentation detailing why someone should invest in you and your project. Known as a *prospectus* or *business plan*, this presentation should be informative and entertaining. Putting together a prospectus not only helps get you financing for your film, but it also helps you see your goal more clearly. Keep in mind that, even though the prospectus is a written presentation, you should be prepared to verbally pitch your movie idea and its commercial potential to the investor as well.

You can write your own plan from scratch (using a program such as PowerPoint) following the advice I give in this section, or you can get software programs with specific templates to help you design an informative plan. For example, you can download PlanMagic at www.planmagic.com for $99.95, or Business Plan Pro at www.businessplanpro.com for $99.95. If you want a software program specifically geared for a film prospectus only, then Movieplan is a good choice! It's only $39.95, and you can get more details at www.movieplan.net. You can also use web-building software such as Wix.com to put together your prospectus directly online.

If you upload or build your prospectus online, make sure that you have a private link or a private password, because the prospectus should only be for the eyes of your potential investors and not a solicitation to anyone who finds your website.

The following sections explain what information your package should contain. (*Note:* Be sure to include a table of contents page directing the investor to the appropriate sections of interest along with page numbers.)

An investor's main focus is to make a good return on his or her investment, while at the same time knowing the associated risk. This is why you should concentrate on presenting to your investor the money-making possibilities should he or she invest in your project. An investor is more concerned with making a profit and looking at your production as an investment; a studio or distributor is looking at the whole picture — a film with a strong story that also has commercial potential.

Synopsis of your story

Most investors are only interested in knowing the gist of your story and the commercial viability of producing it into a film. Your synopsis should include references to the money-making potential of this particular type of story. A page or two is an appropriate length for a synopsis, not much longer than that.

At the end of the synopsis, be sure to note that the screenplay is available upon request (be aware that an investor not familiar with screenplay formatting may find the script difficult to read).

Information about you: What's your history?

Your prospectus should include information about your background and achievements. Investors want to know your credits and experience, if any, with regards to filmmaking. If you have made other films before this, list how they fared financially. Also list related skills such as educational background and financial achievements that help support why you're capable of making this film and using the investor's money to finance your production. Be sure to include any documents, such as newspaper articles or copies of award certificates, that support your filmmaking accomplishments and educational degrees.

Info about your cast and crew

If you've already signed on cast and crew, include their resumes. If you don't know for sure who will sign on as members of your cast and crew, list the people you plan to approach. It's only important to list crew like a cinematographer or makeup person who has impressive credits on other successful films that will add to the production value of your film.

Also include a *letter of interest* from any actors or name stars who've expressed interest in your project. A letter of interest shows that there is interest from someone who could potentially help the commercial success of your movie by appearing in your production. See Chapter 8 for more on letters of interest.

Your budget and profit projections

Investors obviously want to know how much the production will cost to complete. You can include a budget *top sheet,* which is a one-page summary of the entire budget broken into specific categories, or you can provide the full detailed budget with a breakdown of every category. See Chapter 4 for more on budgeting.

Your profit projections estimate how much your film could make in sales, based on other movies and studio and/or independent productions similar to your movie's budget and genre. You can find this information in weekly box office reports on such online sites as www.boxofficemojo.com, www.boxofficereport.com, and of course www.boxoffice.com.

PROSPECTING A WEBSITE

The Internet is a great tool for promoting your project. In the past, filmmakers spent a fortune photocopying their prospectus for their movie and then paying for postage or courier charges. Now all you have to do is tell your potential investors to check out your website. Investors across the world can check out your project in a matter of seconds, after you tell them about your website. (For examples, check out my official websites at www.bryanmichaelstoller.com, www.FirstDogFilm.com, and www.AmazingWizardofPaws.com. **Note:** These films have all been financed and produced, so these are now promotion for the finished films). Having a website gives you the ability to link to and cross-reference certain information. If you're talking about a particular actor, you can link to the actor's website. Or you can create a link to a certain location or piece of equipment that takes the viewer directly to that information.

Investigating Investors

There's an art to finding investors. You need to know who to approach and how much to ask them for, in terms of dollars and cents. You also need to keep their interests in mind when presenting your project. Are they looking to make a lot of money? Or are they satisfied with making a small return on their investment with the association of being involved in the moviemaking business?

Locating potential investors: Show me the money!

So who makes a good investor? Anyone! Your parents or relatives, a coworker, an acquaintance you met at a party or seminar, your doctor, lawyer, or dentist, your boyfriend or girlfriend — or their boyfriend or girlfriend, and anyone you do business with, such as the shop owner down the street.

People are always looking for different ways to invest their money. Some play it safe and put it into interest-bearing accounts or long-term CDs. Others like the excitement and risk of playing the stock market, buying property, or the fun of investing in a movie. Anyone who has a little (or a lot) of money to invest may be willing to take a chance and back your project; you just have to ask. (I discuss ways to successfully approach potential investors later in this chapter.)

REMEMBER

Investors are out there — you just have to find them. And remember, timing is everything. Someone may not be prepared to invest in your film today, but they may be tomorrow. Don't give up — keep asking.

>> **Whether you're at a cocktail party, a screening, or even at the photocopiers, let everyone you come into contact with know that you're looking for investors for your movie.** You never know who knows whom. Maybe Johnny's dad wants to get involved in financing a small movie — you never know until you ask. Word of mouth is the best way to find financing for your film.

>> **Get a mailing list of potential investors from a mailing list company.** Try www.DirectMail.com and search consumer lists and family income above $80,000 or so a year. Addresses can be sent to you in the form of mailing labels or email addresses. I prefer regular mail because emails look like spam and often go into a spam folder. You pay for every 1,000 names and addresses, which can start at $49 and up per 1,000 names.

>> **Look up Investor sites online.** There are services such as www.Invstor.com that, for a fee, connect entrepreneurs with investors. There are also targeted filmmaker sites such as www.Slated.com and www.Stage32.com that match filmmakers with potential investors.

You don't have to find a millionaire to invest in your film. Everyday people are willing to invest some of their savings and/or extra earnings — just look at all those who go to Las Vegas to take a chance on the tables.

Approaching a potential investor

After you know whom to approach for financing, you need to know how to approach them. Meeting an investor is like going out on a first date — you have to impress on the initial date, or you don't get a second one. Your first meeting with a potential investor will probably be over the phone or possibly email. You need to sell the investor on getting involved with you and your film so that you can move to the next step and have a face-to-face meeting or at least by FaceTime or Skype depending on where they're located. The potential investor may request a hard copy, or a link to your prospectus or business plan before wanting to meet in person. This is why your presentation package is so important: If it intrigues the investor, you'll get that meeting and have a chance to close the deal.

Keep in mind the following when approaching investors:

>> **Be enthusiastic** about your project, but be sincere.

>> **Be honest** and don't guarantee that they'll get rich from investing in your movie. Even let them know that investing in movies is risky and there is no guarantee on a return. If you prove that you can be trusted, they may invest in *you* — and fund your future projects.

Don't ever guarantee investors that they'll recoup their investment and make a profit. Nothing in life is guaranteed, especially getting rich off making a movie. You don't want to mislead them. If you guarantee they'll make money and they don't, they could legally come after you stating you made false promises to them.

>> **Be prepared.** Before calling, be ready to answer any questions the investor may ask. This can include what your movie is about (be ready to pitch your story), budget amount, shooting schedule, post-production to release schedule, and how long it will take for them to see a return (if any) on their investment. Before your face-to-face meeting, review all the material in your package so that the investor will know that you know what you're talking about.

>> **Be respectful.** Assure the investor that you will treat his or her money as if it were your own.

>> **Follow up** with a thank-you note to the investor for taking the time to meet with you and for considering your proposal.

You have to look at it as a win-win situation. People get excited about the idea of getting involved in financing a movie. It's a lot more exciting (and definitely more glamorous) than buying $5,000 in toilet paper stock. You could be doing the investor a favor. The investor has the potential of making money with your film (also the potential to lose his pants — but you probably don't want to say that). But again, be honest, and let them know investing in any kind of movie is a risk — there's no guarantee they'll get their money back or make a profit — but that it's your honest intention to make money for them with your movie.

You can also entice your investors by offering to give them an executive producer or associate producer credit in your film's opening credits. If so, be sure to mutually agree in writing the appropriate credit that your investor will receive on the movie. You can have as many executive producer or associate producer credits as fits the number of investors.

After you've found investors, a company agreement between you and your investors should be drafted before anyone hands over cash for you to produce your movie. When the investor agrees to participate in the financing of your movie, it's time to move on to forming a production company and ironing out the details of putting your project together.

Keeping the Securities and Exchange Commission in mind

To protect investors and investments from misrepresentation or fraud, the Securities and Exchange Commission (SEC) regulates companies or individuals seeking to raise financing. SEC regulations prevent the fund-raising company from misrepresenting the project (and committing other fraudulent acts) so that investors can make informed judgments on whether to invest and how much they want to risk.

As you raise funds for your project, you have to follow SEC rules and guidelines that ensure potential investors are property informed. These rules deal with things like

>> How to present your investment opportunity.

>> How to inform the SEC of your business activities, or if your production has to be registered with the SEC.

>> How you identify yourself to investors (to make sure that you don't misrepresent your intention and that you conduct all business activities in a legal manner).

REMEMBER

If you plan on soliciting money from investors that you do not know personally or if you're soliciting from a number of potential investors (not just one) from a list or through referrals, you may need to register with the SEC and follow their rules and regulations. (If the money is from your immediate family, friends, or a limited number of people, you may be exempt and won't need to be regulated by the SEC.) The SEC rules have adjusted to the new online sites that help entrepreneurs find funding, including crowdfunding sites — so you may not need to register with the SEC depending on where your funding is coming from and how much you are trying to raise. You should inquire to see if you have to register and if so the SEC will review your registration to make sure you're abiding by the rules and regulations of soliciting for funds. You can find all the information you need, along with forms to fill out and register at the Securities and Exchange Commission website (www.sec.gov).

WARNING

If you should register with the SEC but don't, you could be fined if you don't comply with the rules and regulations of soliciting funds. Do your research and study the SEC website to determine if your funding sources require you to register with the SEC.

Starting a Production Company

When you find an investor who believes in you and your project, you need to set up a production company through which to run the financing. You often need your investors to help finance the start-up of the company as well, so it's best to wait to form your production company at the time you find an investor.

WARNING

If you don't set up some form of a production company, you're what's called a *sole proprietorship*, and don't have the protection that a production company may provide. Setting up a corporation or limited liability company (LLC) gives you a little more protection personally from lawsuits and other headaches. The company can act as a shield so that, in the event you're sued, only the assets of the company — and not your personal assets — are vulnerable. Each situation is different, so always consult a lawyer versed in company start-ups about your options and risks.

Being in the right company

You have lots of choices when it comes to the type of company you want to form, each of which has its own advantages and disadvantages:

>> General partnership

>> Limited partnership

>> Corporation

>> Limited liability company (LLC)

>> Joint venture

REMEMBER

As you choose the company that best suits your situation, consider these three main factors:

>> **Liability:** Who will be responsible in case of a lawsuit or bad debts? You and the company partners, or just the company?

>> **Taxes:** What kind of tax structure does the company have? Does the company pay tax or do the taxes flow through to you and your partner's personal taxes? Your accountant can give you more information on how taxes work with the type of company you set up.

>> **Ownership:** Who owns the movie and any other assets of the company?

Limited partnerships limit the relationship

A *limited partnership* limits one of the partner's liabilities and tax responsibilities (usually the investor in this case). The main or *general partner* is responsible for the company, while the *limited partner* remains silent and lets you do all the work. For example, an investor gives you the money to make your movie, but he or she is not involved with the creative decisions or production of the movie.

REMEMBER

In a limited partnership, only the investor's investment is at risk. Because the investor isn't responsible for any activities that are performed by the limited partnership, he or she isn't liable if there are any lawsuits against the production company or the general partner.

Howdy pardner — Striking up a partnership?

A *partnership* is the merging of two or more people with the same goals in business who sign an agreement to achieve those goals together. Also known as a *general partnership,* this agreement gives each partner equal authority and equal liability (as opposed to limited authority in a limited partnership) for the company's activities.

Incorporating the idea of a corporation

A *corporation* is a professional entity that is separate from you as an individual. The corporation reports to the IRS regarding taxes, and it is liable in case of lawsuits, bad debts, and so on. A corporation protects the company owners, the filmmaker (that would be you), and your partners (to an extent) by what's called the *corporate shield.* In the event of a lawsuit, only the corporation assets are liable, not the assets of the individuals who run the company.

The costs of starting a corporation vary, depending on whether you use a corporate attorney or incorporate on your own. It can cost as little as $20 or as much as several hundred dollars, depending on where you incorporate and how. You can incorporate through an online service like www.incorporating.com (Bizfilings) or www.legalzoom.com that guide you through all the steps of incorporating. Regardless of whether your company makes a profit or not, you may be responsible for annual minimal taxes. My corporation in Los Angeles, California, is taxed a minimum tax of $800 a year.

TIP

Two good places to incorporate are Nevada and Delaware. Those who form corporations in Nevada, regardless of whether their offices are there or not, do so because the advantages are substantial:

» There are lower or no tax fees for running the corporation.

» There are minimal tax obligations (no state taxes).

» Owners can remain anonymous from the IRS and public records.

» There is low maintenance in running a Nevada company.

» Owners don't have to reside in Nevada.

Some people choose to form their corporation in Delaware because, although it has a small fee to incorporate (more than Nevada, but less than any other state) and annual tax obligations, you can incorporate relatively quickly and easily, and company owners remain anonymous. Delaware is also known to have the highest amount of corporations that are *not* physically in the state. All paperwork, which includes setting up the corporation, filing taxes, and accounting, can be done through the mail or online.

Let's see about an LLC: Limited liability company

A *limited liability company* (LLC) combines the best of a corporation and a limited partnership. It protects the filmmaker's assets that are separate from the LLC in case of a liability suit. An LLC is also easier and cheaper to form than a corporation. Usually the owners of the LLC are listed as members without official corporate titles. An LLC is taxed similar to a corporation, or you have the choice of directing profits and expenses through to your personal taxes. As with a corporation, your LLC has a minimum $800 tax each year, regardless of whether your company makes a profit.

Joining together: Joint ventures

A *joint venture* usually involves two companies already in business who join together on one production. These companies can be corporations, partnerships, or LLCs. Many studios nowadays are doing joint productions because the cost of a studio film with big-name talent has skyrocketed. A joint venture is similar to the structure of a partnership (it's like a joint partnership).

FICTITIOUSLY "DOING BUSINESS AS"

If you form a company as a division under someone else's company (or a company you currently own), you may want to use a fictitious business name called a DBA (short for *doing business as*) or sometimes an *AKA* (short for *also known as*). A DBA or AKA is kind of like a pseudonym.

To register a DBA, go to your city's county clerk's office or download the form from their website (check your local government web pages for your county clerk's website). A DBA costs between $10 and $100 to register, depending on what state and county you live in, and it expires five years from the date you file it. You can also register and file your DBA using www.legalzoom.com (they charge a flat fee of $99 plus state fees), without leaving your computer. You have to announce the name in a local newspaper to make it official and legal — which costs extra (you run it for four weeks in the new businesses classified section). The clerk's office will give you the information for the newspapers and periodicals that provide this service.

Other things to do to set up your production company

When setting up a company, you need to consider some other items on your to-do list:

- ›› **Opening a checking account (specifically for your production):** If you have a checking account specifically for your production, you can monitor the film's production expenses, and your investors can see a proper accounting of where their dollars were spent.

- ›› **Creating a company name and logo:** A logo gives your production company a professional appearance and credibility, and of course a name identifies it and expresses what kind of company it is.

- ›› **Printing business cards and stationery:** Business cards and stationery add to the professional image and credibility of your new production company.

- ›› **Hiring an attorney to look over all agreements:** An attorney can help to protect you as best they can from lawsuits and negligence.

Going Escrow

When you've found your financing and set up your production company, as explained in the earlier sections of this chapter, you may want to consider an *escrow account.* An escrow company monitors the bank account that's been set up with the funds for your production. You don't want to be a week into filming and find out your investor hasn't sent the next installment of the budget (this actually happened to me). Having the money (entire budget) in an escrow account ensures that the money is indeed there and available.

The *escrow holder or agent* follows the specific conditions of a written agreement signed by you and your investors instructing what, where, when, and how the funds will be released. These instructions usually include a payment schedule for disbursement of funds with regards to the production of the movie, from pre-production all the way through post-production. An escrow account is also a security blanket for investors, ensuring them that there will be no suspicious tapping into the bank account and that all funds go towards the production of the movie only.

Contracting Your Investor

Drawing up a formal agreement between you and your investors is the final step in securing financing. This agreement is often an adjunct to your business formation agreement (whether it be a corporation, an LLC, or a form of partnership). It spells out exactly the understanding between you and your investors with regards to the financing of the movie and the participation (if any) in your production company. This is where you would also talk about putting the money in escrow, or getting the full funds into the production bank account before commencing pre-production and principal photography.

Every type of legal agreement has a standard contract. These agreements are called *boilerplate* agreements, meaning all you have to do is fill in the information pertaining to your specific project and budget. You can also add specific items or concerns that you or your investor want to address. You can find boilerplate agreements in Mark Litwak's book, *Contracts for Film and Television* (for more information go to www.marklitwak.com). *The Complete Film Production Handbook* also has every conceivable agreement relating to film production. Movieplan is another software program with investor and company formation agreements (www.movieplansoftware.net).

TIP

Even if you do use boilerplate agreements, I recommend that you have them reviewed by an attorney to make sure you've covered yourself. (You also have the choice of using an attorney to prepare your contracts from scratch, but this will cost you more than starting with a boilerplate agreement.)

All investor agreements should include the following information:

>> **Profit:** An investor can receive anywhere from 10 to 40 percent from the profits of your picture. This is negotiable between you and your investor(s).

>> **Responsibilities:** Spell out the responsibilities of you and your production company and the responsibilities of the investor regarding financing.

>> **Recoupment:** This is when and how long it will take before the investors will see their investment back (but never guarantee they will), plus any profits, and how it will be dispersed between you and the investors. Recoupment, if any, can happen soon after the film is completed, or it may take a year or more, depending on the commercial viability of the film and the aggressiveness of your distributor.

>> **Expenses:** Expenses can include your company overhead, distributor's percentage fee, distributor's advertising and marketing costs for your movie, travel costs, film market and festival costs, legal fees, and any other expenses you specify in the agreement pertaining to the production.

>> **Auditing:** Does the investor have the right to audit? If not, who does?

TIP

>> **Bonus:** As an incentive to your investor to want to invest in your project, you may want to include a special added bonus on top of the investor's standard recoupment of his investment. A bonus can be in the form of an additional percentage on profits, or a quicker return of his investment before certain expenses are paid, and so on.

Tapping into Alternative Sources

If you aren't having much luck finding private investors, or you need supplemental funding to match funds you've already raised, you do have some additional options.

Pre-selling your movie

You may be able to *pre-sell* your movie, based on a great script or star talent. You first find a distributor, who then takes your film idea, the script, a great poster, or the trailer and gets deposits upfront (usually 20 percent of the total selling price) from buyers who like the idea and who will pay the balance (the remaining 80 percent) when the film is delivered to them (see Chapter 19). By having a distributor pre-sell your movie, it gives you some money to start your production, and shows that the buyers are seriously interested.

TIP

A three-minute *trailer* (a commercial for your movie showing the highlights — see Chapter 19) or a scene from your script, can help pre-sell your movie to potential investors or buyers (such as a studio or distributor). A trailer can be shot for little or no money, by getting your actors to work for deferred pay (see Chapter 4) and getting your equipment and locations donated.

Dolly Parton wrote and recorded four original songs for my movie *First Dog.* These songs (and her name) were a great promotional tool when putting the production together. Dan Aykroyd provided the voice of Dexter the Computer in my feature film, *The Random Factor,* which gave me a bit of star power to entice a distributor to pick up the film. Ed Asner played Santa Claus in my movie *Santa Stole Our Dog.* Because Ed played Santa in *Elf* with Will Ferrell, this helped me get a distribution deal with Universal Pictures Home Entertainment.

Getting a grant

When I was 13 years old, I applied to a government council that financed short films. I was turned down because I was too young. I then applied to a fund that encouraged children to make their own films — they, too, turned me down, telling me I was too old. That was my first and last attempt at trying to get a grant. I don't recommend this route because it involves a lot of time, research, and paperwork — not to mention waiting (as long as two years) to know if you received the grant. But, on the other hand, you may get lucky and find it's just the thing for you.

TIP

A grant is easier to obtain if your concept is about a cause or supports a charity and if it's a short film or public service announcement (PSA).

Getting a loan

One alternative to private financing is applying for a loan. The bank might ask you to mortgage your home to give you some extra cash. You could ask your bank (or credit card company) to increase your credit limit to give you more room for charges on your credit card account.

WARNING

Although mortgaging your home or upping your credit-card limit could help finance your movie, I don't recommend going this route because the risk is too great. Think about it: If you borrow heavily on your credit card, you're going to have some astronomical monthly payments that you'll have to make until you break even on your movie, which may never happen. And if you mortgage your house, the worst-case scenario is that you could lose your home — don't do it!

Kickstarting your Indiegogo: Crowdfunding

Kickstarter (www.kickstarter.com), Indiegogo (www.indiegogo.com), and Go Fund Me (www.gofundme.com) are some of the sites that could help attract funding for your project. This is a fairly new form of raising money for entrepreneurs. Many successful campaigns have benefited from crowdfunding. New products, inventions, movies, short films, books, and so on, have all reaped the rewards of this unique type of funding.

Many of these crowdfunding sites allow you to keep the profits on your movie which you do not need to share with your contributors. Instead, you provide *perks*. These can be anything from a copy of the movie on DVD or a private link to the completed movie on YouTube or Vimeo to branded T-shirts, your backers' names in the end credits, or even a cameo for your backers in the movie, depending how much they pledge. For more details on Kickstarter, check out *Kickstarter For Dummies* by Aimee Cebulski (Wiley).

Bartering: Trade you this for that

Bartering is a form of trading. In bartering for your movie, a company gives you the use of its product (on loan or to keep, depending on what it is), or an individual lets you use a particular element (like a location or prop) that you want to use in your movie in exchange for giving them a credit or placing the company's product on camera. Bartering is one way to bring your budget down, but it's not the way to finance your entire production.

When I was 11 years old, I funded my little Super-8 movies by bartering. For my film stock, I contacted different camera stores that sold Super-8 film. If they would donate ten rolls of film for me to make my movie, I would list them in the ending film credits. All through my teens, I bartered for on-camera products, including film stock, costumes and even food. When I was 17, I made a film called *Superham* and raised some of the financing from a local car dealer. In exchange, the car dealer got a front presentation credit introducing the film. You can try bartering for the following products and services:

» Clothing

» Editing equipment and/or an editor

» External hard drives, memory cards, or film stock

» Food and drinks

- **»** Hotel accommodations

- **»** Post-production services

- **»** Locations

- **»** Products featured in actual scenes

- **»** Transportation (including cars for the production and airline tickets)

Bartering in the movie business also includes *product placement.* Product placement is when a company places its product in your production and either lends it to you, gives it to you, or pays you for featuring it in your movie (especially if a major star interacts with the product). For example, while shooting my film *Miss Cast Away and the Island Girls* (featuring a cameo by Michael Jackson), I approached The Sharper Image about highlighting one of their remote control robots in my movie. The company was interested in the product exposure and provided two robots to use in the movie at no charge.

Product placement in the form of goods and services can save you hundreds, even thousands of dollars depending on what they are and what it would cost you if you had to actually pay for their use. If a food company donates sandwiches, this could save you hundreds of dollars in feeding your cast and crew. If you feature a local pizza place in your movie, they might give you free pizza to feed everyone on set!

Some companies, such as Premier Entertainment Services of North Hollywood, California, specialize in placing products in movies and television (check them out at `www.pesfilmtv.com`). If you contact a product-placement company, it will request a copy of your script and comb through it, deciding where it may be able to provide on-camera product for you, based on the client products it represents. There is usually not a charge for this service as the product placement company gets their fee from the companies that provide the products for your project.

Chapter **6**

Location, Location, Location

As a filmmaker, you have the power to take your audience on a trip to exotic locales — a remote island, a picturesque small town, or deep into outer space. Therefore, picking the right locations at which to shoot — or creating just the right environments on soundstages or on your computer — is very important to your movie's success.

In this chapter, you find out how to discover great locations to use in your production — some of them free of charge. Depending on your budget and the setting of your story, you need to decide whether to shoot on location or on a controlled indoor soundstage, so I give you some advice about making that choice as well. Finally, to make sure that you and your production is protected, I explain the types of insurance and city permits that are usually required when shooting on location. Police and firemen may be required, too, and they may show up if you *don't* hire them!

Locating Locations

After you've locked down your script — meaning there are no more changes — comb through it and determine where you want to shoot your scenes. Some software programs, like Movie Magic Screenwriter (www.screenplay.com), actually break down your script for you by pulling out all your scene headings and generating a list of location settings from your screenplay. Of course, you can also go through the script yourself and jot down all the locations without having to use a computer. After you have a list of the settings for your movie, you can start looking for the actual locations that will fit your story.

REMEMBER

You're casting your movie with actors who have a lot of character, so why not find locations with character, too? Don't list generic locations like a bookstore or a restaurant; go with specific settings that will be memorable to your audience, such as a quaint boutique bookstore or a French café with a patio overlooking a park. Does your lead character live in a small, messy apartment or a lavish house on gated grounds with an Olympic-sized swimming pool?

TIP

As you're shooting the principal photography on your movie, see whether you need to show the exterior of the setting where certain interior scenes take place. These outside shots are called *establishing shots,* and they help keep your film from having a claustrophobic feel to it. If the locations are all interiors, the audience is going to feel like they're closed in the entire time — it will feel very disorienting and claustrophobic. Give them some breathing space. Establishing shots can also be part of your *second unit* shoot (see the section "Shooting Second-Unit Locations," later in this chapter for more information).

Managing location managers and scouts

A *location scout* searches out the perfect locations for your movie. Anyone can be a location scout, but someone who does it for a living will be familiar with every type of location, saving you weeks or even months of searching for the right place. Contact your local film commission (if there's one in your city) and ask if it can recommend a location scout, or call your city permit office and ask if it can refer you to a location scout. You can also go online and find a location scout at www.crewnet.com, which conveniently lets you search by state and crew position. If you can't afford a location scout, hire someone who's eager to drive around, make phone calls, and search the Internet — or do it yourself, but remember: Finding the right locations for a film takes time.

A *location manager* manages the locations after you've found them. He or she looks after getting the appropriate releases and permits for your locations and makes sure that the proper insurance is in place (see the later section "Securing Your Locations," for more on releases, insurance, and other location-specific particulars). Your location manager can also double as your location scout on a lower-budget production. If you go this route, make sure to find someone who is detail-oriented and has a good eye for scenic locations.

TIP

Locations Hub (www.locationshub.com) is a service that provides a search engine that lets you track down virtually any type of existing location in the world without having to leave your desk.

Most states have guides or directories listing production services available to filmmakers interested in shooting in their cities. The guides are usually put out by the state film commissions (which you can find by calling your city hall) to encourage productions to use local businesses to help the state's economy. Many cities, including Tucson, Arizona, and Washington, D.C., allow filmmakers to film at government-run buildings as an incentive to make movies in their city. Laws change, so always check, and make note that even if you are allowed to film for free, you will still need to obtain a permit to show you have permission (but the permit is often free as well).

TIP

Don't forget to put the word out to friends, family, and acquaintances that you're looking for locations. You never know who may have a great location that you can use for one of your scenes. For example, my friend Noah let me shoot almost my entire Christmas film at his house. For some reason, he doesn't return my phone calls anymore . . .?

Evaluating potential locations

Filming on a soundstage or in a warehouse (discussed later in this section) is not always practical — you just may not have the budget to do it. Sometimes you can find a location where you can shoot for free or for a price that's within your budget. By shooting on location, you don't have to start from scratch and construct sets for every scene in your movie (not practical at all on a low budget). Whether you're in Los Angeles, New York, or a small town in the Midwest, you're sure to find vacant buildings that can work wonders for your story and that are just waiting to be razed or renovated. From an old restaurant that's been shut down to a bank that's closed its doors, you can usually negotiate with the building owner or the government to shoot on this existing set that's just sitting empty.

Here's a list of things to consider when scouting locations:

>> Is parking available for cast, crew, and equipment vehicles?

>> Are bathroom facilities (in a public park or a local restaurant) nearby — or will you have to rent Porta Potties?

>> Is it in a location that's appropriate for sound (you don't want a location that's too close to the freeway, a construction site, a noisy airport, traffic, factories, and so on)?

>> Is there available electricity to plug in your lights (If not, you'll need a generator) unless you're using LED lights with rechargeable batteries.

>> For out-of-town shoots, are there affordable accommodations nearby?

>> Does it have space available to set up a picnic area for feeding cast and crew?

AFCI.ORG

The Association of Film Commissioners International (AFCI) can help you find answers to important location questions and even put you in contact with worldwide government contacts for on-location shooting. AFCI also puts on location trade shows, where you can meet state and worldwide film commissions all under one roof; check its website at www.afci.org (not .com, unless you're studying to be an electrician) for dates and locations.

>> Can you get permission to shoot there, and if so, do you need a permit? Can you afford to shoot there?

>> Does using the location site require the hiring of a police officer to stop foot or street traffic?

>> Is a photocopy store nearby (for copying the next day's schedule), unless you're sending all schedules electronically to everyone's email?

>> Do cellphones work in the area? If not, is there service nearby?

>> Is there Internet access and/or can you get permission and the password (for email, location directions, and research)?

REMEMBER

Finding the perfect location that works both inside as an interior and outside as an exterior may be difficult. Remember that you can shoot the exterior of a house and then use a different house's interior, or even construct the indoor rooms on a soundstage. Doing so gives you a more controlled environment.

TIP

You may be able to get a location for free if you can offer something in exchange. If you're shooting away from home and you give a hotel a credit or even feature the hotel on camera, you could get free accommodations or at least a discount for your cast and crew to stay there. I've done this on many of my out of town shoots. Lodging can be expensive, and many independent productions can't afford to put up cast and crew. So writing in a scene where you actually see the hotel, or adding a big thank you in the end credits, may be worth it.

Taking location pictures: Shooting in Landscape mode

Now that you always have a camera in your pocket (your smartphone, of course), you can snap some great location pictures to show your cinematographer and other crew members what locations you have to choose from. And you can email your photos immediately to anyone who needs to see them, while saving the snapshots in full, crisp color to your computer. Photos are also helpful in planning your shots after you choose the locations you want to use. With Gorilla software (www.junglesoftware.com), you can even import your actual location photos right into the project management section; include details on your location as well as driving directions. The great thing about some smartphones is that when you take a picture at a location, the smartphone operating system uses its built-in GPS to remember and make note of the exact location where the photo was taken — and can bring up a map pinpointing that location later.

Sounding Off about Soundstages

Soundstages are a convenient way to shoot interior scenes mainly because you don't have to worry about unplanned sounds interrupting your takes. A soundstage is basically a soundproofed room. All exterior sounds are blocked out of an industrial soundstage after the doors are closed. A soundstage is an acoustic environment that has padded walls that absorb sound to prevent an echo or reverb in your dialogue, as would happen if you shot in an uncarpeted room. Another major advantage of shooting on a soundstage is that you can set up several interior sets for different locations in your script without having to move your whole production team. You can have a courtroom, a cell block, an apartment, a coffee shop, and an interior fast-food restaurant all on the same soundstage.

Finding — or creating — a soundstage

When you see an airport or interior airplane scene in a movie, chances are it was shot on a controlled soundstage. My friends at Air Hollywood in Los Angeles (www.airhollywood.com) house several airplane bodies that have removable walls and seats for convenient filming. Air Hollywood also has a full airport terminal that includes X-ray machines, a magazine store, and a bar. I like shooting at Air Hollywood because I've never experienced a flight delay or had to use the air-sickness bag, and they've never lost my luggage either! When I shot a scene at Air Hollywood for my film *Santa Stole Our Dog*, instead of telling my cast and crew to turn off their cellphones, I suggested they put them on *airplane mode!*

To find a sound stage, do a search on the Internet (look for *sound stages* or *warehouses*), or order a copy of the *Creative Handbook*, which lists soundstages in larger cities throughout the U.S. (at www.creativehandbook.com; the *Handbook* is free if you meet their criteria).

REMEMBER

A soundstage can also be a warehouse, a school gym, or a vacant apartment — any place where you can build sets and hold a decent-size crew. Of course, if the room or building is not soundproofed, you have to deal with outside noises. I once shot an office scene in an IKEA store where mock-up rooms are set up for customers. Many furniture stores use these types of displays, which make perfect sets — if you can get permission from the store and keep the customers quiet (and don't forget to hide the price tags!).

TIP

You can make your own soundproofed room, or at least cut down on the reverb, by putting up *foam sheets* on the walls, or on stands (outside of the camera's view) close to where the actors perform their dialogue. These foam sheets absorb reverb and prevent sounds from bouncing back. You can also rent *sound blankets* (the kind used by moving companies). Sound blankets also help to prevent echo and reverb by absorbing sound the way carpeting does. You can hang them outside of the shot or lay them on bare floors (when you're not showing the floor in your shot).

Putting up walls: Using flats

If you're going to shoot on a soundstage or in a warehouse, you have to construct your sets from scratch. You may need to hire carpenters or people with construction knowledge, or you can do the building yourself with the assistance of volunteers. If your budget allows, you could bring in a *production designer* (sort of like an interior designer) and maybe even a person versed in architectural design. If there are professional movie soundstages in your city, there is a good chance you may find existing standing sets such as a jail cell, bar, courtroom set, doctor's office, and so on.

Soundstage sets usually involve *flats,* which are separate moveable walls constructed of wooden frames with support stands to keep them upright. When you go to a theater to see a stage play, you often see sets created with flats. Putting together a simple room, such as an apartment, by using flats is fairly easy. TV shows often use flats, like Sheldon and Amy's apartment in *The Big Bang Theory* (great show, too bad it had to end). Flats can also simulate exterior walls made of brick, logs, concrete, or stucco. Of course, if you have an elaborate set, like the interior of a dry cleaner or an ancient church, using the actual location is easier and cheaper (refer to the earlier section "Locating Locations" for details).

The advantage of shooting on a soundstage using a set constructed with flats is that you can remove the fourth wall where the camera is, which allows more room for your crew and equipment to comfortably shoot the scene. *Saturday Night Live* uses flats with the fourth wall open for the audience and TV cameras. The problem with flats is that they're big, bulky, and very heavy; you need a truck to transport them and several helpers to carry and set them up — unless you're shooting at a professional soundstage that provides wall flats for you.

You can build your own flats or find them at your local theater company. If you're in Los Angeles or New York, try one of the movie studios for renting flats, or you can find scenery houses and set-design companies listed online or an entertainment directory like the Los Angeles 411 (www.la411.com), New York 411 (www.newyork411.com), or the *Creative Handbook* (www.creativehandbook.com).

TIP

You can make your own flats by building a wood frame out of light plywood. Then you paint or wallpaper it, set it up, and bring in some furniture and set decoration — sort of like home decorating. If you're looking to create an exterior scene, you can attach faux paneling from your local hardware store that resembles brick, log, concrete, or some other surface. You can cut out your own windows and put a scenic background outside the window to simulate an outside setting (or put some branches outside the window to suggest a tree). You can see how to construct sturdy flats in the *Stock Scenery Construction: A Handbook* by Bill Raoul (Broadway Press, 1998). Figure 6-1 shows a basic example of a flat and how it should be supported.

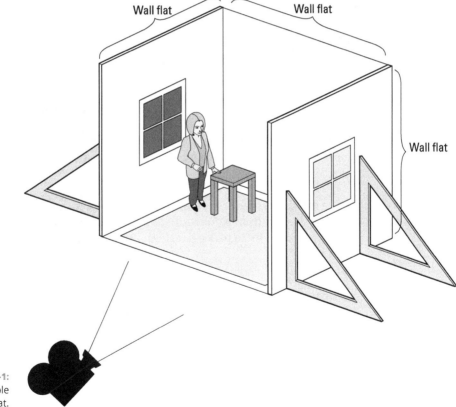

FIGURE 6-1:
An example
of a flat.

Shooting in the United States or Crossing the Border?

You may not have the luxury of deciding where to shoot your movie: Your hometown may be all that you can afford. However, you may face the decision whether to shoot on locations in the United States or take your production to Canada to take advantage of the exceptional government rebates and funding programs (not to mention the expanding U.S. dollar in Canada). For information about shooting in Canada, go to these websites: www.telefilm.ca, or www.OntarioCreates.ca. You may even be able to consider going somewhere else in the world (if the cost of transportation and accommodations is still less than shooting in your hometown). This section examines the pros and cons of both options.

Researching U.S. government incentives

Shooting outside the United States — often in Canada — has become much more common because of the many government incentives (tax and labor rebates). Also, because the dollar may be worth more in other countries. Canada averages a 25–30 percent increase on the American dollar. So your $100,000 budget could stretch to $125,000 in Canada.

This phenomenon, known as *runaway production,* has become a concern for cast and crew in the U.S. who lose work to foreign workers. Runaway production is also a government concern, and local agencies are interested in keeping the film industry within the United States by sponsoring incentives to encourage filmmakers to shoot locally.

Making movies is good for the economy; businesses, including restaurants, hotels, and parks, benefit from it. To entice filmmakers, many states (including California) offer some of these perks, but check first to make sure:

>> They may not charge location fees for state owned property.

>> They may offer tax rebates to filmmakers who shoot locally. A tax rebate reimburses the sales tax you paid for expenses related to your production.

REMEMBER

Tax incentive programs are always changing, so always check for updates. Usually, you're reimbursed after submitting receipts and proof of sales tax payment.

If you aren't located in a major city that has a film commission set up by the government, you can contact your local city hall to find out if there are any incentives for filming locally (waived permits, tax rebates, and free locations, for example).

Hundreds of Hollywood productions shoot in Georgia because they offer generous tax incentives of up to 30 percent. Georgia, Arizona, and 26 other states are *right-to-work* states. Right-to-work states are usually exempt from forcing labor rules and contracts. *Note:* Laws change all the time, so if you are interested in shooting in a right-to-work state, research the latest laws and stipulations of working there.

Traveling to Canada

Sometimes shooting a movie in Canada, as many U.S. studio movies and television shows are doing, has its advantages. They include:

» Rebates on federal and provincial sales tax.

» Lower rental costs on locations.

» Government rebates on labor (up to 35 percent).

» Rebates on post-production services, digital animation, and visual effects.

» The currency exchange stretches your budget, depending on the economy, as much as 35 percent.

The downfall of shooting in Canada is the added expense of having to fly your cast and crew there (unless you hire them locally) and put everyone up in a hotel. You need to decide whether it's more economical to shoot in Canada or stay at home.

Locating Stock Footage

Want an aerial shot of a city lit up at night? An explosion over the ocean? Chances are you can find the perfect footage already shot and just insert it into your film. That's what *stock footage libraries* are all about. Just like locating a sound effect from a sound-effects library or a piece of music from a music library (see Chapter 16 for more on sound and music libraries), you can license existing footage (usually without actors in the shot) to integrate perfectly into your movie. A *license* gives you permission to feature particular footage from a film library in your film for a specific fee. Digital Juice has its own Stock Library (www.digitaljuice.com). I often use stock footage from Video Blocks, which has a vast, affordable library and some unique location shots I can't find anywhere else (www.videoblocks.com).

I've used stock footage from the Pond 5's Digital Library (www.pond5.com) in many of my projects. They have every piece of footage imaginable, from old black-and-white vintage scenes to astronauts and outer-space footage. You can view Pond 5's entire digital library online and easily purchase and download the footage onto your computer. You can preview footage and even download samples with watermarks to see if they work in your movie before you purchase. Stock footage clips usually start around $15 and average around $50 per clip. However, a very unique clip could cost upwards of $200 or more — for example, a clip of a dog catching a frisbee might cost you $39, but a unique clip of a jet fighter taking off, which is not something you can easily find and film yourself, might cost you $149. After you license the footage for the flat fee, you have nonexclusive rights to use it in your movie.

REMEMBER

Stock footage can raise the production value of your movie and make it look like a much bigger-budget film. If you have an aerial opening shot, the audience isn't going to know that you didn't shoot it, or that you paid less than $199 for the footage from a stock footage library, as I did for the opening of my film *First Dog*. For that film, I used footage of the camera flying past the Washington Monument, catching the sun's rays and then revealing the majestic White House on Pennsylvania Avenue.

Most footage from a stock library has been shot on high definition 2K or 4K digital at 24 frames per second. If you shot your movie on digital, or even on film, you should be able to closely match the licensed stock footage to your surrounding shots by color-correcting and adjusting the exposure (lighting) in editing during post-production.

TIP

Stock footage libraries don't just license their footage; they're always looking to buy footage to add to their extensive libraries often on a daily basis. Have you shot anything that may work for a stock footage library? You can earn a little money back to cover the expense of shooting the footage and possibly make a little profit, too. My movie *The Random Factor* (with Dan Aykroyd as the voice of "Dexter") required an opening scene with an ambulance racing through the streets. I couldn't find a stock library that had all the shots I needed, so I shot the footage myself, used it in my movie, and then ended up licensing it to a stock footage house.

Virtual Locations: Creating New Worlds on Your Computer

Need to shoot on another planet? Traveling to the moon isn't economical, and besides, you get motion sickness in outer space. Does the location you need exist only in your mind? Try creating it on your computer.

Turbosquid (www.turbosquid.com) offers up 3D landscapes, architecture, and even 3D objects, pretty much anything under the sun (including the sun). You can find basic and detailed 3D models ready for use, or models that can be redesigned or embellished upon.

Bryce is a great 3D software program by Daz 3D (www.daz3d.com), which has a free downloadable version that enables you to create realistic-looking scenic backgrounds, from tree-topped mountains and rolling hills to alien outer-space terrain complete with hovering planets. Figure 6-2 features a frame from my sci-fi film *Light Years Away* starring Christopher Knight (a.k.a. Peter Brady) and Meadow Williams *(Apollo 13, Den of Thieves)*. You can create your virtual locations in Bryce and then superimpose your actors into the background using a blue- or green-screen process (see Chapter 17 for more information about blue-screen). Santa's magical North Pole workshop was created by my friend Robert Chapin for my film *Santa Stole Our Dog* using Adobe After Effects, Maya, and Nuke. There is also a revolutionary effects software used by many of the Hollywood studios called Houdini.

FIGURE 6-2:
A virtual alien location created with Daz 3D's Bryce software, and Santa's Northpole workshop created in *Adobe After Effects*.

© Astrolite Ent. 2008 Light Years Away — Christopher Knight, Meadow Williams, ©2019 Winterland Ent. Santa Stole Our Dog

Securing Your Locations

After you find the ideal locations for your production, you need to have a formal written agreement between you and the property owners granting you permission to shoot at the location and outlining the specifics (for how long, how much, and any restrictions). You need to be guaranteed the use of the property and make sure that no surprises await you when you show up to start shooting. There are services that can assist you in securing locations, either through the city's permit office, a location service, or your local film commission (which you can find by contacting your local city hall office).

SHOOTING OUTDOORS

Weather is the number-one concern when shooting outdoors (unless you live in California, where it never rains, at least according to the song). Your favorite cable network becomes the Weather Channel or you find you're always checking your reliable weather app. Rain, snow, hail, and wind can ruin any shoot, or at least make it extremely difficult. Hot or cold environments can also affect your camera's performance. Condensation can form on the camera's lens when moving from a cool outside environment to a heated interior. Be prepared to shoot indoors at the last minute (with a backup secured location standing by) if you do get rained out, or be prepared to shoot your scene and have your actors acknowledge the weather in the scene if it is windy or storming.

WARNING

Make sure that the person who signs the agreement to let you use the location has the full authority to do so. There should be a clause in the agreement that clarifies the person signing is an authorized signatory, so he's held responsible if it turns out he misled you. I once planned on shooting in a laundromat in a strip mall. When we arrived at the location, I found out that the owner of the laundromat didn't ask permission of the mall owner he leased his laundry coin service from. I ended up having to renegotiate with the owner of the strip mall.

You can have an attorney draft a one-page location contract, or Movie Forms Pro has 110 production forms which include a location agreement (www.movieforms.com).

Acquiring permits

To shoot on most public locations, you need a permit from the city or state (this is separate from the agreement with the location owner), whether you're filming outside or inside. You don't want to be shooting with cast and crew and have a police officer show up asking for a permit and you don't have one. If this happens, you could be asked to leave, leaving you and your cast and crew out in the cold. Other than California, permits are usually inexpensive, averaging a few hundred dollars; many cities' film commissions encourage movie productions and waive the permit fee. Check with the city or state permit office to find out if the fee can be waived. If you can't find a permit office, start by calling city hall. I like shooting in Arizona. Even though you have to apply for location permits, many of those permits are free — no charge!

TIP

If you're in Los Angeles, the permit office is listed under Film LA (`www.filmla.com`). For New York City, go to `www.nyc.gov` and in the City Agencies drop-down list, select "Film/Theater." If you live outside of the big metropolitan cities, do a search on *local film commission* to see if your town has one.

WARNING

Under no circumstances should you ever sneak onto private property. Trespassing is illegal, and you could be arrested and thrown in jail. Your cinematographer can roll the camera documenting you being hauled off to prison, and you will end up calling your attorney from your "cell" phone.

Ensuring you're insured

What if someone trips and knocks over a light stand, causing the hot light to ignite the drapes and burn down the location? This is when you'll be glad you bought location insurance under general liability coverage. If people know better, they won't let you shoot on their property until you present them with a *certificate of insurance*. This certificate is issued by an insurance carrier under a general liability policy, proving that the location you're using is covered in case you or your production company cause damage. General liability insurance doesn't really cost you money — it saves you money in the long run. See Chapter 4 for more information about all the insurance you should consider purchasing for your production.

GEE! PS

I have one in my car, and now I can't live without it. It's a GPS (global positioning satellite system) navigating device — and it even works with voice command, so I just tell it where I want to go. They're portable, so you can pack it in your suitcase and pop it in your rental car in another city. The service is free (no monthly satellite fees), unless you want additional services like real-time traffic alert, but some systems come with traffic included. Most people now have reverted to just using their map direction app on their smartphone. (I still use my GPS device because it doesn't eat up my smartphone battery or disconnect when using my phone for the radio or phone calls). You just punch in your final address, or use voice command, and the GPS device or app calculates your trip. Whether you're trying to find a location in your city or one across the country, GPS satellites know exactly where you are and direct you to your final destination. Most GPS devices and map apps have millions of points of interest (POI). You can find local restaurants, hospitals, police stations, gas stations, and more in your immediate vicinity. Most speak in friendly voices and different accents, and even recite the street names — and don't worry, they'll never talk to you like a backseat driver.

Mapping out your locations

When your locations are set, you need to make sure that your cast and crew can find them. Usually the first or second assistant director supplies location directions to the cast and crew. Internet mapping sites such as Google Maps are also handy — but always double-check Internet directions. If you use `www.google.com/maps`, you can not only get turn-by-turn directions, you can even click on "Satellite" and see aerial photographs of the location. Click on "Street View" to see an actual street level photo of the address. Some map websites and apps even advise you the best time to leave to avoid traffic. Once you know the address, there are some great GPS apps, such as Waze and Google Maps, that will help you find the best route to your location.

Policing your locations

If you need to stop cars or direct traffic around the area you're shooting, police would be required. Police are also usually required when you're shooting on city or state properties as well (be careful when using the word *shooting* around police officers). Some states offer discounts and rebates on police officers' salaries when shooting on government property.

WARNING

Always have the police direct or stop traffic. You have no authority to do so, and you will either get arrested or some angry commuter will give you a hands-on lesson in road rage. Also, my mom taught me to never play in traffic.

MOVIE TRAILERS (NOT THE COMING-ATTRACTION KIND)

A movie trailer can be a midsized RV or an oversized Winnebago. A trailer is a luxury not always available to the low-budget filmmaker. On studio pictures, the stars always have their own private trailers with all the comforts of home: a kitchen, a bathroom with shower, and a bed. On a bigger budget film, the co-stars often are provided individual small dressing rooms contained in a *honey wagon* that is towed by a semi-tractor truck. On a low-budget production, trying to get even a small RV to use as a production trailer when you're on location isn't a bad idea. The trailer can be a sheltered place to take meetings, a place for actors to have some private space or even take a nap between takes if they don't have their own trailers. Also, a trailer can be a place of refuge when the weather outside is too hot, or too cold, or just a comfortable place to retreat when you need to get your bearings for the next shot.

Fire!

If you're dealing with explosions, firearms, or any potential fire hazard, you're required to have a firefighter on the set (and, of course, a pyrotechnician who is skilled with explosives and gunpowder and, if required by law in your area, licensed). Depending on which city you shoot in, you may get a reimbursement or rebate on the salary you pay to a firefighter.

Shooting Second-Unit Locations

Second-unit photography is footage that isn't shot at the same time as your principal photography and usually doesn't require your main actors (or allows you to use doubles for a distant shot). Second unit is often filmed after your main shoot, when you've had a chance to make a list of additional shots to weave into your main shots, such as establishing exterior shots of certain locations.

If your story is supposed to take place in New York, but you live in a small town in the Midwest and you're on a tiny budget, you can't afford to take your whole cast and crew to New York to shoot, for example. Instead, buy yourself one plane ticket. Pack your portable digital camera and shoot some establishing shots that you can cut into your movie.

For my film *Miss Cast Away and the Island Girls* (a.k.a. *Silly Movie 2*), we shot most of the footage along the beaches of California to save money, but myself and two friends flew to Hawaii to shoot second-unit footage. We shot footage from a helicopter of the islands (through a helicopter tour guide service — with my friend Tim hanging halfway out the helicopter) and establishing shots of the ocean waves hitting the tropical shores, and cut these into the final movie.

KEYING IN BACKGROUNDS

Another inexpensive way to look like you shot your movie in another town or abroad, is to *key* them in (the process known as *chroma key*). Shoot your actors against an all blue or green background and then superimpose (composite) them over any static background footage (stock footage or footage you have shot). You then remove (make transparent) the blue or green behind the actors, allowing your scenic background footage to appear behind them instead. See Chapter 17 for details on using blue or green screen. For my Christmas movie, *Santa Stole Our Dog*, my main actors look like they are making

(continued)

(continued)

their way through a winter wonderland, but in fact they were shot against a blue screen in sunny hot California. I conveniently superimposed them in front of background plates I shot in Canada during a snowstorm.

Here's a scene from my film *First Dog* with my dog Little Bear shot in front of a blue background and then superimposed in front of my second unit footage of the White House. You can also buy footage from a stock footage library, such as Pond 5 (www. pond5.com) and superimpose your actors in front of that footage without having to leave your house.

Courtesy Stellar Entertainment/First American Cinema ©2008

Chapter **7**

Crewing Up: Hiring Your Crew

As a filmmaker, you may be the creative driving force and the master of many, or Jack of all trades, but you can't make a movie all by yourself. Whether you have a 2-person crew or 30 people assisting you in your vision, you need to find people who are as passionate about your movie as you are. In this chapter, I list the positions required on an independent production along with a description of each crew position and what traits, skills, and knowledge are needed. You discover the advantages and disadvantages of hiring an independent contractor versus an employee, along with great tips regarding crew members who may take a pay cut if they get other perks. You can be the producer, director, cinematographer, writer, editor, and even the star of your film — but you can't go it alone: You need a crew to help with lighting, grip equipment, props, wardrobe, sound, and so on.

Something to Crew About

Every film production needs a crew, because one person alone just can't do everything. An independent production, depending on the budget, doesn't require as large a crew as a big studio motion picture. Digital cameras nowadays require less lighting than film stock, which helps cut down on lighting and grip equipment. If you love overworking yourself, you can even operate the camera and sound yourself, as well as position the lights and move the equipment around. Even if you're shooting with film, you can still get away with a small crew; you just may need to add a few more positions — such as first and second camera assistants, because you won't have auto-focus and because you'll need someone to load and offload the film stock. The second assistant camera person will also probably be the person running the film to the lab to be developed. You also will need a sound mixer because you will not be able to record sound into the film camera. In addition you may need an extra grip and best boy for more lights, since film is not as sensitive to light as a lot of the new digital cameras are.

The following sections list the main production team you should try to assemble, whether you're shooting on film or digital video. Having some understanding of what the other people on your crew do — like the cinematographer, the producer, the editor, the dolly grip, and the prop or wardrobe person — can improve your working relationship with them and, in the end, result in a smooth and professional looking production.

REMEMBER

To decide what role *you* take, think about what you enjoy doing most. If you like putting things together, and if you are organized and reliable, then you'd probably make a great producer. If you like things a certain way and under your control, if you are a visionary with a good imagination, and love working with all kinds of people, then your calling may be directing. If you love telling stories and are always jotting down great ideas that come to you, writing screenplays may be for you. Maybe you're a "triple-threat" — someone who writes, produces, and directs.

Producing the producer

A *producer* is responsible for putting the project together and sometimes finding the financing. Without the right producer, the movie may never come to fruition. A producer, who is often the filmmaker (the person responsible for the project being produced in the first place), is the first one on the project and the last one to leave. The producer is responsible for hiring the crew and working with the director to hire the actors. The producer helps "produce" all the elements required to put the production together.

Some projects have an *executive producer*. This person earns the title by either handling the business of the production, being the actual financier of the project, or being someone without whom the project would never have come together. In television and studio features, the executive producer is often a representative of the studio or network who carries a lot of authority.

An *associate producer* is usually a glorified title reserved for someone who contributes an important element to the production — such as finding the financing or the name stars. Agents and managers often get an associate producer credit for bringing a star or major element to a project.

Directing the direction

Everyone wants to direct, don't they? Even my dog has a T-shirt that says, "What I really want to do is direct," and is also a member of the DGA (Dog Actors Guild of America)! A *director* has to be a multitalented multitasker. The director is captain of the ship, the leader of the pack, and is responsible for making all the creative elements come together (see Chapters 13 and 14 for more on what a director does). Many first-time filmmakers can take on the job of directing, and if you do your homework (like reading this book) and are passionate about making your movie, you'll find it a rewarding experience. If you'd rather hire someone else to direct, start collecting demo reels — whether they're short films, features, or commercials — from prospective directors. YouTube is a great place to discover up-and-coming directors.

TIP

When searching for a director, ask these questions:

- ❯❯ **Does he or she tell a story well?** Is the story logical in its sequence of events? Did the director tell an intriguing story and do it effectively?

- ❯❯ **Are the actors' performances believable?** Do they come across as sincere? Do you care about the characters in the movie?

- ❯❯ **Are camera shots and movement effective?** Does the director use effective angles? Are the shots interesting but not distracting to the story? Does the camera movement enhance the shots or distract from them?

- ❯❯ **If the film's a comedy, is it funny?** Does the director have a good sense of comedic timing? Is the comedy funny or too silly?

- ❯❯ **Is the direction consistent?** Do the shots have a certain style? Do all the elements, shots, dialogue, setting, and so on have consistency, or does the work seem all over the place?

Assistant director

Many people have a misconception of what an assistant director does. He or she does *not* assist in directing the movie. An *assistant director* (also known as the A.D.)

is more of an assistant *to* the director. The assistant director keeps the set moving and the production on schedule. The assistant director's duties include:

>> Breaking down the script with the director (to schedule the shoot days).

>> Relaying the director's technical instructions to the cast and crew.

>> Getting the shots ready by making sure that all production personnel and actors are in place and ready when the director needs them.

>> Working with the extras on a small budget, and relaying instructions for the extras to the second assistant director on a bigger production.

>> Making up the *call sheets* (lists of which cast members work the next day and any special equipment or elements needed for the shooting). On bigger productions this is usually handed off by the first assistant director to the unit production manager.

>> Calling the actors who need to work the next day (on larger productions, this task is performed by the unit production manager).

>> Getting the set settled to start shooting (asking if sound and camera are ready and then calling to the sound mixer to roll sound and the camera operator to roll camera — things that must be done before the director cues the actors or action begins).

REMEMBER

The director — never the assistant director — calls "action" and "cut." The assistant director's authority ends (except for cueing the background extras) when the director calls for *Action!*

Second assistant director

The *second assistant director* (the second A.D.) is an assistant to the assistant director and is also responsible for a fair amount of paperwork — especially if it's a union shoot, because there are strict rules and regulations, and everything has to be documented properly. I liken a second A.D. to an executive assistant — this person does paperwork, works on the computer, and helps to make the boss's job easier.

Some of the second A.D.'s paperwork includes handling call sheets, collecting from the camera department the *camera reports* (shots and footage for the day's shoot), collecting talent releases for background players, and so on. The second assistant checks everyone in at the beginning of each day's shoot, calls the actors for camera when they're needed on the set, and then checks everyone out at the end of the shoot.

My sister Nancy was the second A.D for my film *Undercover Angel,* and her job was crowd control. For the final dramatic scene in the film, Nancy rounded up almost 1,000 extras, which was no small task.

Stepping over the line producer

The *line producer's* job is to work with the budget and line up, and keep tabs on the items in the budget categories that make up your production. The line producer works with the producer in getting good deals on equipment, props, locations, and other elements that make up the budget. On a small production, the line producer can often have the job of producer and even unit production manager. On bigger-budget projects, each is a separate position.

REMEMBER

Line producing an independent low-budget film is actually an art form; it requires great skill because you have to work with what you have and can afford. When interviewing potential line producers, find out what budget amounts they've worked with on past productions. Have they worked on budgets similar to yours? If you're shooting a low-budget movie, you need to hire someone who's had the experience of line producing an independent production. A line producer who has worked on a multimillion-dollar budget may have difficulty relating to a small budget. Also make sure you get references from a producer or director whom your prospective line producer worked with in the past.

TIP

You can find a qualified line-producer (and many other crew and staff positions) by checking out the Los Angeles 411 (www.la411.com) or the New York 411 (www.newyork411.com). These industry directories are some of the finest resources for productions in the film and television industry.

Uniting with a production manager

The *unit production manager,* also known as the UPM, works closely with the line producer and assists in getting good deals on equipment and other elements for the shoot. The UPM also ensures that all equipment is on set, on time. A UPM is kind of a co-line producer (in fact, most low-budget productions have no UPM, only a line producer). A UPM on a low-budget production will often take a lower salary to get a better credit as a line producer.

Supervising the script

Someone with a good eye, a decent memory, a knack for recalling details, and a keen sense of observation is the kind of person you need for *script supervising.* Also known as the *continuity person,* a script supervisor must know the script inside and out to ensure that wardrobe, props, and hair match from shot to shot. Without the script supervisor, a cup of coffee may suddenly appear in an actor's hand, props may simply disappear mid-scene, and chairs may magically seem to have rearranged themselves. Preventing this from happening is one of the jobs of the script supervisor. That's why they take tons of reference photos with their smartphone to remember how the makeup scar looked in the last scene, or which earrings the actor wore when she left the party scene — so she'll still have them on when she arrives home.

Some of the script supervisor's duties include making sure:

>> Action matches from shot to shot.

>> Screen direction is correct (see Chapter 14), meaning when one actor is supposed to be looking at another actor, they're facing the proper direction.

>> Wardrobe, props, hair, makeup, wounds, and scars match from shot to shot (still photos taken with a smartphone) help match actors' appearance from shot to shot).

>> The director has shot enough coverage for each scene (for example, that appropriate close-ups were shot for important emotions, or certain angles were shot to show the full impact of the action).

>> Actors say their lines verbatim from the script and are corrected if they change a line or assisted if they forget a line or two (or three).

>> Lenses and frame sizes used for each shot are noted so the director will know whether he has shot enough coverage. This is also helpful to the editor when cutting the picture together and knowing what coverage there was for the scene (giving the editor more cutting options).

>> The editor receives assistance with scene notes and other details to help edit the picture together in a coherent fashion.

Ask to see a candidate's script-continuity notes to see whether the candidate is organized and detail-oriented and whether his or her notes are legible. Getting referrals and talking to a director who's previously worked with this script supervisor is always a good idea.

Directing photography with a cinematographer

The *director of photography* sees the world through the single eye of the camera and helps you envision your movie from script to screen. On low-budget productions, *you* may even be the director of photography. The director of photography is often referred to as the D.P. (or the D.O.P. in Canada) and is also called the *cinematogra-pher.* If you're shooting a low-budget production, your cinematographer will often be the camera operator, as well. Only on bigger-budget and union productions does the cinematographer have someone else operate the camera.

REMEMBER

If you're interviewing potential cinematographers, request to see his or her *demo reel* (a clip usually viewable via a link to YouTube or Vimeo that features samples of the cinematographer's work). A demo will often have short samples of the D.P.'s work from different projects, preferably showing a diverse style from project to project. Maybe you can see the candidate's work on his or her website. Every cinematographer has a demo reel — if the one you're talking to doesn't, beware. That's like a screenwriter without a script. Also see whether he or she has references from other filmmakers. A good place to find a cinematographer (and other crew members) is at www.stage32.com.

Your cinematographer is one of the most important players on your team. After all, the audience doesn't care how much work went into getting each shot; all they see is the final product. So look for the following attributes when choosing a director of photography:

>> Does their demo reel reflect a style that you like?

>> Do they know how to light scenes to convey the appropriate mood — or is their lighting flat?

>> Are shots framed esthetically, or are they awkward? Is the camera movement subtle or jarring?

>> Are they pleasant and personable? Will they be easy to work with?

>> Are they knowledgeable about the technicalities of the camera and lenses, and can they work quickly without compromising quality?

>> Do they have a gaffer and other crew members they like to work with?

>> Are they willing to work long hours with low pay? Will they work on deferment (meaning some of their salary is deferred)?

>> Do they own a film or digital camera (and maybe some lights) to use on your production?

REMEMBER

Nowadays, many cinematographers have their own cameras. Some own digital cinema cameras or DSLRs (which look like still cameras but have digital recording options). You may be able to get both a camera and a cinematographer for the price of one — definitely a plus on a low budget. (For more on motion-picture film and digital cameras, see Chapter 10.)

First assistant camera

The *first assistant cameraperson,* or first A.C., works alongside the camera operator or director of photography — whoever is operating the camera — and changes camera lenses, inserts camera filters, cleans the shutter gate for dust and particles (if it's a film camera), and adjusts the focus. This position is also referred to as the *focus-puller,* because that's the most important duty of the first A.C.: to make sure everything that's supposed to be in focus is in focus. This is a very skilled position, especially when the actor moves to or away from the camera, or the camera moves to and from the actor: The A.C. has to *pull* focus to keep the actor from going out of focus.

TECHNICAL
STUFF

An assistant cameraperson often uses a tape measure and a precision focus knob on the camera to ensure that all images that are supposed to be in focus are. They should be prepared to *rack-focus,* meaning focus from one element in the same shot to another, with precise timing and accuracy. An assistant cameraperson on a digital production often takes measurements using the camera's focus through the lens by using a video monitor to see what the camera sees. Many digital cameras have an auto-focus setting that actually tracks the actor and keeps them in focus. Auto-focus tracking is not always perfect, and sometimes there is a lag, so the A.C. often manually adjusts the focus after rehearsing with the actor and camera movement.

Second assistant camera or D.I.T.

The *second assistant cameraperson,* also known as the second A.C., is required to load and unload the film magazines (if you're shooting film rather than digital), being extremely careful not to expose your precious film to the light as he or she unloads your footage and readies it for development at the film lab. If you're recording to memory cards for digital HD, the second A.C also doubles as the *D.I.T. (digital intermediate technician).* The D.I.T.'s job is to transfer the digital recorded footage to an external hard drive so you can reuse the cards, and to make sure there are no drop-outs or technical issues with the footage. The second A.C. is also responsible for slating the clapboard for syncing sound to picture when shooting film or when doing *double-sync sound* with digital (see Chapter 12 for more on syncing sound), and for logging camera reports that detail what shot was recorded on what film roll (or memory card, if you're recording digital). When shooting with film, camera reports are crucial because they accompany the exposed film to the lab and provide instructions if any special developing and/or printing is required.

REMEMBER

If you're shooting digital with a small crew, your second assistant cameraperson is also your D.I.T. guy.

Going with your gaffer

Your *gaffer* works closely with your cinematographer to make sure the mood and lighting of each scene works effectively. Often the gaffer is also an electrician or has experience and knowledge of electricity and voltage. Ask your cinematographer if he or she has enjoyed working with a certain gaffer in the past. This saves you a lot of time and trouble. You want to have people who are familiar and comfortable working with each other.

Best boy is your best man — or woman

The *best boy* works closely with the gaffer, dealing with electricity and powering the lights. He or she (yes, a best boy can be a woman) also runs the extension cords and checks that everything is plugged in correctly. The gaffer sometimes can recommend a best boy he or she has worked with. If not, ask the cinematographer or another crew person. In the end credits on all my movies, my dog Little Bear has a credit as *good boy* next to the best boy's credit.

Electrician is electrifying

An *electrician's* main job is tying your lights directly into the electrical circuit box to avoid a power overload. If you're doing a digital shoot in a small location and using LED lights, chances are you may be able to plug directly into the wall plugs and you won't need an electrician to monitor the set. (Many LED lights also run on rechargeable batteries.) LED stands for *light emitting diode,* which is a powered diode as opposed to a bulb. That's why LEDs rarely burn out, and why they use extremely low voltage and wattage — about ten times less than a regular incandescent bulb. Checking with an electrician first isn't a bad idea, though — and it's not safe to play with live electricity. You don't want to blow a fuse or, even worse, start a fire. On a smaller shoot, you can hire an electrician from `Yelp.com` or `www.handyman.com` and pay him or her for only an hour or two of work at each new location.

Getting a grip

Grips are the production set's manpower: They move camera and grip equipment and help position lights and stands according to the gaffer and cinematographer's instructions. Having a few grips on hand speeds up your setup and saves time and money. My friend Peter Emslie wanted to work on a project I was developing for Dolly Parton, and he eagerly volunteered to be the dolly grip! A *dolly grip* is in charge of setting up the *dolly* (which is used to move the camera during shots) and the tracks the dolly moves on; he or she skillfully pushes the dolly while the camera is recording.

Sounding like your sound mixer

Sound is very important in any movie. The *sound mixer* is responsible for recording the actors' dialogue on set and ensuring that it's clear and comprehensible. The sound mixer on a production shooting film or on digital, has a separate sound machine, either a digital audio recorder like a four-track audio Zoom H5 handheld that records to SD cards, or a Nagra, which uses audio tape (see Chapter 12). The sound mixer also has a mixing board that allows the ability to input several microphones (for miking several actors within the scene) and mix them into the recorder to get the appropriate balance of all mics. Sound mixers also make sure that the recording is free from interference (background noise that interrupts the dialogue, for example, or hissing or electrical interference on the actual line when using wireless mics).

REMEMBER

Even when shooting with a digital camera that records audio into the camera, many filmmakers prefer using a sound mixer either to monitor the audio going into the camera or to record what's called *double-sync sound* into the mixer's separate digital audio recorder. This is why a clapboard is used, so the separate audio can have a reference to the picture that is synced up at the *clap*.

I've worked with sound mixers like Al Samuels, who did the film *Swingers.* Al's production sound was so good that little or no re-dubbing of dialogue was required by the actors in post-production. I've also worked with sound mixers who recorded completely unusable sound on-set because they didn't know how to mix correctly, didn't hear the interference on the wireless mics, or didn't instruct the *boom* person (see the following section) to position the microphone correctly, resulting in most of the dialogue having to be rerecorded during post-production (see Chapter 16 sound mixing).

Booming the sound

A *boom person* anticipates the actor's performance on set in order to position the microphone at the right distance and angle to get clear, crisp dialogue while at the same time not letting the mic and boom creep into the shot. The boom held by the boom person is a long pole (sometimes called a *fishpole*) with the microphone positioned on the end. The job requires skill, and without the right operator, the recording will suffer. Because the boom person and the sound mixer must communicate clearly with each other, your sound mixer often recommends or brings his own boom person — someone he has worked with before.

Propping up the prop master

The *prop master* is in charge of any object that an actor interacts with — such as a telephone, a lamp, a gun, or a glass of champagne. On smaller productions, the prop person can also be the *set dresser* (the person responsible for items the actors don't interact with, such as flowers on a shelf, placemats on a table, picture frames on a mantle). The prop master can also double as the *greensman,* in charge of plants, flowers, even trees — anything that requires a hand with a green thumb, including plastic plants.

TIP

When interviewing people for the position of prop master, you want to know whether the person has access to *prop houses* or other places that can provide props for free or at a low rental cost. A prop person also needs to be organized, reliable, and detail oriented. If you're not close to any major production centers, check into local theater groups where you'll likely find a candidate to provide you with props for your production.

Dressing up the wardrobe department

Your *wardrobe person* should have the skill to sew from scratch; on an independent budget you can't always afford to purchase or rent certain wardrobe or costumes. It's also important to have someone who can take-in or lengthen pants and other clothing for a better fit on the actor. It's also helpful if this person has contacts for inexpensive clothing rentals. The wardrobe person is also in charge of making sure the actors are wearing the appropriate wardrobe in each scene to match continuity. They number the wardrobe or outfits for each scene and keep track of what the actors were wearing in the last scene and whether there are any wardrobe changes for the next scene.

On low-budget productions, the actors usually wear their own clothes, which the wardrobe person has selected by looking through their closets (with their permission, of course). Wardrobe has to be checked out each day and checked in at the end of each day — even something as simple as boots (if the actor takes them home and forgets them the next day, continuity won't match). The wardrobe person keeps clothes hanging on a wheeled rack like the ones you see in a department store. Each piece of wardrobe is tagged and marked for which scenes it is to be worn in. The wardrobe person also makes sure the actor's wardrobe is kept clean (or dirty, depending on what the scene requires). The wardrobe person is also in charge of dressing the stunt double in the same wardrobe as the star. If wardrobe is going to get dirty, wet, or damaged in a scene, it's up to the wardrobe person to have doubles of the same clothing for additional takes.

Making up is hard to do

Makeup is often overlooked on low-budget productions, but it shouldn't be. The wrong makeup or coloring can cause disastrous results on the final product. An experienced cinema makeup artist knows how to work with different skin tones and make them look even-toned under different lighting conditions. Make sure the makeup artist is versed in film and digital makeup. You don't want, say, a fashion makeup artist, who may exaggerate the actor's makeup instead of making the actor look natural on camera. You especially don't want your male actors to look like they're wearing makeup — unless they're *supposed to* look made up. Makeup can make circles under the eyes vanish, blotchiness on the skin disappear, blemishes go away, or bruises appear. Never use an inexperienced makeup person. Bad makeup will distract your audience — it's happened on one of my films. With special effects makeup, your makeup artist can create a deformed character, age an actor, and make creatures come to life with the aid of *prosthetics* (latex appliances attached to the face — see Chapter 17).

REMEMBER

Be sure to allow for a makeup kit rental fee in the budget for makeup supplies including sponges, powder, puffs, and tissues.

Gopher this, gopher that

A *gopher,* professionally called a *production assistant* but also known as a *runner,* is usually a student or eager beaver who wants to get on a movie set. They go-pher this and go-pher that. The position doesn't require skill as much as it does eagerness to work on a production set. Reliability and hard work are the main prerequisites of a good gopher. The difference between a gopher and an apprentice is that the gopher is hired to work on the set, and often an apprentice is working for free to gain the experience and to learn about the filmmaking process hands-on.

TIP

Gophers are easy to find. Post ads at the local colleges and in trade magazines, flyers, and on Internet film blog and crew sites like `www.crewnet.com`, `http://media-match.com`, `http://castandcrewcall.com`, and `www.productionhub.com`. Also check out `www.studentfilmmakers.com` for crew posting under their Classifieds section.

TIP

Instead of sending your production assistant to grab food for the crew, and to keep them working on-set where you really need them, you can use special App services via your smartphone for Door Dash (`www.doordash.com`) and Grubhub (`www.grubhub.com`) to pick up meals from restaurants. Some online services will even pick up items from the store or pick up deliveries and bring them to you. Lyft, which is a passenger ride service, is known to run errands like doing pickups and deliveries.

Keeping your composer

The *composer* scores music to accompany the images of your film and to help set a mood. Finding a composer is a lot like finding your cinematographer: As soon as you hear a sample of a composer's sound, you'll know immediately whether you like what you hear. Collect CDs or audio file samples from composers to hear their work. You can find composers through the various music organizations — BMI, ASCAP, and SOCAN (see Chapter 16). If you go to `www.crewnet.com` or `http://media-match.com/`, you can click on "Composers" and find a list of potential people who could score your movie.

REMEMBER

The composer sets the mood of your film. Are you intrigued by their style and sound? You want to make sure you both have the same vision for your movie. After you select someone, sit down and discuss the type of music you hear in your head for certain scenes. I often give my composer a rough idea of songs and movie soundtracks I like, and tell him or her to compose in that style. For my film *Turn of the Blade,* I told my composer, Greg Edmonson, that I liked the sexy sound of the saxophone used in the *Lethal Weapon* soundtrack. This gave him an idea of the style I wanted, and he was able to give me a similar feel for my film. Another thing I have done is to put temporary (*temp*) music over my movie's visuals to give my composer an idea of the type of music I am thinking for certain scenes. Because I'm not going to use my temp music in the end, I can pull from known soundtracks and recognizable songs.

WARNING

Never use copyrighted music without permission. If you want to use a commercial song or soundtrack, you need to license it (see Chapter 16). You can be inspired by music that's out there, but don't copy it or even get too close to copying it — you don't want any legal problems.

Editing: Cut that out!

When interviewing a potential *picture editor*, a person who is experienced at cutting images together to form a visual story (technically and creatively), ask to see a sample of something he or she has cut together — either a short film or a feature-length movie. Ask if any of their clips are on YouTube or Vimeo to view. Here's a list of things to look for when interviewing a potential picture editor for your project:

>> **Technical knowledge of nonlinear editing software** (including expertise in all aspects of exporting final footage for distribution). Nonlinear is the technique of having your individual shots as separate entities and available to be assembled in any order. Nonlinear editing software includes Avid, Adobe Premiere, DaVinci Resolve, and Final Cut Pro X.

>> **A nonlinear (computer) editing system,** which is usually a desktop or laptop computer (PC or Mac) with adequate speed and memory.

>> **Good pacing (timing)** to their cutting (with no lags or slow spots in the action).

>> **Effective use of cutaways** (reaction shots, or parallel scenes happening at the same time).

>> **Seamless cuts** (no jarring cuts or jump-cuts that look like frames are missing).

>> **Tight scenes** (no laborious entering and exiting of actors, or silent pauses that seem too long).

>> **Effective transitions** from one scene to another.

TIP

Another advantage to hiring an editor is that they can start editing the picture as soon as you start providing footage from day one. This can speed up your post-production schedule. If you have to shoot *and* edit your movie, you won't have time to start editing until you've finished shooting the entire film. The other advantage to having someone else edit is that they can let you know whether you should shoot extra footage, such as an insert or a close-up, before you leave that location.

And the rest . . .

Depending on the size of your budget, there are other positions that you may need to fill. On a low-budget production, many of the following could be you or someone filling one of the positions mentioned earlier in this chapter:

>> **Casting director:** This person breaks down the script and suggests actors suitable for each role. The casting director looks at submitted headshots and resumes and selects actors to come in to audition. Often, in a low-budget production, the filmmaker is also the casting director.

>> **Location scout:** The location scout breaks down all the locations in the script and finds the actual locations to shoot the movie. The filmmaker can also be the location scout. I've driven around town many times looking for the perfect place to shoot.

>> **Transportation person:** This person is solely dedicated to driving the crew and cast around from hotel to set or parking area to set. If it's a small production, everyone usually drives his or her own car, or sometimes you have another crew member pick you up, and you carpool! You can also use Uber or Lyft to conveniently pick up and drop off your cast and crew.

>> **Production designer:** A production designer designs the overall look of a movie. Although some films (for example, *Batman* or *The Martian,* where a whole world had to be created from scratch) depend on a production designer, most small-budget films don't have the luxury of having one.

>> **Stunt coordinator:** This person is skilled to either perform stunts him- or herself or coordinates with others who are trained stunt people. If your film includes stunts, don't try to save money here. Always hire a professional stunt person who is skilled in even the most basic of stunts. Try to avoid stunts on a

low-budget movie; they can be expensive and risky *and* raise your insurance package. With the advances in special effects software, you may be able to create a virtual character in post-production to safely perform your stunts (many of Spider-Man's aerial stunts are performed by a virtual, computer-generated Spider-Man).

» **Post-production coordinator:** The post-production coordinator coordinates the completion of the movie, schedules when the picture editing and sound elements are to be done, and sets a finishing date for the final production so distribution plans can begin. On a low-budget movie, having a dedicated post-production coordinator is a luxury. Usually, the filmmaker performs these tasks.

» **Still photographer:** You need to think ahead and hire an on-set still photographer to take photos that can be used for publicity and eventually in the artwork for the poster and/or various streaming services. If you can't afford a professional photographer, allow crew members to take photos with their smartphones with an agreement that you can use them for publicity purposes. Distributors (Chapter 19) request production stills to use in posters and in *one-sheets*, also called *sales-sheets,* which are flyers advertising your movie. You also need photos as publicity stills for film festivals, newspaper, websites, and magazine articles.

Finding and Interviewing Your Crew

You're ready to make your movie and you know the positions you want to fill. Now how are you going to find the people to help you put it all together?

» **Place an ad requesting that people apply for crewing up your film.**
You can post an ad in one of the online film and digital publications, like *Videomaker Magazine* (www.videomaker.com), StudentFilmmaker.com, and Mandy.com. You can run an ad in your local newspaper or neighborhood flyer. Search Facebook, and put a social network call-out for crew. Go on a local TV show or news program and get the word out that you're looking for crew. Post ads at local schools and colleges and on blogs that are geared to independent filmmaking.

» **Get ahold of the Los Angeles 411 or New York 411 directory.** In addition to crew listings, these directories list other production resources. Check out www.la411.com or www.newyork411.com.

>> **To find crew throughout the United States and Canada, go to** www.crewnet.com. You can also try www.media-match.com and www.productionhub.com and www.stage32.com. Craig's List (www.craigslist.org) is a great place to find crew — just click on your town or city and then, under the Jobs listing, click the category TV/Film/Video. You can post an ad on the sites (some are free to post) and request resumes via email or through the jobs site account you set up.

After you start getting resumes from potential crew members, you're ready for the interview process. You're not just looking for skills, but also for personality and temperament. For the types of questions to ask and skills to verify, see the earlier discussions on the respective positions.

TIP

Get references from all potential crew members, even if you don't plan on contacting their references. If they have nothing to hide, they'll gladly volunteer letters of reference or contact names. If they say they have no references, beware!

Creative Ways to Pay Your Crew

Now that you've found your crew, you have to figure out how to pay them. When you're shooting a low or no-budget movie, you don't have a lot of money to throw around, if any. No one is being forced to work on your production, especially if there is low or no pay. But you can save dollars on hiring your crew and still have a win-win situation for both parties.

TIP

When you are ready to pay your crew, you can use a payroll company, or write the checks yourself at the end of each production week. If you are working with freelance storyboard artists, editors, or effects people who are in another city or across the world, you can pay them instantly using PayPal just by knowing their email addresses.

Paying later: Deferments or points

One of the ways to save money on cast and crew is to set up an arrangement whereby you pay crew members some of their pay later for the work they perform on your production. There are two ways you can do this:

» **Deferments:** With *deferments,* you *defer some of* the crew members' salaries. Deferments work by paying your crew a small amount up front (if possible) and another amount in deferred pay if and when you start seeing a profit from your film's sales. I recommend using deferments especially if you can pay something small up front; that way, you haven't taken complete advantage of the crew member.

» **Points:** *Points* are similar to deferments, except that instead of a deferred salary of a specific amount, you reward the crew with one or more points to be paid if and when the film starts to make money. One *point* may be 1 percent of the profits of the movie. If the movie makes a lot of money, points continue to add up and continue to be paid as long as the picture makes money.

Offering points or negotiating deferments are good incentives to offer crew when you don't have enough money to pay them what they're worth up front. Doing so also lets you save money up front, money that you can put up on the screen (into the actual production) and enhance the production values of your film.

TIP

I recommend deferments over points, because points obligate you to pay out every time money comes in from the picture, which can be a lot of extra paperwork and expense to keep track of. Deferments, on the other hand, are usually a specific dollar amount; when that amount is reached, your obligation is fulfilled and the crew member doesn't receive any more.

Racking up credits

Your potential crew may not be excited about the pay, if there is any, but you may get them excited about working on your movie by giving them a credit that they haven't been able to earn yet.

Getting a credit with more prestige on your production can help your crew get better positions on the next movie they work. For example, a gaffer who has studied to be a cinematographer may take a cut in pay, or no pay, if he or she gets a chance to be the director of photography on your movie (make sure he or she is qualified though). An art director may be excited — and willing to accept less compensation — to get a production designer credit.

Hiring student bodies

Another way to save on your budget is to go to school. Many students still in or fresh out of college would love to work on a production to gain experience and get their first film credit on their resume and to post on IMDB (www.imdb.com), the go-to Internet Movie Data Base. Some colleges even let their students earn a school credit if your production meets their educational requirements. If you're making a low- or no-budget movie, a student assistant in each department can be an asset to your production.

Paying a kit fee

Another way to save a little bit of money is to split up the salary you pay your crew member by paying him a kit fee. A *kit fee* is like a rental fee for the equipment that the crew member brings to your production. What's great about a kit fee is that it can save crew members on taxes that would otherwise be taken out of their salary, because rental fees in most situations don't count as crew labor — and so they may agree to give you a discount on their salary for paying them this way. You can pay kit fees for

>> Your makeup artist's kit with makeup supplies

>> Camera equipment from your cinematographer

>> Lighting equipment from your cinematographer or gaffer

>> Props provided by your prop master

>> Your sound mixer's own equipment

Hiring crew as independent contractors

You can save yourself and crew members a little money and extra paperwork if you're able to hire each crew member as an *independent contractor*. This way you don't have to withhold any taxes on crew members' salaries, and you don't have to pay social security and benefits since they're operating as freelance workers. Check with the laws in your state or province to see what distinguishes a freelancer from an employee, because laws are always changing. An *independent contractor* works independently without an employer constantly looking over his or her shoulder. Location scouts, wardrobe designers, freelance writers, and storyboard artists can all easily be independent contractors.

REMEMBER

You have to send each independent contractor a 1099 tax form at the end of each year in which they worked for any payment over $600. You can get standard 1099 tax forms at most stationery or office stores, or order online from companies that sell tax forms like Deluxe (www.deluxe.com) or forms you can fill out online at www.irstaxfilings.com. Your accountant may also be able to provide you with 1099 forms.

WARNING

When crew have to work specific hours on set, as opposed to working on their own time, you may have to hire them as employees. At that point, you're required to issue W2 forms, which then requires either hiring a payroll company or enlisting a bookkeeper or accountant to do all the payments and tax withholding, including workman's compensation and so on. Check with an accountant who can advise you which crew members can be hired as independent contractors and which ones should be hired as employees.

Union or non-union — that is the question

If you're doing an independent low-budget movie, you may not want to deal with the additional expense and paperwork involved with hiring a union crew. Unions are very strict, and if you default on any of their regulations, it could slow down, or shut down, your production. Plus, unions require you to pay minimum salaries, which may not be in your budget.

A lot of independent films can't afford to shoot with union employees and have to pass up experienced union crew, unless that union member wants to work on the production (and declare *Financial Core* — see Chapter 8) and take a pay cut in doing so. If you do a union production, you have to follow all union rules to a "T." And be prepared for penalties, including paying for overtime, and so on. You don't need that headache on an independent production — and most of the time you can't afford it anyway.

Putting Out a Contract on Your Crew

You should always have a signed agreement between you and each crew member. Movie Forms Pro (www.movieforms.com) has all necessary crew deal memos. You can also find sample deal memos online, but always have an attorney review them.

Whether the crew member is an independent contractor or an employee, a written agreement prevents any misunderstandings and clearly spells out exactly what's expected of the crew member, including the following:

>> **Position and title:** Define the title they get in the production credits.

>> **Salary:** Specify what they are getting paid (if anything) or getting in deferred pay or points (if any). Note that you may be able to pay non-union

independent contractors a flat fee, whereas union employees usually require hourly pay. See the next section for more on union employees.

>> **Employment status:** Specify whether the crew are working as independent contractors or employees. Make sure everyone fills out a W9 form, with their correct contact info and social security number (download and print out copies of the W9 form at `www.irs.gov/pub/irs-pdf/fw9.pdf`).

>> **Work hours and workweek:** Set out how many hours a day (8 to 12) and how many days a week (5 to 6) are required during production.

REMEMBER

Specify *turnaround* time (time off between shoots) in the crew contracts — and make sure it's enough. Turnaround time usually means at least ten hours before the crew member has to return to the set. You need to respect your crew and show you appreciate their dedication to your film, especially if they're working hard for little money (and they're going to need some proper rest after a long day's shoot).

>> **Copy of completed project:** Promise the crew member a copy of the movie on DVD or a private Internet link to view when it's completed.

TIP

Boilerplates are preexisting contracts that have already been drawn up by an attorney or used for previous productions. All you have to do is fill in the blanks with the crew person's name and other relevant information. My recommendation: Use boilerplates as a guide and then consult an entertainment attorney who can review them and add or subtract where necessary.

One book that I find very informative is *Contracts for the Film & Television Industry* by Mark Litwak (published by Silman-James Press). Mark is a prominent entertainment attorney in Los Angeles who works very closely with independent filmmakers. In addition to his series of legal books, check out his website at `www.marklitwak.com`. Mark's industry book contains contracts that are useful for TV and movie productions, including a three-page crew deal memo (again, I recommend consulting a lawyer to review any boilerplate contract before using it — doing so protects all parties).

REMEMBER

Contracts need to be specifically tailored to your production. If you're in a town that doesn't have an entertainment attorney, you can always find an attorney who is familiar with the film industry via the Internet in Los Angeles, New York, or Toronto. You don't even have to meet face to face. You can send forms and contracts via email. I'm in Los Angeles and so is my entertainment attorney who I've worked with for over twenty years — and in the last five years I've only seen him in person twice (and one of those times was when I ran into him at a department store).

Chapter **8**

Assembling Your Cast of Characters

The time has come to breathe life into your screenplay's characters and have them jump off the page. In this chapter, you discover how to find the perfect cast for your movie and how to talk to agents, managers, and casting directors. You find out what to look for in actors (and their resumes), what to expect when you meet actors, and how to read them for the part. I also give you some important tips to relay to your actors so that you get the best audition from them. You may just discover the next Al Pacino or Sandra Bullock. You may also want to pick up a copy of *Breaking into Acting For Dummies* by Larry Garrison and Wallace Wang (published by Wiley) for more tips on the auditioning and casting process.

Hooking Your Cast and Reeling Them In

Casting is one of the most important decisions you make when putting your movie together — it's half the game. So how do you go about finding your cast of characters? There's no shortage of actors (or wannabes), and there's no shortage of places to find them. You can discover your leading lady or leading man on the street, through a mutual friend, at a talent showcase, online, or even at your family reunion (who knew Cousin Ellie had that star quality you were looking for all along?). You can also find actors by contacting agents, managers, and casting directors; calling casting services; and scouring online actor directories. The following sections tells you how.

Calling all agents

Just because an actor has an agent doesn't mean the actor is working a lot. An agent is more of a legal representative for actors — someone to protect the actor from being taken advantage of on the set and to make sure she receives payment for services rendered. An agent usually does all the contractual work with you for the actor he or she represents, whether it's a detailed agreement or a simple one-page *deal memo* (see "Agreeing with Actors' Agreements" later in this chapter).

REMEMBER

An agent usually collects the actor's payment and takes a 10 percent agent commission fee before paying the performer. A manager can charge 15 percent or more as a commission fee. This is important for you to know, because sometimes an agent and/or manager asks for the actor's fee, *plus* the agent and manager fees on top.

Most agents won't consider a project for a client until they've received and read the screenplay, along with a written offer (and know the money's in the bank). If the agent doesn't like the script (or the offer) or thinks her client isn't appropriate for the project or part, she'll decline.

TIP

If the agent *likes* your project, this is a good time to ask who else he or she represents that may be good for your picture. For my movie *Undercover Angel,* I asked the agent who represented Yasmine Bleeth (the actress playing the lead in my film) who else he represented that he could recommend to play the male lead opposite her. This is how I ended up casting Dean Winters (of HBO's *OZ, Law & Order, John Wick*).

Casting through casting directors

Casting directors are always on the lookout for new talent to feed the myriad of productions being produced. In Hollywood, the casting director has a lot of power because if an actor doesn't get past her, he'll never have a chance to meet the filmmakers. A casting director not only filters the piles of pictures and resumes that are submitted but also schedules auditions with the chosen ones. This saves the filmmaker from having to see everyone who walks through the door — even the ones who can't act their way out of a paper bag (which by the way my dog can do very well). A casting director also builds relationships with talented actors whom he's seen perform in the past at showcases or other film and TV projects, and he keeps a roster of these talented individuals on file should an appropriate part come along for them to try out for.

I'M D.B.

A service that everyone in the film industry uses is the IMDb, which stands for *Internet Movie Database* (www.imdb.com and www.imdbpro.com). Every actor who has ever worked is listed on IMDb. Even my mom, who plays Mrs. Claus in my movie *Santa Stole Our Dog*, has an IMDb page now. Not only can you get actors' complete resumes of films, TV, and stage work, but if you subscribe to *IMDbPro*, you can find out who represents and/or manages them along with contact info. The site also lists production companies, distributors, producers, directors, writers, production crew, and, of course, almost every movie ever made. It's a plethora of information right at one main Internet address. *IMDb* is free, and *IMDbPro* is $149.99 a year, but you can get a free one-month trial by signing up.

REMEMBER

The casting director is only the guard at the gate — the bouncer outside the club — who the actor needs to get past in order to get to you, the filmmaker. The casting director does *not* make the final casting decision; she only filters the talent or suggests name actors that she can approach for your picture. The director or producer makes the final decision on cast.

Placing casting ads

One way to find talent for your film is to place casting ads. A *casting ad* is similar to a job classified ad, but instead of seeking someone for an office position with the proper qualifications, you're seeking an actor with acting experience who qualifies for a very specific acting role. You can place an ad on a job board at a theater company or at local colleges and high schools. Some larger cities even have periodicals devoted to scouting talent. For example, if you're in one of the major cities in the U.S. like Los Angeles, New York, Chicago, or Philadelphia, you can place an ad in *Backstage*, a weekly periodical for actors and industry professionals. *Backstage* also has an online service where you post your casting ads immediately, making them available to online subscribers (www.backstage.com). In addition to placing a casting ad, you can also search the tens of thousands of actors who have posted their pictures, resumes, and even acting demo reels to the online site.

When you post an ad looking for actors for your movie, list the following information:

>> Log line of your movie (one- or two-line synopsis of the story)

>> Character's name and age range (such as 24 to 29)

>> Character's body type (balding, skinny, chesty — preferably not all three!)

- **»** Character's idiosyncrasies (knowing that the character has a lisp, a twitch, or a type of attitude is helpful to the actor in the audition)

- **»** Character role (lead, supporting, or day player)

- **»** Acting experience (required or not)

- **»** Whether you're seeking union or non-union actors (many independent low-budget films can't afford to hire union actors and follow union regulations under the restraints of a small production — see Chapter 4)

- **»** Pay or no pay (important to mention)

- **»** Benefits such as a copy of the movie and meals on set (important, especially if you offer no or low pay)

- **»** Contact information (where actors can send their pictures, resumes, and online demo reels if they have one)

Through online submissions, pictures and resumes can be delivered in seconds instead of the days necessary when actors used to mail them through the post office. Nowadays, an attached email photo can be viewed immediately in color and in high photo quality with an included YouTube or Vimeo link to view the actor's online acting reel.

Calling casting services

A casting service is a service that hooks the filmmaker up with the actor — a win-win situation. A filmmaker puts out a call for a particular type of acting role, and a casting service gets that call out to the agents, managers, and actors who could fill that role. Nowadays, many casting services use the Internet, because it's faster than using snail mail or courier services. Many cities have casting services, and the best way to find out is to talk to agents in your area. If any type of casting service is available, agents will be using it.

CATTLE CALLING

Round 'em up! A *cattle call* is a casting call where anyone can show up and be seen by the producers (like you've seen on *American Idol* and *America's Got Talent*). My dog recently went to a cattle call for canines (he has his Dog Actors Guild {DAG} card). You can place a cattle call casting ad in your local newspaper, in an entertainment trade magazine like *Backstage*, on the Internet, or through a casting service. Depending on the film and the roll being offered, actors can wind around the block. If you're offering generic parts that can be filled by almost anyone, your cattle call could cause a stampede!

BREAKING INTO BREAKDOWN SERVICES

If you're in the Los Angeles, New York, Toronto, or Vancouver areas, I suggest contacting Breakdown Services. Breakdown Services lets casting directors, producers, and directors send out a call for a certain type of character(s) needed for a film or TV production. The specified criteria relate to physical description and acting abilities.

You submit a breakdown of your cast to Breakdown Services, which then posts the list on its site, Breakdown Express (www.breakdownexpress.com). The many agents and managers who subscribe to the breakdowns can then access it. Breakdown Services also has a service called Actors Access (www.actorsaccess.com), which allows actors to see certain casting notices on the Breakdown Services Breakdown Express website and submit their pictures, resumes, and demo reels directly to you.

Placing a breakdown ad is free if your production is union; if your production is non-union, the fee is $100 unless you're paying actors at least $100 a day; then the casting ad is free.

Accessing actor directories

If you're looking for an apartment, you can browse through an online rental directory, complete with photos and even videos. If you're looking to buy a new home, you can look through an online real-estate site. Well, actors have their own directory, too. You can flip through pages of a directory that features actors' photos and contact information, all at your fingertips. Actor Hub (www.actorhub.com) is a great resource, and www.filmlocal.com also has a nice directory. Actors Access (www.actorsaccess.com) is a popular directory used by Hollywood casting agents and producers. Central Casting (www.centralcasting.com) is an excellent source for finding background actors, formally known as "extras." These are the people milling around in the background to help round out your scene.

Screening an Actor's Information

After you've received an actor's submission, you need to evaluate whether this actor is a potential candidate for one of the roles in your movie. Some of the things you'll consider as you review the actor's picture and resume:

» Does the actor look the part?

» Does he or she have the qualifications (acting experience) and/or some professional training — or are they a natural with star quality?

>> Does he or she have any special skills listed that may help add believability to playing that part? (Roller-skating? Juggling? Doing accents?)

>> If the actor submitted a demo reel, is his or her performance believable or stiff and amateurish?

>> Is the actor union or non-union? If an actor is union, you have to follow union rules and pay the actor appropriately (see Chapter 4). Many low-budget films can't afford to hire union actors. Some union actors are willing to work non-union by going *financial core* (that is, temporarily resigning from SAG-AFTRA, which the union doesn't encourage).

Headshots and resumes

You can tell how serious an actor is by how he submits his picture (called a *headshot*) and resume. I've received folded photocopies of pictures in letter-size envelopes (saving the sender on postage). Online, if the actor has obvious unprofessional photos and doesn't have a demo reel (even a simple 30-second monologue or just a clip of the actor talking to the camera), he or she is not being serious about acting as a career choice. If an actor doesn't take him- or herself seriously enough to submit professional materials, you can't take him or her seriously either. The only actors who probably don't need a professional headshot are those auditioning for the role of the headless horseman in *Sleepy Hollow!*

TIP

When you receive pictures and resumes from actors, especially if you receive them in the mail (which is much rarer these days), make sure all pertinent information is on the resume, including a contact number for the agent, manager, or actor. More than once I've received a resume that didn't include the actors' contact information — not even a phone number or email address! Because I couldn't contact these actors for an audition, I had to cast them into a trash-can instead!

Also, make sure the pictures and resumes you receive in the mail or in person when meeting the actor, are stapled together (many arrive unstapled). If not, you may want to staple them yourself (and deduct the staple from their salary if they get the job). That way you don't lose track of what resume belongs with which picture.

Reading and reviewing resumes

Following are things you should find on an actor's resume that will help determine whether he or she is qualified for one of the roles in your movie:

>> **Height, weight, hair, and eye color.** Since the photo doesn't say, "actual size," the resume should include height. Before the Internet, actors used to

submit photos in black and white (cheaper for the actor to print a few hundred), and therefore their resumes used to include hair and eye color, too. Even though the photos are usually in color now, the resume should still list eye and hair color. The reason for this is if the actor's vitals are part of a search base where casting is looking for a blue-eyed blonde, or a dark-haired, dark-eyed bad guy. Also, sometimes resumes get separated from their photos accidentally.

>> **Union affiliations if any.** Don't let non-union status cause you to reject an actor. Just because an actor may not be in a union doesn't mean he isn't a good actor. Every successful actor at one time was not in a union.

>> **List of credits.** See what experience the actor has. Just as important as acting experience is the experience of being on a set and knowing the rituals. But you can also discover an up and coming talent too who has no or few credits.

>> **Commercial credits.** Usually a resume says, "Commercial credits upon request." You are welcome to request them.

>> **Online demo reel.** Does the actor have a sample acting reel of previous work or a test scene to show his or her on-screen persona — even a 30-second intro showing off his or her personality?

>> **Stage work.** Lets you know whether the actor has any live-performance experience (keep in mind that stage play acting is quite different from motion picture acting).

>> **Training and special skills.** Anything that may enhance the character you're considering the actor for.

>> **Contact information (agent, manager, cellphone, website, and email address).** Many good actors don't have an agent or manager; you can contact them directly if they provide their email or website address.

Sometimes you find an actor with very little experience who ends up being perfect for the part. I never judge an actor by a lack of credits on his or her resume. Request a demo reel or call them in — you can't tell personality from a resume.

Heading toward headshots

An actor's physical *headshot* is usually an 8-x-10-inch color photo with a resume stapled to the back. Headshots used to be submitted in black and white because color was so much more expensive, and it was a style that worked at the time. Now with the Internet, everyone can afford to email or upload a color photo. *Zed cards* are a series of different shots on one card. Even though they're submitted more for modeling work, I like to see several shots of an actor, if available, just to get a better idea of what he or she looks like.

I've rarely met an actor who looks exactly like his or her photo. Don't hire an actor based solely on a headshot — always meet him or her in person! I've made this mistake and regretted it — I ended up having to put the actor in the back of the shot — out of focus!

When you look at an actor's photo, do you see some personality? Is there a gleam in the eye? I've received headshots where the actor looks like he's a frightened deer in a tractor-trailer's headlights, or she's putting on a goofy face that immediately warns me she may be an over-actor.

Recording their act

An actor may submit a *demo reel* with his resume and headshot. More often than not, their demo reel is available on the Internet. A demo reel is often a short clip available for viewing on YouTube (www.youtube.com) or Vimeo (www.vimeo.com) that features a selection of acting scenes, usually between three and five minutes in length, in which the actor showcases his or her acting skills. Smartphones have excellent digital cameras built in, so there's no excuse for an actor not to have even a sample scene.

Spinning an actor's website

Not only do the actor's tools include a headshot, resume, and a demo reel, but many also have either a personal web page or a website. Many actors' Internet sites put up pictures (including headshots) and resumes for filmmakers to reference. One such service is www.hollywoodsuccess.com, which posts actors' pictures and resumes from all over the country. I'm surprised by how many people call themselves actors but don't have a website and/or a demo reel. Wix.com makes it easy and free for an actor to set up his or her own website. An actor without a website and/or demo reel is like a writer without a script.

You'll know an actor is serious and professional about her career if she also has an electronic resume on a personal web page with the following:

>> Several photos to give you an idea of her look

>> An updated list of credits and skills to get an idea of her experience in front of the camera

>> Her email address or her agent's email address so that you can easily make contact

>> A streaming demo reel to give you an idea immediately of her on-camera persona (many actors' websites now link to YouTube or Vimeo, where you can see scenes they've uploaded of their performances)

Auditioning Your Potential Cast

The audition is the first face-to-face meeting between you and the actor. First impressions are always the most important — especially in the casting process. The audition not only gives you a chance to "test" the actor, but it also lets you see if he really does resemble his photo — minus the magic of a professional photographer and airbrush artist and gives you an idea of whether this person can take direction. Have him read some lines from the script, and then tell him to try it a different way — with an accent or using a different tone or attitude — to see if he can take direction.

TIP

Nothing compares to a meeting in person, but if distance is a problem, a webcam meeting is the next best thing! I've auditioned actors using Skype and iChat (through Apple iPhone, iPad, and computers). Auditioning remotely is the next best thing to conducting an in-person audition, and you can get a good sense of the actor's personality. I've also had actors record themselves on their smartphones reading a few pages from the script (*sides*), and then uploading the footage with a private link on YouTube for me to review.

Creating a friendly environment

Always conduct auditions in a place of business — never in your home, no matter how small your production. Having people come to your home is a bit suspicious and, besides, it's not professional. Why would you want every Tom, Dick, and Harriet coming to your private residence anyway? You can find an office, conference room, dance studio, or rehearsal hall to rent for a few hours at a reasonable price ($10 to $40 per hour), or borrow an office space through a friend. If you're only auditioning one specific actor, whom you think might be the perfect casting, arrange to meet them in person at a coffee shop.

REMEMBER

If you're personable with the actors, they'll be much more comfortable talking with you and more likely to be themselves. People tend to mirror people — so if you're uptight, they'll be uptight or uncomfortable. Be professional, but be respectful and friendly; not only will the casting process be easier for the actors, but it will also be more effective for you.

Inspecting an actor's etiquette

When you meet an actor for the first time, he or she will probably make some kind of impression on you. Is this someone you would like to work with? There are several things you should look for in an actor:

>> **Is he punctual?** Does he show up on time for the audition? If not, this could be an indication that he's not reliable or at least not punctual.

>> **Does she have personality?** The number-one most important trait of an actor is personality. A strong personality in general helps infuse personality into the character the actor is playing. Would you say Sandra Bullock and George Clooney have personality — I should say so!

>> **What is he like before the reading and after?** How an actor acts before and after the reading often impresses me more than the reading itself. It gives you a chance to see if that person has a sense of humor, funny quirks, or interesting mannerisms.

>> **How is she dressed?** An actor should dress appropriately for an audition. She doesn't have to wear a uniform or costume that suits the character, but if she's trying out for a biker chick role, leather pants and a sleeveless shirt are okay. If the role is an attorney, wearing a suit helps the casting director "see" that actor in the role a lot easier. I've had actors show up in baseball caps and shorts, like they're on their way to the gym and they're doing a favor by stopping in to see me.

>> **Does he conduct himself professionally?** An actor should be polite, cordial, respectful, and pleasant at an audition.

Actors who send a thank-you note (or postcard or email with their photo) after you've met always stand out. Less than 5 percent of actors have sent me thank-you notes over the past 25 years, but I've actually singled out actors who do, and hired some of them because their note reminded me of our meeting. It tells me they're thoughtful, probably reliable, and they take their acting career seriously. This is someone I *want* to have on my set.

Slating on camera

You may want to record the auditions so that you have a reference of all the people you auditioned. You can use your smartphone, or even the same digital camera you're using to shoot your movie with. When you record the auditions, always have the actor start by *slating*. *Slating* means that the actor introduces him- or herself on camera and then gives a contact number (cellphone, or agent or manager numbers, or email address). Slating saves you the time and trouble of tracking down and matching up to pictures and resumes. Another advantage to recording the auditions, you can share the footage with your colleagues and see if you all agree on the same actors.

Avoiding bitter-cold readings

Some directors have actors do a cold reading of *sides* (two or three pages from the script) without any study time on a first audition. This is effective when you want to see how actors work with no preparation. If you want to get a better idea of their performance abilities, then give them at least ten minutes with the material before expecting them to perform it for you. I am not concerned how well an actor memorizes the lines — so I tell them not to worry if they mess up on the dialogue. I'm not hiring them for their memorization skills, I'm hiring them for their personality and acting abilities.

TIP

To help calm the actors' nerves and bring out their personality, talk to them for a few minutes before they read; doing so helps you see whether they're personable and have a quality that the audience will be attracted to. Then have them read to see whether they can inject their personality into their reading. I often tell actors it's okay if they miss or add some words if it keeps them from staring at the script pages. I'm not looking to see how well they can memorize words; I'm looking for a natural performance that impresses me during the audition phase.

Monologues leave you all by yourself

Actors have been conditioned to bring *monologues* to perform at auditions for the casting director, producer, or director. I'm not a fan of monologues because rarely do you have a scene where the actor is talking for three minutes straight with no interaction from other characters. Monologues are more suited in auditioning for stage plays, as they tend to make the actor *project* (reach and speak louder).

TIP

When an actor prefers to do a monologue, do what I do: Have the actor pick someone in the room to talk to, and then have that person sit or stand at the distance he would if he were in the actual scene. This helps the actor better target his voice level and emotions. You can also have the other person silently react, so the performing actor has some interaction with a live person. Doing this eliminates another problem: Many actors who perform monologues make the mistake of talking to the casting director or person conducting the auditions (the director or producer), something akin to looking straight into the camera, which is a no-no! It always makes me uncomfortable as well when the actor looks directly at me while performing. If you're conducting the auditions, you want to observe the performance, not feel like you're part of it.

Making the Cut: Picking Your Cast

Choosing your final cast is not always the easiest job for the filmmaker. The actors you decide on have the responsibility of carrying your movie. They are the blood that keeps your film alive.

Calling back

When you like an actor who has come in for an audition, you call her back for a more personal meeting. This is appropriately called a *call back*. The call back gives you and the actor a second chance to become familiar with each other and for you to see whether she's appropriate for the role you're considering her for. During a call back, you usually have more time to sit down and talk to the actor and get a better feel of her personality. You can take time to have her read some more pages from the script as well, or even read opposite actors you've already cast for the other parts.

Screen testing

A *screen test* is an actual dialogue scene from your movie that you have the actor perform so that you can see how he comes across on camera. A screen testing usually occurs only when you're seriously considering a particular actor but aren't sure whether he can effectively play the role. Screen testing also lets you see how comfortable the actor is in front of the camera (and working with one of the other actors you may have already cast) and how well he takes direction.

TIP

Shoot a convenient and no-cost screen test with your smartphone. The picture quality is great and the lighting doesn't have to be perfect. You are looking only at performance here.

And the winners are . . .

After you've found the actor who's going to breathe life into the character, the first thing you have to do to hire that actor is call the actor's agent (if he is represented by one) and tell her you're interested in casting her client. The agent then contacts the actor and tells him the good news. If an actor doesn't have representation, you can call him directly and personally tell him that you're looking forward to working with him.

REMEMBER

Make sure that the actor or the actor's representatives understand all the details of the job. Be up front. If there's low pay or no pay, let them know this right away. (Some agents want their actor clients to get parts and build up a *reel,* various scenes of their work, and they're glad to negotiate a deal that you can afford.) Let them know that you will give them a DVD copy or a private YouTube link of their scene when the movie is completed, and that you'll feed them well on the set.

The next thing you need to do is contract that actor, which means arranging a legal agreement between your company and the actor. You can find more information about agreements in the next section.

TIP

After you select your actor(s), contact the other actors that you *seriously* considered before you chose someone else. Actors are sensitive, and knowing that they were seriously being considered lets them know they are worthy. You can even let them know that you will keep them in mind as a backup should your first choice not work out and that you may possibly cast them in future projects (which I actually have done). Don't turn down second choices until your first-choice actor has agreed to do your movie and is signed on. You still have to deal with egos, agents, and managers, and your first-choice actor may suddenly become unavailable.

Agreeing with Actors' Agreements

Once you cast an actor, it's important to get a written agreement between you and the actor, and/or her representative (agent). The agreement protects both the actor and you, the filmmaker. It spells out the terms regarding what's expected of both parties and is signed by you and the actor. The actor plays the assigned role, for a certain period of time, and gets paid (or doesn't). This agreement also contractually obligates the actor to your production; she can't take another project unless you don't fulfill your end of the agreement.

WARNING

If the actor is a minor (and I don't mean a coal miner), a guardian over the age of 18 must sign on his or her behalf. Otherwise, the contract can't be enforced — it's like not having a contract at all. Without a contract, a minor actor has no obligation to you or the production. He can even not show up on set, and you don't have a legal document to enforce.

Contracting union players

If you're hiring union actors with the Screen Actors Guild-AFTRA (SAG-AFTRA), you have to use their contracts, which lay out strict rules and regulations that you have to abide by, including guild salaries (close to $1,000 a day) to its union members. There are special SAG Indie agreements for independent productions that may fit into your budget; you can read about these in Chapter 4.

REMEMBER

If you're doing a union production using SAG-AFTRA (www.sagaftra.org) (SAG merged with the American Federation of Television and Radio Artists), or the Alliance of Canadian Cinema, Television & Radio Artists (ACTRA, www.actra.ca), you have contractual union stipulations to abide by. You can get details on the various contract agreements on their websites. The Screen Actors Guild has several special contracts for lower-budget productions (www.sagindie.org) (see Chapter 4); check out its website for details. If you're shooting a very low-budget production, you may want to avoid the paperwork hassles and extra costs of becoming a signatory to one of the unions and go non-union.

Contracting non-union players

A non-union actor's agreement can be issued in two phases. The first phase involves a *deal memo.* The second phase involves the formal *long-form agreement.* Both of these are explained in the following sections.

The deal memo

The deal memo is a short, preliminary contract or agreement usually made up of a few sentences stating that you're interested in hiring the actor for your movie and that a more formal agreement will be drawn up in the near future. The main purpose of a deal memo is to outline the main points of your deal without having to wait for the attorneys to do their thing. You may be able to find an appropriate agreement from an entertainment book, such as Mark Litwak's *Contracts for the Film & Television Industry* (see his website, www.marklitwak.com). Regardless of where you get your contracts, always have an attorney review them before sending them out to be signed.

In addition to a deal memo, you may want to give the actor a monetary retainer to show that you're serious about hiring him. The retainer can be $1, $100, or a $1,000 — depending on how badly you want to retain that particular actor for the part. The retainer legally attaches the actor to your project so you can start planning your shooting schedule or concentrate on casting the other roles. If the actor has name value, having him committed to your project may be of interest to potential distributors and/or investors.

TIP

If you're lucky enough to interest a big-name actor in your movie, ask her for a *letter of interest,* which is a letter from the talent saying that he or she is aware of the project and is interested in being a part of your production contingent on salary requirements and schedule. (Usually, you write the letter, and the actor signs it.) Often, the first thing a distributor or studio asks is not "What's the story about?" but "Who's in it?" A letter of interest from a recognized actor could help get you financing and distribution.

The long-form agreement

After contract points are negotiated in detail, a formal agreement, usually called the *long-form agreement,* is drawn up by your attorney. An actor's formal long-form agreement should include the following points:

» Name of the character role the actor will play

» The number of shooting days or weeks involved

» Salary (plus any deferments, and/or points)

» *Per diem* (pocket money if on location)

» Perks (such as a trailer, a manicurist, a masseuse, or candy!)

» Automatic Dialogue Replacement (ADR) availability (for re-recording additional actor's dialogue in post-production)

» How the actor will be billed on the film and poster

» Does the actor have first right of refusal on publicity stills?

In addition, the contract could specify that the actor will receive a DVD copy or private online link of the project when it is completed.

REMEMBER

Make sure that your agreements let you use the actors' *likeness* in *perpetuity,* which means forever. You don't want to have to track them down ten years later to renew.

Securing releases from extras

In addition to written agreements with your main talent, you also need to have releases signed by *extras* (any other individuals appearing on camera). Yes, *everyone.* Even if people are walking by in the background or sitting at a bar, you need to have them sign a release. A release can be a simple one-paragraph letter giving you permission to use the person's likeness in your film. (Don't forget: As with lead roles, an extra's release should allow you to use his or her likeness *in perpetuity* so you don't have to track him or her down years later to renew your rights.) A studio or distributor releasing your film will require that you have these releases. If you're shooting in a public area and non-actors walk by in the background — you only need to have them sign a release if you can make out their faces. If they are a blur, or way in the background unidentifiable, you can use them for free!

A short release can read as follows:

> For value received, I, [PERSON'S NAME] hereby consent that all photographs and/or images of me and/or voice recordings in whole or in part for [YOU THE FILMMAKER/COMPANY], may be used by [YOU THE FILMMAKER/COMPANY] and/or others including distributors, with my consent for the purposes of illustration, advertising, broadcast or publication in any manner in perpetuity.

Make sure to include the date and have both parties sign the agreement. Having an attorney review this and any other agreements with regards to your production is always a smart idea.

WARNING

If you feature people in your film who didn't sign a release, they can legally keep you from showing the footage that they appear in. So don't forget, always get a signed release — even from your mother, if she's in your movie!

UNION ACTORS WORKING IN NON-UNION PRODUCTIONS

A union actor may decide to do your project even if it's non-union. *Financial core* (FiCo) was established by the Supreme Court of the United States to protect union members from coming under fire from their own union if they take non-union jobs (they cannot be sanctioned by the union; they still have to pay their dues, and they lose some of their voting privileges). Financial core encompasses all U.S. unions, not just the ones related to entertainment. Search the Internet for *financial core* to get the latest updates on this controversial topic.

Many times low-budget productions only go union if they have name actors (that can make your film more commercial to distributors). Many actors will work non-union to get a good part (though the unions definitely discourage it). The Screen Actors Guild puts out some low-budget agreements to help independent filmmakers cast union members in low-budget productions — and still allows you to use non-union actors in the same production as well (see the guild's website, www.sagindie.org). Also see Chapter 4 for more information on low-budget agreements.

Chapter **9**

Storyboarding Your Movie

f a picture is worth a thousand words, then a storyboard literally speaks volumes about your film. What's a storyboard? A visual illustration (hand-drawn or created with computer software) of the separate shots that will make up your movie. If you've ever read the Sunday comics or comic books, you're already familiar with storyboards.

This chapter shows you the advantages of storyboarding and how to break your script down into separate shots that become illustrated panels. You find out about the elements that make up a storyboard panel and the different sizes they come in and why. You see how a professional presentation of your movie in the visual form of a storyboard helps you sell your concept to an investor or studio. Don't think you can draw well enough? I provide suggestions for making your own storyboards with the help of some great software products. If you don't want to draw or use software products, I tell you how to find the right artist for your project and what you should expect to pay.

Understanding the Basics and Benefits of Storyboarding

Storyboards, which consist of a series of separate panels or frames, each one representing individual shots in your movie, provide an illustrated version of your screenplay — they tell your story with pictures. By storyboarding your movie, you, the cast, and the crew can visualize what the shots are going to look like before you even start shooting.

Storyboards serve as a visual reference and are helpful in the following situations:

>> Making a presentation to a client, such as an investor or a studio

>> Helping your cast and crew see your vision of the shots so that they're on the same page you're on

>> Showing your cameraman (director of photography) exactly what type of framing you want for each shot (more on framing later in this chapter)

>> Scheduling your shots for each day

>> Determining whether you have any unique shots that require action or special effects

>> Budgeting (planning ahead with storyboards saves you time and money)

TIP

Having trouble picturing what a storyboard is? Look at a favorite movie of yours on DVD or streaming on your computer or television — and hit the still frame button every time there's a new shot. This exemplifies what each storyboard incorporates for each camera shot. The storyboard frame or panel represents the first frame of each individual, continuous shot. If there is movement in the shot, then the storyboard will have arrows representing the movement — whether it's the actor or the camera that moves.

The storyboard's individual shots make up scenes, and scenes make up the whole film. You can have a few dozen storyboards for specific shots only, or 1,200 or more designed for your entire film — it all depends on the type of material you're storyboarding. For example, an action picture requires more precise planning; extensively storyboarding makes it easier to see and coordinate the shots. It also lets you cover the action from numerous angles and preplan those angles in storyboard panels to heighten the excitement. You can also storyboard any stunts, so the crew can see exactly what's going to happen on set. Steven Spielberg storyboarded almost 70 percent of his shots for *Indiana Jones and the Temple of Doom.* (He had help — although Spielberg draws initial concepts for his storyboards, he usually enlists the skills of a seasoned storyboard artist to realize his vision even further.) I discuss the benefits of hiring a storyboard artist later in this chapter.

On the other hand, not every filmmaker relies on storyboards. Sometimes the story doesn't require the details of each shot to be illustrated. A love story, such as the romantic comedy *The Silver Linings Playbook* may not demand hundreds of detailed storyboards because the shots are not as complex as those in an action or effects picture — although some simple storyboards showing angles and types of shots are always helpful.

Each panel of a storyboard shows you exactly what's needed for that particular shot, eliminating the guesswork for you and your crew. For example, storyboards let you know how big your set needs to be. If you plan to have aliens exit a spaceship, storyboards give you and your crew an idea about whether you need to build the whole ship or just the door area (the wide shot of the whole ship can be created in post-production via computer effects). Another example — does your storyboard show a large crowd in the stands watching a football game — or just a small section? From your storyboard panel, you know that you only need a small crowd and not a whole stadium full!

REMEMBER

You don't need to have storyboards rendered in full color unless you use them to impress a client or investor when selling your idea. Often, completed panels are acceptable in pencil, ink, or even charcoal, and can be basic or even crude — as long as they depict your vision as the director accurately.

STORYBOARDS ARE LIKE COMIC BOOKS

When I was a kid growing up in the '70s, I was an avid reader and collector of comic books. I spent endless hours absorbed in my Spider-Man, Batman, Richie Rich, and Archie comics. Little did I know that years later I would work with comic panels, or storyboards, to map out my shots for a film. Reading comic books at a young age taught me how to break a story into shots and angles — and I was learning about movement within a single shot or panel that I would one day apply to my filmmaking ventures. Once you start storyboarding, you'll never look at the Sunday comics the same way again!

Setting Up to Storyboard

Before you create your storyboards, you have to perform certain tasks and make certain decisions. First, begin by evaluating your screenplay and picturing it in terms of separate shots that can be visually translated into individual storyboard panels. Then you determine what makes up each shot and also which images need to be storyboarded and which ones don't. After you start storyboarding, you'll need to determine whether you're shooting for a TV movie or a theatrical release, which may affect the frame dimensions of your panels. Read on for the details!

Breaking down your script

The task of turning your screenplay into a movie can be very overwhelming. But remember, a long journey begins with a single step, so begin by breaking the screenplay down into small steps, or shots. A *shot* is defined from the time the camera turns on to cover the action to the time it's turned off — in other words, continuous footage with no cuts. Figure out what you want these shots to entail and then transform those ideas into a series of storyboard panels. If an actor or a camera is to move within the shot, you use arrows to show the movement, and sometimes you extend the dimensions of the storyboard panel to show the parameters of that movement. Stepping back and seeing your movie in individual panels makes the project much less overwhelming.

Evaluating each shot

You have several elements to consider when preparing your storyboards. You first need to evaluate your script and break it down into shots. Then, as you plan each shot panel, ask yourself the following questions:

>> What is the location setting?

>> How many actors are needed in the shot?

>> Do you need any important props or vehicles in the shot?

>> What type of shot (close-up, wide-shot, establishing shot, and so on) do you need? (See Chapter 14 for specific information about shots.)

>> What is the shot's *angle* (where the camera is shooting from)? Is it a high angle? A low angle? (Chapter 14 has more on angles.)

>> Do any actors or vehicles need to move within a frame, and what is the direction of that action?

>> Do you need any camera movement to add motion to this shot? Does the camera follow the actor or vehicles in the shot, and in what direction?

>> Do you need any special lighting? The lighting depends on what type of mood you're trying to convey (for example, you may need candlelight, moonlight, a dark alley, or a bright sunny day).

>> Do you need any special effects? Illustrating special effects is important to deciding whether you have to hire a special-effects person. Special effects can include gunfire, explosions, and computer-generated effects.

Organizing a shot list

After you determine what makes up each shot, decide whether you want to storyboard every shot or just the ones that require special planning, like action or special effects. If you want to keep a certain style throughout the film — like low angles, special lenses, or a certain lighting style (for example, shadows) — then you may want to storyboard every shot. If you only want to storyboard certain scenes that may require special planning, keep a *shot list* of all the events or scenes that jump out at you so that you can translate them into separate storyboard panels.

REMEMBER

Even if you've already created your shot list, you aren't locked into it. Inspiration for a new shot often hits while you're on set and your creative juices are flowing. If you have time and money, and the schedule and budget allow, try out that inspiration!

Framing storyboard panels

Before you actually draw your storyboards, you need to create a space for them to call home. The shape and dimensions of your storyboard panels will be determined by whether your movie is going to a high definition TV screen, or a theatrical screen in a movie theater. These different dimensions can affect how much information is drawn into your storyboards and what will ultimately be seen on the appropriate screen.

TIP

A really fun and free storyboard program called Storyboarder can be found at www.wonderunit.com/storyboarder. This may be the only storyboard program you need. As with most storyboard programs, you can inject your screenplay into the program so you can organize the parts of your script you need to storyboard. The developers of Storyboarder are also working on a revolutionary program called Shot Generator, which works in a virtual reality world. It's a game changer for storyboarding that allows you to enter a VR world, move your actors around, pose them, and even add objects in the frame, and then output them into individual storyboard panels. The amazing software is free, and the VR headset is under $400.

A storyboard panel is basically just a rectangle containing the illustration of each individual shot (one of many that you envision for your movie). Here are some quick steps to design your own storyboard panels:

1. **Decide which shape and size of panel to use.**

   A television storyboard panel, like the screen on an HD television set, resembles a rectangle, (16x9 dimensions) or 1:78 aspect ratio. This has replaced the old square analog TV screens with an aspect ratio of 4x3. Theatrical feature-film storyboards are rectangular in shape but narrower on the top and bottom. This is also referred to as *widescreen* or *letterbox* (because it resembles the dimensions of a standard letter envelope). When widescreen films shot in 2.40:1 (wider format than that of 16x9) appear on HD televisions, a black bar appears on the top and bottom of the image (see Figure 9-1). Many filmmakers now shoot for the wider framing, which works well for theatrical films and high definition TVs. With wider framing, the image will be shrunk down slightly so as not to cut off any of the image on your TV, thus causing the picture to have black bars at the top and bottom of the picture. TV and streaming movies are often shot to fill the entire dimensions of your 16x9 television. Theatrical releases are often the movies that are shot in the wider screen format causing the black bars on the top and bottom of your television screen.

   TIP

   You can storyboard panel templates in different format sizes on the Internet — but it's just as easy to create your own. You can draw four to six on a regular 8 ½-x-11-inch piece of paper (keeping them at a legible size), or a better idea is to design and print blank storyboard panels using your desktop computer.

FIGURE 9-1:
A penciled storyboard of an obsolete (square 4:3) analog format TV panel from *The Frog Prince,* and a widescreen panel from *First Dog* using the sketch mode in FrameForge 3D.

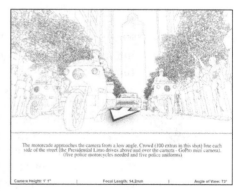

2006© Stellar Ent. (Artist: Tom Decker); 2012© First American Cinema, (Artist-Alexander-Sasha Yurchikov)

WIDENING THE SCREEN TO BE SEEN

Old analog TVs had an aspect ratio of 4:3. The picture was slightly wider than it was high. This is the aspect ratio that was designated to conventional television since the advent of the medium. The new dimensions for television broadcast are for high definition TV at 16:9 (equivalent to 1:78), where the width is almost twice the height of the now defunct analog TV screen. Motion pictures are projected in theaters in a 2.35:1 ratio (which is often referred to as *letterbox* or *widescreen*). Motion pictures conform well on HD 16:9 televisions (with top and bottom cropping). Some foreign countries use aspect ratios such as 1:66 and 1:78, which are variables on the letterbox format and can be reduced (or cropped) to fit on virtually any television set.

2. **Draw the shape of the panel and add a thick black or grey border (approximately 1/2 inch in width) around the panel.**

   Placing a border around each panel helps you to see each panel as a definitive separate shot and subliminally creates the illusion of a TV screen or darkened theater around your shot, giving you an idea of what that individual image will look like.

3. **Create a *description panel* by drawing an empty box just below the bottom of the frame panel.**

   Use the *description box* to write down important information that describes in detail what the illustration doesn't show or enhances what is drawn in the frame (see Figure 9-1). For example, include any important dialogue, camera directions, scene numbers, or special-effects instructions.

Deciding What to Include in Each Panel: Putting Pencil to Paper

After you create your storyboard panels, you need to decide exactly what you want your shots to look like. First, determine what the best angle is to capture the drama in a particular shot and whether you're going to move the camera. Also, think about lighting effects (shadows, special lighting, and so on) and other special effects that can be clearly exemplified in your boards. You should also draw any physical elements that will be inside the frame, including special props and, of course, your actors.

Choosing the right angles

You need to decide where you want to position the camera for the best *coverage* (the best angle to see the action). Angles have a subliminal effect on your audience (see Chapter 14 for examples of what the various camera angles look like in the frame and what effects they have):

>> **A low angle,** in which the camera is positioned on the ground looking up at the actor, can make an actor appear bigger and more menacing. So in your storyboard panel, you draw the low angle looking up at the actor with the ceiling or sky behind him.

>> **A high angle** that looks down on an actor can make the character appear innocent (like Rocket Raccoon in *Guardians of the Galaxy* — though he's not innocent!), small (as in *Ant-Man*), or weak. The storyboard sketch must make it clear that you need to have the camera up high.

Make a note if you will require special equipment, such as a high tripod or a crane to get your high-angle shot (check out Chapter 14 for more information about types of dollies and cranes).

Imagining camera and actor movement

Camera movement emphasizes a feeling or mood in a scene, and your storyboard panels should depict any such movement in each shot. (Check out Chapter 13 for additional tips on camera movement.) This is also a good time to decide if your actors are going to move within the frame as well. You can plan basic actor movement in the storyboards and save detailed movement of your actors, called *blocking* (see Chapter 13), for when you're actually on the set.

Arrows can show an actor's or object's movement within a panel. Arrows can also show the direction of your camera movement, whether it pans up, down, dollies left, or dollies right. Arrows also convey the camera moving in or out of the shot or leading or following an actor or vehicle. Figure 9-2 illustrates the use of arrows in a storyboard panel from my film, *First Dog.*

Boarding your special effects

Special effects can be costly, especially if they aren't planned properly. By story-boarding your special effects, you see exactly what they entail. For example, if a giant dinosaur looms up into the frame for one shot, as in *Jurassic World*, you know the shot requires at least the head of the creature and some blue sky behind it.

You and your special-effects team know exactly the elements you need for that shot (and the creature knows he doesn't have to worry about what shoes to wear that day). Now, if in the next frame, you have the dinosaur from head to toe, chasing pedestrians through the streets, your special-effects team has a lot more work to do.

FIGURE 9-2:
The use of arrows
for movement
within the frame.

Storyboarding is also important to see how the camera needs to move during the effect, which can be tricky when the frame has computer-generated images. If the shot consists of an explosion with an actor in the same shot, then you can see by this panel that either you have to have the actor as far away from the explosion as possible (unless you don't plan on using the actor in any more shots — LOL!) or you need to add the actor to the shot during post-production via green screen (see Chapter 17 for more on green screens). By illustrating these effects or stunts in a storyboard panel, you have a better opportunity to actually see what elements are in the shot and what safety precautions may be required.

REMEMBER

Use the description panel (explained in the earlier section "Framing storyboard panels") to detail exactly what is required for a shot. In the previous example, the description panel would note that explosives are set in the alley behind the dumpster and that you will superimpose the actor into the shot during post-production. Additional information may mention that the dumpster lid is made of light plastic, and it isn't hinged to the bin, so it can fly into the air on detonation (that reminds me, I forgot to take out the garbage).

ANIMATING ANIMATICS

Animatics is a form of storyboarding that incorporates your individual panels and turns them into a moving picture show (animates them). Animatics can be as simple as a QuickTime or AVI presentation with zooms and pans of the storyboard frames (called the *Ken Burns effect*). On a more sophisticated level, you can animate your storyboard panels, with your characters and vehicles moving within the panels, and add in narration or dialogue, along with music and even sound effects.

The early *Star Wars* movies used animatics, which helped showcase the shots and effects to the cast and crew. Doing an Internet search on *Star Wars animatics* will bring up many videos of the animated storyboards behind the pre-production. For *Iron Man 3*, a combination of amazing inked and computer-generated storyboard panels were pre-visualized into exciting animatics. (Search *Iron Man animatics* online.) Many animated movies like *Toy Story* used animatics because the character styles already existed (although cruder and simpler drawings were used to illustrate the characters' movements within the shots). TV commercials also rely heavily on animatics because a client is more easily convinced if he can see a moving visual presentation that resembles the final product. Of course, it's also easier to do an animatic for a 30-second commercial than a 90-minute movie.

Storyboard Fountain (www.storyboardfountain.com) makes a free storyboard program that lets you draw your own panels and even animate them. Reallusion (www.reallusion.com) makes a program called Cartoon Animator that works great for creating characters to use in animatics. Adobe After Effects and Photoshop are also great programs for designing animatics from scratch.

Sketching out the actors, props, and vehicles

As you inspect each shot, you see what actors, props, and vehicles are required. If you decide that one storyboard panel is a close-up of an actor, you sketch that one actor, and only that actor, in the panel. You may decide that you want a two-shot (see Chapter 14 for more information on different types of shots), so you need to frame two actors in this panel.

Looking at lighting and location

Lighting can emphasize a certain mood or tone in a shot. So, when drawing your panels, point out any special lighting techniques. If it's a dark chase through an alley, cryptic shadows and endless darkness add to the suspense and need to be illustrated in your storyboards. You can give more detail in the description box below each storyboard panel about what you're trying to show in the illustration.

You don't need to draw actual locations in detail unless something in the setting is crucial to the shot, or a character interacts with it somehow. If a car is driving down the road, you only need to draw the road and not the surrounding trees and buildings. If an actor enters a room, you only need to draw the door from which the actor enters. Some scribbles or lines on the walls can show that the scene is taking place inside. If you're using a software program to design your storyboards, the program can repeat a background location so that you don't have to redraw it by hand every time (see "Designing with storyboard software" later in this chapter for more information).

TIP

There are some nifty apps that let you create storyboards using your smartphone. For instance, Storyboard Animator by Keely Hill, a free app for the iPhone, lets you draw storyboard panels and then automatically scroll through them to create a basic animatic of your story.

I Can't Draw, Even If My Life Depended on It

Many people are not trained artists, and some of us can only draw stick people (who look like skinny actors who don't eat — I know a few of those). But never fear, in the following sections, I outline a few solutions — like using storyboard software or hiring an artist — for the artistically challenged.

Designing with storyboard software

If you're not satisfied with drawing happy faces on stick people, but you still want to create the storyboards yourself, try using storyboard software. Storyboard design programs give you a library of predrawn generic characters (male, female, children, animals) that you can choose, click on, and drop right into your storyboard panels. You can manipulate the size and shape of each character and even rotate the character's position. Along with a cast of characters, these programs also usually provide a library of common props and generic locations to place in your frames as well. A few different software programs are available to help you out:

>> **Shot Pro** is a software program that you can download at www.shot professional.com. It works on your computer and can be transferred and worked on with your smartphone. It also has an option to use your

smartphone as a face motion capture to get realistic expressions on your actors. You can even create animatics with this program.

>> **Storyboard Quick and Storyboard Artist** from PowerProduction (www.powerproduction.com) costs $299.99. This easy-to-use program makes for quick storyboarding.

>> **Studio Binder** has a free and cool software program called Shot Lists & Storyboards that allows you to import your drawings into empty panels and add script and notes to each storyboard. You can also import photos taken on your smartphone to create storyboards from posed stills of your friends (acting out the script), instead of drawing your elements. Shot Lists & Storyboards is available at www.studiobinder.com.

>> **FrameForge 3D** is the Ferrari of storyboard software (www.frameforge.com). The program turns your storyboard elements into a virtual world, allowing you to manipulate your actors, change camera angles and location settings without having to redraw them every time. The program is so sophisticated, it lists how high your camera is off the ground and what type of lens is being used (wide angle, telephoto, and so on). You can also make animatics with this software.

TIP

Another way to create storyboards if you're not an artist is to take photographs! Get several of your friends together and have them act out your screenplay in still pictures. The most economical way to do this is using your smartphone's camera. Have no friends? Use dolls, toy soldiers, or puppets — whoever your real friends are. George Lucas shot amusing crude video storyboards with dolls of his *Star Wars* characters for his original *Star Wars* episodes.

There's an amazing free app for your smartphone called Blocker by AfterNow. It actually drops three-dimensional actors into your real locations while looking through your smartphone. You can then position those virtual actors and even circle around them as they magically appear as images inside your smartphone. You can photograph them to create still images that can become your 3D storyboards.

Drawing the help of a professional artist

You've been reading this chapter and thinking to yourself, "I can't draw well enough to put my shots into storyboards" or, "I'm not computer literate; I won't be able to run the storyboard software programs." Don't panic! If you aren't happy with your stick characters in your storyboard panels, and you can afford it, you can always hire a professional storyboard artist.

STORYBOARDING WITH STORYBOARD QUICK

One of my favorite storyboard software programs is Storyboard Quick by PowerProduction Software. A great feature of Storyboard Quick is that you can input your entire screenplay so that every piece of dialogue has its own storyboard panel. It's a great way to break down your script. Storyboard Quick works for both PCs and Macs. And it stands by its name — you can create storyboards quickly!

Storyboard Quick lets you choose what elements you want in your separate panels. You can drag and drop from a library of different characters and put them anywhere within the frame. You can resize your characters to any size and turn and flip them in any direction. Storyboard Quick comes with libraries of images that include characters, props, and locations (such as various rooms, beaches, mountains, deserts, and even interiors of vehicles). You can also buy add-on libraries for additional prop, character, and location images. You can get more information on Storyboard Quick at www. powerproduction.com.

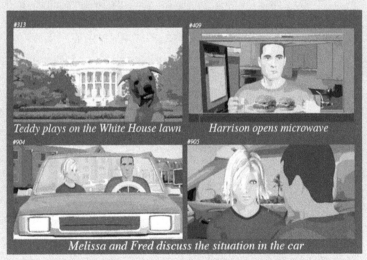

Teddy plays on the White House lawn   Harrison opens microwave

Melissa and Fred discuss the situation in the car

© PowerProduction Software/©2008 Stellar Entertainment,
Undercover Angel, First American Cinema, First Dog

A storyboard artist is very much like a crime sketch artist. You describe in detail what your shot looks like, and the artist does his best to put your vision on the page. The artist starts by sketching very rough pencil drawings and making any special notes during your meeting — with you looking over his shoulder to see that he's on the right track. He then goes home (or wherever he feels most comfortable drawing) and returns later with the completed panels. A storyboard artist can ink in the pencil drawings or leave them a little rough, depending on your taste.

REMEMBER

If you ask a storyboard artist to *conceptualize* (meaning to design the look of a piece of equipment, a wardrobe, or a vehicle, like a spaceship), you want him to render it in full detail and color for optimum presentation.

Discovering an artist

Lots of talented artists are out there who would be glad to storyboard your movie. Even an artist who has never done storyboards can still sketch some great panels after getting a basic understanding of camera shots and lenses. If you decide to hire a professional artist, there are several ways to find one:

» Art schools are a good place to find budding talent.

» Cartoonists who work for a local newspaper or online magazine or blog may enjoy a change of pace.

» *Picture Book* is an annual online reference guide (specializing in children's illustrations) packed with hundreds of artists' samples and contact information. You can check it out at www.picture-book.com.

» *RSVP: The Directory of Illustration and Design* is similar to *Picture Book* and also features hundreds of artists' sample work. You can find out more information at the website at www.rsvpdirectory.com.

» Famous Frames, Inc. is a company that specializes in providing storyboard artists for independent and studio feature films. Find the company at www.famousframes.com.

» *Animation Magazine* features interviews and articles on cartoonists and also has helpful ads and classified sections that list artists available for freelance work. For print and digital subscription information, go to www.animationmagazine.net.

» An Internet search for *artists* and *cartoonists* can also turn up some valuable contacts, such as www.anythingcartoon.com.

Assessing the artist's qualifications

You need to keep in mind several things when interviewing professional artists to storyboard your shots:

» **Be sure to ask whether he or she has ever drawn storyboards before.**
Working with a storyboard artist who is versed in camera angles and lenses and has a basic knowledge of cinematic language is best.

- » **Make sure the artist draws in a style that works aesthetically for the style of your film.** If your movie is a comedy, the style should be light and even have a slight cartoonish feel to it. If it's a serious drama, the illustrations should look mature and depict a more formal style with shadows and more serious undertones.

REMEMBER

  Request samples from other movies the artist has storyboarded to see not only whether you like her style but also whether she has an understanding of the process. Her current work should speak for itself (a picture's worth a thousand words!).

- » **Assess your compatibility.** It's very important that you get along as a team so that the artist can translate your shots more accurately and effectively into the storyboard panels and that they understand your vision. Keep in mind that even though you call the shots, you may get some great ideas and suggestions from the artist.

- » **Negotiate a fair price.** You want an artist who will work at a reasonable rate that fits within your budget. Often on independent films, storyboards are a luxury, so you want to make sure you have enough money to pay for a storyboard artist. Sketches per panel can range from $3 for a rough thumbnail pencil sketch to $50 for a detailed black-and-white ink rendering. Remember, though, the price is completely negotiable between you and the artist.

- » **Make sure that the artist's turnaround time works for your schedule.** *Turnaround* means the time it takes from working on the rough sketches with the artist, until they come back to you with the final rendered storyboard panels.

TIP

Don't limit yourself to only local artists. You can work with an artist across the street or across the world via email and have the storyboards scanned and sent to you as an attachment — or for bigger files they can be uploaded for you to download on your end using a web service such as Hightail (www.hightail.com). If you go this route, discuss the shots and style in detail with the artist first — through Skype or FaceTime if you can, and make sure his rough sketches match your expectations — he can then email you low-res files of what he's working — or hold them up to the camera if you're doing video conferencing — so that you can verify he's on the right track. You can even pay your artist using PayPal (an Internet service that lets you send or receive payments anywhere in the world). All you need is his email address. Check out PayPal (www.paypal.com) for more information on this payment option.

FRAMEFORGING IN 3D

FrameForge is a phenomenal 3D storyboarding program that creates a virtual world of your movie. You build your sets, create your characters, and add props and vehicles, all in a 3D virtual world. Once you build each set/location and cast your storyboards, all you have to do is move the virtual camera, and the program creates your angles and camera shots for you. By moving the virtual camera the images in your storyboard panels will show the correct dimensions, emulating what they would look like with those actual lenses and shot sizes (lens and angle perception), and the program also calculates and lists lens sizes and camera height in the description panel. With a simple click of your mouse, on output you can even change the three-dimensional panels to look more like two-dimensional penciled sketches.

The program also lets you view an overhead (bird's-eye) view of your shot, showing the placement of your camera setup and actors within the scene.

There's a Core version for the truly independent filmmaker, and a more intricate and higher priced Pro version (that many studios have used, such as on *Pirates of the Caribbean* and *Jurassic World*). If you are a student, teacher, military, or veteran, you can get a great discount. You can order expansion packs (at additional cost) that include Crime & Justice (police and swat teams), Military Pack (soldiers, terrorists, battlefield armaments, and military vehicles), and Stock Set (furniture, landscaping elements, and structural elements). Check it out at www.frameforge.com.

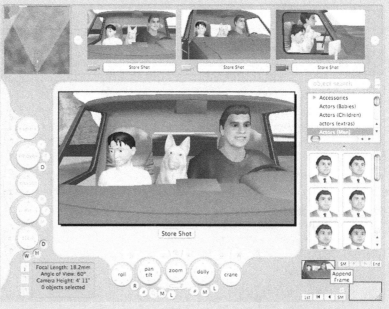

© 2010 First Dog, courtesy Stellar Entertainment/First American Cinema

3

Ready to Roll: Starting Production on Your Movie

You discover that the creative elements to making a movie are the same whether you shoot with a traditional film camera, your always-at-the-ready smartphone, or a high definition digital camera (at 24-frames) that closely emulates a film-stock look.

I show you the meaning of "Lights, camera, action!" You're sure to find the chapter on lighting illuminating, and I'll have you tuned in on the sound production chapter.

I give you the right directions on directing your actors and then direct you onto your movie set.

Chapter **10**

Shooting through the Looking Glass

With the magical box called the movie camera, you can capture your story, turn it into pictures, and show it to audiences all over the world. In this chapter, you see the difference between motion-picture film cameras (which are going the way of the dinosaur) and high-definition digital cameras (becoming the norm). This chapter also explains how the single eye of the camera sees, and how you can harness that distinctive eye to get the best picture possible. I help you choose the correct lenses to capture your shots and use them to their full benefit. Finally, you find out how to add filters (when and why) and other accessories to add to your filmmaking toolbox.

REMEMBER

The 21st century has brought some amazing technological advances to mankind, including digital filmmaking. All the filmmaking techniques and creative skills described throughout this book can be applied to digital filmmaking, or when using a venerable film camera. The only difference is in the type of equipment and the technical means of getting a finished product. The aspects of creativity pretty much remain the same.

Choosing the Right Camera

Before shooting begins, you need to decide whether you want to use a motion picture film camera (that uses film *celluloid*), a digital consumer camcorder (an inexpensive type you use to record family events — including your handy smartphone's internal camera), or a more advanced high-end consumer technology of digital cinema cameras that shoot variable frames (including 24p frames per second) that more closely emulate the look of shooting with a film camera.

Rolling with film cameras (the old-fashioned way?)

The *film camera* (also referred to as the *motion-picture film camera*) has been around since the late 1800s. Because the film camera runs film stock through its housing, it can be a much bigger and heavier (and noisier) piece of equipment than a digital camera. Film cameras generally rely on manual focus and exposure, and manual dial-in settings.

REMEMBER

Film has a nostalgic feel to it, creating the illusion (in a subliminal way) of something that's happened in the past — the feeling of reflecting on a cherished memory. Film photographs a softer, more surreal image than the sharp, sometimes harsh and unflattering picture that video cameras can present.

TIP

You can cut your film costs by buying 16mm or 35mm *recans*, rolls of film that have been put back in the film can by a production company that ended up not using all the film stock it purchased. You can buy recans or film ends (under 400-foot reels) at prices much cheaper than the cost of new film stock. It's getting more difficult to find recans these days as most recan companies have gone out of business due to the new age of digital photography. You can sometimes find recans on Craig's List or eBay — but you're taking a chance if it hasn't been professionally tested to make sure it's still good. You can get brand new film stock up to 30 percent off retail prices if you're a student with I.D. — through special student programs offered by both Kodak and Fuji Film. Check out their respective websites at www.kodak.com and www.fujifilmusa.com.

REMEMBER

These days, shooting on film stock is more expensive — not only because you are using physical celluloid film, which costs per the minute (as opposed to virtual digital files on reusable SD cards with a digital camera), but also because you have to have your film stock manually scanned into digital files before you can edit on a nonlinear system and perform all your post-production duties. Scanning to digital files can run as high as $500 per hour, which can add up. The other problem with using actual film is that it can't help but collect dust and hairs via built-up static electricity — you can't fight physics. You have to actually stop on individual scanned frames and remove any particles that have adhered to your film by erasing them digitally. You don't have this issue with digital files.

Reading the camera magazine

You can't read a film camera magazine because it's not the type of magazine you may be thinking of. Instead, a *camera magazine* is a housing that looks like Mickey Mouse ears on the top of the motion-picture film camera; it holds the raw (undeveloped) film celluloid that winds off the reels into the camera and past the exposure gate. The magazine is sealed tight and perfectly light-proof (so the film isn't accidentally exposed and ruined by the light). After the film winds up on the back magazine during shooting, it can be detached easily from the camera and downloaded by the assistant cameraperson (see Chapter 7 for details on crew responsibilities). The exposed film is then sealed in a film can and sent to the lab for developing. The equivalent for a digital cinema camera is a tiny SD card (about the size of your thumbnail) for some cameras, and a little bigger card (about the size of a matchbox) used for digital cinema cameras such as the Arri Amira.

STAYING UP TO STANDARDS WITH ASA AND ISO

ASA and ISO are both measurements of light in terms of speed and sensitivity. ASA stands for *American Standards Association*, and has mainly been replaced by ISO, which stands *for International Organization for Standardization.* You can buy film for your motion picture camera in a variety of speeds. *Film speed,* in relation to American Standards Association (ASA) and International Standards Organization (ISO), refers to how quickly the film responds to light. The higher the ASA or ISO rating, the more sensitive the film stock is to light. Some film stocks can actually "see in the dark." An ASA of 800 is more light sensitive and can expose darker images than, say, a film speed of 200 ASA. (When you buy film for your 35mm still camera, you have the same choices of ASAs or ISOs as well.)

In the past, higher ASA films that worked well in shooting low-light situations often had a grainy picture quality. Kodak has made some amazing developments over the years, producing high-speed films such as Vision3 500T color negative in 16mm and 35mm formats with much less grain and very sharp, crisp picture quality.

In terms of digital cameras that are solely measured by ISO, light sensitivity is determined by the camera's electronic CCD and Lux capability and not by the digital card or external hard drive recording the footage (see Chapter 11 for more information on Lux).

VIDEO-ASSISTING JERRY LEWIS

Jerry Lewis directed and starred in many of his films, but he had difficulty gauging his performance while doing double-duty as director. He needed to find a way to see what he shot while he was filming so he wouldn't be surprised a day later when the footage came back after being developed at the lab.

In 1956, Jerry attached an analog video camera to the motion picture film camera so that he could capture his scenes on video at the same time the film camera was rolling. He could then immediately play back the video footage as a reference to see whether he needed to adjust his performance and do another take with the film camera. This is how *video assist* was born. Jerry Lewis created a new technique that virtually every filmmaker shooting with a film camera uses to this day.

Video tapping

With a film camera, you can record the image on film stock and watch the footage on a monitor at the same time, if you have a *video tap*, also known as *video assist*. Nowadays, film cameras come with a video tap, which enables a video signal to record exactly what the film camera is seeing through the lens. Video assist saves time and money, by letting the director see on a TV monitor the actual camera movement and framing by the cinematographer. If it is recorded to an external hard drive, you can also play back a shot on the monitor so that you can decide whether it needs be reshot. This videotaped footage is only for reference and not for final release — that's why you're shooting film!

Another advantage to shooting with a digital camera instead of a film camera is that you automatically have the equivalent of "video assist" where the images being recorded can immediately be viewed on a monitor, recorded to a digital card, and then downloaded to an external hard drive.

Recording with digital cameras

Video images are captured by a digital camera and recorded to digital SD cards, or the camera is connected directly to an external hard drive that reads and downloads the footage as it's being recorded by the digital camera. When using a digital camera, you also have several types of cameras and digital formats, which can determine how the final image looks:

>> **DSLR cameras:** A *digital single lens reflex (DSLR)* camera resembles a 35mm professional still camera (which it is). It not only takes breathtaking high quality HD still images, but it also shoots digital moving images as well. DSLR

cameras often use SD cards that are inserted into the camera for recording digital images. An external hard drive can also be attached to the DSLR camera for downloading footage directly to the hard drive as the camera is recording in real time.

>> **Digital 24p cinema camcorder:** This is also a digital camera that looks more like a movie camera (and bulky) as opposed to a DSLR camera. It may have more sophistication than a DSLR camera, and is solely meant to shoot digital movies as opposed to also taking still photos like the DSLR camera. A digital 24p cinema camera also closely works to emulate the look of a film camera without the expense of film stock, lab and printing costs, or *telecine* (transferring-to-video) costs. By recording the equivalent of 24 frames per second, this type of camera gives the digital video image more of the soft and pleasing look associated with film and simulating an almost subliminal 24 frame shutter effect as with film moving through a 24 frame projector. Many DSLR cameras also can shoot 24 frames per second, in addition to other frame rates.

TECHNICAL STUFF

The "p" in 24p stands for *progressive*. What it means is that each frame is scanned in a progressive continuous manner, resulting in a better quality image (higher resolution), as opposed to *interlace*, which scans and processes every other frame and then interlaces the missing frames to fill in the gaps. Progressive requires more processing, which in turn requires more memory and demands more storage. The advantage of interlace is less processing and memory, but it compromises picture quality, with the possibility of artifacts, flickering, or strobing.

Digital high-definition consumer cameras, including DSLRs, start as low as $200 (for various Canon Vixia camcorders), and average around $1,200 (for a Black-magic Cinema Camera) and up for *prosumer* or more professional digital cinema cameras, including the Panasonic Lumix GH5s for around $2,000 (the GH5 — without the "s" is about $500 cheaper). Prices are definitely becoming affordable for the independent filmmaker — especially if you just want to shoot your movie using your efficient smartphone.

Then you have the Lumix S1H, considered a professional cinema camera because it shoots at full-frame as opposed to 4/3 like the Lumix GH5 and costs around $4,000. A purely professional cinema camera like the Arri Amira (used to shoot many of your favorite TV series) can set you back upwards of $40,000, not including lenses, batteries, digital cards, and so on. An Arri Alexa (used for many of your favorite feature films) costs closer to $70,000 before lenses and accessories.

REMEMBER

Prosumer is a term coined by certain manufacturers to mean a cross between a professional and consumer level product. A prosumer camera can be used in a professional capacity — exceeding home-movie standards in terms of picture quality and end use — but is also more affordable, falling within the consumer price range.

Going over the advantages of digital cameras

Shooting your movie with a digital camcorder or DSLR has many advantages:

>> **A DSLR is lighter and smaller (and more portable) than a film camera, and even lighter and more portable than a digital camcorder, in that it resembles a normal 35mm still photography camera.** A digital camcorder usually falls between 4 and 8 pounds. A film camera (with film magazine and lenses) can weigh upwards of 15 to 60 pounds. With a DSLR camera, you can attach it to a consumer stabilizer for steadying your shots, wherein a larger and heavier digital camcorder or film camera requires a much more sophisticated and expensive gimbal.

>> **You don't have to reload bulky film magazines every ten minutes as you have to do when shooting with a film camera.** For digital cameras, an SD card, depending on the storage space of the card, can be anywhere from ten minutes up to an hour (depending on what *codec* you are using). An SD card is also easy to pop in and out in a matter of seconds. You can also attach, via a digital cable, an external hard drive to your digital camera and can record for much longer periods of time only limited by the size of the external hard drive's capacity.

>> **You can reuse SD memory cards (and they're cheaper than shooting on film).** An SD card can be used over and over again after you download the digital files off the card. After downloading (and maybe an extra backup or two of your footage to other hard drives) you just erase the SD card and start recording again.

TECHNICAL STUFF

Cameras that record digital files use interchangeable memory cards, and/or can record to external hard drives that connect to the camera. There is usually a setting in the digital camera that lets you choose the *codec* you want to record in. A codec is the type of file and the information of how it's recorded. Some of the standard digital codecs are ProRes 4444, QuickTime, H264, H265 (which is overtaking its predecessor H264), and MP4. These files are in digital *wrappers* that contain the characteristics of the codec. ProRes 4444 is a higher quality codec that doesn't lose some of the details that a lower format like QuickTime or MP4 might — but ProRes files can be quite large (especially in 4K) as opposed to smaller QuickTime files that are more compacted and easier to upload and download.

>> **You see the image instantly on the camera's built-in video monitor.** With this capability, you don't need a video assist tap (see the earlier section "Video tapping" for details). You can also plug in an external monitor (often with an HDMI or mini-HDMI cable) to your digital camera to view a larger image. Many digital cameras like the Panasonic Lumix GH5 lets you view your footage wirelessly through Wi-Fi on your smartphone or tablet.

SMART SHOOTING WITH YOUR SMARTPHONE

TIP

Smartphones that function like miniature computers with a camera built in first came onto the horizon in 2007 and continue to evolve beyond our wildest imaginations. Many independent filmmakers shoot their short films on their smartphones, and some have even shot feature-length movies — a few have actually made it into the Sundance Film Festival. Smartphones shoot in high definition and many now shoot up to 4K. Your footage can be transferred to an external hard drive or directly to your computer's internal drive — and most editing programs accommodate the digital format of your smartphone footage.

When shooting your movie on your smartphone, remember to turn your phone horizontally and shoot in landscape mode (not portrait mode). *Landscape mode* is when you turn your phone sideways so it mimics the wide frame of the cinema screen as opposed to the vertical way (*portrait mode*) you normally hold your smartphone. Also, set your smartphone on airplane mode — this turns off the phone and text functions so your shoot is not interrupted by a text or phone call!

REMEMBER

The advantage of connecting a television monitor to your digital camera is to get a better idea of what your final picture will look like (instead of trusting the three-inch camera monitor and *hoping* your actor is in focus). Make sure your TV monitor has been adjusted correctly (calibrated) for proper skin tones and other coloration. Most digital cameras have an HDMI or mini-HDMI output so you can connect directly to any HD TV or monitor. Many digital cameras now come with Wi-Fi so that you can wirelessly view your camera's footage on a smartphone or tablet — or even on a smart TV that has Wi-Fi.

» **You can plug in a microphone and use the digital sound recorded directly into the camera.** If using a digital camera, your sound will be professional digital quality! Be sure *not* to use the camera's built-in omnidirectional microphone because then you will record everything behind and in front of the camera — and your actor's dialogue will get buried among the sounds of traffic and other distracting noises in your environment.

TIP

Make sure the camera has an input for a separate microphone (most do). Depending on the camera, the input for the microphone will either be a 3.5mm -plug or an XLR input. You rarely want to use the microphone that comes attached with the camera because you'll hear everything in front of and behind the camera (this is called an *omni-directional microphone*). See Chapter 12 for more on microphones.

>> **You don't have to take the footage into a film lab and have it developed.** This saves time, money — and hassle.

>> **You can import the digitally recorded footage directly into your editing system.** You don't have to transfer from film to digital files — it's already in a digital format, and you can start editing!

REMEMBER

It can be extremely expensive for an independent filmmaker to transfer film footage to a digital format. You would have to go into a professional facility that can do this (it's called *telecine*). This can cost anywhere from $300 to $500 per hour. And remember, you are not just transferring the length of your final film, but all the footage and endless takes you shot, which could be many, many hours.

>> **You can manipulate it to more closely resemble film shots.** Software programs like Magic Bullet Frames from Red Giant Software (`www.redgiant software.com`) can make digital video footage look more like you shot it on film or if you want to experiment with the color, texture, and mood of your images. There's also a company called Filmlook (`www.filmlook.com`) that can run your movie through its patented digital process (and also color-correct) to make it look more like it was shot on film. There are digital cinema cameras that simulate film and 24-frame motion (see the following section). Red Giant Software also makes a product called Instant HD that can resize and emulate the look of high definition from footage you originally shot in bygone analog format.

Taking a close-up look at digital cinema camcorders (24p)

Panasonic has a 24p (24-frame progressive) camera called the Lumix GH5s (see Figure 10-1). Priced around $2,000. This DSLR camera can give you a traditional video look equivalent to 30 frames a second or, using the touchscreen, you can change it to emulate 24 frames per second to resemble the texture and look more similar to a celluloid film image. Sony, Canon, and Blackmagic also make affordable 24p digital cameras that are worth investigating.

TECHNICAL STUFF

The Blackmagic Pocket Camera and many digital cameras of today use technology similar to the digital cameras George Lucas used in his *Star Wars* films *The Phantom Menace* and *Attack of the Clones* of the late 90s–early 2000s, in which Lucas proved that the picture quality of digital cinema camcorders can emulate closely the look of film. In 2001, Robert Rodriguez shot *Spy Kids 2* entirely with digital camcorders and said that he'd never use film again. Other directors, like Spielberg and Tarantino, still prefer to shoot on film. You can't beat the look of film; that's why all the camera manufacturers are constantly trying to create that perfect film-look digital camera.

TIP

Shooting on digital files with a digital cinema camcorder saves you a lot of money over shooting on film. If you can't afford to buy a digital cinema camera like the Lumix GH5 for around $1,400 (or the GH5s at around $2,000), or the Blackmagic Pocket Camera for around $1,200, you might be able to afford the Lumix GH7 for around $500. Otherwise you can rent a digital camera from a camera rental facility. Or better yet, find a cinematographer who owns one of these cameras — you'll get a package deal — a cinematographer and a camera!

GOING PRO WITH GOPRO

Think of all the unique and fantastic shots you could get if your camera had no limitations due to its size and weight. That camera is called the *GoPro*. GoPro's line of cameras have been featured as perfect for endurance sports videos and fast action footage — Red Bull is a major official sponsor for many athletic events — but it's more than that. The camera also has dozens of accessories that complement its functionality — from attaching it to virtually any object or subject, to leak-proof watertight housings for underwater adventures.

(continued)

(continued)

Because it fits in the palm of your hand, the powerful mini 4K GoPro camera opens up a new world of movie-making possibilities. Using an app on your smartphone, you can remotely view and control this little fits-in-your pocket device, which you can put virtually anywhere. From a point-of-view shot looking out from a toaster or mailbox to a football's view as it soars through the goalposts; from the point of view of a lion as it sneaks towards its prey to a turbulent shot of a bike chase from the perspective of its cycling pedals. Every filmmaker should have this camera as part of his or her arsenal. It's a must-have for second unit filming, for special, never-before-seen shots, or even for your principal "A" camera.

Back in 2002, the GoPro company started out with one of the smallest cameras ever created. This miniature camera was originally created as a wrist camera by an avid surfer to capture firsthand the thrill of riding the perfect wave. It wasn't until around 2009 that the GoPro HD Hero was introduced, and now it has evolved into the perfected GoPro HERO7. The camera has shot unique perspective footage from around the world endless times, and captured things never before possible — where cameras had never gone before — and in pristine digital 4K video. GoPro footage is nothing short of breathtaking — just check out the GoPro website (www.gopro.com) for clips of what has been shot with this tiny camera,. If the footage doesn't blow you away — nothing will. *You* can get some amazing shots too — all it takes is your imagination.

ALEXA, TELL ME ABOUT THE ALEXA

Hollywood is all abuzz with the advent of the Arri Alexa digital camera. It was developed to aggressively compete with motion picture film cameras — without having to use expensive film stock. The *Avengers* movies were all shot with the Alexa (including the Arri Alexa 65mm IMAX camera for *Avengers: Endgame*). This camera was also used in some scenes *for Mission: Impossible – Fallout.* The Alexa starts between $70,000 and $100,000 and will put you back another few thousand on accessories and lenses. There's also the less expensive Alexa Mini, which is a smaller, more run- and-gun version of its big brother, costing around $36,000. Arri also developed another cinema camera called the Amira — that one will only set you back about $40,000!

Arri's Alexa and Amira cameras are the most widely used digital cameras by TV producers and theatrical studio productions. The Amira, a similar camera as the Alexa, is used in 90 percent of the TV shows you see today. The Alexa has a new 4K version, as well as an Alexa Mini, which can be used when a smaller, lighter, and more portable professional camera is required.

Arri has a unique proprietary science when it comes to its digital cinema cameras. Their cameras have a subliminal 24-frames-per-second shutter feeling, which, along with Arri's unique color science, brings their digital cinema cameras to the head of the pack. Arri also develops their own uniquely designed camera lenses that work seamlessly with all their cameras.

Other studio films shot with the Arri Alexa include: *Skyfall, The Wolverine, Dunkirk, San Andreas*, and *Mission Impossible – Rogue Nation* (digital and film cameras), to name just a few.

Arri Amira

Arri Alexa Mini

Courtesy Arri

With the advent of digital technology using 24p (24 frames per second, progressive) to emulate a film-look (without having to use film), more and more productions are being produced on video recorded to digital files. In the past, these productions had to be expensively transferred to film stock to be played in a regular movie house projecting 35mm film. Today, very few movie theaters are even equipped with 35mm projectors anymore. Instead, most commercial movie theaters have been retrofitted with sophisticated digital projectors. Your digital movie can now be converted to a digital file on a portable hard drive called a DCP (Digital Cinema Package). The other great thing about a DCP is that it contains all the settings for your movie; designated audio channels and volumes, set exposure for projection, screen size aspect ratio, and so on, so your film projects an image that you intended your audience to see. DCP's can also be *locked,* meaning they require a password key to allow the theater to show your film on certain dates determined by you (this is extra protection from your movie being pirated). Also, it no longer requires four or five large bulky metal film containers (weighing a ton and expensive to ship) to be sent to theaters all over the country. Many movie theaters can also project DVD and Blu-ray discs as well.

Most prosumer digital cameras shoot with a 16x9 screen size, or allow you to emulate an anamorphic or CinemaScope letterbox image similar to the shape of the wide stretched screen in a movie theater (this is also a good format if you're planning on premiering your film in movie theaters). The camera settings on a digital camera allow you to put a black border at the top and bottom of the screen to create a narrower, rectangular-shaped frame of 2:35.1 (see Figure 10-2 for different aspect ratios). The other option is that you can shoot your movie in 16x9, and then create a separate theatrical framed version in post-production by cropping the top and bottom of your image to the CinemaScope 2:35.1 dimensions, or by using software that does it for you. Chapter 9 shows you the various screen shapes.

FIGURE 10-2:
Aspect ratios —
old Analog TV, HD
TV and Theatrical
dimensions.

©2019 Santa Stole Our Dog, *Actor; Gary Bosloy*

Movies on Amazon Prime and Netflix have black borders on the top and bottom of the picture when viewing on your 16x9 HD TV. This shows you the full letterbox format from when the film premiered in movie theaters.

Do You Need Glasses? Types of Lenses and What They See

Camera lenses are sized in millimeters, which represent the circumference of the lens or the ring size that attaches to the camera housing, in order to control the size of your shots. (Note that camera formats are also referred to in millimeters, as in 35mm, 16mm, and Super 8mm; here, millimeters refer to the width of the film stock the camera uses — are you confused yet?) The assortment of lens sizes needed depends on the camera format being used. For 35mm film cameras, a set of standard lenses for picture area consists of the following: 18mm, 25mm, 35mm, 40mm, 50mm, 75mm, and 100mm (see Figure 10-3 for examples). Today's lenses tend to look the same from the outside, but the glass and specifications inside are configured differently for wide to close-up views, as in the example of Arri's lenses. Note the lens type is marked with a large number; a 16mm lens, 32mm, 50mm, and a telephoto 85mm lens.

FIGURE 10-3: A wide, medium, and telephoto lens for an older model 35mm Arri film camera, compared to a super-wide, wide, medium, and telephoto lens set for an Arri digital camera.

Each lens serves a purpose and gives a different image size when attached to the camera. A lens can also change the characteristics of the image. For example, a wide lens like the 18mm makes things appear more spacious by slightly bending the image (squeezing more information into the shot). A wide lens is effective for shooting establishing shots to make rooms and areas look more expansive than they really are. A telephoto lens tends to flatten and compress images and make things appear closer together. Telephoto lenses are good for bringing distant objects closer to the camera (using magnification similar to a low powered telescope).

Lower-priced cameras come with a fixed lens that is a permanent part of the camera (as with your smartphone camera) or a GoPro Camera and can't be detached (unless you take a hacksaw and cut it off — but you don't want to do that now, do you?). Professional-model and higher-priced digital cameras, like the Lumix GH5, use *interchangeable lenses,* which allow you to detach the existing lens and screw on different-sized lenses (telephoto, wide-angle, zoom, and so on). In most digital cameras, the lens functions are similar to a film camera's lenses (if the camera accepts interchangeable lenses), but they are measured differently. (See the section "The normal lens sees what you see," later in this chapter.)

Pocket Camera Osmosis

The OSMO Pocket is a nifty miniature camera, smaller than an electric toothbrush (and weighs about the same), which shoots 4K footage rivaling cameras ten times its size. (See Figure 10-4.) You can't brush your teeth with it, but it will easily fit in your mouth! Created by DJI, the leader in stabilized camera systems including aerial drones, the OSMO was designed for single-hand use and even has a touch-screen built into the handle that doubles as a viewing monitor. The camera works with the DJI Mimo app to expand and open up the experience of working with this pocket camera even more. The OSMO Pocket camera shoots digital video with some high-tech sophistication. The camera can track objects or people with smooth and steady stabilization using a three-axis handheld gimbal. The OSMO pocket makes every shot look like a professional movie crew (a teenie-weenie one) was behind the lens.

FIGURE 10-4:
The miniature
OSMO Pocket
camera by DJI.

TIP

Currently, 2K high definition is the standard digital recording format at 1,920 x 1,080 pixels (2,048 x 1,080 is also considered 2K). Many digital cameras now have the capability to record 4K, which is 3,840 x 2,160 pixels. One of the greatest advantages to recording in 4K is the ability to reframe your shots in post-production without sacrificing picture quality. By recording in 4K and delivering your movie in 2K, you can zoom into your shots during editing and reframe them without creating soft or grainy images. You can also finish your film in 4K, which some distribution outlets such as Netflix are starting to require as the norm in their delivery specs.

The normal lens sees what you see

A 50mm lens on a 35mm film or still camera, and a digital camera (that has a full-frame chip equivalent to a 35mm frame of film) is known as the *normal lens*. It's equivalent in perspective to what your eye sees (look through the lens and open your other eye, and you will be seeing about the same size image). This normal lens does not create any distortion and presents an image that most closely resembles what you see without the camera. Many filmmakers prefer this lens when shooting actors. Depending on your subject, a normal 50mm lens can be more complimentary to your actor's features (a wide lens may make your actor look heavier or distorted, a telephoto lens may flatten your actor's features).

For cameras other than 35mm film cameras, or digital 35 and Super 35mm full-frame digital cameras (the chip is full size compared to a 35mm frame of film, as opposed to micro 4/3 chip on a consumer camera, which is closer in size to a 16mm frame) the size of the normal (50mm) lens is smaller. Table 10-1 shows the measurement of normal, wide-angle, and telephoto lenses for various types of cameras.

TABLE 10-1 **Normal Lens (50mm) Measurements for Various Camera Formats**

Camera	Type of Lens	Measurement
35mm film and 35mm and Super 35mm full-frame digital equivalent	Normal lens	50mm
	Wide-angle lens	18mm
	Telephoto lens	100mm
16mm	Normal lens	25mm
	Wide-angle lens	9mm
	Telephoto lens	50mm

(continued)

TABLE 10-1 *(continued)*

Camera	Type of Lens	Measurement
Super 8mm	Normal lens	15mm
	Wide-angle lens	7.5mm
	Telephoto lens	30mm
Digital prosumer video	Normal lens	25mm
	Wide-angle lens	9mm
	Telephoto lens	50mm

Notice that 16mm and digital 4/3rds camera lenses translate the same.

REMEMBER

Digital video lenses on consumer cameras vary in width and thread sizes depending on the particular make and type of camera, so check the manual that comes with the camera. Most professional digital cameras, including DSLR cameras, use PL (positive lock) mounts and can therefore use a variety of 16mm or 35mm motion picture lenses.

TECHNICAL STUFF

Most digital prosumer cameras and consumer DSRL cameras have what is called a 4/3 microchip (equivalent to the size of a 16mm film frame). More professional digital cameras have a full-frame chip (similar in size to a 35mm film frame). The difference is not only in the improvement of quality with a full-frame camera, but also in that the lenses are measured differently. A full-frame camera has a similar 35mm-sized frame inside the camera and therefore uses regular lenses that would normally be used for a 35mm still or motion picture film camera (as with the professional digital cameras like the Arris Alexa or Panasonic Varicam). The micro 4/3 digital camera has a smaller window inside (about the size of a 16mm film frame) requiring a smaller measurement that is often half the size of a full frame lens. For example, a normal 50mm lens on a full-frame camera would be a 25mm normal lens on a 4/3 camera body.

Short or wide-angle lens

A *wide-angle lens,* also called a *short lens,* consists of a curved glass that bends the light coming into the camera and pushes the picture back to create a wider frame than what you see with the naked eye.

When using a 35mm camera (film or digital full-frame equivalent), a wide-angle lens is lower in number than the 50mm normal lens. (For other type of cameras, the numbers for a wide-angle lens are much lower — refer to Table 10-1.)

Therefore, a 40mm or 25mm lens (on a 35mm film or full-frame digital camera) pushes the image farther back to appear as if you're farther away than you really are. The image is reduced so that more of your subject or scenery can fit into the frame. Wide-angle lenses make locations and sets appear more expansive (more picture information is squeezed into the frame). However, wide-angle lenses can create some distortion, so the closer you are to the subject, the more noticeable the distortion is.

A *super wide-angle lens* is sometimes referred to as a *fisheye* lens because it resembles a bulbous fish eye. Often these lenses are 18mm or lower for a 35mm film or a full-frame digital camera. On a 4/3rd digital camera you would use a 9mm lens. This type of lens (see Figure 10-5) distorts the picture and makes everything look rounder. Usually you only want to use a really wide lens when you want to create an effect like someone looking through a peephole in a door, or for comic effect when you want a character's nose to be bigger and his or her face distorted.

You can add a wide-angle lens to your consumer camera by screwing a *converter lens* (with threads) onto your existing camera lens so that you can go even wider than the permanent lens on your camera allows.

Super wide-angle lens

Super wide-angle lens in action

FIGURE 10-5: A super wide-angle lens (left), and a super wide-angle lens in action (right and bottom).

Going long with telephoto

A *telephoto lens* (also called a *long lens*) is higher in number than 50mm for 35mm film and digital full-frame cameras. Therefore, a 75mm lens gives you an image that appears to be closer than the normal lens (50mm) does. If you look through the camera with a 75mm lens and open your other eye, you'll see the image closer in the viewfinder than it really is in person. Many cinematographers like to use a 100mm telephoto lens as their go-to long lens.

INSTA360 SEES VIRTUALLY EVERYTHING IN 360!

The *Insta360 One X* is a small, lightweight camera (about the size of a thin smartphone) that sees 360 degrees. It's affordable for the independent filmmaker who's interested in virtual reality movies for under $400. This little camera, with built in stabilization, records digitally internally or wirelessly through Bluetooth and Wi-Fi, or to an internal SD memory card. The camera stitches together a flawless 360 degrees of its environment that can be viewed and experienced through virtual reality glasses, or with a cursor or your finger viewed on a smartphone or computer screen.

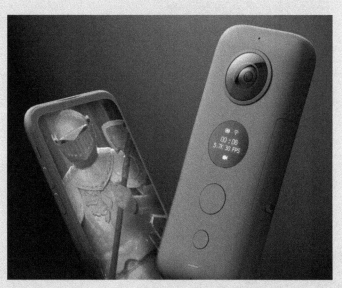

Photo of Insta360 Camera courtesy Arashi Vision US LLC

TIP

A telephoto lens is often used for close-up shots (and depending on the camera and exposure), helping to throw the background out of focus. (See later in this chapter for more on what is known as *depth of field*.) An out-of-focus background lets the audience concentrate on an actor or object in the frame without being distracted by the surroundings. A telephoto lens is also used to capture close-ups of buildings or objects that are at a fair distance from the camera. A pair of binoculars (or a low power telescope) works similar to a telephoto lens by bringing the subject closer. Explosions, car stunts, and other dangerous situations can be safely captured on camera from a distance using a long lens.

Zooming in on zoom lenses

A *zoom lens* does the work of several lenses in one. You can frame a wide-shot, a medium shot (usually framing your subject just above the waist to slightly above his or her head), and also a telephoto close-up shot by using a single zoom lens. Most affordable consumer camcorders come with a zoom lens that's permanently attached to the camera (cannot be unscrewed and replaced with other lenses). A zoom lens saves the time of removing and attaching different lenses and of having to make sure no dust gets inside the camera while changing lenses.

TECHNICAL STUFF

Feature film cinematographers prefer using *prime lenses,* which are the individual lenses (a separate wide, medium, and telephoto lens), instead of a zoom lens that has the ability to *mimic* different focal lengths. Prime lenses tend be better quality and the ground glass more precise with less distortion. Prime lenses also tend to avoid the flat, compressed feeling you might get with an inexpensive zoom lens.

Clearing the Air about Filters

You've heard the term, "seeing life through rose-colored glasses." Well, in a nutshell, that's what *lens filters* are all about. They're like sunglasses for your camera. But each lens serves a different purpose: You can change colors, set moods, and correct the picture. By placing a filter in front of your camera lens, you can magically change or enhance an image by

>> Removing annoying glare

>> Changing the color of the sky

>> Softening the subject through the lens

>> Adjusting the exposure (darker)

>> Correcting the image color

>> Making colors pop (stand out)

TIP

The Tiffen Company (www.tiffen.com), one of the largest and most recognized filter companies, puts out a line of quality filters. Table 10-2 gives you some examples of what Tiffen filters can do. Companies like Red Giant (www.RedGiant.com) also make special software that allows you to create virtual filter effects in the post-production phase right in your computer.

TABLE 10-2   **Tiffen Company Filters**

Filter	Effect
Pro-mist	Softens the image
Polarizer	Reduces or eliminates glare
Star	Causes light sources to sparkle
Neutral Density (ND)	Lowers the exposure, making the picture darker
85 and 80	Color-corrects the image
Sunrise (half)	Adds warm sunrise degradation to the sky (the bottom part of the filter is clear, and a warm color — orange or yellow — gradually gets deeper toward the top of the filter)
Blue Sky (half)	Adds richer blue to the sky (the bottom half of the filter is clear, and the upper half gradually becomes a deep sky blue)
Full Orange	Warms the entire image
Full Blue	Cools the entire image (also emulates nighttime)

Lee Filters (www.leefilters.com) is a company that offers similar filters, and Samy's Camera (www.samys.com) also carries a wide variety of filters and camera accessories.

Sliding-in or screwing-on: Types of filters

Filters come in two format types and can be used on both film cameras and digital video cameras: slide-in or screw-on. Each has its advantages, as explained in the following sections.

Whenever you put a filter or additional lens over your camera lens, you need to adjust the exposure because the camera is now working through more levels of lenses to give you a good picture (see the "Exposing Yourself to Exposures" section later in this chapter).

Screw-on filters

You screw a screw-on filter directly onto the camera lens (you need to match the lens circumference millimeter size to fit your specific camera). Screw-on lenses don't require a bulky matte box, as do slide-in filters, which keeps the camera portable and lightweight.

Slide-in filters

Slide-in filters require a *matte box,* a device that you mount in front of your camera lens. The filters, which are approximately 1/4-inch thick and 4x4 inches in size (square as opposed to the round screw-on filters), conveniently slide in and out of the matte box. A matte box can also be used for inserting effects masks, like looking through keyholes, binoculars, or a telescope view.

The advantage of a slide-in filter is that it works with any camera (and lens) because it doesn't depend on having to screw a fitted sized lens directly onto the camera. Instead a standard 4x4-inch filter slides into the matte box. Also, using multiple filters in a matte box is easier.

Slide-in filters for the matte box are quicker and more convenient than screw-on filters — you just drop the filter in the slot. Slide-in filters can also be turned sideways, something you can't do with most screw-on filters. Both types, however, allow you to use multiple filters at the same time if you want to use a combination of filter effects like a warm color filter, plus a filter that softens the picture image. I recommend you don't use any filters that you could add in post-production, because using a filter with the camera can't be undone in post-production. During editing, however, you can experiment with post-production filter software to see what results you can create.

Coloring with filters

The main purpose of corrective filters is to correct the film or video image so that the colors resemble what the human eye sees, whether you're shooting indoors or outdoors. Without proper color balance, your picture will have a slight off-colored tint to it.

On a film camera, the color filters you use depend on the film stock you're using and the color temperature of your lighting source (see Chapter 11 for details on color temperature). For example, a number *85 filter* color balances *tungsten* (film stock designed to be used indoors) for outdoor filming so that your scenes don't have a blue hue to them. A number *80 filter* color-corrects daylight film being used indoors so you don't have a yellow, red, or orange tint to your picture. Chapter 11 also discusses color corrections and effects using *gels,* which you can place in front of your movie lights. In addition, film footage is color-corrected or adjusted by the timer in the lab or while transferring your film footage to video via telecine (see Chapter 15).

REMEMBER

If you're using a digital camera, you can manually set the color balance by pointing the camera at a white card or object to establish a point of reference for your camera. Or you can use the automatic white balance that sets the correct color balance for you (but the exposure can fluctuate if you move the camera within different lighting conditions). After establishing what the color "white" should look like, your camera then recognizes (with its artificial intelligence) the correct colors of other objects.

One of the advantages that digital has over film is that you immediately see on your LCD or TV monitor the results of the color correction. You don't have to wait for the film to come back from the lab to see whether you got it right. In the post-production stage, you can do additional color-correction tweaking right on your computer. Most editing software like Final Cut Pro comes with color-correcting software. In addition, a myriad of software companies like Red Giant (`www.redgiant.com`) and FX Factory (`www.fxfactory.com`) feature software plug-ins that let you create all kinds of visual looks and corrections using their filtering software. Blackmagic provides a free industry-standard color correction and editing software called DaVinci Resolve. It works on both Mac and PC platforms.

TIP

Get a color chart from Kodak (it resembles a colored checkerboard) or the *Macbeth* color chart (you can purchase this chart on Amazon for under $20). You can photograph the chart at the beginning of each camera roll (each slated take) to use as a color reference when color-correcting your movie in post-production.

Day for night and night for day

Sometimes you can't conveniently shoot a night scene at night or a day scene during the day. By putting on a blue filter during an overcast day (and/or avoiding showing the sky in the scene), you can fool your audience into believing that the blue cast is night. You can also do this in post-production to tweak the night-look just right.

To create the look of daytime after the sun has gone down, you use large lights called *HMIs* (or the brightest lights you can find), which simulate sunlight.

By keeping your shots fairly close on your subjects and avoiding the horizon in the frame (such as keeping the actor against a building), your audience will think the scenes were shot during daylight hours.

Neutral about neutral density filters

A *neutral density filter,* also known as an ND filter, is used to reduce the amount of light coming into the camera lens — much like a pair of sunglasses cuts down on the amount of light hitting your eyes. In bright-light situations, an ND filter helps to avoid an overexposed picture that can blow-out your whites to the point of obscuring picture details in post-production. These filters come in various gradations, each one darker than the next. You screw on, or slide in (if using a matte box), a neutral density filter in front of the camera lens. If you're shooting with a digital camera, many come with a built in neutral density filter you can electronically turn on by flipping a switch or choosing in the menu.

Polarizers

Certain surfaces, like a metallic robot, a shiny car, or sparkling windows, can cause distracting reflections. *Polarizers* usually take care of this problem. If you're shooting someone through a car windshield, for example, you often get a glare, making the driver difficult to see in the car (see Figure 10-6). A polarizing filter can be adjusted until the glare is minimal or completely eliminated. Polarizing filters, much like sunglasses that filter out glare and make images easier to see, only work at the time of shooting. You can't remove glare in post-production and bring back detail to an image that was never there when shooting.

FIGURE 10-6: Without polarizer (left) and with polarizer (right).

Exposing Yourself to Exposures

Exposures control the amount of light entering the *iris* (also called the *aperture)* of the camera lens, which reacts to the light and opens and closes to allow more or less light into the camera. The human eye pupil works similarly, but the response is automatic. The film camera's eye needs human assistance to adjust the settings for focus, exposures, and so on. Most digital cameras have advanced circuitry and do a lot of this for you (when set on automatic) but there are times when you want to control your settings manually.

TECHNICAL STUFF

When you look outside on a bright day, the iris of your eye shrinks to a smaller circle because the eye has plenty of light to see. The iris of the camera works the same way when you manually adjust it, or let the automatic intelligence of the camera take over. Concentrated light is directed through the tiny aperture of the camera causing objects to appear in sharp focus (this is also why people who don't have 20/20 vision see better during daylight hours than at night) or when reading on a backlit tablet. Have you ever noticed that when you turn off the lights in a room, your eyes take a moment to adjust? That's because your brain is telling your eyes' pupils that they need to open wider to compensate for the lack of light. The iris of the camera works the same way and has to be opened up wider (either manually or automatically) to allow for more light to enter the lens to be able to expose or "see" an image with enough light.

REMEMBER

Your smartphone uses artificial intelligence to color correct your shot, keep it in focus, and adjust the exposure. Wow — now, that *is* smart!

F-stopping to a "t"

The various sizes of the iris as it opens and closes to light are measured in f-stops. You can manually set these settings to get a proper exposure (allowing enough light to enter the lens to record a proper image — not too dark, not too light). Or you can use the automatic setting on your camera. The disadvantage to using the automatic setting is that the lighting will fluctuate as you move the camera within different lighting conditions. (If you take a lens and adjust the f-stops while looking directly into the lens, you can actually see the iris adjusting in size, similar to the iris of your eye as it adjusts to light.)

Figure 10-7 illustrates the *aperture* opening of different exposures. The higher the number, the smaller the opening of the iris. F-stops are also measured in t-stops, which are more accurate for digital video because they measure exactly how much light is entering the lens. Most camera lenses are marked with both f- and t-stops on the side of the lens.

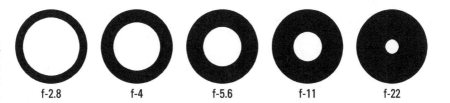

FIGURE 10-7: A series of aperture settings at different exposures.

f-2.8　　f-4　　f-5.6　　f-11　　f-22

Shuttering to think

Shutter speed affects how the motion of an image is captured on film (celluloid) or recorded to digital files. High shutter speeds are appropriate for shooting fast-moving subjects, such as a car chase or a competitive sporting event. By setting your camera for a higher shutter speed, you avoid having your subject blur or smear in the frame. For example, if you pause the footage on your DVD player, DVR, or while streaming a movie off Amazon or Netflix, the subject looks like a clear still photograph rather than a blurred image moving across the frame. Slower shutter speeds are best for low-light situations where the image needs more time to absorb adequate light to get a properly exposed picture.

On a film camera, the standard shutter speed at 24 frames per second is 1/50 of a second. So, on an independent film, shot in digital, I choose to shoot at a shutter speed of 1/50, which creates the illusion of running close to 24 frames per second. You can adjust the film camera shutter up to 1/1,700 of a second. On a digital camera, the standard shutter is 1/60 of a second (equivalent to a digital camera shooting 30 frames per second), and on some cameras, like the Panasonic Lumix GH5, the shutter speed can be adjusted as fast as 1/15,000 of a second.

REMEMBER

Shutter speed is different from *film speed* and *ISO* settings. Film speed for film (known as *ASA*) and ISO on digital cameras is more sensitive to light the higher the number. So, for example, film stock with an ASA of 800 sees in the dark better than a 200 ASA film stock. On a digital camera, 2500 ISO sees better in the dark than a setting of 200 ISO. But the higher the ISO number the more grain you will start to introduce into your image (though the newer digital cameras are pretty amazing with minimizing the grain at high ISO settings). Also, remember that exposure (your aperture setting to allow light in) is also different from shutter speed, film speed, ISO, and ASA. I used to get confused by all these terms, and I bring them up here so maybe you won't get confused and you'll know they each do their own thing. You're welcome!

Focusing a Sharper Image: Depth of Field

Depth of field deals with the depth of focus in your shot. In other words, what distance in front of and behind your subject are in acceptable focus? Knowing how depth of field works helps you to compose more interesting shots. The left shot in Figure 10-8 was taken with a 50mm lens set at 8 feet (with a small aperture setting of f-16), resulting in the actor and background both being in focus. The right shot was taken with a 100mm lens (with an f-stop of f-4) with the actor 25 feet from the camera. Notice that the actor is in focus, but the background is out of focus.

FIGURE 10-8:
With a medium (50mm) lens, everything is in focus (left). With a telephoto (100mm long lens), the background is out of focus (right) depending on your exposure and shutter speed settings.

©2008 Astrolite Ent. & ©2019 First American Cinema Little Bear and Ed Asner in Santa Stole Our Dog

TIP

Make sure the eyepiece on your camera is focused to your eye. Otherwise, you can't tell if your subject is in proper focus. Most consumer and prosumer digital cameras have built-in LCD or OLED screens that work as an internal monitors for you to view your shots.

The type of lens, shutter speed, and f-stop all affect the area in the frame that will be in focus. Table 10-3 shows the range of focus (what will be in focus at different exposure f-stop settings) within the frame, using a 50mm lens (normal lens) on a film camera or a professional full-frame digital camera.

TABLE 10-3   **The Distance Range in Focus at Different F-Stops**

Lens Setting	F-4	F-5.6	F-11	F-22
15 ft.	11 ft. to 23 ft. 8 in.	9 ft. 11 in. to 30 ft. 9 in.	7 ft. 6 in. to 20 ft. 8 in.	5 ft. to infinity
8 ft.	6 ft. 8in. to 9 ft. 11 in.	6 ft. 4 in. to 11 ft.	5 ft. 3 in. to 16 ft. 11in.	3 ft. 11in. to infinity

Lens Setting	F-4	F-5.6	F-11	F-22
5 ft.	4 ft. 6 in. to 5 ft. 8 in.	4 ft. 3 in. to 6 ft.	3 ft. 9 in. to 7 ft. 5 in.	3 ft. to 14 ft. 1 in.
2 ft.	1 ft. 11 in. to 2 ft. 1 in.	1 ft. 11 in. to 2 ft. 2 in.	1 ft. 9 in. to 2 ft. 3 in.	1 ft. 7 in. to 2 ft. 8 in.

The higher the f-stop, the larger the area that the camera sees in sharp focus. The advantage of shooting outside, where you'll have more than adequate light on a sunny day, is that it raises your *depth of field*, meaning your subject and the foreground and most distant objects will remain in focus if your shutter speed is normal (around 1/50) and your lens iris is around F-16 or F-22.

You can find cinematography books at your library, local bookstore, or charts on the Internet that contain every conceivable depth-of-field situation for film and digital cameras and the various lens and exposure settings. You can also find an excellent (and fun) Depth of Field Simulator at www.DOFsimulator.net. This is an interactive simulator that lets you play with different lens sizes, f-stops, and the distance from your actor to the camera — and see how the different situations and settings affect your depth of field and the focus results of each.

REMEMBER

Most digital cameras give you the option to focus manually, and this is your best bet. Zoom in as close as you can to the object you want to concentrate on, focus as clearly and precisely as you can, then zoom out and frame your image. Now you know your subject is in focus, regardless of objects or things moving behind or in front. Many digital cameras can now find the focus for you just by pressing your finger on the image of the LCD camera screen of the person or subject you want in focus. Some cameras also have settings for *follow-focus*, meaning the camera will attempt to keep the subject in focus as it or the camera moves. You'll notice I said *attempt* — the technology is still not perfect for auto follow-focus — sometimes the camera can focus and other times there is a lag, or it focuses on something you don't want in focus. Camera manufacturers are always working to perfect this technology — but it hasn't happened yet as I write this.

You have to be careful if you use the automatic focus because certain situations can fool it:

>> **Shooting through a cage or a fence:** The camera doesn't know whether to focus on the bars or the object behind it.

>> **Images that aren't centered in the frame:** The camera may try to auto-focus on an image that's in the foreground or background, but not the main subject.

>> **Fast-moving objects:** These can trick your auto-focus into trying to follow-focus the image, but it can't keep up.

TIP

Most consumer and prosumer digital cameras now allow you to use auto-focus after setting an area in which the camera will attempt to follow within the frame. This means you can position a zone square around your actor's head, and if the actor doesn't move too quickly within the frame, the camera will keep his or her face in complete focus — especially if the actor moves towards or away from the camera. Some digital cameras do this very well, keeping focus with little to no lag time — others are still waiting on updated software to help them be more consistent with this feature. Using an auto-focus setting like this is especially helpful when you are the only cameraman and you don't have a second person (assistant camera) to adjust the focus as your subject moves within the frame.

Chapter **11**

Let There Be Lighting!

ittle did Thomas Edison know that the simple light bulb he invented in 1879 would take on so many shapes and *color temperatures* and be instrumental in controlling the look of every image captured on film or video (including digital files). Without the proper lighting and exposure, your actors will be sitting (or standing) in the dark.

Lighting, the focus of this chapter, is the technique of creating a mood getting the right exposure, and capturing the most aesthetically pleasing images for your waiting audience. Here, you develop a feel for the lighting spectrum, color temperatures, and the distribution of light and dark — painting with light, as you will. You also get a short primer on lighting safety.

Lighting Up Your Life

Lighting brings life to your shots. Light lets your audience "see" where your actors are and where they're going. Instead of just flipping on a light switch in a room with one overhead light, you have the power to control the lighting in your shots by positioning a myriad of lights (on stands, the floor, tabletops, the ceiling) virtually anywhere to illuminate your scene. Lighting can bring an inviting aesthetic beauty to your shots, a bright and exciting feel, or a deliberate dreariness, depending on the final results you're looking to achieve. When lit correctly, your lighting will pull your actors away from the walls and furniture, creating a more inviting dimensional environment. Creative lighting can reach behind your actors and separate them from the background. You can create depth and perspective with proper lighting and control the mood of the scene by coloring your lights with gels.

REMEMBER

Don't be afraid to experiment with light. Pick up your lights on their stands and move them around your subjects. Watch what light does to your actors as you lower, raise, and tilt your movie lights at different angles toward your subjects. See how you can create a mood with shadows and make your actors look more pleasing by bouncing light off the ceiling or using other lighting tricks and tools, like scrims and glass diffusion, discussed later in this chapter.

Shedding Some Light on Lighting Jargon

Before delving deeply into this chapter, take a minute to review two important lighting terms.

Big foot-candles: Lighting for film cameras

Motion-picture film cameras measure the illumination of light falling on a subject in *foot-candles*. One foot-candle is the amount of illumination produced by a single candle at a distance of 1 foot away from the subject. For example, if your light meter (see the "Measuring with light meters" section later in this chapter) reads 200 foot-candles, that means that your light source is equivalent to the illumination of 200 candles falling on your subject from 1 foot away. The exposure is also determined by the speed of the film, which in turn controls your exposure (see Chapter 10 for information on stops and exposures).

Lux (and cream cheese): Lighting for digital

A *lux* is the European equivalent of a foot-candle, but instead of being the equivalent of a single candle at a distance of 1 foot, one lux is the illumination of 1 square meter (European measurement) per single candle. Digital cameras measure light in lux.

REMEMBER

Electronic digital cameras are much more sensitive to light than motion-picture film cameras are, so you can more easily shoot in low-light situations (such as the Lumix GH5). With proper lux levels for low-light cameras, the camera is able to dig into the darkness to give you an acceptable image that's not grainy or muddy in appearance. This is similar to the newer fast-speed films, with less grain, which have been developed for motion-picture cameras (see Chapter 10). *Fast-speed film* refers to the film stock's ability to respond to light, not to how fast the film moves through the camera.

Digital cameras contain chips — not edible potato chips, but digital chips — known as *CCDs*. CCD stands for *charge-coupled device* and is a circuit that stores data and converts what the camera records into an electrical image. CCDs are also light sensitive, allowing the camera to "see" into dimmer environments and produce acceptable images. A one-chip camera lends itself to home movies and non-broadcast projects, while a three-chip camera is suitable for professional broadcast with colors and a digital image that is cleaner and sharper than one-chip cameras. Three-chip cameras used to be more expensive, so if you decided you wanted one, you had to dip deeper into your wallet (chip and dip). But today, one-chip cameras are long gone, and three-chip cameras are common and affordable for most budgets.

REMEMBER

A standard lux rating averages around three lux and is affected by the CCD and the lens speed. CCDs are light sensitive and determine the lux in a digital camera. A 60-watt incandescent light bulb (or LED 6 watt equivalent) is equal to 10 lux, so a 3-lux camera is extremely sensitive to light when recording.

Taking your color temperature

Different types of light radiate different color intensities, called *color temperatures,* which affect how the camera records the light. The color temperature of the lighting affects the final colors in your movie. Color temperature is determined by the intensity of light that radiates from your movie lights, practical lights, or the sun; don't confuse it with thermal temperature that measures hot and cold.

When you're imagining how color temperature works, think of a blacksmith heating up and shaping a horseshoe in a forge. As the black mass heats up, it turns different colors. Turn on your gas stove and notice that the flames are fluorescent blue with a lighter blue outline. This is how color temperature works.

Our eyes adjust to the colors of light, something the camera can't do without some assistance. That's why gels, white balance, and filters (see Chapter 10) are used to get the film or digital camera to see what the human eye sees. The camera has a mechanical eye (with film cameras) or an electronic eye (with digital cameras) that has to be programmed so that lighting will look natural to what the human eye sees. Many camcorders can emulate what the human eye sees when you set them on automatic.

REMEMBER

Every color has a temperature that's measured in *Kelvins* (named after Lord Kelvin, who discovered the system). Kelvin is a rate of measurement in degrees, similar to Fahrenheit and Celsius, and it's usually shortened to °K. Warmer colors like red and amber have lower Kelvin ratings. For example, sunlight is yellow, orange, and red — a lower Kelvin rating than the blue Kelvin rating of the moonlight. Film is a sensitive material that lets light burn its color into it. The higher the temperature in °K, the cooler the color. In other words, the hotter the temperature, the bluer the hue; the lower the temperature, the warmer the hue (reds, oranges, yellows). Table 11-1 shows standard Kelvin ratings.

TABLE 11-1

Kelvin Ratings of Light

Light Source	Average Color Temperature (in °K)
Candle	1,600
Sunrise/sunset	2,000
3,200 Standard indoor lights	3,200
Early-morning/late-afternoon sunlight	4,200
Midday sunlight (hottest)	5,500
Light shade/overcast	7,200
Full shade/hazy day	8,000
Dusk	9,500

REMEMBER

The average color temperature of your indoor lights is 3,200°K (a warmer look), and the average lighting provided by the sun during daylight hours is about 5,500°K (a cooler white/blue hue).

Illuminating with soft light versus hard light

Soft light is any light source bounced off a reflective surface or a translucent material between the lights and your actors, thus creating a softer effect. You can create soft light in a number of ways:

>> By simply bouncing light off a ceiling or a white card or by using a portable lighting device that has the bulb facing into a reflective housing that bounces the light back out.

>> By placing a translucent cloth-like material in front of the bulb to filter any hard, direct light from falling on your subject, and also cuts down on unwanted shadows — this is called *diffusion*. A lampshade is a perfect example of this type of soft light; rarely does a room have exposed light bulbs (naked bulbs should not be seen in public!). The company Rosco, www.rosco.com, makes a line of light diffusion and color correction filters called Cinegels, which includes cloth diffusers. PRL Lighting (www.prllighting.com) encloses its LED lights with a soft covering called a *soft box* to diffuse and soften as well as minimize shadows when illuminating your subject.

Hard light creates a harsh, bright look on your subject and should be avoided — it's not flattering to most subjects. An example of hard light is the intense rays of the sun. Most professional cinematographers prefer shooting outside on cloudy days (rather than sunny days), because the clouds diffuse the sunlight and add softness to everything. On larger productions, the lighting crew actually stretches a large white translucent tarp on a metal frame over the outdoor set to diffuse the harsh rays of the sun falling on the actors. On close-up shots, you can easily hold a translucent cloth like a white bedsheet in the path of the sun above the actor to diffuse the harsh sunlight and create a soft, more complimentary light on your actor's face.

Seeing your eye light

The sparkle in an actor's eye can make or break a close-up. A small light, called an *eye light*, often attached to the camera can help bring life to an actor's eyes by brightening them up and adding a little glint. The Lustra L50 LED light doubles as an on-camera light using a shoehorn adapter that attaches to your camera (see Figure 11-1). The light panel is 7 by 4 1/2 inches with the thickness of about two decks of cards, and weighs only 15 ounces. It fits comfortably and conveniently on most cameras. You can use the dimmer switch to control the intensity of the light, helping to naturally brighten any subject in a close-up and fill in shadows on the face. The Lustra L50 contains 50 individual internal LED bulbs within its housing and comes with a power supply that can be plugged into any regular outlet — or it can run cordless using a rechargeable Sony battery. The Lustra L50 retails for around $199, and you can get it at www.prllighting.com.

TIP

A little trick that I've discovered is to use my iPhone's flashlight app to create an eye light or fill light onto my close-up subject. It's pocket portable and doesn't need to be plugged in. You can either use the flashlight app on your phone, or open a blank white screen and turn the brightness up; you'll be surprised at how much illumination it throws on your close subject!

Painting with Light

Lighting your movie is similar to painting a picture with brush strokes onto a blank canvas. An artist brushes on light to create a mood and cast light on the subject or objects in a painting in much the same way you set up and position your movie lights. You throw light onto your set and subjects. In order to create a three-dimensional look to your shots, you need to understand the basic lighting setup, shown in Figure 11-2, that helps separate your subjects from the background that could otherwise cause a flat-looking image:

>> **Key light:** The main light (and often the brighter source than your other lights) that you set up first and then supplement with two or more other types of lights.

>> **Back light:** Also used as a *hairlight,* the back light is directed at the back of your actors to pull them out of the background. It can also create a soft halo around your subjects.

>> **Fill light:** You use the fill light to fill in or supplement the other lights for a more natural look. This light also helps soften shadows.

>> **Background light:** As its name implies, the background light lights your background to separate it from your actors and to create more depth in the shot.

Spotlight on Lighting Equipment

You can light a scene in many ways. Turn on a corner lamp. See the light find your subject. Now turn on an overhead light. Each lighting source enhances and sets a mood for your shot. A candlelit dinner wouldn't be half as romantic if the room were bathed in bright light. A haunted house wouldn't be nearly as scary if it were as bright as day inside.

PRL Lighting makes some great portable lighting kits like the Lustra L50 3-Lite kit that comes with three portable LED lights engineered for uniform color with a dimmer switch on back to control light spread and intensity. The kit includes accessories like softboxes, gels, and light stand mounts. You can view the company's line of light products at www.prllighting.com.

Shining light on halogens, LEDs, incandescents, fluorescents, and HMIs

Most professional movie lights used to only use *halogen* bulbs (also called *halogen quartz*), which are usually at a color balance of 3,200K (see the section "Taking your color temperature" earlier in this chapter). Inside each bulb is a *tungsten coil* that heats up the halogen gas in the bulb to create a steady, non-flicker consistent light, giving an even color temperature — thus, ensuring a consistent color balance for the scene. Halogen lights can be expensive, are delicate, and eventually burn out, unlike LED lights.

Don't ever touch a halogen bulb with your bare hands — even if the bulb is cool. The oil on your fingers creates a spot on the surface of the bulb that eventually weakens the glass and causes the light to explode. Also, halogen bulbs can be extremely hot and can burn you!

LED stands for *light emitting diode*. Yes, that's right — it's actually a diode that lights up. LED is not a bulb, and therefore never burns out (everything has a lifespan, so it could last up to 25 years). Most incandescents have been replaced by the cost-saving and efficient LED lighting technology — and fluorescent lights are also being overtaken by LEDs, including even the familiar fluorescent tube lighting (LED tubes are lined with diodes around the tube). LEDs have lower wattage and thus save money on your electricity bills. A 6 watt LED bulb is equivalent to a 60 watt incandescent bulb. Because LEDs require very little power to run their diodes, they are a perfect match for using rechargeable batteries, which is extremely convenient, especially if you're on a run-and-gun shoot — or if you don't have immediate access to a power outlet.

An *incandescent (tungsten)* light is a light source that you probably use to use every day in the form of your household light bulb. An incandescent also contains a tungsten wire filament that heats up, but unlike the halogen lamp, the bulb doesn't contain halogen gas and so isn't as energy-efficient as halogen bulbs. Average household incandescent bulbs have color temperatures of around 3,000K, depending on the wattage. Halogen bulbs last two to three times longer than a regular incandescent light bulb and burn at higher temperatures. In today's modern world, most incandescent bulbs have been replaced with long-life and power saving LED bulbs.

Fluorescent lights, often called CFL (Compact Fluorescent Light), are energy-efficient bulbs that last up to ten times longer than incandescent bulbs and give out less heat. But, now fluorescent lights are being superseded by the even more energy efficient LED light technology. The color temperature of fluorescent bulbs are similar to incandescent/tungsten Kelvin ratings.

TIP

An *HMI* (short for *hydrargyrum medium-arc iodide*) is a powerful, expensive, bulky and very heavy light used to emulate sunlight (it has the same color temperature as sunlight) at around 5,600K. The bulb is made up of mercury vapor and metal halides that burn at very high intensity to create extremely bright lighting — so run away fast if you drop it! An HMI is used to supplement real sunlight when the sun is setting or on overcast days. You can also shine an HMI through the windows on your indoor set to create the appearance of bright sunshine beaming in, or you can place it outside a window at night to simulate daylight outside. You can also use an HMI to fill in shadows on an actor's face caused by the sun. An HMI can also be used to light up a city block at night. Keep the HMI balanced for tungsten (blue hue) to simulate moonlight instead of sunlight. Some companies have developed LED versions of the HMI and boast they are good alternatives — and of course cheaper, smaller, and lighter.

When you're working on smaller interior sets, like an office or bedroom, a portable lighting kit usually suffices. A *lighting kit* typically consists of three to four small LED lights with collapsible stands that you can adjust to whatever height you need (see the "Gathering light on accessories" section later in this chapter). I have several great lighting kits that I ordered off the Internet from PRL Lighting (www.prllighting.com) and Neewer kits (available through Amazon). Lighting kits, like the Lustra Lite kit in Figure 11-3, usually come neatly encased in a sturdy case or backpack that you can carry conveniently to your shoot.

TIP

Pick up a couple of LED *work-lamps* between $30 and $80 from your local hardware store; they're cheaper than renting professional studio lights or a complete lighting kit. Some come with included sturdy metal stands, and the lights are usually bright enough to light a small outdoor parking lot. Some even work with rechargeable batteries!

Filming the light of day

If you're shooting with a motion-picture film camera, you need to make sure the color temperature of the film stock matches the color temperature of the light you're filming under. *Daylight* film is color balanced for the Kelvin temperatures radiated by the sun.

Image courtesy of PRL Lighting

Indoor film is balanced for tungsten lights. Tungsten halogen lights are usually rated at 3,200 Kelvin and are consistent in the color temperature they radiate. Household incandescent lamps have a color temperature of around 3,000K, depending on the wattage. LED lights come in a range of temperatures from daylight (bright white) to warmer indoor colors.

REMEMBER

If you're shooting with a 16mm or 35mm camera using indoor film stock and you have sunlight coming through the windows, you need to use an 85 (amber-colored) filter (see Chapter 10) to color-correct the daylight. If you're using outdoor film stock indoors, you use an 80 (blue-colored) filter to color-correct your indoor lights for the outdoor (daylight) film stock.

Most digital cameras have an automatic white balance function with which you can set the white balance that determines a precedent for all other colors to be correct.

You're on a roll with gels

Instead of, or in addition to, using filters over the camera lens (see Chapter 10), you can change the color temperature on-set by placing rolls of colored *gels* over the lights (or in the case of sunlight, over windows). You can mix and match different colored gels with different lights and pinpoint certain colors on certain objects or people in the scene. For example:

>> A blue gel on a light creates a blue hue to simulate a moonlit night.

>> A warm yellow/orange gel can add to the warmth of a romantic scene in front of the fireplace.

Gels are often used to color-correct light sources in order to balance the correct colors when using motion picture film stock. An 85 amber gel converts incoming sunlight to indoor color balance to give you correct coloring with your tungsten lamps for your indoor scene.

Gels create artistic hues on set, diffusing and controlling the lighting environment designed by the cinematographer and the gaffer. The company Rosco puts out a free color-swatch booklet that has close to 300 gels, called Cinegels, with actual samples in a little flip book — visit Rosco's website at www.rosco.com to request the free swatch book.

Gels come in rolls for a reason: You may need to use a lot of them. They are made of thin, light celluloid and are usually tolerate in hot lights, being heat resistant (although if you're using LED bulbs, the heat is minimal unlike with halogen bulbs). For example, if you're shooting indoors and have a big, bright window in the shot, you're going to get a blast of overexposed light if you don't do something. You can put a gel over the window to color correct and also cut down the light.

TIP

When filming indoors on a bright, sunny day, I have actually used window film from the hardware store to cut down on the harsh light coming through the windows. These rolls of thin plastic are normally used to cut down on heat and UV rays and for privacy (much like your car tinting). There are different shades, light to darkest, and I find the medium shade works great and has a natural look on film. Often the film applies easily to the window with static cling and water. You can also tape them up on the outside of the window, but make sure it's stretched and secure so the gel doesn't flutter in the breeze, giving away there is something over the windows.

Reflecting on reflector boards

You can't control the sun when you're filming outside, other than knowing what position it will be at any given time of day. But you can control the direction of the sun with a little portable shiny device called a *reflector*. If your subject can't face the sun, you use a reflector board to catch the sun's rays and bounce the light back onto your subject (see Figure 11-4).

Neewer (available through Amazon) makes different sizes of portable pop-open reflector discs that collapse to the size of a steering wheel and come in a variety of sizes. You can find reflector discs in different colors for different uses, such as white, soft gold, silver, and translucent reflective surfaces. You can also diffuse the sun's harshness by placing a translucent reflector between the sun's rays and your subject. Check out Amazon for all the types of reflectors and prices available.

TIP

You don't need to run out and buy a professional reflector board if it's not in your budget. Instead, you can use a white foam card or flexible piece of shiny aluminum. You can also find sheets of Styrofoam at your local hardware store for insulation that have one side covered in a tinfoil type of material. You can use either side as a reflector board, depending on the intensity of the light you want to reflect. Mother Nature herself makes a great reflector in the wintertime — it's called snow. (Even Mother Nature is into snow-business.) The white snow helps to reflect sunlight off the ground and upward to get rid of shadows under an actor's eyes, nose, and chin.

WARNING

If the sun is behind your actor and you don't use a reflector board, you'll most often end up with a silhouette of your actor (referred to as *backlit*) because the light of the sun behind the actor is much brighter than the light in front of your actor. The camera's auto iris exposes for the brighter image and leaves your subject in the dark. Silhouette shots can be effective for scenes such as an actor on a camel crossing the desert hilltops against a burning sun.

Opening barn doors: No cows or chickens here

You may need to control the spread of light falling on your subject from a lamp with *barn doors*. Barn doors resemble miniature black flags and shade the light as it beams out of its housing. A typical barn door has between two and four metal, hinged doors that open up like — you guessed it! — barn doors.

Cooking with cookies, scrims, and diffused glass

When using movie lights, sometimes the light is too broad and bright and you want to control the intensity. There are many ways to do that: using cookies, scrims, and diffused glass placed over the lights to soften or create a lighting effect:

>> **Cookies:** These *cookies* aren't edible, but they kind of look like an oversized cookie cutter. Cookies break up light or simulate the shadow of tree branches, window blinds, and so on. They come in a variety of shapes, and you can easily make your own. A *gobo* is similar to a cookie, but it doesn't have a distinct pattern and usually blocks the light in sections. A light blocking gobo is called a *flag*.

TIP

For an inexpensive cookie, take a small branch off a tree (the one the gardener was going to trim anyway) and clamp it to a stand, putting it in the path of your light. The branch casts an abstract shadow, simulating a tree outside a window.

>> **Scrims:** *Scrims* resemble the mesh in a screen door or window. They cut down on the intensity from bright set lights and are placed in a holder or on a stand in front of a movie light.

TIP

For an inexpensive scrim, go to your local hardware store and buy some black mesh used for patio screen doors or windows. Cut it to fit in front of your lights, and clamp it in place with a stationery binder clip from an office-supply store.

>> **Diffused glass:** *Diffused glass* diffuses the light source when you place it in front of your light. Diffused glass may be frosted, bubbled, or textured like a glass shower door. This texturing creates a softer light on your subjects that makes them look better than under a harsh light with no diffusion. Wax paper, positioned not too closely to your lights (unless they're low-heat LEDs), works great for diffusing the light on your subjects.

Waving flags and snoots

If the first thing you think of when you hear the word *snoot* is an elephant or an anteater, you're not far off. A *snoot* directs light through its trunk-shaped funnel and produces a concentrated beam of light similar to a spotlight. It is used a lot in shooting miniatures, because the light can be pinpointed on small areas.

A *flag*, on the other hand, probably makes you think of the country's flag flapping in the wind with the sun shining brightly behind it. In filmmaking, however, the sun can be flagged by a flag. A flag is a (usually) black, opaque piece of material that is stretched over a wire frame to block light from a movie light or the sun that's glaring into the camera lens. A flag works just like your hand does when you use it to keep the sun's glare out of your eyes or like your car visor does when you flip it down while you're driving.

Measuring with light meters

To accurately record an image on film stock, you need to use a light meter. A *light meter* resembles a battery tester, only you dial the film stock you're using into the meter and then take a light-meter reading of the lighting on your set. The meter tells you the correct exposure to set your camera at. If you're shooting on digital, the camera often works as its own light meter and can automatically read the amount of light coming into the lens. There are limitations on the internal light meter inside your digital camera, though.

Light meters read the intensity of the light on the subject in foot-candles, letting the cinematographer know what his *f-stop* or *t-stop* setting should be (more on *f-* and *t-stops* in Chapter 10).

Some light meters give you both *reflective* and *incidental* readings (see Figure 11-5):

>> **Incidental light meter:** An *incidental light meter* reads direct light shining into the meter from the actual light source — in other words, the light pointed at and falling on your subject. These meters are quite accurate and aren't fooled by large areas of light and dark in the same shot. Your digital camera cannot read incidental light because like your lights, the camera is pointed towards your subject.

>> **Reflective light meter:** A *reflective light meter* measures the reflected light off the subject and back into the meter. A *spot meter* is a reflective meter that reads the light in a particular spot so that you know how light falls in different places over your subject and can choose an average reading — even if you

have large light and dark areas that normally confuse a meter. A digital camera works similarly to a spot meter as it reads the light reflecting into the lens. It allows you to zoom in on a particular spot and get an accurate reading without having to use a separate reflective light meter.

TIP

When you're using a digital camera, take a light reading and then set your exposure manually. This way, if the camera follows a subject moving from a darker to lighter area, the camera doesn't try to automatically adjust the exposure and cause the picture to flutter between light and dark.

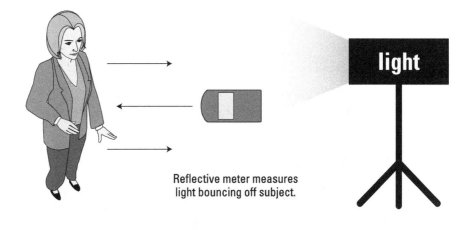

Reflective meter measures
light bouncing off subject.

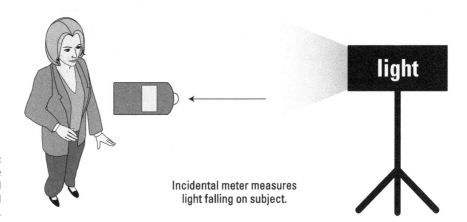

Incidental meter measures
light falling on subject.

FIGURE 11-5:
A reflective
light meter and
an incidental
light meter.

In the App Store for the iPhone, you'll find a nifty little app designed by Adam Wilt called Cine Meter II. For only $25 dollars (instead of $400), you can turn your iPhone into an actual incidental and reflective light meter! It uses your iPhone's built-in camera to read the light and give you all the information that an expensive light meter does. Chances are, you'll always have this light meter with you.

Your digital camera can only read *reflective* light similar to a reflective light meter. Your camera cannot read *incidental* light because the meter needs to be pointed from your subject towards the light that is coming at them. Incidental light meters are more accurate. Also, separate light meters can calculate other equations that your camera cannot read automatically such as color temperature, exposures, lux, or foot candles.

Gathering light on accessories

In addition to all the complex, technical lighting tools detailed in the preceding sections, you also need to think about a few low-cost, simple accessories that are a necessity on the set.

>> **Clamps and clothespins:** You use clamps and clothespins to hold diffusion cloths or scrims over your lights, as well as to clamp things to your C-stands. Clothespins can be helpful to clip light things together, attach or hang props, and so on. Your local hardware store has a variety of grips and clamps in all shapes and sizes. Binder clips from your office supply store also work well.

>> **C-stands and lighting stands:** *C-stands* can be lifesavers on a movie set. You can adjust these stands to varying heights, as well as adjust the extended folding arm post into many positions for holding flags, cookies, *scenic backdrops* (see Chapter 17), or props. *Light stands* are adjustable in height and usually have three extended legs that spread out to help balance the weight of the light securely so it doesn't topple over.

>> **Sandbags:** *Sandbags* may not seem important — after all, they just lie there like a lump of sand and don't look very impressive. But when you have unbalanced light stands and other pieces of equipment tipping over, you may wonder how you ever survived without them. A sandbag is simply a filmmaker's paperweight. A standard sandbag weighs about 15 pounds and resembles a cowboy's saddlebag.

You can rent sandbags, buy them for about a dollar a pound, or make your own. To make your own, fill empty plastic sandbags (you can find these at most hardware stores for under $1 each, or on Amazon) with play sand (you can buy 50 pounds for around $4). Many local fire departments have free sand bags and sand (you have to fill them yourself — you've got to work a little for something free) they give away to minimize flooding during storm season. Head over to your neighborhood fire department for some free sandbags (it's always good to have some on hand anyway and be prepared for rainy season when you're done shooting your movie).

REMEMBER

An *expendable* refers to an element that can be used up and replaced. Light bulbs (halogen, fluorescent, incandescent) eventually burn out, break, or just plain don't work. They are expendable and have to be replaced. LEDs can last up to 20 years or more (if they're not dropped or damaged) so they are not considered expendables. Tape (gaffers tape, masking tape, Scotch tape, double-sided tape) glue, batteries, and even gels (which eventually fade, melt, rip, or wear out) fall into the expendable category, as well.

Blowing a Fuse: Taking Safety Precautions

Gaffers and electricians (see Chapter 7) are trained to not overload the electrical circuits. Lots of lights (especially halogen bulbs) can use a lot of voltage and need to be distributed properly. You don't want the fire department showing up after you've blown the fuse for your entire neighborhood.

TIP

Plug in your lights using several different circuits. Don't plug them in using the wall plugs in the same room. Be creative in your distribution. Get a lot of extension cords, also called *stingers* on-set, and plug into different rooms, so you don't overload one individual circuit. You may have to have your electrician do a *tie-in*. This means that he plugs the lights directly into the fuse box and surpasses the electrical outlets at your location. The advantage to using LED lights is that they are very low wattage compared to incandescent and halogen bulbs — so on a small shoot you rarely have to worry about blowing a fuse.

REMEMBER

You're not always going to be near an electrical outlet, and if you're shooting outdoors as night is falling, you may need to supplement your lighting. Even if you're shooting a night scene, you still need lights to get a properly exposed image. Some indoor locations may not let you use the electricity, or you may be shooting in an older house or building that can't take the voltage required by your lights. You can often run LED lights off rechargeable batteries because they're low voltage. Sometimes you need to run lights, whether they are LEDs or halogens, and you still need to plug them in. In such cases, you can run them off a portable generator. Generators run on gasoline. Don't forget to have a can of gas ready to refill the generator. You don't want to use the old excuse, "We ran out of gas."

Chapter **12**

Sound Advice: Production Sound

You've heard the expression "A picture is worth a thousand words." But with the right sound accompanying the picture, it can be worth 10,000 words! The right music or soundtrack can enhance even the dullest images. Sound and picture should complement each other. It's kind of like a relationship: You may be all right on your own, but together you're a dynamite team. Radio dramas were exciting to listen to, and silent pictures entertained audiences, but it wasn't until radio and silent pictures were married that things really started to sizzle. And the honeymoon is still going strong.

Getting a clear professional dialogue track on your movie requires the expertise of someone skilled in the art of sound recording. A *production sound mixer* will have the knowledge of what microphones to use and how to control the audio levels to give you the cleanest audio tracks. If you don't have the budget to hire a professional sound mixer, you can train yourself, or hire someone interested in taking on the task of recording your audio — but you have to read this chapter first!

Testing, Testing, 1, 2, 3

Without sound you're just shooting a silent movie, and silent movies are a thing of the past. The sound elements for your film are made up of a series of sounds:

>> Actors' dialogue

>> Environmental atmosphere (ambience)

>> On-camera sound effects

These elements have to be recorded properly to create a pristine soundtrack for your film. If you're making your movie with a digital cinema camera, then you have the option to record the sound onto the digital files that record your images into the camera, keeping picture and sound as one. Or, for more controlled and professional sound recording, you may want to use a separate sound system, as you would do if shooting with motion picture film stock — which then will be married to your picture in the post-production phase. You can also do both, and one can be used as a backup.

Assembling a Sound Team

Just as it's important to have someone who knows how to operate the camera and give you great-looking images (see Chapter 7), it's also important to have someone skilled at recording production sound so that the audience "hears" your movie. You can record the sound yourself or hire someone eager to do sound for you, but if you can hire someone experienced in this field you'll have fewer headaches in the end (getting clear crisp sound for the final product) unless you hire a deaf sound person (see the sidebar "On the Røde to great sound" later in this chapter). The other advantage to hiring a skilled sound mixer is that he or she may own a recorder and microphones, saving you the time and trouble of renting or buying them elsewhere.

Mixing it up with your mixer

No, a mixer is not your personal bartender during production. A mixer mixes the sound elements on-set, which consist of dialogue between actors and accompanying production sounds, like footsteps or doors closing, that help guide the addition of enhanced sound effects in post-production.

A *sound mixer* uses a mixing board to control and adjust volume levels of each actor (if several mics are used on-set) and the quality of the sound — not too low, not too high, no interference, and so on. When shooting on film, the mixing board is connected to a sound recorder as 35mm film does not record audio onto the film like digital files do. When shooting digital you can also do separate audio into a digital recorder, or you can connect your microphones directly to your digital camera and record audio internally, keeping picture and sound connected as one. Sound mixers train their ears to pick up any distracting noises, such as background noise, wireless mic interference, feedback, or hissing, that can ruin the recording of sound during a shot, and then they adjust or fix it out of the sound mix.

The sound mixer's duties include:

>> Recording usable actor dialogue, and adjusting each actor's volume if each actor has their own designated microphone or lavalier. (A *lavalier* is a wireless mic that clips onto an actor's collar or cleverly hidden elsewhere so as to not be seen by the camera. For more on lavaliers, see the section "Wireless microphones," later in this chapter.)

>> Recording room tone (known as *ambience*), at the end of each take, to be used in post-production.

>> Announcing each take (called *slating* the take) and keeping a written log for the picture editor to follow in post-production (see Chapter 15).

>> Recording any necessary voice-over (off-camera narration heard over a scene) or *wild lines,* lines repeated for clarity after the scene has been shot.

>> Recording special sound effects on set that can be used in the final movie or replaced and/or enhanced with an effect from a sound-effects library.

>> Playing back music and lyrics for lip-syncing (on a musical number or on music videos).

WILD AND CRAZY LINES

Dialogue has to be clear. If the audience can't hear an actor's dialogue, they'll lean over to the person next to them and whisper, "What'd he say?" and miss the next bit of dialogue. You don't want that to happen. If the sound mixer thinks that a line has been stepped on by another actor or that some background noise interfered, he or she has the actor repeat the lines, now called *wild lines,* after the director has yelled "Cut!" and the camera has stopped rolling. Replacing those lines in post-production is easier than reshooting the whole take if it's otherwise usable except for that line or two. Recording the actor's line on-set ensures that the sound can be easily matched into the existing take.

Making room for the boom operator

The job of a *boom operator* is to hold the microphone attached to the tip of a pole called the *boom* (often referred to as a *fishpole*, because it resembles one) out over the actors (or just out of camera frame so it's not in the shot) and to find the best direction from which to capture the actors' dialogue. The boom operator works closely with the sound mixer and is usually guided by the mixer (through head-phones) as to where to point the microphone for optimum dialogue recording.

The duties of the boom operator include:

>> Directing the boom and mic in the most favorable position to pick up the best dialogue recording

>> Being familiar with the scenes, knowing which actor speaks next, and pointing the microphone directly at that actor from above or below the camera frame

>> Placing hidden mics or lapel mics on the actors when it's difficult to pick up good sound with the mic outside of the shot (especially in wide shots)

>> Setting up and testing the wireless mics used in wide shots

REMEMBER

Don't underestimate the skill of the boom operator. On my film *Turn of the Blade*, we had someone fill in for my boom man one day. This guy was so bad, he kept creeping into every shot — he almost became part of the cast! Often, your sound mixer can recommend someone he or she has worked with before who doesn't need to be fitted by your wardrobe person.

TECHNICAL STUFF

A professional boom pole is often made of the lightest but strongest of materials, like aluminum. The K-Tek Avalon boom pole is made of aluminum, and it also has a built-in XLR cable input so there's no outer dangling cables. The Avalon boom is available at www.ktekpro.com.

The lighter the boom pole, the easier it is for the boom-pole person to hold it up for extended takes. Røde makes several boom precision-balanced poles, including the Boom Pole Pro. It extends via locking connectors from just under three feet to up to ten feet long, weighs only 18oz and is made of carbon fiber — it's not only feather-light, but also gorilla strong. The pole has a rubber tip on the bottom for non-slip resting and has a standard thread at the tip for attaching a *shock mount* (which floats the microphone with rubber bands or flexible stabilizing bars to absorb and limit vibrations), in which you then cradle your microphone. Another great trick is you can run your microphone cable inside the boom pole to avoid messy hanging cables knocking against the outside of your pole. Røde carries a host of different boom poles, and one that should fit your budget (www.rode.com).

Choosing Analog or Digital Sound

Just as you have a choice of film or digital video formats (see Chapter 10), you have a choice of audio-recording formats: analog or digital. As you've probably discovered, your music CDs sound better than your old analog cassette tapes. CDs are in the digital domain, and you don't lose any generation in quality when making copies as you do when dubbing analog cassette tapes.

It's much easier to record your audio using digital equipment and spare the trouble of using older analog technology. Digital machines are more compact, they use fewer batteries than some of the older bulkier analog recorders (like the Nagra), and most record internally or to hard drives or SD memory cards. Finding a digital recorder in a small town is also easier than finding an analog recorder for film use. If you're shooting with a digital camera, it also acts as a camera and a recorder all in one unit, and your sound will automatically be in the digital realm.

Analog: The sound of Nagra Falls

The Polish word *Nagra* means "to record." A Nagra, from the company of the same name, is an analog recorder that uses 1/4-inch magnetic tape on reel to reel (Nagra makes digital recorders as well). Analog Nagras were once the number one choice of recording mixers on almost every film ever made in Hollywood, but now with the advent of digital technology, filmmakers have more choices (and less-expensive alternatives) when choosing a recording machine for their productions. An analog Nagra keeps in perfect sync with the film camera because it has a crystal-sync device within its housing. *Crystal sync* is an electronic device that is found in both the motion-picture film camera and the separate sound recorder and provides for precise speed control. Digital audio recorders don't require crystal sync, because digital audio runs the same speed as your digital picture files when set to the same frames-per-second recording.

TIP

A Nagra requires up to 12 batteries at a time, and those 12 batteries may have to be replaced every day. My advice is to move up to the new technology of digital audio recording and leave analog behind.

In the field with digital recorders

Digital field recorders are portable handheld recorders (about the size of a cell phone) with no moving parts. Audio is recorded onto a memory card or internal hard drive usually as BWF (broadcast wave format — an extension of WAV files) files. The audio files can then be transferred to an external hard drive. The ZOOM H5 Handy Recorder is an all-digital sophisticated handheld recorder that has dual stereo mic capsules attached (and can even be conveniently attached to your camera or a boom pole), or doubles as a separate digital recorder for plugging in external microphones. The recorder only requires 2 AA batteries (as opposed to the 12 D-size batteries for an old analog Nagra recorder). You can get more information on ZOOM digital recorders at www.zoom-na.com. Professional digital sound recorders can be expensive, anywhere from several hundred dollars to a few thousand dollars to buy.

Zoom also makes an affordable smartphone attachment, the iQ7, that virtually turns your iPhone or iPad into a professional digital recorder, which works alongside the Zoom Handy Recorder app from the App Store. (See Figure 12-1.) The app also allows you to immediately email the audio recording files to yourself or any email address, which you can then conveniently drop into your editing program.

FIGURE 12-1:
A zoom recorder and a smartphone zoom audio attachment and recording app.

If you're in Los Angeles, you can find sound houses that rent digital field recorders. If you're in a smaller town, you may find a local music equipment store that can rent you a digital recorder. If you hire a professional sound mixer, chances are he'll have all his own equipment, including a sound recorder and a set of appropriate microphones.

Sound mixers used to lug all their sound equipment on a sound cart. Today, unless your mixer is using an older analog Nagra, they no longer need to push and pull around an awkward cart. Some sound mixers just hand-hold their digital recorders, because they're light and portable, or just rest them on the nearest flat surface. Some sound mixers attach straps to their recorders for convenience; others attach their lights or heavier recorders to a vest like the Stingray Harness by K-Tek (www.ktekpro.com).

REMEMBER

You don't have to worry about buying or renting a digital field recorder if you're shooting with a digital camera. You can plug your sound directly into your camcorder and you'll get pristine high-quality sound married to your digital footage. Just remember to monitor your audio meters so they don't over-modulate. But, the advantage of having a separate audio recorder and sound mixer is having a dedicated sound person constantly monitoring and adjusting the audio for the best recording.

REMEMBER

WAV stands for *waveform audio format.* This is the type of uncompressed file format that sound is digitally recorded to for television or motion picture productions. BWF files (broadcast wave format) is a form of WAV files that is also used with certain digital audio recorders. Audio files can be recorded to a hard drive, memory card, or CD/DVD data discs. AAC (advanced audio coding) audio files are compressed (smaller files than WAV) and though they don't contain as much information as uncompressed WAV files, AAC files take up less memory and are almost as good as WAV files (but have some slight loss in quality) if you need to save on storage space. MP3 (MPEG audio player 3) is another sound format that is more synonymous with music files but the files are compressed, making them smaller, and like ACC they have some loss in quality — so you should stick with WAV files for your movie. It is a lossless format that does not compromise your audio.

Recording with Microphones

Recording crisp, clear dialogue is an art because sound is a very sensitive element, moving in waves similar to the circular ripples that spread out when you drop a rock in water. Recording these sound waves — as dialogue or other audio elements — so that they can be heard with optimum quality requires the proper microphone. If you're shooting on digital, you can plug the appropriate external microphone directly into the camcorder for better audio-recording results and override the camcorder microphone.

Dialogue, background sounds, crowd noise, or a live musical performance all require a different type of microphone. And a sound mixer is trained to know which type of microphone is appropriate for each situation. The sound mixer's arsenal of microphones includes

>> Shotgun microphone (a directional microphone hearing audio from the direction of which the microphone is pointed)

>> Omni-directional microphone (picking up audio from all directions)

>> Lapel (lavaliere) microphone (concentrated on the person on which it is clipped to)

The following sections describe how these microphones work.

REMEMBER

Every type of microphone has a *listening pattern* that determines from which direction the microphone hears sound. For example, if you have a shotgun or directional microphone, its listening pattern is that of a narrow tube; it hears only what's directly in front of it. Anything outside this directional pattern can't be heard clearly by this type of microphone. Figure 12-2 shows what the listening patterns look like for omni-directional and directional microphones. You can often find an illustrated pattern of your microphone's listening pattern in the manual that comes with it.

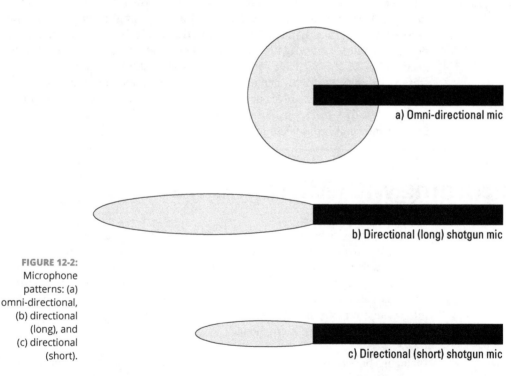

FIGURE 12-2: Microphone patterns: (a) omni-directional, (b) directional (long), and (c) directional (short).

All types of microphones can usually be rented from your local instrument music store or a sound rental house, if you have one in your area.

REMEMBER

The microphone that comes attached to your camcorder is not very good for professional sound recording. The main reason is that many camcorders have an omni-directional mic that picks up sound not just in front of the camera but from the sides and behind. That means the mic will pick up everything — from you behind the camera whispering to yourself, to Joe flushing the toilet in the next room. That's why most camcorders have an input to plug in an external microphone. The microphone that comes attached to your camcorder is usually appropriate only for recording events such as parades, birthday parties, vacations, and family get-togethers — but definitely not for professional use such as a feature film or movie short.

Shooting with shotgun (directional) microphones

A *shotgun microphone* resembles Han Solo's light saber, only it doesn't light up — and it doesn't make a very good weapon. This type of microphone should be mounted in a shock mount holder (suspended by rubber bands or flexible plastic mounts (similar to the way your car's suspension works) for shock absorption. The shock mount should also have a shoe for attaching the microphone onto a boom pole, camera, or tripod.

A shotgun is a *directional* microphone, such as the SGM-250 from Azden (www.azden.com) or the NTG3 by Røde (www.rode.com). A directional microphone picks up sounds directly in front of it, and it filters out sounds to the sides and back. It's like a bullet being shot from a gun — the line the bullet travels is the direction from which the microphone picks up sound. You use directional microphones to record actors' dialogue.

Shotgun mics come in two types:

>> **Long shotgun** has a long, narrow directional pattern that picks up sounds at a distance directly in front of the microphone, which is effective when actors are in a wide shot and the microphone can't get too close without ending up in the shot.

>> **Short shotgun** has a narrow directional pattern with a shorter reach for sounds closer to the microphone. This mic works well for medium and close-up shots when the microphone can be closer to the actors and still be out of the shot. This is the most common type of microphone used for recording actors' dialogue on-set. If you can only afford to buy or rent one, this is it!

TIP

A shotgun microphone (refer to Figure 12-3) is usually covered by a *windscreen* (a tube-shaped piece of foam that slides over the length of the microphone). On windy, outdoor shoots, you use a windscreen resembling a furry ferret (my dog's still trying to figure out what kind of animal it is) that absorbs wind before it hits the mic's sensitive diaphragm.

If you don't protect your microphone with a windscreen, you'll hear a shallow, soft banging from the air movement. A windscreen helps to absorb or filter out wind, as well as an actor breathing too closely to the mic. Additional stability is having the microphone float on a *shock-mount* to minimize microphone movement and any vibration.

FIGURE 12-3: Microphones: (a) the Røde camera mic with foam windscreen attached; (b) the Røde directional mic with a shock-mount and furry wind screen; (c) the Azden SGM-250 shotgun (directional) microphone.

Omni-directional mics

Omni means "all," and that's exactly what an *omni-directional* mic hears. Like the human ear, this mic is unable to decide which sounds to listen to and hears everything at once — and at the same volume level. Use omni-directional mics for events, crowds, plays, and environmental background recordings (see the sections "Recording with Microphones" earlier in this chapter and "Capturing On-Set Ambience" later in this chapter). Most built-in microphones on camcorders are omni-directional.

Lapel microphones

A lapel microphone (also known as a *lavaliere,* or *lav* on-set) can be worn on a lapel or cleverly hidden in a person's clothing, such as on a tie or in a pocket, sometimes behind the ear, and is small enough to not be intrusive. Wireless lapel mics are often used on actors for distant shots requiring dialogue. Most sit-down interviews on television and documentaries use lapel mics.

Røde (www.rode.com) makes a revolutionary wireless lavaliere microphone system called Wireless GO. Instead of using radio frequencies, which can often introduce hiss, buzz, or crackle interference, Wireless GO uses digital 2.4GHZ transmission — so you may never want to use wired microphones ever again! In the box, you'll find a lapel microphone transmitter, and a separate receiver that plugs in to your camera, or even to your smartphone. The batteries last about seven hours, and the range is up to 230 feet.

Wireless microphones

Shotgun and other microphone types (including lapel mics) can be wireless and work on radio frequencies, or the 2.4GHZ band that occupies the same space as Wi-Fi using the Wireless GO by Røde. Wireless mics can be used to pick up the actors' dialogue for distant shots, when a boom or mic cables would otherwise end up in the shot.

TIP

ON THE RØDE TO GREAT SOUND

Røde Microphones make a myriad of sound products, from professional microphones for feature films; handheld wireless mics for interviews and news reporting; and wireless miniature lavaliers for TV and film. Røde has a microphone for any situation and any budget (www.rode.com).

Røde microphones actually saved one of my productions from what could have been a disastrous situation. I had hired a professional sound mixer who had all the bells and whistles — directional mics, omni-directional microphones, wireless lavaliers, a fancy boom pole, and an expensive digital sound recorder. Ninety percent of her audio was unusable! Had I hired a deaf sound person? Actually, no — she just was not monitoring the sound or watching the audio meters, and apparently didn't know how to use her professional sound equipment properly. The wireless mics had static interference, the boom pole mics had rattling from the boom operator's hands, and the directional mics seemed to be pointed in the wrong direction! Thankfully, I had placed backup Røde

(continued)

(continued)

microphones on-set (backups are always a good idea) and plugged them directly into my camera. For some scenes where the actor's dialogue may have been too far away from my backup Røde microphones, the microphones still recorded a guidance track that could be heard and used for *looping* (replacing) any of the actor's dialogue in post-production. (See Chapter 16 for more on looping and ADR.)

Røde created a revolutionary wireless lavalier microphone using 2.4GHz digital transmission that occupies the same space as Wi-Fi. Using this digital technology, the Wireless GO lavaliers won't introduce interference, such as static, as regular lavaliers that depend on radio frequencies often do.

Even if you have a professional sound mixer on-set recording separate audio into a sound recorder for your production, it's always a good idea to have a backup microphone also recording audio on-set. You can use the on-camera microphone (don't ever turn it off) even if the actors are too far away for a clean recording, because it will record the actors' dialogue, which can be used as a guide to redo the dialogue in post-production (looping/ADR, see Chapter 16) should your sound mixer's recordings be unusable.

Using Your Headphones

You and your boom operator should always use professional cushioned *head-phones*, which cup the ear and block outside noise to make sure that your sound is coming through clearly and that there's no interference or buzzing on the line. You can use *earbuds* (which fit in the ear) such as apple's wireless AirPods, but you get a less accurate indication of the sound recording because some background noise still makes its way in. You can also find wireless Bluetooth headphones (like SkullCandy). I've used them on-set and during post-production, and I love not having to deal with dangling cords.

REMEMBER

Always verify your sound recording through headphones. At the start of each day's shoot, record some test audio and play it back in the headphones to make sure your microphone and recorder are working properly (this includes your camcorder's audio if you're shooting on digital and plugged directly into your camera). I've had too many shoots where I forgot to bring headphones or earphones, and just assumed that the camera was recording sound. One time, the microphone didn't have a battery and didn't record any audio. Another time, the external microphone wasn't plugged in properly to my camcorder; instead, the camera was picking up sound with the built-in camcorder mic, and you could hear everything in front of and behind the camera (all of it louder than the talent on camera). Mark my words, the audio gremlin is out to get you, so always double-check that your sound recording is working.

Walking and Talking: Walkie-Talkies on Set

Communication on-set between crew members is extremely important. Everyone is running around, and it's not always easy to find the grip or makeup person when you need them. That's where walkie-talkies come in handy. You would probably lose your voice after yelling back and forth on the set without them. Rather than rent expensive walkie-talkies, you can find some great long-range ones (up to three miles) on Amazon for under $30.

TIP

Nowadays, you can use the same two-way radio technology of walkie-talkies — but instead with your smartphone. Zello and Intercom are two great walkie-talkie apps that turn your smartphone into a handy two-way radio walkie-talkie on-set. With these apps, you can even use your earphones or AirPods to monitor the channel and keep aware of all set instructions. This is much more convenient than making a phone call or texting a crew member every time you need them. Also, the walkie-talkie apps let the entire crew (who have the app) hear instructions at the same time:

>> Communicating at a distance with crew who can be scattered about

>> Driving scenes (when the camera and the actors are in separate vehicles)

>> Helicopter shots (for communicating with the ground crew)

>> Signaling the police (or an assistant) to hold traffic or pedestrians during a shot

Listening for Quiet

In addition to the windscreens used with shotgun microphones to keep the wind from becoming part of your film's soundtrack (refer to the earlier section "Shooting with shotgun (directional) microphones"), sound teams use additional equipment to ensure that the actors' dialogue comes through loud and clear.

Shushing the camera: Barney hears you

A *blimp* or *barney* is a casing that fits snuggly over the film camera magazine containing the film stock to muffle the sound of the camera cranking the film along — kind of like a silencer for the camera. If you shoot with a digital camera, you don't have to use a barney because digital cameras are completely silent.

Silencing footsteps with sound blankets and foot foam

If you have actors walking on hardwood floors or concrete, especially women in high heels, you need to put *sound blankets* on the floor. Sound blankets are like the heavy padded sheets used in moving vans for covering furniture. Sound blankets soften and absorb the sound of the actors' footsteps on a bare floor, preventing the actors from stepping on their lines — literally. These blankets absorb errant sound waves and prevent your dialogue from sounding tinny or picking up too much reverberation. Of course, you only put sound blankets on the floor when the actors' feet are not in the shot. You can also drape sound blankets over vertical stands or hang from the walls to help absorb reverb off bare walls.

REMEMBER

Actor's footsteps are added in post-production, when you do *foley* (see Chapter 16). You rarely use the actor's footsteps from the actual shoot.

A thick comforter can be substituted if you don't have access to professional sound blankets. You can also purchase *foot foam* from a sound rental company, or easily order over the Internet. This product is a foam rubber or felt backing of varying thickness that can be cut and adhered to the bottom of your actors' shoes, enabling them to walk on hard surfaces without making excessive noise and allowing the camera to show their feet as well.

TIP

If you're on a limited budget, you can silence your actors' shoes by using double-sided tape to attach thin pieces of carpet or underpadding to the bottoms of their shoes. Applying the soft fuzzy side of Velcro to the bottom of footwear is another good trick (and it comes with adhesive backing). Be mindful of what surface your actors walk on, and use non-slip rubber instead of Velcro or carpet on the bottom of their shoes if you think there's a possibility of slipping.

ACOUSTICS AND CARPETING

Recording sound in a gymnasium or a house with hardwood floors makes it difficult to record proper sound without getting a tinny sound or reverb. The sound bounces off the reflective surfaces like radar. If you have a choice, shoot your scenes in carpeted rooms or be prepared to put down sound blankets. Also, hang some blankets or foam sheets over stands to absorb some of the sound that bounces off the walls and floor.

Slating with the clapper board

Slating is a familiar sight to most people, although many probably don't know what it's for. A person with a black-and-white board, called a *clapper board,* stands in front of the camera and says something like, "Scene 1, Take 3," claps the board down creating a loud "clap," and then ducks out of the way. Slating not only visually identifies the scene number, shot number, and production information (required for the editor), but it also is used to sync up picture to sound when using a film camera or separate audio with a digital camera (as explained in the following section).

When shooting motion picture film and separate sound (or digital and a separate audio recorder), you sync up picture to sound by matching the sound of the clapper clapping down with the image of the clapper board completely closed in the first frame. Syncing the clap with the picture in this one frame marries the sound and picture and puts it perfectly in sync.

TIP

If you've misplaced your clapper board or can't afford one, you can clap your hands together (just once — don't applaud!) to give a sync mark to match the sound to the picture. You won't be able to identify the scene number and shot number, though, unless you announce it or write it on your hand each time. Even better, check out the myriad of clapper board apps such as ClapperPod SP or NoBusSlate.

Syncing picture and sound with timecode

Timecode is a series of electronic-generated numbers — hours, minutes, seconds, and frames (for example, 01:28:22:06) — each representing a specific frame of your movie when recorded into digital files or when transferred from film onto tape or digital files. Even if you have thousands of frames in your film, after it's transferred to tape or recorded onto digital media (smart cards or hard drive), each frame has its own personal identification number that can be punched into a computer to pinpoint that specific frame. These timecode numbers are generated on BWF-compliant audio files (explained in the earlier section "In the field with digital recorders").

REMEMBER

Timecode numbers can be used to sync shots (which is quicker than eyeballing the clapper board and matching it with the sound of the clap) if you're using a *timecode slate* (a clapper board that displays the timecode numbers read from a timecode audio recorder). You simply punch in the timecode numbers displayed on the special timecode slate, and the picture and sound automatically sync up.

TIP

There are also special software plug-ins that can actually sync up your dialogue when you don't have a shot slated with a sync clap. Red Giant software (www.redgiant.com) has Plural Eyes, a plug-in that can match the visuals of your audio waveform of your actors' dialogue (even if it's low or badly modulated) to the visuals of your professional recorded waveform. It's like matching up and replacing an original document over a bad photocopy.

Capturing On-Set Ambience

Ambience is the background sound of a particular environment. These distinctive, individual sounds accentuate a scene and help dialogue and sound effects blend together, while smoothing out the soundtrack to sound rich and full. You need to record ambient sounds just as you do dialogue.

While shooting on location, the sound mixer usually has the cast and crew be quiet for a moment or so and records *room tone* (recording outside ambience is called a *presence track*). An omni-directional microphone, as opposed to a directional microphone, works well for recording ambient sounds. Room tone can include the low hum of an air-conditioner, the almost inaudible sound of a refrigerator, or ocean waves. The ambient sound can then be *looped* (repeated over and over in post-production) and layered under the dialogue, which is recorded separately, to create a realistic-sounding scene. Ambient sounds can include:

>> **Factory:** Sound of machines whirring and air-conditioning buzzing

>> **Carnival:** People laughing and tinny carnival music playing

>> **Library:** People whispering, pages turning, clock ticking (yes, even a quiet library has ambient sounds)

>> **Freeway:** Sound of bustling traffic and horns honking

>> **Meandering stream:** Sound of water babbling and birds chirping

>> **Restaurant:** People talking and utensils clattering

>> **Park:** Sounds of children playing, dogs barking, birds chirping

TIP

If you can't afford to shoot in an actual restaurant, you can fake it right in your own house or apartment. Set up a corner with a table and chairs and add ambient sounds that you've recorded at a busy restaurant. Maybe have a friend, wearing an apron, walk past the frame. When you add the ambient restaurant sounds in post-production, it will seem like your actors are in a corner of a busy restaurant. Just don't pull back with the camera and reveal your dog sitting on the stairway anxiously waiting for table scraps!

Reporting Your Sound

Sound reports are production forms that the sound mixer fills out. They provide information about the audio recorded on-set, including which audio tapes or digital files contain which sound takes. Making sure that sound reports are filled out properly is critical for providing precise notes to the editor when matching up the sound to the picture (if you didn't record directly into the camera, but instead used a separate audio recorder). You can get sound report forms where you rent your sound equipment (or find lots of free templates online), but your sound mixer will probably have them, too. Of course, you can also create your own on your computer using Excel or any word-processing program.

TIP

I recommend you always back up your sound files, whether you're recording to analog audio tape or to digital files on a hard drive or memory cards. It's inexpensive to clone your audio files to a backup drive or transfer your sound files to CD or DVD discs. Audio files are usually not large files, at least not like video files. Just as you should back up your computer files for security, you should back up your sound files without exception. Better safe and "sound" than sorry.

Chapter **13**

Directing Your Actors: . . . And Action!

When I was 8 years old, I was fascinated with magic and puppets. Then I picked up my dad's Super-8 movie camera and learned to manipulate my puppets on camera. The magic of filmmaking! Actors are kind of like puppets, and the director is the puppeteer pulling the strings through the magic of the movie camera.

The independent filmmaker in the world of low-budget filmmaking is sometimes a triple-threat — producer, director, and writer. So when I talk about the "director," I'm referring to the filmmaker as well. Chances are you're at least one of these — or possibly all three.

This chapter uncovers the secrets of working with actors after you've cast them in your movie. Your actors will look to you, the director, for advice and guidance. Discover how to create a comfortable environment in which the actors' trust you. Find out how to speak the actors' language, explore the story's subtext, and define each character's backstory with your cast. See how *blocking* (where your actors move on-set) can enhance a scene, and discover how to pull the best performances from your actors.

Getting Your Actors Familiar with the Material — and Each Other

The director's job is to understand the script and to make sure that the actors comprehend the overall story and how the characters they're playing fit into it. You as director need to discuss certain things with each actor to make the character clearer in the actor's mind:

>> **The character's goals:** What drives or motivates the character and makes him or her tick?

>> **The *subtext* (what the character isn't saying):** What is the character saying indirectly (not through right-on-the-nose dialogue)?

>> **The *backstory* or *ghost* (the character's past):** How is the character affected by his or her upbringing?

>> **Idiosyncrasies of the character:** Does the character have any unique quirks — special personality traits that stand out and make him or her different?

>> **The introversion or extroversion of the character:** How would the character behave in a situation? (Would the character step back or step forward?)

>> **The character's dress and grooming style:** Is the character neat or a slob? Does he or she care?

>> **The character's views on life:** Does the character have strong opinions? Is the character a leader or a follower?

>> **The theme of the story as it relates to the character:** Is accomplishing the goal necessary to the character's survival?

I talk more about helping actors prepare for their characters in the section "Preparing Your Actors before the Shoot" later in this chapter.

Remembering that familiarity breeds content

The director's first job is to make the actors feel comfortable because the actor/director relationship determines whether the performances and relationships on screen are believable.

An ensemble show like *The Big Bang Theory* had a successful cast that worked perfectly together — they really were friends, even after working together for so many seasons. But when making a movie, you don't have the luxury of the cast getting to spend a lot of time together, so arranging a few informal gatherings for your cast is a good idea. A launch party for the movie is always a good idea because it gives everyone a chance to meet and greet before starting work on the film. Dinner with the main cast, coffee, or even a walk around the block helps break the ice and can make a big difference when the actors do scenes together. I once set up a ping-pong table off-set so the actors could play a fun game between takes, which is a great way to get to know someone and let loose.

Reading through the script: The table read

The *table read* is an informal get-together for the cast and director (and other prime production people) in which they sit down at a big table and read the script from beginning to end. This is the first time you'll hear the script come to life — kind of like a radio drama without the sound effects and music — and it's an important stage during which the actors are heard together in one sitting. Have the actors read through the script several times and study their characters before coming to the table read.

REMEMBER

The whole cast should be at the table read. This is the one rare occasion when the entire cast and the director are in the same room together. Because most films are shot out of context, it also may be the only time the actors hear the story from beginning to end, giving them, and you, a sense of the story's continuity. This helps the actors make choices and understand the story better when on the set and shooting a scene out of context. The actors can refer back to the table read and know what came before and what follows after.

During the table read, you hear what works and what doesn't. If it's a comedy, does everyone find it funny? This is also the opportune time to answer questions from the cast as they read through the script together.

Adjusting dialogue to make it read naturally

Often, a screenplay contains dialogue that doesn't quite sound natural because the writer couldn't try it out with real actors. If an actor is uncomfortable saying a line, you should probably change it — you don't want an awkward performance that doesn't come across as believable. Use the table read, discussed in the preceding section, to discover and correct these types of problems instead of waiting until you're on the set. The table-read may also spark some additional ideas, in addition to dialogue adjustments, that you may want to make a note of.

Being a Parent and Mentor to Your Actors — with No Allowance

Actors work from inside their character and can't see how their performance is being perceived. Even the most successful actors need guidance from their director. Many actors admit that they're like lost children: They are vulnerable, sensitive, a little insecure, and open to guidance — all assets of a great actor.

Above all else, to get the proper performance, trust must exist between you and the actors. The more the actors trust you, the more they will allow you to dig in deep and pull great performances out of them. The actors also need to respect you as they would a parent and a mentor. Without the actors' respect, gaining their trust and getting great performances from them is very difficult.

REMEMBER

A director needs to understand actors. Read about acting. Observe acting classes and study actors in films and on TV. Doing so conditions you to appreciate where an actor is coming from. Empathizing with your actors more helps you make better choices when directing your actors. Also, check out the book *Breaking into Acting For Dummies* by Larry Garrison and Wallace Wang (published by Wiley) to get a better handle on the actor's side of things.

LIFE'S A STAGE

We've all been actors at least once in our lifetime. At the age of 7, you probably put on your best performance for that trip to the ice-cream shop or feigned a temperature to get out of going to school. Remember that dramatic temper tantrum at 6, when you had to go to the dentist or get your hair cut? When you were young, you had no inhibitions and you weren't self-conscious — that's why children often make great actors. Kids are great at make-believe.

Actors are really just hypnotizing themselves into believing that they are the character in the screenplay. (In high school, I tried hypnotizing all the girls in my history class, but it didn't work).

What about in the courtroom? The lawyers who present their cases, and their clients — guilty or not guilty — often pour out believable performances to influence the judge and jury. Many people who are psychosomatic actually get sick because they've convinced themselves that they're sick. The mind is a powerful thing. William Shakespeare said, "Nothing is good or bad, but thinking makes it so." If you believe it, it must be true. An actor can use this power of the mind when adapting a character.

REMEMBER

The actor should be treated with respect. A director gives guidance and support. The director is *not* a dictator!

Preparing Your Actors before the Shoot

You've done the table read and, if you're lucky, you have a little time to work with the actors one-on-one before everyone sets foot on the set. Preparing your actors includes rehearsing, but rehearsing is only a small part of the preparation. You need to share tips and tricks with the actors so that they give the best and most believable performances in your movie.

As explained earlier in this chapter, the director makes sure that the actors understand the characters' goals, desires, and purposes in each scene. The actors and director need to be on the same page and agree on the meaning of each scene.

REMEMBER

Casting is half the game. A director shouldn't have to teach actors to act. A director should guide and give direction only. It's up to the actors to come to the set as professionals and know how to utilize an actor's tools. See Chapter 8 for details about casting the right actors in your production.

Rehearsals, yea or nay?

Preparing your actors for the shoot involves some form of rehearsal. You can repeat each scene until it feels right. Or you can do exercises and give tips to loosen up the actors. Rehearsing can mean having the actors — especially those who have a friendship or association on screen — spend time with each other in order to become more comfortable around one other. It can be *blocking* the actors' movements for the camera (see the section "Blocking, walking, and talking" later in this chapter) and coming up with the right *business* for each actor in each scene (see the section "Taking care of business" later in this chapter). If you do rehearse with your actors, remember that the purpose of rehearsing is to make the planned look unplanned.

WARNING

Too much rehearsing can take away a scene's freshness and spontaneity. Steven Spielberg, like many other directors, is apparently not a big fan of rehearsing too much. The other problem with over-rehearsing is that if you see a better choice for blocking, dialogue, and so on during shooting, it may be hard for the actors to change what they've conditioned themselves to do during rehearsals.

Sometimes you can use *not* rehearsing to your benefit. One of my films featured a comical musical number spoofing *Pirates of the Caribbean,* and I wanted it to be a funny uncoordinated dance number. My sister Marlene asked when we were rehearsing, and I told her we weren't!

REMEMBER

Not every scene needs a rehearsal, just like not every scene needs to be storyboarded (see Chapter 9 for more on storyboarding). Don't beat a scene to death. As a director, I like to let the actors give their rendition of the performance first — that gives me something to mold and shape.

Some actors require a lot of rehearsal, and others prefer very little. An actor may need rehearsals even if the director doesn't like to rehearse. Some actors' performances get better the more they rehearse, and some get worse (they become less believable, and their performance becomes flat and mechanical). An actor's training and experience can determine how much rehearsal time, if any, he or she requires. Some seasoned actors, such as James Earl Jones, who played a Canadian judge in my film *Undercover Angel,* are consummate professionals and require very little direction and no rehearsal for the role. (See Figure 13-1.) By being observant, you can see whether the actors need time to warm up or if they're up to speed on the first take.

TIP

When you rehearse with your actors, allow them to hold something back from their performance. Have them save a freshness for the camera.

FIGURE 13-1:
James Earl Jones being directed by the author on the set of *Undercover Angel* (Stellar Entertainment).

Rehearsing the characters, not just the lines

The actors should think about the characters they're playing, not just the words they say. An actor needs to imagine himself or herself as the character and figure out what the character wears, what the character's opinions are, and how the character reacts in certain situations. An actor can rehearse a character while driving, having lunch, and so on without having to study the script or the character's dialogue.

As the director, you can direct the actors to inject their personality into the characters — to imagine their blood pumping in the characters' veins. Encourage them to become their characters, to pull their characters off the page and bring them to life!

Actors should study people's quirks and idiosyncrasies and find little unique traits to add humanity and dimension to the characters they play. Frank Abagnale, Leonardo DiCaprio's character in *Catch Me If You Can,* always peels the labels off bottles, telegraphing his nervousness and youthful energy. It also shows Tom Hanks's FBI agent, Hanratty (who knows of Abagnale's label-peeling habit), that Frank is nearby. My friend Donald Petrie, who directed *Miss Congeniality,* was with Sandra Bullock at dinner one night when she laughed and let out a loud snort. Don told her that would be great for her character — and it ended up in the film.

PROMPTING DIALOGUE

Sometimes an actor needs help delivering a speech during a scene, reciting a lot of words and facts that are difficult to memorize, or, if you're shooting a documentary or infomercial, talking into the camera. The solution? A teleprompter.

You see actors reading off teleprompters all the time on TV. All the awards shows prompt the actors with their intros and presentations, and most times when you see a political candidate or a host talking into the camera, chances are, they've never memorized a word they're saying — they're reading it word for word off a teleprompter screen. That's why you often see the talent squinting or putting on their distance glasses before they start talking.

PromptSmart is a really cool smartphone app that lets you email or paste a script into the App on your smartphone. The app displays the words of your script in virtually any size font, lets you control the speed of the scroll, change the colors, and so on. It even has voice-control and scrolls as you speak! You can also download it to your iPad or

(continued)

(continued)

tablet – or even better, mirror your smartphone with the teleprompter app to a large TV screen for easier viewing. You can find the PromptSmart app for free by going to your smartphone's app store. So get going, be smart — and prompt!

Caddie Buddy makes a convenient, affordable and portable teleprompter device to work with any teleprompter app. It works with most digital cameras (DSLRs, camcorders, smartphones) and sets up in minutes. The teleprompter glass reflects your script off your tablet or smartphone in front of the camera (to which it is invisible, but your actor can read the text while looking into the camera lens). I think this is a must-have for anyone who makes YouTube videos, documentaries, instructional videos, or any other video in which they look into the camera as if talking directly to their audience. Check out this great teleprompter at www.caddiebuddy.com and click on Teleprompter.

Discovering the characters' backstories

Backstory is the history of a character. It's also referred to as the *ghost*. What haunts the character from childhood? What kind of family did he have? What type of upbringing? What skeletons does the character have in his closet?

The director should encourage each actor to imagine and develop the ghost of his or her character, but the actor doesn't need to share it with the director as long as the history works for the actor and helps bring dimension to his or her performance. The backstory can become the actor's personal secret, making the fictional character more real to the actor.

TIP

I'm sure you've seen stories of well-known actors who, in order to portray real-life characters, actually meet and follow that person around to study them (of course, only if they're still alive!). Julia Roberts studied and met with Erin Brockovich for the movie of the same name. Sandra Bullock met with Leigh Anne Tuohy, and ended up winning an Academy Award for her portrayal of her in *The Blind Side*. Jennifer Lawrence studied Joy Mangano, the inventor of the Miracle Mop, for the movie *Joy*. Christian Bale studied footage of Dick Cheney before he was dramatically and unrecognizable transformed through extensive prosthetic makeup into the former vice president for the movie *Vice*.

REMEMBER

Knowing the backstory or ghost helps an actor make dramatic choices for the character during each scene when decisions need to be made. For example, if Jonathan was abused as a child, now as an adult he may flinch every time someone makes a sudden move around him.

Reading between the lines: Subtext

Subtext is what's being said between the lines. Rarely does a multidimensional character say things right on the nose (although they do it all the time in bad scripts). Subtext is an element that an actor's character will probably deliver through many passages of dialogue. It's important for the director to make sure that every actor understands the subtext of the scene.

Subtext is relayed onscreen through the actors' body language and the dialogue metaphors that their characters choose during the scene. When a character says that she doesn't mind, does she? When Sally says she's really happy that Noah's getting married, is she *really* happy for him? What does her body language tell us as we see her twisting a paperclip into a pretzel as she says, "Everything's fine"?

In *The Big Picture,* Kevin Bacon's character, Nick, is making lunch for his girlfriend, Susan (Emily Longstreth), whom he broke up with earlier in the film. The two are talking about their grilled-cheese sandwiches, but the dialogue and action in the scene are actually revealing the subtext of them starting up their relationship again. In *San Andreas,* Dwayne Johnson's character, Raymond, reminisces with his ex-wife, Emma (Carla Gugino), about all the good times they had together. The subtext shows us they still have feelings for each other and telegraphs that they might just get back together when the shaking stops.

Exercising and warming up your actors

Much like going to the gym, actors need to warm up both physically and mentally before getting into the real workout of shooting their scenes. Stretching limbers up the body, and doing breathing exercises opens up the mind. Many actors forget to breathe properly before starting their scenes. It's amazing what a few deep breaths can do to calm an actor before performing a scene or getting into character.

Keeping it natural, naturally

TIP

A great exercise is to have your actors whisper their lines in rehearsal and then perform the scene again using normal volume. Overacting is much harder when you whisper, and it's always easier to bring up a performance than to bring it down. Bruce Willis was very believable in *The Sixth Sense,* and he virtually whispered his whole performance.

Another thing to note is the distance between your actors. If they're in close proximity to each other, they don't need to raise their voices for everyone in the room to hear. I was working with two actors who were speaking too loudly across a table, which made the performance unnatural. So I told them to pretend they were in a busy restaurant and didn't want anyone eavesdropping on their conversation. It worked like a charm. Lowering their voices toned down their overacting.

TIP

I discovered an exercise that helps actors act more naturally. If you're not getting a realistic performance from your actors, give each one a yo-yo. Have them recite their lines while trying to do tricks with the yo-yo. It's some kind of left brain, right brain (no brain) exercise that I've found takes the actors' minds off trying too hard. Then when they put the yo-yos away, they return to a more natural delivery of lines.

Improving through improvisation: "I made that up"

An excellent exercise to get actors to think beyond what's written in the script and delve into what a scene is really about is to have them ad-lib or improvise the scene. Doing the scene without the script — just making up what the scene is about — helps the actors feel the emotion and sense of the scene and really think about what they are talking about, as opposed to reciting memorized lines. When you feel that the actors have gained some insight by improvising, have them follow the script again.

Acting is reacting

Many actors are too focused on anticipating their lines and don't listen to the other actors. But acting is like ping-pong or tennis: You have to react to the ball coming at you or you miss it every time. Speechless characters can be just as intriguing in films as those who speak. A good example is Elisa, a mute character in Guillermo del Toro's *The Shape of Water*. Without dialogue, a character is a sounding board for another character, and someone who communicates through her physical expression, which can be as powerful as her verbal expressions. Good actors emote without saying a word.

TIP

As a director, become more aware about how you act and react to things every waking hour. Acknowledge how everyday things affect your emotions. This sensitizes you to how an actor works. Which emotions are verbalized and which ones are shown through expression? Which ones are subtle and which ones are over the top? Use these feelings to help get your thoughts across to your actors when directing them.

Speaking with body language

Have your actors study body language. An actor not only speaks with words but with his or her body. Body language can be very powerful. People cross their arms when they're shy or being defensive. They slump when they're feeling down or have no energy. People move differently when they flirt. Next time you're streaming or watching a movie on TV, turn the sound off and notice the actors' body language. It's a universal language without words. Notice how you can even tell how a dog is feeling by its body language — is it happy and wagging its tail, or lethargic and acting depressed?

Remind your actors that true character is revealed more by what a character's actions are when he or she is alone than when around others. The tough biker enters his apartment, sits down next to his cat on the couch, and pets the animal in a very caring manner — showing a sensitive side that no one sees when he's in public.

Directing Actors during the Shoot

Directing actors on-set involves more than just helping them perform in character. It includes telling them where to move within the frame, giving them proper direction and motivation for the scene, and answering any questions that help the actor better his or her performance. The actor should trust you and look to you for guidance.

Never yell at your actors. If an actor is doing a scene incorrectly or not to your satisfaction, take him or her aside quietly and discuss the situation in private. Do not correct or critique an actor's performance in front of the rest of the cast and crew — at least not so anyone can eavesdrop. The actor will appreciate the fact that you discuss direction in private. Actors especially are self-conscious. You don't want to embarrass them in front of the rest of the cast and crew or upset them and have to deal with a moody actor who won't come out of his trailer.

Encouraging your actors to ask questions — but not too many

You want your actors to feel that they can ask questions because you don't want them second-guessing things on the set. But if an actor gets too dependent on the director and asks questions before every take, encourage the actor to start trusting his or her performance and answer some of those questions on his own. To keep the need for questions to a minimum, be specific in your directions. Ambiguous directions can cost extra takes when an actor misunderstands you.

Remind the actors before shooting a scene where the scene is in the story and what came before it, especially if you're shooting out of order. Doing so helps the actor recall how she felt in the scene before this one and match her emotions to reflect the former scene. If Mary was sullen in the last scene because Gary had to fly out of town, then Mary would still be holding her feelings in the next scene.

Reminding your actors that less is more — more or less

Sometimes it's better for actors to do less in terms of expression and emphasis in their dialogue. They should feel the emotion and let their body language and tone set the mood (but without exaggerating their body movements either — like waving their arms around or using their hands too much when talking).

Stage actors have to *project* their performance to a live audience, which involves emphasizing dialogue and increasing volume because the audience is at a distance. Yet when an actor projects in front of a camera, the performance can come across as stagy or not believable. A camera can pick up subtle emotional clues: a blink, a tear in the eye, or a simple twitch. So giving less is more in film. Let the projector project, and not the actor.

I once read a newspaper review of a film that said, "Great acting!" To me, that's a contradiction. Great acting should be invisible. Last time I was in an office store, I complained to the store clerk that I couldn't find the invisible tape. Get the idea? If it's invisible, you shouldn't see it.

TIP

When it comes time for an actor to let loose for a big scene, make sure that you keep that actor fresh until the big moment. Save an actor's emotional performance for the close-up. If you know that you're going to go into a close-up when the actor wells up with tears, you don't want the actor to give her best performance in the wide shot. You still want to shoot the wide shot, so your editor can cut into the close-up.

Also make sure that your actors flow each mood into the next. They'll need your guidance on this. When happiness turns to anger, the audience needs to see it building up — it can't just come out of nowhere. It's like a teapot coming to the point of boiling: It happens gradually until finally the steam shoots out under the pressure. When a singer carries a note higher and higher, it's a gradual ascension. A character would only "snap" from one mood to another if he were crazy or unstable.

Feeling the words, not just memorizing

What did you have for lunch three days ago? I can guarantee that you had to think about that. It took some *pre-thought.* Did you look down or away to catch your thoughts? As a director, remind your actors to use pre-thought when recalling things. Too many actors seem to roll off numbers and recall incidents without any pre-thought because they've memorized the script so well. They don't show that they're thinking — only acting.

ROBOTIC PERFORMANCE

Without an on-screen personality, an actor comes across as a robot, programmed to recite words without feeling or expression. Encourage your actors to bring their uniqueness to the role, to plug their own DNA into the character they're playing. Think of an actor as an empty computer with unlimited software choices. Look at successful and unique actors like Arnold Schwarzenegger, Steve Martin, Sandra Bullock, and Dwayne (The Rock) Johnson. All could have followed earlier advice to get rid of the accent, the white hair, the attitude, acting style, and so on, but they retained their own looks and personalities with great success.

Along those same lines, many actors enter a scene and put too much into a simple "hello." Direct your actors to have a more matter-of-fact delivery. Don't enter the scene saying "hello" like you've rehearsed it 100 times and it's the most important thing in the world.

Also make your actors aware if they're enunciating each word too perfectly. Precise enunciation is reserved for narration, professional speeches, and presentations. Let the actors run their words together. Many actors tend to put too much space between words to make sure that they're being clear, but it doesn't sound natural or believable in films — unless they're playing a newscaster in your movie.

Blocking, walking, and talking

Blocking is how the actors move on-set and how the camera covers that movement. The blocking for a scene is sometimes done in rehearsal, but sometimes it's done on the set just before shooting a scene (see Chapter 14).

Establishing blocking is like breaking down a scene into separate blocks. An actor moves first from the window to the table, then from the table to a chair, and then from the chair to the door. Movement keeps a scene from becoming too static and makes the actors' performances seem more real. In real life, people rarely stand or sit in one place too long. It's almost like coordinating a dance routine — without the dancing — unless you're shooting *La La Land*.

REMEMBER

The best time to decide on blocking is when you have the actors together for rehearsal, or on the set as the camera and lights are being set. Have the actors do their lines and see what motivates their movement. Often blocking comes automatically. It feels right for the actor to stand up at this point, or sit down, or move toward the window during a specific piece of dialogue.

Cheating is a technical term for framing things better for the camera, or for making the shot look more aesthetically pleasing — when an actor needs to turn slightly to one side for a better shot, for example, or when two actors need to move closer together to make a shot work. You cheat the lamp into the shot behind the actor's close-up so that it frames better in the picture, for example.

Taking care of business

An actor's performance is made more real when he or she is preoccupied with moving and doing *business*. Business is what actors do with their hands, or the action that occupies them while they're performing a scene, such as drinking, fiddling with keys, doing the dishes, or tidying up. A director usually gives each actor an idea for his or her business, but sometimes the actor has a good suggestion as well.

Business takes away from an actor's self-consciousness. It gives the actor something to do with his or her hands. Some actors use their hands too much, waving them all over the place. By holding a book, a pen, or a drink, the actor doesn't have to worry about what to do with her hands. It's a diversion, like the yo-yo exercise mentioned earlier in this chapter.

GORILLA TRAINING

Sometimes an actor has to wear heavy prosthetic makeup (like a mask) or a complete body costume, like a monster or gorilla suit. Body language can have a big impact on a performance, especially when makeup limits facial expressions.

I did a cameo in the film *Naked Gun 21/2,* playing a gorilla when Leslie Nielsen comes crashing out of the zoo entrance in a tank followed by runaway elephants, giraffes, and two gorillas. (The gorillas had to be actors in suits because using the real animals wasn't safe.) For a week, I studied the mannerisms and body language of a gorilla — I was in "gorilla" training!

In a full body suit, an actor has to project his emotions to reflect how the character is feeling. Anthony Daniels has performed in a tight robot suit throughout the *Star Wars* movies for over 40 years. Peter Mayhew played Chewbacca in a heavy, furry, wookiee costume and still stole audiences' hearts for over four decades. Nowadays, an actor's mannerisms and body language are often transferred to a computer-generated character using *motion-capture*, as was done with the Hulk in *The Avengers* movies, or even with Iron Man or Spider-Man in many of their action scenes.

Matching actors' actions

Make sure that your actors repeat the same blocking and business when filming from different angles. In post-production, the editor needs to cut the two angles together, and as long as the actor does the same thing in both shots, the editor can have a choice of where to make the cut. If an actor is talking and raises a coffee cup to his lips, it has to match other camera shots taken from another angle. The actor has to raise the cup at the exact same line of dialogue, or the two shots won't cut together properly (and this will really frustrate the editor, who may not be able to cut the two shots together smoothly). The script supervisor helps the actors remember what their actions were in each shot so they match when the scene is shot from a different angle. (You can find more on the script supervisor's assistance to the actors and director in Chapter 14.)

WARNING

Continuity mistakes can make a film look really unprofessional — even though the pros make them all the time. Out of all the actors I have worked with over the years, only my dog Little Bear has been able to match his actions consistently better than the human actors. Continuity means that things need to remain consistent from one angle to another, or the audience will get confused. A sandwich has to have the same bites taken out of it when covered from a different angle. An unwrapped present shouldn't still be wrapped in a different angle. In one shot in the movie *Fatal Attraction,* Glenn Close has unwrapped a present, but when the camera cuts to another angle, the present is still wrapped! If an actor exits one room wearing a blue shirt buttoned to the neck, he should enter the next room wearing the same blue shirt still buttoned to the neck.

Commending the actors

Giving your actors feedback after you shoot each scene is very important. An actor is always looking for a response — attention is one of the reasons people become actors. Actors often feel isolated and hurt if they don't receive acknowledgment.

If an actor doesn't receive any feedback from you, even a simple, "That was great," she'll feel that her performance didn't live up to your expectations. If you believe that your actors can do a better take, tell them, "That was good, but I know you can do better." Treat the actors delicately, and you'll get great performances from them.

REMEMBER

A professional and thoughtful director compliments the actors' work and encourages them to give the best performances possible, but rarely will an actor return the compliment. The filmmaker usually gets his praise at the film's premiere.

Chapter **14**

A Sense of Direction: Directing Your Movie

A director is an *auteur* — the true author of a film. The creative force behind the movie. He or she is not unlike a god, a creator, a leader who takes all the credit — or all the blame! If you as a filmmaker take on the task of the director, shaping and molding all the elements into a movie, your passion for the story should be undeniable; you'll be involved with it for quite some time. A director lives movies in the daytime and dreams movies in the nighttime.

This chapter breaks down the mystery behind what a director does to produce a movie. You see what makes a great director and how to translate a script to the screen. You discover the cinematic language of directors, from making decisions on the set to subtext, symbolism, and pacing.

You also find out when to move the camera (after all, it's a *motion* picture) and why, as well as what special equipment, including tripods, dollies, and cranes, helps you get the desired shot. Directing a film is a laborious task, so be prepared to run an exhausting, but exciting, marathon.

Focusing on Directing

The director of a movie must work closely with the actors in a creative capacity, pulling the best performances from them (see Chapter 13, which talks about directing actors). The director also needs to have some knowledge of the camera and lenses, and how to use them to set a mood and capture the magic in each scene. Having the final say on the locations, casting, script, and often editing of the final picture makes the director the keeper of the film and stamps it with his or her personal signature.

Directing traits

A director is a father, mother, psychologist, mentor, and ship's captain. To succeed in this role, you must be good at confidently giving directions in an authoritative manner — without being a dictator. Certain traits make for a successful director. Some people are born with these traits; others acquire them through observing and studying and learning to be more aware of everything around them. The following list of traits will help you be a better director:

>> **Being mentally strong:** The director needs to be emotionally and mentally strong in the sense that he can control his emotions. By keeping calm, the actors remain calm. If the director is uneasy, the actors pick up on this. It's very similar to a dog watching his master and sensing that something is wrong. It's important to be sensitive to the actors' needs. A director should also never lose his sense of humor (hopefully he has one in the first place!).

>> **Being a problem-solver:** A big part of a director's job is problem-solving — and doing it on the spot. You need to make decisions quickly and wisely, because not making a decision is a decision. Take a deep breath, make a decision, and move on.

>> **Setting the tone:** The director sets the tone on-set with the cast and crew. A friendly family atmosphere creates camaraderie among the cast and crew that is ultimately reflected in the final production. Actors often subliminally mirror their director. If the director is frantic, uptight, and nervous, the actors' performances are affected. If the director is confident, organized, and decisive, the actors feel a sense of security. And if the director earns an actor's trust, the actor is more willing to try different things.

As your film's director, you need to show confidence. You are the leader, and the cast (and crew) will look up to you.

REMEMBER

>> **Having an eye for detail:** A good director has an eye for detail and can visualize the screenplay as a moving picture even before setting foot on the set. The director can help the actor find little nuances, subtle expressions

to make his or her performance unique. When deciding on props and set design, the director looks for details that add character and dimension to be used in the scenes.

>> **Timing and pacing things right:** With the help of the script supervisor (see Chapter 7), the director makes sure that the shots and scenes are shot at a proper pace. The script supervisor carries a stopwatch and accurately times each shot to get a better sense of how long the scene will run on screen.

REMEMBER

The world tends to slow down on screen — probably because the audience's attention is concentrated solely on the screen and the camera doesn't blink. The director's job is to pace the movie by controlling the pacing of the actors' performances and the number of shots in each scene. The more shots in a scene, the faster the pace feels and the less it seems to lag.

Training yourself as a director

A director, no matter how experienced or successful, is a student of film. You are continuously learning and studying — experiencing life and bringing those experiences to your work. One of the most important things you can do to become a better director is to study films and cinematography to see how others tell their stories cinematically and figure out at least the basics of lenses and shot composition.

REMEMBER

Seeing what other directors do can trigger new and original ideas, especially if you study films in your genre (see Chapter 2 on film genres). That's why you should watch lots of movies — not to copy, but to be inspired. Here are a couple of tips to use when watching movies and TV shows:

>> **Read the script in closed caption.** One of my favorite things to do when I have time to watch TV or stream a movie is to view the closed-captioning. Doing so enables me to read the script on the bottom of the screen as the story unfolds. You can study performances (as well as camera moves) and see how the script is structured — literally.

>> **Watch a silent film.** I like to turn the sound off once in a while when watching movies (no one wants to watch films with me for some reason). Movies are all about motion. If a film is done right, you can tell what the story is about by the visuals. If you watch *Back to the Future, Jurassic World,* or *John Wick* with the sound off, for example, you get a sense of what the characters are going through, the emotions, and so on. If you watch a soap opera on TV and turn the sound off, though, all you get are talking heads — and no idea what's going on — unless someone pulls out a gun!

Here are some other things you can do that can translate into making you a more effective director:

>> **Read books (this includes e-books).** Read voraciously and on every topic; you never know what may come in handy.

>> **Watch people.** See how their moods affect their body language and how they react to strangers and to friends.

>> **Experience life.** Take in the world around you. The more experiences you have, the more original ideas you can bring to your films.

>> **Ask questions.** It's the only way to get the answers.

>> **Observe acting classes.** This is called *auditing*. See how acting coaches teach.

>> **Take classes.** Force yourself to study subjects you normally would have no interest in. When you take active interest in a topic, you'll be surprised at the curiosity it generates in you. For convenience, you can even enroll in online classes.

>> **Travel.** See the world and the lifestyles of other countries.

>> **Study paintings.** Look for inspiration in terms of composition and lighting. Take a trip to your local museum.

DIRECTING YOUR SLEEP, EXERCISE, AND EATING

Directing a movie is like going into battle (with a small army). You've got to be well prepared. Exercising, eating right, and getting plenty of sleep is crucial to being a strong director and leader on your film. You're training for a marathon and you need to get in shape and be alert with all your senses if you want to survive your shoot and make a great film. Even Steven Spielberg had a trainer/exercise coach in his earlier days to keep him in top shape to handle his strenuous directing duties.

Try to get at least some form of exercise — even if it's walking the dog around the block each morning. Cut down on sugar and any foods that have a lot of starches or carbs to avoid major sugar crashes. Use Uber Eats, Grub Hub, or Door Dash to order meals from your favorite healthy restaurants when you don't have time to cook or eat out.

Do your best. Sometimes I do have to give in to a Red Bull or other energy drinks when on a long and grueling shoot.

Translating Script to Screen

A screenplay is the blueprint of what ultimately becomes a motion picture. The director's task is to translate this blueprint to the screen — to "build" the movie. Each scene can be interpreted in many different ways, and if the director is not the screenwriter, he or she must understand what the writer is trying to say. The director also needs to fix any holes in the story, know how to translate words into visuals, and add or delete scenes to make the story stronger.

REMEMBER

As a director, you have to be passionate about the material — dissect it, understand it completely.

Understanding the screenplay

As a director, you need to understand exactly what the story is about and what the motivation and goals of each character are. A director looks at each scene and asks, "What's the purpose of this scene? What's the underlining reason — to impress the girl, to prepare for the big race?" Just as the actor asks the question, "How does this scene relate to my character?" the director asks a broader question, "How does this scene relate to the story as a whole?" Sometimes the director finds that the scene doesn't add anything to the story and ends up cutting it. Other times, the scene may need to be enhanced or another scene or two may need to be added before or after this particular scene to strengthen it and the story.

By asking questions, you're forced to seek the answers. This adds more dimension to the story and characters. It helps you make choices in your direction and step back to see the whole picture.

REMEMBER

A scene's underlying purpose is often revealed by subtext. *Subtext* is the meaning behind the words — it's reading between the lines. You need to understand not only what the characters are saying, but also what the subtext reveals. What does the scene really mean? How do the characters really feel? Subtext can mean the opposite of what a character says verbally. A character may say, "I hate you!" when his actions reveal the opposite emotion. Meaning conveyed through subtext can also be more powerful than meaning conveyed through dialogue. Instead of Karen saying she misses her daughter, it's much more effective to use a visual of her picking up her child's favorite doll and looking at it sadly.

Symbolism is a type of metaphor in which one thing is used to represent something else, such as an idea or an emotional state, or to convey a deeper truth. In cinema, visuals are often used symbolically and can be very powerful. In the screenplay

I adapted for *They Cage the Animals at Night* from the novel by Jennings Michael Burch, I incorporated symbolism in these ways:

>> Little Jennings is locked in his room with the same key that was used to lock the stuffed animals in the cabinet at night. In this instance, the use of the key symbolizes that Jennings is just like a caged animal.

>> The setting of the orphanage resembles a prison with barbed wire around it. Without ever stating the fact in words, the orphanage's setting symbolizes the imprisonment of the orphans.

Rewriting or adjusting the script

If the director isn't the screenwriter, he or she often embellishes the story and adds his or her own creative vision and style to the script. Enhancements to the script include adding or deleting scenes to support other scenes in the story, along with filling any holes in the story. In addition to strengthening the script in terms of better character development (Jimmy finally realizes he can do it on his own at the end) or story repairs (Sarah shouldn't run into Mark at the train station because it's too contrived to the story), you may also need to do some adjusting because of budget limitations.

As you're prepping the movie, you may find that consolidating several locations into one makes the production more economical. You also may find that you eliminate some of the secondary characters that aren't crucial to the story and save having to pay additional actors.

Visualizing your screenplay

After you've done your directorial homework of understanding the emotional and psychological aspects of the screenplay, you now must turn the words on paper into visual shots. As you read your screenplay with your visual mind open, certain portions will jump out at you, calling for a specific shot or a certain angle to express what's going on in that particular scene. Sometimes it's a simple *close-up* or *two shot* (see later in this chapter) or it's a dramatic image that calls out, like the powerful end shot in the original *Planet of the Apes* (1968) when the camera pulls back to reveal the Statue of Liberty half-submerged in the sand by the ocean's shore.

Translating the script into visuals is something that the director does alone, unlike the table read, which involves the entire cast (see Chapter 13 on actors). To get the creative juices flowing and to better understand the characters and story, isolate yourself from civilization and escape into the world of the screenplay.

TIP

Take a pencil and a ruler and partition the individual scenes in the script. Draw a solid line across the page at the beginning of each scene. A new scene always appears in all capitals and starts with *EXT.* or *INT.*, then the setting (i.e., a magic bookstore) and then is followed with either *DAY* or *NIGHT* (i.e., *EXT. MAGIC BOOKSTORE – NIGHT*). You can find tons of screenplay format examples and margin settings by searching the Internet for *screenplay formatting*. Separating your film into separate blocks makes tackling the scenes one at a time easier.

Mapping Out Your Plans for the Camera

Part of a director's homework includes making notes, sketches, or diagrams of how he or she envisions the shots in each scene. You can use various techniques to plan shots, including storyboards, written shot lists, schematics, notations on the script, and models.

Designing storyboards

Some directors start directing even before stepping onto the set by creating a comic-book version of their movie utilizing *storyboards*. Storyboards are visual frames that outline the composition of each shot. Some directors prefer to design shots with storyboards, but they require a lot of time and an artist's hand (although you can draw stick figures or use storyboard software). Other directors prefer to save storyboarding for special-effect shots and action scenes only (see Chapter 9 for more on storyboarding).

Creating a shot list

A shot list, sometimes referred to as a *dance card,* consists of written directions that describe the details of each shot. Usually, it is scribbled on index cards for convenience. Sometimes the director prepares the shot list well in advance, and sometimes it's done right before the next day's shoot. A shot list contains the scene and shot number, which the director checks off as shots are completed. Here's an example of a shot list for Scene 45 from my film *Undercover Angel* (more on types of shots in the section "Taking Your Best Shot" later in this chapter):

Harrison looks up from typewriter — **camera dollies** in for a **close-up.**

Jenny gets up and goes to the door — **camera follows** her and stops.

Harrison gets up — **camera leads** him to *Jenny* at the door.

Two shot — **over the shoulder** of *Harrison* talking to *Jenny.*

REMEMBER

As the director, you may want to do both a shot list and storyboard your scenes to illustrate the actual framing and position of the action.

Sketching schematics

Schematics show a basic floor plan with an overhead view of where the camera and actors will be placed for each shot within a scene. I use dotted lines with directional arrows showing actors' movement. If you have several camera angles, number each camera shot in the schematics to show exactly where the camera will be placed.

You can draw schematics on separate pieces of paper and numbered to each shot and scene or you can sketch them on the page opposite the scene in the screenplay. In Figure 14-1, the director's schematic shows the actor's position and direction of movement with the camera placement and movement as well. If you prefer to use a software program, FrameForge 3D (which I talk about in Chapter 9) not only creates virtual three-dimensional storyboards, but it also creates accurate overhead schematics of all your camera setups and even calculates the height and movement of your camera shots. Check it out at www.frameforge3d.com.

TIP

When planning your schematics, you can use different-sized coins (pennies, dimes, and nickels) to represent different actors and move them around on your hand-drawn or computer-generated floor plan. After you decide on the actors' movement within the scene, circle the coins in place and then choose the best camera placement to cover the action (but then put those coins into your budget — you're going to need every penny!).

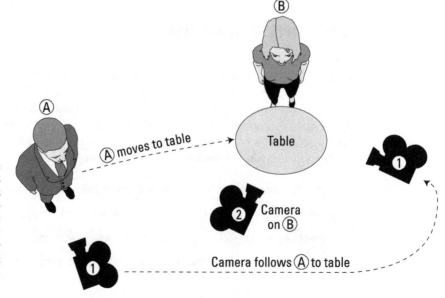

FIGURE 14-1: A director's schematic shows where the camera and actors are and shows any movement that takes place during the shot.

Making notes on the script

You can circle, box, underline, and highlight certain words in the script to show different instructions, such as when to use a close-up, dolly-in, or tracking shot. (See "Taking Your Best Shot," later in this chapter, for information about the different types of shots directors use.)

Planning with models (not the high-fashion kind)

To get a three-dimensional idea for your shots, you can place dolls or miniature plastic soldiers on a tabletop to find the best camera angles. Doing so helps you visualize where to position the actors to get the best coverage. Just be prepared to explain why you're playing with dolls when someone walks into the room unexpectedly.

Continuing Continuity with Your Script Supervisor

Directing a movie is like piecing a jigsaw puzzle together. It's up to the director and the script supervisor to make sense of it all (see Chapter 7 for information about hiring your crew). The *script supervisor* works alongside the director, keeping track of *continuity* (the logical order of things, actions, wardrobe, and characters that need to be consistent from shot to shot or scene to scene) and following the script to make sure that the director doesn't miss a scene or a planned shot.

REMEMBER

Forgetting a scene is very easy because a script is usually shot out of sequence. Without a script supervisor to mark the script and follow what has been shot, it's not uncommon for a scene or two to be forgotten. Even the lowest budgeted production should have a script supervisor. The director has enough things to worry about, and forgetting whether the actor exited right or left in the last shot is very easy to do — but it's the script supervisor's job to remember and make written notes of those types of details and more. The script supervisor can be the director's best friend (next to his dog).

Got a match?

The director sometimes has an actor repeat his actions so they match when the same action is shot from a different camera angle or with a different frame size. This is called *matching.* It's important for the actor to match his actions exactly so that the two shots can be cut together seamlessly, ensuring continuity. An effective way to cut shots together is during movement on camera; if an actor lifts a coffee cup to his lips in a wide shot, the filmmaker (or your editor) may choose to cut to a close-up of the cup coming up to the actor's lips. But the action must be repeated exactly in the wide shot and again in the close-up for it to match in the editing room. The script supervisor takes note of the actor's *business* (see Chapter 13) and reminds the actor to repeat the same action at the new angle.

Inserting coverage and cutaways

As the director, you should be versed in the power of coverage, cutaways, and inserts — and know the difference between them.

Coverage

Coverage is catching the same action from different angles so that the continuity of the shots is logical. It can be done with several cameras or, as is often done, by placing the camera at different angles and repeating the action.

TIP

When covering the action, the director needs to set a shooting ratio (and if you're shooting film, how much film stock to usable footage). An average shooting ratio on a low-budget film is 3:1 — three takes to get one good one. Setting a shooting ratio is important, because this lets you pace how much raw film stock you need to purchase (and what to budget for). If shooting to digital files, then you only need to be concerned about having a few SD memory cards to swap out (and erase and reuse) or the appropriate size hard drives, and how many. A production that is budgeted for 3 takes per shot needs to have approximately 270 minutes of film to end up with roughly a 90-minute finished film (3 takes at 90 minutes = 270 minutes of film stock needed). Again, this is all moot (and so much cheaper) if you're recording to digital files.

If you're shooting on digital, you have more leeway than film, because you can use SD memory cards over and over again (of course, after you download the recorded files to an external hard drive) — and you can even play back the shot right away to see whether it worked to your satisfaction and then decide if you want to try another take. If you're shooting on digital, you need to budget for at least two memory cards and a few external hard drives to store your final footage for editing.

Cutaway

A *cutaway* is a shot of something the actor looks at or something that is not part of the main shot — such as a clock on the wall or another actor's reaction to what's going on in the scene. You can use a cutaway to save a shot that doesn't work in one take and to hide what would otherwise end up being a *jump-cut* (the action appears to be missing frames and jumps). You can use part of Take 1 before the cutaway and the end of Take 2 after the cutaway, for example. If one actor is on the phone, you can cutaway to the person being spoken to on the other end. Cutaways are also used in interview situations: the guest speaks and then there's a cutaway to the interviewer nodding (this allows tighter editing of the guest's answers).

TIP

Use a cutaway after a gag to show a reaction. It helps to emphasize a funny moment for the audience, allowing them to share their reaction with an on-screen character. Showing a reaction also lets the audience know how to react to something if it can be interpreted in several ways. An effective use of a cutaway is the Wicked Witch in the *Wizard of Oz* watching Dorothy and her friends through a crystal ball. You can also use a cutaway to condense time — he walks toward the exit, cut to a cutaway of the cat watching him from the stairs, and then cut back to the actor now on the street and getting into his car.

Insert

An *insert* is similar to a cutaway, except that it's usually part of the same location where the dialogue or action is taking place, but often shot separately from the main shoot or after the actors have left the set. An insert is usually a close-up of a watch, a letter (like the one Harry Potter received notifying him he was accepted at the Hogwarts School of Witchcraft and Wizardry), or someone holding an object, like the remote control for the time-machine DeLorean that Doc operated in *Back to the Future*. When you do an insert of someone turning pages in a book, for example, or a close-up of a watch on a wrist, you can use someone other than your main actor if that actor's not available. Just remember to make sure the hands are alike: same gender, with a similar appearance, and wearing identical rings or jewelry.

Screen direction: Your other left

Screen direction is an important element to be aware of. If a car is driving right to left in one shot, the car should continue to travel in the same direction to its destination. If the camera crosses the *line of action* to the opposite side of the car and shoots it going left to right, the car will appear to be going in the opposite direction, as if it were heading back to where it started from. Paying attention to the line of action, also known as the *action axis* or *180-degree rule,* helps keep the direction of your actors and movement consistent so the audience doesn't get confused. When you watch a football game, notice how the cameras never cross the line; otherwise, it would look like the home team is running the wrong way!

When one actor speaks to her left, you expect the actor to whom she's speaking to look to his right. You create an imaginary line and keep all your elements on one side of the line or the other — but you have to remain consistent, otherwise you'll be *crossing the line* and the on-screen direction will be flipped. If you film both actors as though they're looking to their left, it will appear as though they're looking at something to their left, and not at each other. The camera should not cross the line of action. Many amateur filmmakers often make the mistake of *crossing the line.* See Figure 14-2 for an example.

You can cross the line of action while the camera is in motion (where the change of direction is seen on-screen) because then the audience sees that the camera has stepped over the line, and you don't have an abrupt cut that can be disorienting.

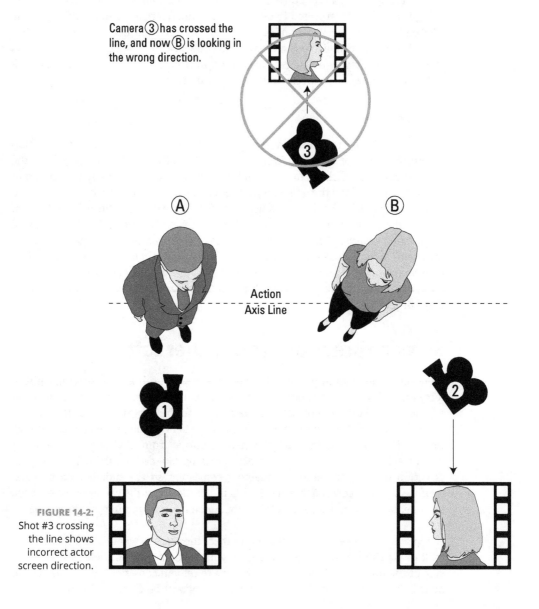

Camera ③ has crossed the line, and now ⑧ is looking in the wrong direction.

Ⓐ   Ⓑ

Action
Axis Line

FIGURE 14-2:
Shot #3 crossing the line shows incorrect actor screen direction.

Taking Your Best Shot

The camera never blinks. That's what cuts (changing from one shot to another shot) are for. But to cut from one shot to another, you have to vary your shots by size and angle so that you don't end up with a *jump-cut*, which would appear as if the shot were missing some frames (see Chapter 15 for more on film editing). Shot compositions, sizes, and angles enhance how you tell your story. You may want a close-up when two actors are talking if the conversation is an intimate one. A wide establishing shot may be appropriate if you want to show that the actors are surrounded by a barren wasteland. A great book to study composition of shots is *The Five C's of Cinematography,* by Joseph V. Mascelli (published by Siles Press).

REMEMBER

As a director, knowing at least the basics of the camera and lenses is advantageous. You should hire someone who is skilled in shooting digital and/or film if you want your production to look professional. The cinematographer's job is to be educated about lenses, exposures, and how the camera functions to get the best images possible (see Chapter 10), but you'll be better able to convey your story visually if you have a sense of what the camera can do.

Each cinematographer and director has a slightly different definition of framing and shot sizes, but the definitions are similar enough to warrant the following list of traditional shots, explained in the following sections:

>> Wide shot (which can also work as an establishing shot)

>> Medium shot

>> Two shot

>> Close-up

Where the heck are we? Establishing a wide shot

A *wide shot* (WS) reveals where the scene is taking place. Also referred to as a *long shot* or *master shot,* a wide shot helps orient the audience. A wide shot also gives the actors room to move within a shot, without the camera having to follow them. Medium shots and close-ups (explained later in this chapter) are often cut into a wide shot for variation.

An *establishing shot* is a type of wide shot that can establish a building before the camera cuts to an interior office. Figure 14-3 shows a wide shot from my film *First Dog* of Danny sitting alone in the Oval Office, and a wide establishing shot from my film *The Random Factor.*

FIGURE 14-3:
An interior wide
shot (left) and an
establishing
exterior wide
shot (right).

Photo of John Paul Howard in First Dog, *First American Cinema, LLC*
Photo of Andrew Divoff and William Richert in The Random Factor, *courtesy of Showbuzz and Gloria Everett*

You don't have to be a psychic to get a medium shot

A *medium shot* (MS) is a standard shot that usually shows a character from mid-chest to slightly above the actor's head. A medium shot is more intimate than a wide shot, but provides more breathing space for the actor than a close-up. It's also used when you have an actor holding something in the frame or elaborating with his hands. Figure 14-4 shows a medium shot of Eric Roberts as the President of the United States in my film *First Dog*.

FIGURE 14-4:
A medium shot.

Photo of Eric Roberts as the President in First Dog, *First American Cinema, LLC*

Two shot: Three's a crowd

A *two shot* can either be a form of a medium shot that has two actors standing or sitting next to each other or an over-the-shoulder shot where one actor's back or profile is closer to the camera than the other actor facing the camera. A two shot can save time and money when you have a dialogue scene between two actors by having them both in the frame as they carry on their conversation. The audience diverts their attention to each actor as he or she speaks, instead of having the camera cut to individual shots of each actor speaking. A two shot is also effective when two characters are walking and talking side by side. Figure 14-5 shows a two shot from *Undercover Angel*.

FIGURE 14-5:
A two shot.

Photo of Dean Winters and Yasmine Bleeth in Undercover Angel, *courtesy of Sunland Studios/Stellar Entertainment*

I'm ready for my close-up

A *close-up shot* (CU), or *single*, is usually from the nape of the neck to just slightly above the top of the head, or trimming the top of their head slightly. If you get in closer, so that the actor's head fills most of the frame, you have a *tight close-up*. Going in even tighter, to a person's eyes or mouth, gives you an *extreme close-up*. Close-ups create a sense of intimacy and the feeling that you're involved in the scene. They also reveal emotion in the eyes or the hint of a smile. Figure 14-6 shows a close-up, a tight close-up, and an extreme close-up.

The director often chooses a close-up to emphasize the intensity of a scene. Emotional or sensitive dialogue is often shot in a tight close-up to emphasize the importance of what's being said.

FIGURE 14-6:
A loose close-up (left), a tighter close-up (middle), and an extreme close-up. Notice the breathing room to the left of the actors in the first two close-ups.

James Earl Jones in Undercover Angel, *courtesy of Sunland Studios/Stellar Entertainment (photo by Bill Grimshaw), Crystal Owens in* Turn of the Blade, *courtesy of Northstar Entertainment, and Sasha Yurchikov in* Amazing Wizard of Paws, *Grand Illusion Ent.*

TIP

When framing an actor in a close-up, give him some *breathing room*. Breathing room puts more space in front of the actor's face in the direction he's looking or talking than behind him. If you don't allow this space, the shot will have a claustrophobic feel to it (unless it's an extreme close-up and you want it to feel claustrophobic). Also, never center a head in the middle of the frame unless it's a news reporter talking into the camera. Centering someone in the middle of the frame creates an awkward composition and creates an off-balance feeling to the shot.

Teeter-tottering angles: Are you high or low?

A *high angle* is usually shot using a crane, standing on a hill, an aerial drone shot, or looking out a window of a high-rise to get an angle looking down. When you shoot from a high angle, your subjects look smaller and therefore insignificant.

In contrast, you shoot a *low angle* from below your subject's height — as low as the ground (or lower if you dig yourself a hole). Low angles tend to make subjects look bigger, more powerful, or menacing. A character appears intimidating if you use a low-angle shot. Figure 14-7 shows an example of each type.

FIGURE 14-7:
High-angle shots make subjects look smaller and less significant (left). Low-angle shots make subjects look more imposing (right).

Nancy-Lynn Stoller, Tiny Lister as Big Mike in First Dog, *First American Cinema, LLC*

TIP

Here's an inexpensive way to get a low-angle shot from the ground: Get one of those beanbag pillows and lay your camera on it. Shape the pillow to cradle your camera safely and align it so that the shot isn't crooked (unless you want it to be).

FINDING THE DIRECTOR'S VIEWFINDER

A personal director's viewfinder is a precision tool that enables you to see the world through the eyes of various types of camera lenses. The director's viewfinder resembles a pirate's spyglass and has built-in interchangeable aspect ratios that you can resize with a simple twist (for framing 16:9 for HDTV or 2:35:1 for theatrical CinemaScope movie theater projection). The finder allows you to "see" through different size lenses that a film or digital camera uses without having to carry a bulky camera around with you. These finders are light enough to hang around your neck or keep in a handbag. These viewfinders can be expensive, but not for you — because I'm now going to introduce you to a director's viewfinder that works on your smartphone via a free app! Through the app store on your smartphone, check out Magic ViewFinder. You'll also see several pay versions (like FilmicPro), if you want to get really technical with your lenses and camera settings.

I'm high on you: The God shot

In a *God shot*, the camera looks straight down on a scene, symbolizing God's point of view looking down on his creation — also showing the audience the big picture. This can be an interior shot or a very effective exterior shot from the sky. It is often used in movies to remind us that a central character is human and sometimes insignificant. The God shot was used effectively and consistently in *The Truman Show* to symbolize the God complex of Christof who created and directed the ultimate reality show documenting the real life of Burbank Truman (Jim Carrey) and televising his personal life unfolding in front of the entire world.

To accomplish a God shot, you need a camera crane or an aerial drone. Or a cheaper way to go is to shoot looking down from a tall structure's balcony or window.

Picture This: Deciding When to Move the Camera and Why

Fred Astaire said that if he didn't dance in a scene, the camera should. Keeping motion in a shot is like choreography for the camera. If you stand still too long and your camera remains static, your audience gets restless (that's why I can't sit still watching a stage play). It's as if you're having a stare-down with the image because the camera never blinks. A moving camera, however, brings energy to the scene. So, when you have a good reason to move the camera, let it dance! It's appropriate to move the camera when:

>> Following a character

>> Revealing something

>> Emphasizing a character's reaction

>> Underlining a dramatic effect

>> Creating a sense of chaos or excitement

REMEMBER

An actor's actions should motivate the camera. Start to move the camera at the same time the actor moves to create seamless camera motion.

Playing with dollies

A camera that needs to be moved is placed on a *dolly* so that the motion is fluid and doesn't bump around. You can rent a professional dolly with a hydraulic stand that acts as a motion tripod, or you can make your own by fitting a flat board with rugged wheels. Put a tripod on the board, and you have yourself a dolly. I use a Manfrotto tripod (www.manfrotto.com), which I secure to the dolly. It's a lightweight but sturdy tripod that has a great fluid head for effortless panning and tilting of the camera.

If you're working on an uneven surface, you need to lay down *dolly tracks.* You can rent them with the dolly, or you can put down boards or mats on the ground to create a smooth surface for the dolly wheels to roll over. Dyno Trek (www.dynoequipment.com) makes a super lightweight tracking *slider* with super-smooth dolling motion. The package comes with 3 feet of magnetic interlocking tracks that break down into 3-foot sections for travel or storage. The motor is battery-rechargeable, and you control it with the Dyno Trek app. The slider was developed to work best with a light camera such as a GoPro or a smartphone — but I've used it with my DSLR camera and it seemed to work pretty well. The Dyno Trek slider system is priced at $299.

TIP

If you can't afford a dolly, borrow a wheelchair. Sit in the wheelchair with the camera (get one of those beanbag pillows to rest the camera on to absorb the shock) and have someone push you for a smooth dolly shot.

I once needed a shot that moved in over a conference table during a scene of the boss talking to his board members. I wanted the camera to move toward the boss at the head of the table. We put the camera on an inexpensive skateboard and slowly moved it over the surface of the table toward the actor. It was one of the smoothest shots in the movie!

Craning to get a high shot

A camera *crane* allows you to raise or lower ("boom") the camera while shooting to get a more dramatic shot. SteadyTracker makes a series of cranes called the CobraCrane. They range from 3 to 12 feet and attach to your own tripod. The CobraCrane uses a cable-and-pulley system with roller bearings, allowing you to tilt the camera for extremely smooth angles in all directions. Check out the Cobra-Crane, which starts at $249, at www.steadytracker.com.

WARNING

When shooting from a crane, you need to be able to view the shot so that you can manipulate it properly. Otherwise, you could end up with something that's unusable (at worst) or not quite what you wanted (at best). When shooting digital files using a crane, you need to either run a video cable from the camera to a TV monitor, or wirelessly via Bluetooth or Wi-Fi, which many digital cameras can do nowadays. If you're using a film camera, then you need to have a *video assist* unit (see Chapter 10 for more information on video assist). I use my iPhone to watch and play back (via Wi-Fi) the crane footage when shooting on my Panasonic Lumix GH5s. You also need a set of inexpensive free weights (from a sporting goods store) to counterbalance the crane to keep your camera in the air, kind of like a teeter-totter.

Stabilizing the camera

A camera steadying device turns the camera into a fluid floating machine. Think of it as a shock absorber for the camera. The brand commonly used in Hollywood is called a Steadicam, made by the Tiffen Company (www.tiffen.com). With technology advances of today, you can now get stabilizing camera systems that used to cost around $100,000 for under $400! Instead of laying down dolly tracks, the camera operator just walks with the camera "floating" on a stabilizing gimbal. A gimbal is great for walking and talking shots with your actors. FeiyuTech makes the a2000 stabilizing gimbal (at around $379 on Amazon) for digital cameras weighing up to five pounds. (See Figure 14-8.) I have one — it keeps all my moving shots steady and smooth — I love it so much I use it whenever I can!

Manfrotto puts out the Fig Rig, which resembles a steering wheel (at $317). (See Figure 14-8.) You can attach small lights, a microphone, and even a camera remote conveniently on the handle for turning the camera on and off and controlling the zoom. Steer yourself to Manfrotto's website at www.manfrotto.com.

I discovered an interesting new device called the Rollocam H2. (See Figure 14-9.) It's an amazing free-roaming slider for most DSLR or prosumer digital cameras. It's an intelligent robot built into a slider that can take your camera pretty much anywhere you program it to go. Road trip, anyone? It has a built-in intervalometer for taking pictures, allowing you to achieve amazing time-lapse sequences. The Rollocam enables face recognition to follow you around on three axes, and is controlled by its free app, weighs only five ounces, and fits in your pocket. It works similar to a slider or dolly on tracks — only no tracks. *Tracks? Who needs tracks!* It costs $249. You can get more info at www.steadytracker.com.

FIGURE 14-8:
The author/director using the Fig Rig on-set (left); the FeiyuTech stabilizer with PRL camera light and the Røde directional mic attached to the gimbal handles (right).

FIGURE 14-9:
Rollocam by Steadytracker.

FLYING HIGH WITH AERIAL DRONES

Not too long ago, an independent production couldn't afford aerial shots without the high-expense safety precautions and costly permits of hiring a helicopter company. That has all changed for the independent filmmaker! DJI, a pioneer in the field (or sky) now leads the pack with its revolutionary aerial camera drones (also known as a *UAV* or *unmanned aerial vehicle*). The new Mavic 2 Pro is a compact but powerful drone that goes above and beyond (literally) in the category of professional drones. The Mavic 2 Pro has its own form of artificial intelligence because it knows to move around and avoid any barriers in the air, whether it be a mountain, a building — or even a UFO! The advanced GPS keeps the drone secure in its flight path and also assists in bringing it back home safely where it originated take-off. The drone's gimbal stabilization keeps the motion steady and smooth with a professional look that would rival any stunt heli-copter pilot. Every shot appears to disobey physics and the drone appears to magically and smoothly float through the sky as it captures amazing footage that resembles an expensive studio production. The drone also has a setting to follow a vehicle, person, or cyclist better than a police high-speed chase copter. The Mavic 2 Pro folds up for com-pact storage and easily fits in a small backpack. It quickly unfolds — ready for take-off with an agenda for breathtaking shots. Can you tell I'm excited about this flying robot camera? You can get your own DJI Mavic 2 Pro by going to www.dji.com.

4

Finishing Your Movie in Post

IN THIS PART . . .

You discover that you can edit your movie like the big studios do, right on your desktop computer.

I introduce you to post-production audio, such as sound effects and musical compositions, which is an important element for making your production sizzle with great sound.

Special visual effects have been greatly influenced by the computer age, and with some ingenuity, you too can create some incredible effects with your camera without exploding your budget.

I discuss the title of your movie and the proper credit recognition for all the cast, crew, and contacts who help bring your film to fruition.

Chapter **15**

Cut to: Editing Your Movie — Shot by Shot

After you've shot your film, you're ready to *cut* (edit) it together. You can edit your masterpiece on your computer and do it affordably. In this chapter, I introduce you to the various editing software programs that enable you to cut your movie without leaving your desk.

In this chapter, you also see how the world of nonlinear editing works and discover the secrets to cutting your picture for the optimum effect — by controlling the story, changing the sequence of events, and playing with time. Sound editing is also important when cutting together dialogue, sound effects, and music; so you see (and hear) all about that, too. I also introduce you to the duties of a film laboratory, if you're still shooting with film stock, and show you how to *develop* a great relationship. If you're shooting digital, you may be able to do most or all of your post-production on your computer, without ever having to step into a professional digital post house.

Editing Your Movie: Putting One Frame in Front of the Other

Editing is more than just piecing together shots into scenes. Understanding the story and the best way to tell it is an art. Editing controls the feel of your film and can make or break the illusion. To edit well, you need to know on what frame to start your shot and on what frame to end it, when to cut to the *reaction shot* (a visual response from another actor in the scene), and when to stay on the main character.

Some of the elements you need to consider when editing are:

>> **Pacing:** The length of shots and scenes gives the entire film a pace — a feeling of moving fast or slow. You don't want your film to lag.

>> **Scene length:** Keep scenes under three minutes if possible, so they don't drag on and seem monotonous.

>> **Order of shots and scenes:** By arranging your shots in a particular sequence, you can dramatically affect a scene's meaning. See the later section "Linear versus Nonlinear Editing" for details.

TIP

>> **Cutting on action:** Most shots cut (or edit) better on action. If your actor is opening a car door, have him or her repeat the action while you shoot it from different angles or shot sizes (such as a close-up or a wide shot). You then can overlap the shots as you cut on the motion. This is also called *matching,* and it helps hide the cut, making the transition appear seamless.

>> **Matching shots:** You want to join static shots with static shots, and moving shots next to other moving shots. If you have a fast-paced car-chase scene and the camera is moving wildly to follow the action, a sudden static shot of a car sitting quietly at a stop light will be jarring. (Of course, that may be the effect you want.)

>> **Varying the angle and size of shots:** A *jump-cut* happens when shots that are too similar in appearance are cut together, making the picture look as if it has jumped, or that the actor has popped from one spot to another. In order to avoid a jump-cut, you need to vary the angle and size of the next shot. One way to avoid a jump-cut is to shoot a cutaway of an actor's reaction or of a significant object on-set that you can use to tie two different shots together. An appropriate cutaway can often save the day.

>> **Showing simultaneous action:** You can cut back and forth between scenes happening at the same time. This is called *cross-cutting.* Or you can make a *parallel cut,* which is showing the simultaneous action with a split screen. This was often done on the TV show *24.*

>> **Choosing the best take (or combining the best of several takes):** You shoot several takes of a particular scene so that you have a choice in the editing room. Obviously, the more takes you have, the more choices. You can also combine parts of various takes — the beginning of one take, and the end of another, for example, if you have a cutaway to insert between them — to create the scene you want.

Choosing an editor: Cut that out!

You need to decide whether you're going to edit the movie yourself or get a fresh pair of eyes to do it for you. Many directors avoid editing their pictures because they're too close to the material and want to bring another perspective to the story. That's why, on a big studio production, a picture editor starts assembling your shots and scenes together as you're shooting, and a sound editor edits the dialogue and other sound elements.

You can place an ad seeking an editor in the classified section of many film and trade magazines like *Backstage* (www.backstage.com) or search online at www.crewnet. com for an editor near you. Look for someone who has at least a few films under his belt and ask to see a sample of his work — does he cut scenes tight so they don't lag? But if you're on a small production, you're probably your own editor. You're in good company, though. Robert Rodriguez (*El Mariachi* and *Sin City)* prefers to cut his own films. For more on hiring an editor for your team, check out Chapter 7.

REMEMBER

One of the advantages of hiring an editor is that he or she can start assembling what you've shot immediately after the first day on the set. This means that your editor can tell you while you're shooting whether you need extra footage: a *cutaway* (a reaction shot or something that helps piece two other shots together seamlessly) to make a scene work better, a close-up of some person or object, or an *establishing shot* (a wide shot of the location that orientates the audience to where the scene is taking place).

Shooting enough coverage

You need to shoot enough *coverage* so that you have plenty of different takes and interesting angles to choose from. Every time you add another angle to a scene, you make it more interesting and less monotonous. Using just one shot in a two-minute scene is like having a stare-down — and that's just dull and annoying (unless it's a bet to see who wins). The camera never blinks — that's what cutting is for. Cutting is like blinking from one shot to the next. When you watch a play, you don't stare at the stage as a whole the entire time; you concentrate on the individual actors as they speak, or on a prop or action sequence that catches your attention.

TIP

If you don't have time to shoot several angles, then create movement in the shot, such as having the camera follow or lead your actors as they're walking and talking. Make the shot as interesting as possible.

Some directors shoot a ratio of three takes to get one shot (3:1), and some shoot ten or more. The editor's job is to find the best take or to combine the best of several takes with cutaways. As you start to piece the movie together, it magically begins to take on a shape of its own, and the story starts to (hopefully) make sense.

Assembling a first cut

The first step is piecing together what is called an *assembly cut, rough cut,* or *first cut.* This is the most basic cut possible, showing the story in continuity (because often the scenes are shot out of order, out of continuity).

Editing the visuals of your movie is very similar to writing a screenplay. The first assembly of footage is like the first rough draft, putting things into perspective and giving you a feel for your story. After you have your basic cut, you start shaping, trimming, and cutting until your film feels complete. Like dancing, there's a rhythm to cutting — it flows, and everything feels like it's falling into place.

REMEMBER

Don't be discouraged if the first cut doesn't excite you. The pacing may seem too slow, the performances may appear dull. I've often been disappointed with a first cut — and apparently, many big studio directors have had concerns after working on their first cuts. After your first cut, you start to get a sense of how to tighten up the picture. You start to cut out long boring exits to the door, pauses that are too long between lines, or a scene that isn't working and that won't be missed if you cut it out entirely. You may even want to reshoot or add a completely new scene to make the picture better as a whole. You need to do a lot of shaping and adjusting before your masterpiece shines through. It's like molding something out of clay — you have to keep chipping away until you like what you see. Also, remember, you are seeing the movie still in its raw form because color-correction, sound effects, music score, special effects, and other elements have not been added yet.

Building a director's cut

The director's contract usually stipulates whether he gets to make sure his vision is followed in the editing room by approving the final cut of the movie. This final, director-approved cut is called a *director's cut.* The director usually views an assembly, or first, cut (scenes assembled loosely in continuity according to the screenplay; see the preceding section) by the picture editor. The director then gives the editor suggestions on where to place specific shots, close-ups, and establishing shots; how to change the order of things; how to tighten a scene; and so on. (See Figure 15-1.)

Usually, a director gets a director's cut based on his clout in the industry. Ultimately, the big studio has the final say in the cutting of a picture if the director doesn't contractually have final cut. Steven Spielberg always gets final say because he's earned that honor and proven himself to know what works and what doesn't. George Lucas always has the final cut because he doesn't report to anyone but himself! With the release of most films on DVD or streaming now, many directors who didn't have the clout to get a director's cut theatrically in their studio contract now have the opportunity to get a director's cut featured as one of the bonuses on the DVD or streaming sites such as on iTunes. Chances are, you are your own studio boss, so you decide who gets final say on editing. You will probably have director's cut because you report to yourself!

FIGURE 15-1: The author working on his "director's cut" on an iMac connected to a big screen TV for checking details.

Photo finish: Finalizing a final cut

Many times a studio screens a version of the movie to a *test audience* (a group of people brought in to watch and rate the picture). The audience members fill out a questionnaire, and the studio (or the director, if they have final cut) evaluates all the comments from the screening and may re-edit accordingly.

THE CUTTING-ROOM FLOOR

Many actors in Hollywood have unfortunately only made the *cutting-room floor*. This expression started in the days when editors physically cut film and literally threw the discarded scenes on the editing-room floor. Today, very few shot scenes are discarded entirely. Instead, these unused scenes are saved on a computer hard drive and often incorporated into the bonus section of the film's DVD or streaming release (including humorous outtake flubs by the actors).

After all the editing is finished and approved, you create the final, *locked* picture approved by the studio — or by the director if he has the authority to make the final cut (which you probably do have if you're an independent director). Now the post-production work on sound begins, and the composer can start timing the scenes that will be *scored* (set to music).

Listening to the sound editor

In addition to editing the picture on your movie, you have to assemble and edit the sound elements. These elements are prepared by the sound editor, who is most often the picture editor and even the final post-production sound mixer on an independent film. The sound elements are put onto separate audio channels (called *tracks*) and then mixed down into a final soundtrack that combines all channels mixed together. Some of those edited sound elements include:

>> Dialogue (may have separate dialogue tracks for each actor)

>> Sound effects (can have unlimited sound-effects tracks)

>> Music (usually one or two tracks for music)

>> Ambience (background sounds like birds chirping, an air-conditioner humming, ocean waves crashing, and so on)

REMEMBER

Dialogue editing is as important as your picture edit. The sound editor has a variety of elements to consider, such as overlapping conversations or starting a character's dialogue over the end of another character's shot. Check out Chapter 16 for more on dialogue and sound editing.

FLATLINING THE FLATBED AND MOVIOLA

Not too long ago, editors would cut their films by actually handling the film itself and physically cutting it, where necessary. They would trim the thin celluloid and glue or tape the scenes together on a moviola or flatbed, which would run the film at the proper speed to see what the final results looked like, and how the picture timed out.

A *moviola* is an upright editing system that resembles a projector morphed with a sewing machine. The actual film is projected into a viewer as it spools onto a top reel. The picture editor physically cuts the film into individual shots and hangs the film strips in a bin for reassembling. A *flatbed* editing system works similar to the moviola, but instead of being vertical, it's a horizontal table with the film reels lying flat on the surface.

Although physically cutting the film is considered nonlinear editing because the individual shots and scenes are rearranged like individual blocks, the process isn't nearly as quick and effective as rearranging the clips digitally on a nonlinear computer editing system. Editing on a moviola or a flatbed has pretty much been replaced by digital nonlinear editing on a computer even if the filmmaker shot on film (the film is transferred to digital files for editing).

Linear versus Nonlinear Editing

Imagine that you've sorted through a set of your recent vacation photos and slipped them into a photo album, one picture per page. You just created a sequential order to your sightseeing photos. But say your mood changes or you decide that the picture of the huge fish you caught looks much better facing the photo of Uncle Bob's minnow, even though he caught it several days before your catch and before the trip to Disney World. No problem. You can just slide the photos out of their pockets and rearrange them. This is nonlinear organization. Of course, if the photos are glued into the pockets, you can't rearrange them. They're now treated together as a whole, and not as individual shots — they're stuck in a linear world and can't be rearranged.

Editing in linear

Linear editing means that you assemble your shots one after another in consecutive order. There is no rearranging. The order of the shots are not interchangeable. Linear editing is used only when the order of shots don't matter, or when something is shot in real time. Rarely does anyone edit linearly when nonlinear is so much easier now with computers.

The only time anyone would edit linearly was if they edited directly onto video-tape. A video deck, used as a *player*, would allow you to transfer footage to a video *recorder* deck to put one shot at the end of another shot. Videotape could not be cut physically like film, so if you wanted to remove or add just one shot somewhere in the middle of your edits, you would have to start over again. Nobody edits on vid-eotape anymore.

Editing in nonlinear

Digital nonlinear editing, first pioneered by George Lucas's Editroid system, opened a new world for the editor. A single editor can now quickly experiment with different variations of a picture that would otherwise have taken a dozen edi-tors many hours, or days, to perform.

In *nonlinear editing,* each shot, and each scene, is its own separate compartment and can be moved around like individual building blocks in any order within your editing timeline. Even the opening scene can easily be moved within seconds to the end of the timeline. Nonlinear editing is easier and quicker; it also allows you to be more creative than linear editing.

Sometimes the order of your shots is dictated by the obvious — like the order of events when getting dressed: You put on your underwear first and your pants second — at least I hope you do. But if you rearrange the order of shots or events, you can change the psychology of your scene. For example, here are three shots in a particular order in your movie:

1. A baby crying

2. The family cat hanging from the ceiling fan

3. A baby laughing

If you start with the baby crying, then in this order, the effect is the cat has stopped the baby from crying, and the child is now amused. Now see what happens when you change the order:

1. A baby laughing

2. The family cat hanging from the ceiling fan

3. A baby crying

Having the baby laughing at the beginning and crying at the end creates the effect that the child is now frightened for (or of) the animal. Quentin Tarantino put the ending of his film *Pulp Fiction* at the beginning of the film, and let the story prog-ress until it picked up the beginning at the ending.

When you shoot footage with your camera, you're shooting in a linear fashion. For example, if you're filming the birth of a baby, everything you shoot shows the birthing process in order. But if you go into the editing room and decide to edit in nonlinear, you can change the order of real time and have the baby go back to the mother's womb (go to your womb!). With digital technology, you can shoot in linear fashion and cut in nonlinear style.

Editing on Your Computer

The same computer on which you write letters, organize your bank account, surf the Internet, and maybe even write your script can now easily be turned into a powerful editing machine. Most computers, both PC and Apple computers, are able to edit a movie in a nonlinear environment and are limited only by the size of their hard drives (but unlimited when using external hard drives).

In nonlinear editing (NLE), you take all your separate shots, arrange them in story order, and then play them consecutively to form a scene. Every frame has its own individual set of *time-code numbers* (numbers generated electronically on the video image or in a computer) or *edge-code numbers* (numbers printed on the actual film stock) that pinpoint its exact starting and ending frames. Computer software can then generate an *edit list* that accurately contains the hour, minutes, seconds, and frames of your shots and identifies each cut made by the editor. With the right editing software, you have the capability to edit your movie without leaving your computer. (For technical tips on setting up your own editing studio, check out *Digital Video For Dummies* by Keith Underdahl, published by Wiley.)

You can also purchase third-party software programs to perform additional functions like special effects, mattes, and process digital footage to look more like it was shot on motion picture film stock. (See "Simulating cinema with software" later in this chapter. Also see Chapter 17 for more on software used for special effects in the post-production phase.)

Hard driving

Your computer hard drive stores all your picture information. Because you'll probably need more hard drive space than the amount that's in your computer's internal hard drive, you may want to purchase an external hard drive or two. An external hard drive these days is often compact — about the size of a paperback novel or not much bigger than a deck of cards. External hard drives connect to your computer via USB 3, USB C cables, or *thunderbolt* for speedy data transfer.

REMEMBER

THUNDERBOLT AND LIGHTNING, VERY, VERY FRIGHTENING!

Thunderbolt is a digital connection (a special cable) that transfers the information from your digital camcorder to your computer, to an external hard drive, or to other equipment with no degradation in picture quality. Most computers now have Thunderbolt, USB 3, or USB C inputs so that you can plug your digital camera directly into them and transfer your footage. The data speed transfer of Thunderbolt is twice as fast as USB 3. Thunderbolt 3 can transfer around 40 gigabytes per second. So the higher the GBPS, the faster the data transfer — which is a good thing if you get impatient easily. USB-3 is becoming a common cable for many smartphones (other than Apple's proprietary iPhone cables).

HDMI stands for *high definition multimedia interface*. Don't confuse HDMI with external hard drive cables. HDMI is used for connecting video and audio from a digital camera, cable box, or digital player (including DVD and Blu-ray players) or a game box to a high definition TV or studio monitor. An HDMI cable is used to send or receive digital video and audio signals for viewing or broadcast.

Most external hard drives can be formatted for either PC or Mac platforms. The *codec* (digital file format) you record in will determine on how much storage space you will need on your external hard drive. Examples of certain codecs are .mov, MP4, H264, H265, ProRes 4444, and so on. Each one compresses your footage differently. Some are large files, some are small. H264 and H265 are known to compress large files into smaller files that maintain quality without much loss from image compression. When capturing or transferring high definition footage (depending on the compression), it can equate to around one gig per minute (or more if shooting above 2K) — so a 500GB external drive in high def can hold up 500 minutes. I like to use at least a 4 terabyte external drive, also known as 4TB — 4,000 gigabytes.

Cutting it with editing software

Without software, a computer has no personality. Add movie-editing software often known as NLE (nonlinear editing) and it becomes a complete post-production editing suite within the confines of your desk space. You can choose from numerous editing programs on the market that allow you to affordably edit your digital footage in a nonlinear environment. Some computers even come with free editing software.

Most software-editing programs use these basic components of nonlinear editing:

>> A bin to hold your individual shots

>> A timeline that allows you to assemble your shots in any order (it resembles individual storyboard panels placed one after another — see Chapter 9)

>> A main window that plays back your edited footage

>> Titling, effects, and transition options

All editing software accepts 2K high definition files, but many also work with digital files up to 4K resolution. 4K takes more CPU (computer power) so even if the software will edit 4K footage, make sure your computer has the right operating system, enough memory, and the correct specifications to run very large files.

iMovie

Many Apple computers come with iMovie, a free, simple-to-use, nonlinear editing software that allows you to cut your movie on your computer. The program also comes with over 80 music soundtracks you can use with your footage. Check out *Digital Video For Dummies* by Keith Underdahl (published by Wiley), which guides you through the steps of using this effective and easy-to-use software to edit your projects.

An Avid fan

Avid, a name synonymous with nonlinear editing, makes the multi-award winning Media Composer software, which works with Mac or PC platforms. The program works with high definition resolution up to 16K. Many studio feature films have been edited on Media Composer software. Avid's software is more sophisticated than other lower-priced editing software, but it also has a longer learning curve. The software includes audio tools for post sound. It also includes titling and graphics, along with a variety of real-time effects. Avid charges a monthly or yearly subscription charge to use their editing software. You can get more details on Media Composer at www.avid.com.

Becoming a pro with Final Cut

My favorite editing program, without hesitation, is Final Cut Pro 10 (FCPX), available for use with Apple computers for $299. (See Figure 15-2.) No monthly subscription. You own it and the free Apple support is as good as it gets. It's a professional and powerful nonlinear software program for cutting picture (2K and 4K) as well as audio. It's much more sophisticated than iMovie or some of the other nonlinear software, and it can produce some amazing results, including titles, effects, transitions, and color-correction. With it, you can repair shaky footage, fix many audio problems, and even create closed captions. The program also comes with an extensive sound effects and music library. This is a whole new reworking of Final Cut Pro, and for those who gave up on FCPX after FCP7 — you need to revisit this amazing software. You can even download and use it for free on a trial basis for a whole month! Check it out at the Apple App Store and download it today (if you use a Mac).

This is not only the perfect nonlinear editing software for the novice independent filmmaker, many feature films have been cut using the software, including my film, *Santa Stole Our Dog*, which was released by Universal Home Entertainment. A lot of great tutorials on YouTube show you how effective and user-friendly Final Cut Pro X is. I won't cut on anything else!

FIGURE 15-2:
Final Cut Pro X
editing software
program.

Resolving Di Vinci

Blackmagic (the ones that make the cool digital pocket cameras) also developed a widely used nonlinear editing program called Di Vinci Resolve. Depending which version you use, or whether you've bought a Blackmagic camera — the editing software may be free to you! Resolve also is known for its powerful color-correcting and -grading software — used by many colorist professionals in Hollywood and abroad.

Wonderful Filmora

Filmora from Wondershare is an affordable one-time buy of $59 NLE software that is packed with lots of power. The program is easy to learn, and you can find lots of helpful tutorials on the Wondershare website. The program has effects and transitions included. The limitation, though, is that no third-party plug-ins are made for Filmora like there are for some of the other editing programs like Final Cut Pro, Avid, and Premiere.

Premiering Adobe

Adobe makes popular software programs for the editing world: Adobe Premiere Pro for picture and sound editing (priced at $239 a year). Check out Adobe's products at www.adobe.com. Unless you edit for a living this can be very expensive because it's a monthly and/or yearly subscription. I have edited with Premiere and definitely prefer editing on Final Cut Pro. I kept running into technical issues with Premiere and found limitations with the software compared to other editing software. Adobe also makes other software like Adobe After Effects (a powerful effects engine) that you can add to your monthly or yearly subscription. Check out Adobe's products at www.adobe.com.

TIP

KB Covers makes really cool keyboard covers, each individually customized to precisely fit over different brands of computer keyboards, including laptops and MacBooks — and are designed to work with many of the major editing software programs, like Final Cut Pro, Avid, and Premiere Pro. Chances are, they'll have a precision fit cover for your keyboard, designed to work with your editing software. It's like a shortcut for editing, because the thin silicone cover converts your keyboard by displaying all the shortcut keys for most editing functions. These covers can definitely speed up your editing game. KB Covers has you covered at www.kbcovers.com. (See Figure 15-3.)

Simulating cinema with software

Many independent filmmakers desperately want to make a movie that looks like it was shot on 35mm film — but they can't afford the expense that comes with shooting on motion picture film stock. There are now software programs that will process your digital video footage in the post-production phase and create the illusion (as best it can) that you shot on 35mm film. These programs emulate the characteristics associated with the look of film stock, such as grain, contrast, softness, subtle shuttle flutter, and saturated colors. The software also pulls down footage shot at 30-frames per second to emulate the 24 standard frames used with motion picture film cameras. FilmConvert is a unique software program that converts and emulates a pretty effective film-look to your digitally shot footage (www.filmconvert.com). Red Giant puts out software called Magic Bullet Looks that has settings to emulate particular Kodak and Fuji film stock emulsions. The software also has other color-correction presets and color-correction controls allowing you to start from scratch. Remember, though, you may get close, but digital will never look exactly like film, because film is organic and digital is electronic — but advances in technology are bringing them closer. Magic Bullet Looks works with many of the popular NLE editing programs, including Final Cut Pro, Resolve, and Avid Media Composer. Check out the magic at www.redgiant.com.

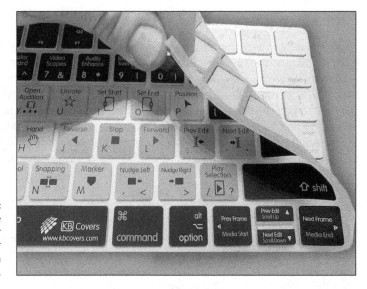

FIGURE 15-3:
KB silicone keyboard cover customized for FCPX for use on iMac keypad.

JUICING WITH DIGITAL JUICE

Digital Juice is literally an editor's tool box! An invaluable arsenal of knicks and knacks to enhance your productions. Everything from animated backgrounds, titles, lower-thirds, royalty-free stock footage, sound effects, music tracks, special effects layers, and on and on. When you open the Digital Juice website, you are opening a portal to a magical world that will enhance any filmmaker's dream. The contents are almost as entertaining as watching Netflix! Pretty much every major studio, TV network, and production house has a subscription to Digital Juice. It's a near-endless array of digital elements available at your keyboard fingertips (and more are added all the time) to download and juice up any production. This is an excellent tool for any editor! A one-time lifetime fee starts at $399, and it's well worth it! To discover more about what Digital Juice is all about, go to www.digitaljuice.com.

TIP

This neat little tip could save your production! I discovered a miraculous software plug-in call Neat Video. It is a magical plug-in that fixes dancing grain or noisy footage that appears to be completely unusable — or at least distracting to the viewer. This amazing and powerful software works with many nonlinear editing platforms like Final Cut Pro and Adobe Premiere. It saved one of my movies where some of my dark, underlit scenes had so much grain and noise they were almost unwatchable and wouldn't have passed broadcast specifications. The Neat Video software quickly smoothed out my shots by removing unwanted grain and noise, and turned some pretty ugly visuals into images of beauty. And the shots passed the strict technical QC test to air on broadcast television and on several popular streaming platforms! Find it at www.neatvideo.com.

Posting your production in your computer

After you finish editing all the dialogue and picture elements for your movie in your computer, you're ready to marry your picture and sound together. If the final production is going to television, DVD, and digital streaming distribution (and not a theatrical release), then you can continue to do most of your final preparations in the computer (color correcting, titles, and so on). If you plan on getting a theatrical release for your picture, then you'll need to have a DCP (digital cinema package) authored by a post-production house. See Chapter 19 for details on DCP, what it is, and how it works.

Outputting your masterpiece

Once you've completed your final cut, you then have to figure out how you're going to get your movie out of your computer. There are a variety of ways to output your movie. One way is to make a QuickTime file. Think of a QuickTime file as a container. It can contain different digital codecs, including ProRes, H.264, and MPEG-4 MOV files. This file can be exported to an external hard drive or authored onto a standard DVD or Blu-ray disc (depending on the size of the file). Most TV networks and streaming platforms will accept delivery of your movie on an external hard drive. A QuickTime file can even be uploaded and showcased on YouTube (www.youtube.com), Vimeo (www.vimeo.com), or Facebook. If you are entering your movie in a film festival, you can often upload the QuickTime of your movie to a private and secure site that the film festival uses to review entries (instead of shipping out a DVD or Blu-ray disc).

If you want to export your edited movie from your computer directly to digital tape which is usually Digibeta tape (sometimes a requirement for TV broadcast or streaming platforms), then you have several options. You can rent a Digibeta tape machine and output the QuickTime file of your movie yourself, or you can take your

QuickTime file to a professional post-production facility and have the people there transfer the QuickTime file to digital videotape for you. In the long run, it's easier to have a post-production house do it, because they will guarantee it's done right.

REMEMBER

In this day and age of entertainment outlets, things have changed exponentially in the last few years. No longer is entertainment limited to a few major TV networks. With advances in digital technology, the Internet, and the explosion of wireless communications — we have unlimited entertainment at our fingertips — literally. Netflix brought a new age of entertainment by offering tens of thousands of movies and TV series available to everyone (with a subscription) on your schedule, and at your convenience. On the heels of Netflix, we now have an explosion of more streaming platforms. Amazon Prime Video, Disney Plus, CBS All Access, Universal, Warner Bros., and even Apple are into the streaming game. I'm just waiting for an implosion. Too many services, too many series and movies. Eventually I think quantity is going to overcome quality. YouTube and Vimeo offers a platform that anyone can upload their short or feature film and can now call themselves a published artist. But looking at the big picture — all these streaming services are going to need content. Maybe this is a good thing for you!

TIP

If you've ever had the challenge of trying to send a digital file to someone (like your special-effects guy) via email but the file was too big, here's a little secret: Check out www.hightail.com. This site allows you to upload and download files. The cost? Files up to 100MB are free; files up to 25GB are $12 a month.

Developing a Relationship with Your Film Lab

If you're working with actual film celluloid, you need a film laboratory. You can find a film laboratory in the Yellow Pages or by surfing the Internet under "Film Laboratories" or "Motion Picture Film Services." If your town doesn't have a film lab, you may want to call a laboratory in Los Angeles, New York, or Toronto. In L.A., try Deluxe Labs (www.bydeluxe.com), Technicolor (www.technicolor.com), or Fotokem (www.fotokem.com). In New York, try Colorlab (www.colorlab.com) and arrange to have your film shipped for developing. When I shot my film *Undercover Angel* in Ottawa, Ontario, I shipped the 35mm film by bus to Deluxe Laboratories in Toronto. The lab developed my film stock and shipped back the *dailies* (see the next section, "Developing negatives, producing prints, and DCP") by overnight express.

A good relationship with your lab ensures that the services it performs — including developing your film negative; transferring your film to digital files, DVDs, or external hard drives (for dailies as well as the final product for TV, streaming and DVD release); transferring your movie into a DCP (digital cinema package — see Chapter 19) for a theatrical release — are performed properly and on a timely basis. Also, don't be afraid to negotiate for the best price you can. Because fewer productions are shooting on film, laboratories have an incentive to give discounts to first-time or independent filmmakers. All you have to do is ask!

Film labs offer the services and equipment outlined in the following sections.

REMEMBER

If you're working solely with digital files, you don't need to depend on the services of a film lab, unless at some point, you need a master digital video transfer to a Digibeta for broadcast and/or DVD copies of your final movie, or a DCP for theatrical showings.

Developing negatives, producing prints, and DCP

If you shoot on film and then edit in your computer, you need the services of a film lab to develop your film negative and then transfer that footage to digital media (digital files, DVDs, or external hard drives) so you can then input that footage into your computer that contains your editing software.

If you shoot your movie on film with plans for a possible theatrical release, the film lab will do a telecine transfer of your film footage. You can skip the process of printing your film stock and actually turn your developed negative into a positive image in the telecine stage. *Telecine* is the procedure of transferring your 16mm or 35mm film stock footage directly into digital files. Nowadays, most film labs have telecine bays where you can transfer your developed film footage by running it through a film projector and scanning it directly into digital files. In telecine, you can play with the colors, correct the exposure, and do lots of other picture enhancements as well. You can then import these digital files of your original film footage into your computer and start editing with your NLE (nonlinear editing) software. You will need the lab again only when you're ready to make a DCP (digital cinema package) for theatrical release.

REMEMBER

Dailies consist of the footage that you shot the day before, which has already been developed by the lab. If you're shooting with a digital camcorder, your results are immediate, and you have no dailies to speak of — you just cue up the thumbnails of your footage, click on the appropriate digital file and play back what you've shot.

Being positive about a negative cutter

If you originally shot on motion picture film, cutting the film negative was one of the last steps before you were ready to make prints of your film for theatrical distribution. Today, very few film negatives are cut; instead, the untouched negative is transferred to digital and cut electronically through a nonlinear editing system.

Some die-hard filmmakers still want to have their negatives physically cut, but it can be expensive and time-consuming. The negative cutter follows your *edit decision list* (EDL), which is an electronic printout of numbers that relate to each edit if your movie was cut on a nonlinear editing system, or the actual edge-code numbers printed on your *film work-print* (a print of your film that can be handled) if you're physically cutting the actual celluloid film.

The EDL on computer disc can also instruct a computer in a professional post-production editing bay to assemble your project into a final edited production onto a digital file. It finds the shots that are to be edited together and matches up the correct numbers at the end of one cut and the numbers assigned to the new cut. This is usually done in a professional editing bay if you off-lined your movie on your computer in a lower picture resolution — possibly because you didn't have the hard drive space to do higher picture resolution.

TIP

The best place to find a negative cutter is through your film laboratory's recommendation. You want a good negative cutter who will delicately cut your film negative, keeping it safe from dust and scratches.

Color-correcting your movie: As plain as black and white

Before you release your movie, your footage has to be graded and color-corrected shot by shot, scene by scene, so that the shots match perfectly. For example, when you're shooting outside, the sun is constantly moving and changing the color temperature of your footage (see Chapter 11 for color temperature info). One shot may not match a previous shot because the tint is slightly different.

You may want to enhance the color of your scenes, such as make your skies bluer or add more saturation of colors, adding more contrast to your footage that requires shot-by-shot adjustment. If you're making a Western or period piece, you may want to pull out some of the color or infuse a sepia tone into the entire production. If it's a war drama, you may want a grainy, drained-of-color look to add to the dangerous and dreary settings.

When color-correcting the actual film negative, a machine called a *hazeltine* or *color analyzer* calibrates the settings of color correction and exposures, which the printing department follows. Your negative footage appears on a monitor showing how the positive picture and color will look when projected on the screen. The person working for the lab who corrects the color is called the *timer.* If you color-correct your film for TV release, streaming or theatrical release the color corrector is called a *telecine operator* or *colorist.*

REMEMBER

If you're editing your movie on a nonlinear editing system in your computer after you've transferred your film footage to digital or originally shot on digital, you can now control and correct the image color with the editing software on your computer. Digital footage is often recorded raw or with basic settings that give you a neutral image without any enhancements. The correction that you make in the post-production stage is usually to enhance the colors and contrast of the images, or to change them completely for effect.

Coloring your world

Every movie requires some tweaking of the visual look. Often, when you're shooting in digital you will be shooting raw, meaning the camera is shooting footage without knowing what colors and shading is correct. You can do some of that in the camera, but you have much more latitude and control when you are in the post-production phase. You have the luxury of time to decide what "look" you want your footage to have. Will the colors be bright and colorful like a family Disney movie? Or will the colors be weak and drained of color in a story of dramatic tragedy? Color-correcting and controlling the lights and darks (contrast) from one shot to another to match the overall look is also important.

L.U.T.s to look up

A L.U.T. stands for *look up table*. Every digital camera's manufacturer, whether it be a Red Dragon cinema camera, to an Arri Alexa, offers a customized L.U.T. A L.U.T. is software with precise settings for each specific camera that you can load into the camera before you shoot — or into the editing program when you are starting to edit your movie. A L.U.T. is a prefigured set of calculated numbers that starts you off with a presentable image for that specific camera. In other words, the L.U.T. gives you a color-corrected and graded image that you can then tweak to your personal taste. It's better than starting from scratch with a raw, washed-out image straight from the camera. For example, Final Cut Pro X offers a plug-in that has hundreds of preconfigured L.U.T.s — you choose your camera from the list, and apply the designated L.U.T. to your footage. You may not even have to color-correct your film manually if you are happy with the look of the L.U.T. after you drop it over your footage. You may just need to do some tweaking shot-to-shot to make sure everything matches the environment.

TECHNICAL STUFF

Most editing programs come with color-correction software built in, but you can also purchase a myriad of color-correction software programs that have pre-sets for different looks, or that let you start from scratch. Red Giant Software has an application called Magic Bullet Looks, as well as a plug-in called Colorista, that contains circles of color that let you choose the correct colors and shades by moving your cursor around the color wheels. Lots of third-party companies make color-correction plug-ins, including FXFactory, whose Color Cone allows you to bend shades and play with any of the colors of the spectrum to give you precise and pleasing aesthetic results.

Cloning, Not Copying; Cloning, Not Copying

In the past, making a *dub* (copy) of your VHS tape (now an archaic format) was as simple as taping from one machine to another or taking the tape to a video-dubbing company (which made dubs in quantity at one time). But the dub never looked as good as the original. It was always grainy and softer in focus — kind of like a photocopy of a photocopy that gets more and more fuzzy. But now, when you make a copy from a digital file to an external drive or author it onto a DVD, you're making an exact duplicate of the original material. You're actually making a *clone* — a copy of the original with no degradation in picture quality. So the clone you send to people looks as good as the original footage.

Most post-production houses offer this service either in-house or through an affiliated company, but you can also do it on your own. Most PC and Mac computers make it easy for you to burn your own DVDs right on your computer. Wondershare makes DVD Creator, which lets you author and burn DVD and Blu-ray copies with over 100 free DVD menu templates to choose from (check out www.wondershare. net). Roxio makes a popular software program called Toast, which, in addition to authoring and burning DVDs and Blu-ray discs, also has settings to compress and convert a myriad of digital formats.

Whenever I need a lot of DVDs, I turn to a company called Disc Makers. They are a premium company that has excellent quality control and shipping. I've used them to make tens of thousands of DVDs when I've sold my movies to Redbox. Give Disc Makers a call — tell them I sent you and they'll give you a deal!

REMEMBER

Blu-ray is a high definition optical disc format that was developed not only to hold more digital information (more than 10 times that of regular DVD discs), but also to hold programs and movies at the highest HD quality available (more on this in Chapter 19 on distribution). The name *Blu-ray* derives from the blue laser light used to read this type of disc. Most studio releases are available on DVD and Blu-ray format (and some even come with a digital file of the movie which is even higher quality). Ultra Blu-ray is a brand new format that supersedes the already-high quality of regular Blu-ray and can display 4K movies. Ultra Blu-ray players are also *backwards-compatible,* meaning they will play regular DVD and Blu-ray discs.

Chapter **16**

Posting Your Movie's Soundtrack: Adding Music and Effects to the Mix

More than 80 percent of the sound in a movie is added *after* shooting, during post-production. All the different types of sound — dialogue, sound effects, music, and so on — are recorded separately and then mixed together to create one soundtrack. If you really want to take notice of sound that's been added, watch an animated film like *Spider-Man: Into The Spider-Verse, The Incredibles, Toy Story,* or *The LEGO Movie* for which 100 percent of the sound was created (an animated picture requires all sounds to be created from scratch to match the images). For an animated film, the actor's dialogue is usually recorded months before the animation is even created, and the animated character's lips are matched to the live actor's dialogue recordings.

Even if your movie features live actors, you need to add sound effects, music, and other sound elements in order to strengthen the production value of your film. Sound effects enhance visual elements, putting some real *punch* into a punch, for example. Music, whether it's licensed songs or composed specifically for the picture, enhances the mood of a film. This chapter explains what these other sound elements are, how to record or acquire them, and how to mix it all together yourself or find a professional sound mixer to make your film's soundtrack sound great.

Finishing Sound in Post-Production

After your movie is *locked* (picture editing and timing of the film will not change, and dialogue is synced up with the picture; see Chapter 15 for details), you're ready to start adding another dimension to your baby: sound design.

The *re-recording mixer*, also known as the *post-production sound mixer*, takes all the sound elements of your production and mixes them down into one master soundtrack that complements the picture. On a tiny budget, you may be the sound mixer, but the job requires some technical know-how and artistic skills and may be too ambitious an undertaking. Finding someone with experience, if you can, is the best route to go. On bigger budget productions, you may have a team that includes three mixers working together. One controls the music, one mixes sound effects, and another handles the dialogue.

The key to mixing the final elements is knowing how and when to feature different sounds and controlling the volume of each element. When dialogue comes in while music is playing, the mixer needs to find an appropriate volume level so that the music doesn't drown out the dialogue or disappear behind the scene. A sound that is too loud or too soft can distract from the action. Sound-mixing a film is similar to sound-mixing a song in which lyrics and instrumentation are combined and balanced so all the elements are heard clearly.

REMEMBER

The more layering of sound you have, the more professional your soundtrack will seem. The effect is subliminal. A good sound mix is transparent and doesn't call attention to itself to your audience — but they're sure to notice a bad mix.

Stirring up the mixer's toolbox

The post-production mixer brings artistic and technical skills to the mix, but the following tools make the job easier:

- » Mixing board (a physical board with knobs and sliders or an equivalent board incorporated into your sound software)

- » Computer (most home computers can accommodate sound software)

- » Sound mixing software

- » External hard drive, or storage discs (CD-ROM, DVD, or Blu-ray) for output of files to sync to your final production

If using a computer, you input the separate audio tracks — containing dialogue, sound effects, songs, and musical score — into the computer and mix them by using special sound-mixing software (again it's recommended you hire a professional mixer if you're not versed on the technical aspects of sound mixing). The tracks are then balanced and output as audio files to an external hard drive, or storage discs. From there, the sound can be transferred to a locked digital master, or to an optical track of your film print (if finishing on film). (See the section "Outputting Your Final Mix," later in this chapter for more information.)

Pro Tools has been the sound-mixing software of choice for professional sound designers. It's the sound equivalent of a picture-editing system like Avid or Final Cut Pro (see Chapter 15) and is actually put out by Avid. A free version called Pro Tools First might be all you need. You can also finalize your sound mix in Final Cut Pro X if you so desire. The software with a myriad of audio tools to fix and enhance your sound mix also comes with a large royalty free sound effects library ready to plug into your audio timeline!

TIP

If you want (or need) to hire a seasoned post-production sound mixer, call local sound studios and ask for contact numbers and/or email addresses. You can also look for a sound mixer at www.crewnet.com and www.media-match.com, which lets you search for any crew position by city or state. I have used Juniper Post in Los Angeles on many of my final sound mixes for my movies. Ben Zarai, my sound mixer at Juniper Post, has given me some phenomenal final mixes. They have also all passed strict quality checks (QC) that many TV stations, streamers, and foreign buyers insist on (including delivering perfect M&E tracks, which I discuss in the section "Separating music and effects tracks for foreign release," later in this chapter).

Mixing the right balance

The sound mixer plays each scene of your movie repeatedly as he or she mixes and syncs the sound elements. These elements consist of:

- » Dialogue

- » Sound effects

>> Foley (footsteps, falls, fight sounds, hand props, and so on that are matched perfectly to the actor's on-screen actions by Foley artists — see "Getting to know Jack Foley" later in this chapter)

>> Musical score (including songs)

>> Voice-over narration

>> Ambience (background environmental sounds)

>> Source music or songs within the scene (on radio, TV, or a performing band), which has to be recorded specifically for the film or with permission to use the source from the originator or owner of the music

REMEMBER

The sound mixer must make sure the dialogue, music, and effects aren't competing with each other, controlling the audio levels so that the sounds balance one another. On a small production, the sound mixer is usually in charge of mixing all the elements, which include dialogue, music and songs, sound effects, Foley, and ambience. The key to a good sound mix is staying focused on the picture so that the audience can stay focused on your story.

The mixer controls a separate track for each individual element, including several tracks of dialogue. The dialogue editor prepares a separate audio track for each actor's dialogue so that the sound mixer can control each actor's dialogue in terms of audio level and equalization individually to get clear-sounding dialogue. On a small production, your dialogue editor is often the same person who edits your picture. Each sound category is marked on the physical mixing board (if it's not a virtual mixing board in your software) so that the mixer knows which volume slider controls which track. A movie soundtrack can have unlimited individual audio tracks on top of each other containing different sound elements, as the mixer can keep layering and mixing (adjusting appropriate audio levels), on as many different tracks until you've got one complete master soundtrack.

REMEMBER

The sound mixer is also responsible for *cleaning up* the dialogue tracks: making sure there is no distracting background noise from the set before, during, or after the actor's dialogue. Also, the mixer mixes in ambience from the take under the actor's dialogue to fill in any gaps or drop-outs in the audio. This smooths out the audio between the actors and creates a seamless track of clean dialogue.

The sound mixer can emulate certain effects through the mixing board or a software program; for example, a *telephone filter* can make a voice sound as though it's coming through a telephone. *Reverb* can add an echo to a voice to make it sound like the actor is speaking in an auditorium, and even make voices sound like they're a fair distance away. In addition to these specialty effects, audio filtering can be adjusted to minimize (or hopefully remove) any *noise*, or hissing, that may be on the recorded audio track.

The mixer also prepares *music and effects* (M&E) *tracks* without the actors' dialogue so that, if the movie is purchased for distribution in a non-English-speaking country, it can be dubbed in the language of choice and still retain the music and sound effects. You can find further details on M&E in the section "Separating music and effects tracks for foreign release," later in this chapter.

A qualified sound mixer has an "ear" for mixing the right volume levels and finding a happy medium between the dialogue, music, and sound effects so they aren't competing with each other. To help ride the proper audio levels of each sound element, sometimes the sound mixer refers to a cue sheet prepared by the sound editor that indicates when each effect will be coming up (so the mixer can anticipate lowering or raising the volume of the upcoming sound element). If you're mixing your own audio, there's a great software plug-in called Voice Leveler by Accusonus, which you can find at www.fxfactory.com. It fixes uneven dialogue levels and smooths out the audio levels to match throughout your entire sound mix. It's only $49 — I like the sound of that!

Looping the loop

Looping, also called *ADR* (automatic or automated dialogue replacement), is the art of replacing dialogue that wasn't recorded clearly on the set or couldn't be recorded properly because the location was too noisy to get good audio. The actor watches on a monitor or movie screen the shot or scene for which dialogue needs to be replaced. Through a set of headphones, the actor listens to the unusable audio replayed over and over again (looped) and then repeats the lines for rerecording, trying to match what's on the screen. (See Figure 16-1.) The best audio take is kept and edited to match the picture as closely as possible. The mixer works magic with equalization and reverb to make it sound as close to the previously recorded on-set dialogue as possible.

REMEMBER

If an actor steps on a line, stutters, or screws up a word during actual shooting, it can be rerecorded in an ADR session and mixed back into the dialogue tracks. Often times, it's not the actor's fault; instead a plane flies overhead, a garbage truck churns its grinding presence outside, or some crew member talks over a take with "When's lunch?"

Creating Sound Effects with a Bang

Turn the sound off on your TV, and you'll realize how much less dramatic the action seems without sound effects (or music or dialogue). Sound effects can be very subtle, like a key jiggling in a lock, or very dramatic, like a thunderous explosion of a missile strike. Almost all the sound effects that accompany a film are added or re-created in post-production. Dialogue is the only sound from the actual filming that's retained all the way to the final picture — but not without enhancement.

TIP

Using a sound effect to suggest an action or event that you can't afford to shoot is often just as effective as showing the whole event. For example, say you want to include a car crash in your movie. A car drives out of the frame, and a few seconds later you hear a terrible crash (another sound effect) — and then a lone tire rolls into the shot. You've created a believable effect — without totaling the car! You can create your own sound effects or license them from a sound-effects library. Do you have an inexpensive aerial drone doubling for the point-of-view of a military helicopter looking down on your subjects? Just add the sound effect of a high-flying helicopter, and you've just upped your production value!

Listening to digital sound-effects libraries

You can find almost every sound effect imaginable in sound-effects libraries. Sound Ideas is one of the world's largest publishers of sound-effects libraries. I'm currently using one of its sound packages called the General 6000 Series. This series contains every imaginable sound effect; you have 40 CDs' worth of sounds to choose from. Other series libraries are also available for direct download via Sound Ideas's website or you can get larger libraries on an external hard drive. Check out its website at www.sound-ideas.com to see the different categories of sound-effects libraries offered. The sound effects are all digitally mastered and include these categories:

>> **Animals:** Dogs, cats, birds, exotic animals

>> **Devices and machines:** Telephones, cellphones, fax machines, coffee makers

>> **Fights:** Punches, jumps, falls

>> **Locations:** Airports, restaurants, schools, playgrounds

>> **Office environments:** Office machines, printers, elevators

>> **People:** Crowds, applause, footsteps, laughing, crying

>> **Toys:** Wind-up toys, race cars, spring-action toys

>> **Vehicles:** Planes, trains, automobiles, boats

>> **Cartoon:** Funny sounds, exaggerated noises, silly boings, swishes, and so on

Some sound-effects libraries let you download individual sound effects for as little as $1 an effect. Many stock footage libraries, such as Pond5's (www.pond5.com), also offer thousands of individual sound effects for downloading. An online search for sound effects can find you pretty much any sound effect you need, ready for download. After they're downloaded directly to your computer, you can easily plug those sound effects right into your editing timeline.

A professional sound-effects library on CD's or an external hard drive can cost anywhere from $100 up to $1,000, depending on how extensive it is. I often use the Digital Juice sound-effects found at www.digitaljuice.com as part of the Digital Juice lifetime subscription. You can browse, search, and preview tens of thousands of sound effects right on your desktop! Chances are, you'll find the sound effect you're looking for.

If you're mixing your film at a professional mixing studio, most times you can use its sound-effects library for no additional charge.

REMEMBER

Creating and recording your own sound effects

If you want to save money and have some fun, you can record your own sound effects. I did that for many of my independent films. I went to the airport and recorded sounds of planes and helicopters taking off and landing; I recorded the sound of opening and closing my fridge door, and hammering a nail into a piece of wood — right on my iPhone. I immediately get pristine digital audio, which I can email to myself and then plug the audio file directly into my editing program.

TIP

You can also record sound effects using your digital camera. Record your sound effects using a good external microphone. Better not to use the camera's built-in attached mic. Just make sure that you use an external microphone appropriate for recording the particular sound effect you want. (Use a directional microphone for concentrated sounds like keys dropping on the ground and an omnidirectional mic for recording ambient sounds like the ocean or a crowded restaurant. See Chapter 12 for more on microphones.) You may want to keep the cap on the camera so you know that you were recording for audio purposes only (but remember to take the cap off while shooting your actual movie!).

You can also record your sound effects on a portable digital recorder like the Zoom H5 handy recorder that records to SD cards for professional digital quality sound. You might want to check out www.zoom-na.com to get more info on its portable sound recorders.

TIP

Don't be afraid to experiment when creating sound effects. Emulate skaters on an ice rink by scraping knives together, or punches by slamming dough on a counter. Make alien sound effects by slowing down, speeding up, or mixing several sounds together. Need the sound of a roaring fire but the real thing doesn't roar? Try crumpling paper into a ball close to a microphone. Waiting for the thunder in a rainstorm? Wait no longer; get a piece of tin or even a cookie sheet and flap it around. Voilà — thunder inside your house! On my movie, *The Amazing Wizard of Paws*, I had an actor running in a suit of armor. The suit was cheap and made of plastic, and it didn't sound like it was made of metal at all. In post-production, I clanked some metal pots and pans together and dubbed it over the picture — and everybody thought it was a real suit of armor! One of my secrets is taking several different sound effects and layering them on top of each other to create unique sound effects that are even more effective than just one single sound.

Getting to know Jack Foley

Named after its innovator, Jack Foley, *Foley walking* is a precise sound-effects technique where an artist (also called a Foley artist) watches the screen and reenacts the actors' interaction with items in real time to re-create the sound effects that accompany the images on the screen. Foley effects include footsteps, clothes rustling, objects being handled, and body impacts.

Foley walkers often use a Foley pit (sophisticated audio post-production facilities usually have such a pit available). A Foley pit consists of separate small floor panels with different surfaces such as hardwood flooring, carpeting, concrete, and even water. The Foley walker has different surfaces at his or her disposal and walks "in place" on these surfaces while watching the actors on screen in order to match their actions. A skilled Foley artist usually watches the scene a few times before acting out the action and then creates the Foley sounds at the same time as the action is playing out on the screen while it's being recorded to digital files.

A professional Foley artist often brings a large suitcase containing items to assist him or her in re-creating sound effects to match the picture, such as various shoes, an assortment of hand props (paper, cutlery, stapler, and so on). Letting the Foley artist know what special elements may be helpful to bring when adding Foley to your picture (for example, coconut shells cut in half can emulate horses hoofs trotting across the pavement) is also helpful. I've seen a few burly Foley walkers put on women's shoes to emulate a woman on screen trekking down the street in high heels. (I can imagine a Foley walker's business card with the slogan, "I'm not a cross-dresser, but I may need to put on high heels.")

Foley is different from using a sound-effects library because it's easier to emulate someone walking up a flight of metal stairs and matching it in one take with a Foley walker. With a sound-effects library, you would have to find individual footsteps and match each step every time the actor moved up one step. This would take more time and more work to sync up.

The best way to locate a Foley artist is by contacting a local sound studio or TV station and asking if it has a list of professional Foley artists. You can also log on to soundlister.com/foley-artist and see if a Foley artist is in your neighborhood.

TIP

If you can't afford a professional Foley artist (which could cost upwards of $35 an hour), you can have fun doing your own Foley. You'll just have to do a lot of practicing. You can put together your own Foley pit by using a square foot or two of different surfaces like tile, wood, concrete, and carpet, plus a bucket with water (for splashing sounds). Just take a trip to your local hardware store to find these various surfaces. You create your own fight sounds by punching into a bag of flour or sand. You can use household items to enhance sounds made by your actors interacting with items on screen, like keys jingling, pens clicking, and cutlery clinking. For my film *First Dog,* I punched drywall nails through each finger of a pair of gloves, and then tapped my fingers while watching the dog onscreen to create the sound of the pup trotting along the sidewalk.

Adding room tone: Ambience or background sounds

Ambience is the background sound that gives your soundtrack fullness and enhances the location environment. Ambient sounds can be the buzzing of an air-conditioner working overtime, dogs barking in a neighborhood, or water dripping in the kitchen sink. Often, the production sound mixer records a loopable ambient track during the shoot (see Chapter 12). The post-production sound mixer can also enhance a scene by adding ambience from a sound-effects library that may have a fuller sound than the original location — like sounds of birds chirping in a park, or a nearby cascading waterfall. Ambience under a scene also covers up any gaps or sound dropouts between dialogue to create a seamless and even flow behind the actors' dialogue.

Scoring Big with Music

Turn on a classical radio station and close your eyes while the orchestral pieces play — you can't help but imagine visual images created by the music. Instrumental music can help evoke and enhance a mood in each scene of your movie and create an underlying emotion that the audience can feel. Add some songs with lyrics, and you've got a movie soundtrack.

Conducting a composer to set the mood

A *composer* can write an original music score to custom fit your film perfectly. He or she composes a theme that identifies your film and enhances the emotion and subtext of your story. The composer should write music appropriate to each scene. You wouldn't have pounding rap music during a romantic interaction of two people having a candlelit dinner. Some musical scores, such as the scores from *Jaws, Star Wars, Jurassic World,* and *Harry Potter* and the emotional orchestral score of *Titanic,* have become easily identifiable because they capture the style and theme of each film so well.

Nowadays, composers can record an entire movie soundtrack without leaving their garage or studio — and without hiring a single live musician. But although synthesizers and samplers have gotten better, they still can't replace the sensation of human breath filling an acoustic instrument or the emotion and passion of an artist breathing life into a musical instrument. Hiring musicians can be expensive, however; so a synthesized orchestra is often a cheaper way to go. Or you can combine synthesized music with real musicians. That's what composer Greg Edmonson did on my film *Turn of the Blade* to create a score that sounded more like a real orchestra.

Music software sounds less synthesized nowadays than it did when synthesizers first came onto the scene because music software these days uses *samples*. Samples are exactly that — they are samples from actual recordings of actual music notes — drums, wind instruments, and strings being strung. These samples can be arranged to form a more realistic sound, emulating a real orchestra.

When the composer is working to create my movie's soundtrack on his computer, I often remind him to add some reverb. This creates the subliminal feeling that the orchestra was conducted in a large hall/studio, the way most big-studio tracks are recorded. It also gives it that big, expansive feeling.

The best way to look for a composer is by calling the local sound-recording facilities in your area. Your local TV station may recommend a composer who works in your town. You can also contact the various music organizations (BMI, ASCAP, and SOCAN) and get a free list of their members — composers, musicians, and songwriters. Crew Net (www.crewnet.com) is a free service that lets you search for a composer (and other crew positions) by city or state. Media-Match (www.media-match.com) also provides a similar service via the Internet. I've discovered some great musical talent (composers and song artists) at VersusMedia (www.versusmedia.com) and composers from all over the world at Soundlister (www.soundlister.com).

If you plan on using any music you didn't commission and pay for, be sure it's in the public domain (see "Finding songs in the public domain" and "Orchestrating the rights to popular music" later in this chapter). If you're not sure of the rights or you didn't pay to use someone else's music, you're making yourself liable for a lawsuit — don't take that chance!

Composing your own music

You can use music software programs that put you at the keyboard — and you don't even have to read music or have ever played a note in your life. SmartSound makes Sonicfire Pro, which enables you to become your own composer, using your own computer (see Figure 16-2). The program gives you custom control over genre, style, and duration. You don't have to be a musician or know how to read music to get professional results. It's easy to use and starts at $199 (depending on how many library music discs you buy with the software). You just input your picture footage into Sonicfire Pro, choose from the music library selections that you own for the style of music (scary, happy, energetic, romantic, thriller), then point and click to cut, rearrange, and control the music and length to match your picture perfectly! Check out Sonicfire Pro at www.smartsound.com.

If you have a Mac computer, then you have a free app called GarageBand. It lets you arrange and play sounds using samples and loops of instruments to create your own music. GarageBand also has over 400 sound effects that you can use in your movie as well.

Another great way to add music easily to your production is through the Create Music website (www.createmusic.com). You do everything online. You move your completed movie or scenes into your web browser, and then through the Create Music website you can access all types of musical scores, which you can input into the timeline and adjust the timing of the music clip to match the length of each scene. There's no software to download; you do it all online on their website.

FIGURE 16-2:
Sonicfire Pro makes importing your movie and then customizing your own music easy. Here I am at a *For Dummies* book signing with a friend.

The sound of music libraries and music software

If you're on a limited budget, you may not be able to afford a composer to write and score original music for your film, and you may not have the patience to use a music program like Sonicfire Pro or GarageBand. That's where music libraries come to the rescue. Just as you can get sound effects from a CD library or online, you can get music of every conceivable type, which you pay a fee to use in your movie. Your project will sound very professional if you use music from a music library. The main disadvantage though is that the music clips will not be timed to end exactly when your scene ends unless you luck out and find a music clip that's the same length as your scene. But you can fade out the music when your scene ends or do a soft audio dissolve between tracks. Some great music libraries can be found at www.pond5.com, www.killertracks.com, and through www.digitaljuice.com, if you have a subscription.

Some music libraries charge a *needle-drop fee,* which is a fee charged literally every time a music cue starts and stops during your movie. But most provide *royalty-free* music, meaning that after you buy the CD or download the file, you get a lifetime of unlimited use of that music cue in your movie — so get out your (music) library card!

Companies such as Music Bakery (www.musicbakery.com) also provides a wide variety of music cues to choose from for your film projects. I've been using Music Bakery's music for years, and I've always been impressed with the selection. Some of the categories that music libraries offer include a variety of musical styles and genres: jazz and blues, orchestral, rock and urban, corporate image music (short music intros appropriate for logos), drama and suspense, and more.

TIP

Music libraries allow you to sample their music via the website so that you can select tracks for your project without having to buy before you hear it (the music cue will have an audio watermark, which is removed when you license the clip). Creative Support Services (CSS) is another music library that provides a broad range of music for film projects. At its website (www.cssmusic.com), you can listen to thousands of music tracks — if you have the time.

Singing original songs

You can enhance your movie and add some energy to certain scenes by slipping in some songs. Finding new talent in clubs and showcases (maybe you'll find the next Beatles or Lady Gaga) can be a lot of fun — not to mention cheaper than having to license a well-known song from a major recording label. You're sure to find bands that will be excited to have one of their songs in your movie. If you offer to let them keep the rights to the song, they may let you use it for free. You really just want permission to use their song within the context of your film — they can continue to own the rights to their song.

Versus Media (www.VersusMedia.com) is a one-stop website to find song artists looking to provide existing or original songs for film productions. Zero Fee Music (www.ZeroFeeMusic.com) provides free songs (to eligible filmmakers) from its song catalog. You only have to list its songs on your music cue sheets (see cue sheets later in this chapter), and when you sell your movie to television, the TV station pays the royalties to the artist's music organization and that's where the song artists may see some payment for their song(s) in your movie.

REMEMBER

Always have some written agreement between yourself and the band. It's best to have an attorney versed in entertainment or music contracts write it up for you. You can find music and song agreements in *Contracts for the Film & Television Industry* by Mark Litwak, along with other staff and crew contract information (buy the book or download contracts from Mark's website, www.marklitwak.com). Your agreement should clearly state that the band is providing you the original lyrics and music in a recording that you can use in your movie (for no charge, or a nominal fee), and the band owns the song that can be used in the context of your film. Any royalties paid by the band's music association (BMI, ASCAP, or SOCAN) is paid from the TV network that licenses the film and follows the music cue sheets to see who gets paid for the music.

Orchestrating the rights to popular music

Music companies have dedicated licensing departments for the very purpose of licensing songs for use in feature films, TV productions, and commercials. A well-placed song can be as lucrative for a band and its recording company in a soundtrack that sells at a store or online as it is having the song in the finished film. But recording companies don't just let you use their music for free; you have to pay a licensing fee.

TIP

Using a recognizable song in your movie can cost upwards of $20,000 for the *synchronization rights* (connecting musical recordings up with film or TV works). You can save some money if you use the lyrics from the song but have your newly discovered band do its own rendition (you still need to license permission to use the lyrics and written composition). Many bands have their own garage studio where they can record a song or two for relatively little money, or they have contacts with professional sound studios that may give them a discount or offer some free studio time as a favor.

Cueing up cue sheets

When you sell your movie to a distributor, you need to provide a music *cue sheet.* This sheet, usually prepared by the composer, is simply a listing of all the music cues in your film. A cue sheet lists the cue number, the time length of the cue, and a brief title or description of what the music piece relates to in the film (for example, David meets Misty). Cue sheets help the music organizations like BMI, ASCAP, and SOCAN monitor their members' contributions to various projects and to send out the appropriate royalties for the use of their music (paid by TV networks and streaming services).

Finding songs in the public domain

Seventy years after the life of the author of a song, its copyright expires, and the song enters the *public domain.* Anyone can use material in the public domain without having to license it from the owner's estate or get permission to use it for professional (and profitable) purposes. Most of Gilbert and Sullivan's famous songs, such as "The Modern Major General," are in the public domain. Titles such as "Pop Goes the Weasel" and "Row, Row, Row Your Boat" are other well-known ditties in the public domain. For various titles that are currently in the public domain, check out www.pdinfo.com. There was a controversy over the song "Happy Birthday." For years, people who used it were fined because it was copyrighted. However, after a ruling in 2015, the song is now in the public domain.

WARNING

A song or musical composition may be in the public domain, but the actual recording may be copyrighted, so make sure to do your research. The best thing to do is to have a composer rescore it and hire original singers and musicians to perform it. I even recommend working with a copyright attorney to make sure you don't run into legal issues.

Outputting Your Final Mix

Your sound mixer prepares separate audio tracks known as *stems* for your movie. Each set of stems consists of different mixed elements that make up your final mix. One set of stems contains the actors dialogue, one set is dedicated to all mixed music, and another set is for sound effects and Foley. When played together, these stems represent your final sound mix and are used in the making of your final release.

After you have your dialogue, sound effects, ambience, Foley, and music pulled together into your final mix, or *printmaster,* you're ready to sync sound to picture by transferring the sound to your film negative at the lab (if you are finishing on film). If your sound has been mixed for a digital release (which most are these days), the final soundtrack can be transferred directly into a digital-editing system via a hard drive, or from storage discs (DVD or CD). Sound files are not as big as video files, so your sound mixer may even be able to email you a folder of the final mixed files.

The final sound output is usually done by someone at the film lab when going to a film print. If you're finishing on digital on a nonlinear editing system on your computer, you can input it yourself, or if you're using an editor, they can input it and sync it up to the final picture.

REMEMBER

If finishing on film, the final sound mix is printed to the *optical track* of your film print. The sound and the film are then married to become one — for better or worse! Most films nowadays though are projected digitally, so even if you finish all your elements on film, chances are your movie will be transferred to a DCP (digital cinema package) on a portable hard drive and delivered to the theaters. However, if you want to use a popular sound format that makes your soundtrack really come to life, you need to run your printmaster through a format-specific encoding process. Dolby Labs licenses its popular Dolby Digital 5.1 and 7.1 surround encoding technology, giving a unique dimensional sound quality to your soundtrack.

Surrounding sound

Sound can be exciting to the ears, especially with the advancement in digital surround sound formats, which include Dolby Digital and DTS (digital theater systems) in both the 5.1, and 7.1 configurations, a three-dimensional sound experience. Standard 5.1 surround configures to three front speakers (left, center, and right), two surround channels (left surround, right surround, and a separate feed for a subwoofer for low-frequency material), to make your audience feel more like they're part of the action; 7.1 surround adds two more side speakers into the configuration for an even more immersive sound experience.

Listening in stereo

The average family does not have the sophisticated sound system attached to their TV or computer to take advantage of hearing that great 5.1 or 7.1 mix you are so proud of. Instead, your audio channels all get compressed down into two stereo channels when they are streamed or broadcast. Also, not all TV networks and streaming platforms output beyond stereo mixes. When you are mixing your final surround audio, you need to constantly check how it will also sound in stereo and that the compressed 7.1 or 5.1 channels mix nicely and cleanly and legibly into a stereo mix as well. With all the ways to view entertainment these days, you never know how your audience is going to be watching and listening to your movie — a tiny smartphone with limiting sound output, a computer with built-in speakers, or a TV with a beefed up, geeked out "octophonic" sound system?

Separating music and effects tracks for foreign release

If you know that you're going to have a distributor sell your movie in the foreign markets (overseas), you also need to make two separate printmasters: one that contains only the music and sound effects (*M&E tracks*) and another with just the English dialogue. Having this version of the printmaster enables a foreign distributor to dub the language of its country into the picture and still have the original music and sound effects tracks behind the dubbed voices. The English dialogue track is used only as a guide for the foreign dubbing actors.

Next time you're on an airplane that flies to a foreign country (including French Canada and Mexico), check the audio channels on the in-flight movie. You can often switch back and forth between languages, but you'll notice that the music and sound effects are the same on both channels.

Chapter **17**

Conjuring Up Special Effects

A *special effect* is something out of the ordinary that is added to a film during shooting or in post-production that entertains, amazes, or adds wonder to the story. Special effects — whether it's dinosaurs in your kitchen or cars turning into giant robots — they don't just happen in front of the camera in real time. They take preparation and skill. Like a magician creating illusions on-stage, you can create illusions for your movie. With special effects on-set through the camera or in post-production, you can fool your audience by making something look like it really happened! This chapter tells you what you need to know.

Creating Effects: In or Out of Camera?

You can create special effects in several ways:

» **In the camera:** To create effects in the camera, you use lenses and filters or you control exposure (see Chapter 10). You can do glass-reflection shots in the camera to create ghost effects, for example, and use forced perspective to make things appear bigger or smaller than they really are and change their perspective. You can add a photo or miniature close to the lens to appear life-size and real. Playing with speed and motion of the camera is another in-camera trick.

GENERATING COMPUTER EFFECTS

Almost every film you see nowadays has at least some computer-generated effects —
even if you don't notice them, such as some of the underwater scenes in *The Shape of
Water*, which were not shot underwater but instead with special lighting and smoke
effects. *A Beautiful Mind* has seamless digital effects, such as the seasons that magically
change right before the audience's eyes while John Nash (Russell Crowe) sits by his
window working on his thesis. Then you have films like *Black Panther* and *Solo: A Star
Wars Story* that have hundreds if not thousands of computer-generated effects created
in post-production, after the main photography of the film has been shot. These
amazing illusions, like the ones shown here from my film *Silly Movie 2*, can be created
entirely on a desktop computer.

© 2008 Bryan Michael Stoller/Island Productions, Silly Movie 2

There are some amazing software animation programs out there, including one called
CrazyTalk by Reallusion. You can virtually take any still photograph of a person or animal
and make it talk or sing! I was able to make my dog sing a song with just a few clicks
(and now he's got a record deal!). You can get more info and a trial download at www.
reallusion.com. Your smartphone might even have a similar animated emoji app that
turns you into an animated talking head during your facetime or video/text chats.

Adobe makes a software program called After Effects that is widely used in nonlinear
editing systems (see more on nonlinear editing in Chapters 15 and 16) to create many
amazing effects. If you're familiar with Adobe's Photoshop software, which lets you
manipulate photos and images, then imagine After Effects as Photoshop in motion. You
can take a still image of a truck, animate the wheels, add suspension in the cab, and create a moving image. For more information, go to www.adobe.com.

PLUGGING IN SPECIAL EFFECTS SOFTWARE

Often referred to as *plug-ins*, there are literally thousands upon thousands of special effects software apps from third-party companies that are designed to "plug-in" to your existing nonlinear editing system on your computer — this includes plug-ins compatible with Final Cut Pro, Adobe Premiere, and Avid's Media Composer editing programs. Some of the software plug-ins I use come from Red Giant Software (www.redgiant. com), FXfactory (www.fxfactory.com), PixelFilmStudios (www.pixelfilmstudios. com), BorisFX (www.borisfx.com), and Core Melt (www.coremelt.com). Plug-ins can do a thousand different things, such as changing footage from day to night, creating soft mattes around your footage, getting rid of actor blemishes and de-aging them using beauty software; changing the wording on signs and billboards; compositing with blue and green screens; and adding mind-bending transitions of every imaginable type (and ones you can't even imagine)! Light lasers, glow effects, reflections, holograms, shadows, sharpening and blurring filters, stabilizing and un-stabilizing (shaking) plug-ins, and even snow, rain, fog, and fire plug-ins.

Many nonlinear editing programs like Final Cut Pro come with a myriad of their own plug-ins, so you may not even need to purchase third-party software to achieve the effects you're looking for. Final Cut Pro includes built-in stabilization for your shots at the click of your mouse, fancy dissolves and transitions, and composite choices as well. Also, Final Cut Pro and third-party software include *presets*. Presets are effect plug-ins that you just drop onto your shot to achieve a pre-set look or effect that instantly transforms your shot without you manually changing or tweaking any settings (but you can still tweak and customize if you want to).

>> **On the set:** Effects created on the set include things like explosions, fire, and gunshots — even weather, like fog, rain, lightning, or snow (if you're creating it). Levitation and superhuman leaps can also be created on-set with wires attached to your actors (like Spider-Man leaping from building to building); the wires are removed (erased) in post-production. You can also use *matte paintings* (elements painted on glass in front of the camera) or front and back projection of locations onto a large reflective screen behind your actors.

>> **With makeup:** These types of special effects include horror makeup, latex appliances to the face, hair pieces, special teeth and contact lenses. Full-body costumes, such as a gorilla or Godzilla outfit, to the amphibian creature suit in *The Shape of Water,* also fall under this category.

>> **In post-production:** Using *opticals* (adding images together when completing on film, or with effects software in post-production when working digitally on a computer. This includes compositing images together using blue or green screen. Also CGI (computer-generated images) are very popular (and much more affordable nowadays) for generating special effects and creating images during the post-production phase.

The following sections of this chapter explain these different effect options in detail.

Dropping in Backgrounds

Often on an independent budget you can't afford to travel to a distant location to be used as a backdrop for your movie, or the location only exists in your mind (like a desert planet with three moons and a pink horizon). Fortunately, with a little know-how, you can place your actors into backgrounds that have either been shot separately (without any actors in the shot, called a *background plate*) or created completely in your computer. This is known as *compositing*, where several elements shot at separate times are combined to look like they were shot together as part of the same shot.

TIP

You can combine several different special effects, such as matte painting, miniature models, blue screen, and background plates, by *layering* them upon each other. It's like laying clear plastic sheets on top of each other, but each one has a different element that complements the previous plastic sheet and its element. After all the elements are blended together, you have a *composite*. Hawaiki Keyer is an amazing software plug-in that helps you create seamless composites (you can get Hawaiki Keyer through www.fxfactory.com).

Turning blue and green

In the blue-screen or green-screen process, the actor does the scene in front of a blue or green background, which is later replaced with a location background, miniature model, or computer-generated background (also known as a *background plate* — see the following section on plates). Imagine taking a pair of magic scissors and cutting away everything that's blue or green. You end up with what looks like a cardboard cutout of your actor that is then placed in front of any background. Your actor looks like she's really there and not in front of a screen at all. Green is used a lot now for the screen color, because that particular hue is not a common color that your actors would be wearing. If you have elves on your set, as I did while shooting *Santa Stole Our Dog*, I used blue screen a lot, because the elves wore green outfits and a character, "Elfis" wore green suede shoes — and they would have disappeared into a green-screen background!

TECHNICAL STUFF

John Fulton was one of the first effects creators to use what is known as the *traveling matte* using blue or green screen. Fulton designed the effects for *The Invisible Man* in 1933 (an updated version, *Memoirs of an Invisible Man,* in 1992, starring Chevy Chase, used the same blue-screen techniques over have a half-century later). Almost every movie today, even if it's a factual story, uses blue or green screen at some point. Alan Horn, CCO and co-chairman of The Walt Disney Studios, who provided an exclusive interview for me earlier in the book, told me that the movie *The Bucket List,* in which Jack Nicholson and Morgan Freeman traveled around the world, was mostly done on green screen and the actors never left California. Fictional and fantasy stories such films as *Star Wars, Jurassic Park,* and the *Avengers* tentpoles depend on the composite screen process to blend live-action actors into wondrous sci-fi and fantasy situations.

Figure 17-1 shows the prehistoric pig, *Jurassic Pork,* generated on the computer. The second image is me in *Miss Cast Away & the Island Girls* (also known as *Silly Movie 2*) against a blue screen (even though it's a black-and-white photo, I swear it was blue). When the two images are merged together and adding a background in post-production, you have what is called a *composite* with the action hero and the dinosaur appearing as if they are in the same shot together.

TIP

You don't have to use a professional blue or green screen — you can just use a plain-colored bed sheet, as long as you don't have that same color in your subject's clothing or hair coloring. Then in post-production, you remove the screen or sheet color and bring in your background plate to merge the elements together. If you want to purchase an effective and inexpensive blue or green screen (like the one I used in the composite shot in Figure 17-1), you can find tons on Amazon that are light and portable so you can easily take it to the set or stage. I even have friends who have painted a bare wall in their apartment completely blue and used it for blue-screen shots.

Dishing out background plates

Background plates are still-image photos or motion picture footage of particular locations. The still photos or moving footage of your background plate is inserted in post-production behind an actor or characters who performed the scene in front of a blue or green screen. Background plates are often shot after the main photography of your movie so that you know what background plates you will need. I've used stock footage of distant or difficult locations to get to, from Pond5 as background plates behind my actors (www.pond5.com). You can also do an Internet search for stock footage libraries to find a background plate that works for your particular shot(s).

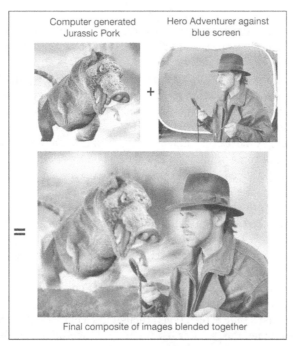

Computer generated
Jurassic Pork

Hero Adventurer against
blue screen

+

=

Final composite of images blended together

FIGURE 17-1:
The author (on right, not left) in a composite shot created from two images.

© Zandoria Studios/William Sutton, dinosaur concept

© Bryan Michael Stoller

TIP

Even your sophisticated smartphone is great for taking high-quality photos or digital footage of locations for background plates. Most smartphones are at least 10 megapixels, and many can even shoot 4K footage for background plates that have movement — such as trees blowing in the wind or ocean waves rolling over a sandy beach.

WARNING

Be sure to always shoot your background plates on a tripod; otherwise, they won't work as good background plates because they will be jiggling behind your actors when you composite them together.

A touch of glass: Matte paintings

Instead of constructing or destroying real cities, buildings, and other backgrounds, you can paint them! In the *Wizard of Oz*, the famous Emerald City is actually a *matte painting*. The grass and field of flowers in the foreground are part of a real set, but the background with the Emerald Castle and sky is painted on glass. A matte painting can actually be in front of the camera, the painted image can be positioned so that the glass and reflections are not seen through the camera lens, and the painting on glass looks to be part of the actual shot. A matte painting can also be photographed in post-production and merged with scenes already shot, which is often easier because you have more time to fuss around with it in the post-production phase.

The Gotham City skyline featured in *Batman* used matte paintings. And the film *Earthquake* used matte paintings to simulate earthquake damage to the high-rise buildings by placing paintings over the existing exteriors to simulate gaps, caved-in walls, broken windows, and partially collapsed buildings. Nowadays matte paintings are often painted digitally in the computer and married to the live-action footage in post-production.

Have you seen scenic backdrops?

Almost every television show or feature film uses billboard-sized scenic back-drops that either are blown up from an actual location photograph or are painted onto a light-durable material like vinyl or cloth material and positioned behind the actors on the set. (See Figure 17-2.) Scenic backdrops are often seen through the windows on stage sets. Or the high-rise building with the huge picture windows and the beautiful city skyline could be a scenic backdrop. An example of a city backdrop at night is of the Hollywood Hills seen every weeknight behind Jimmy Kimmel's desk on *Jimmy Kimmel Live.* Scenic backdrops are sometimes translucent so they can be backlit to give the image vibrancy, especially if it's a night scene. Backdrops save time and money in the long run because they're cheaper. Rather than go to Paris, for example, you can use a scenic backdrop of the Eiffel Tower outside the restaurant window, or hotel room balcony set.

FIGURE 17-2: Cloth backdrop in my living room with dog actor Little Bear, shows the effectiveness and realism of a scenic backdrop.

Scenic backdrops can also be projected from behind or from the front onto a reflected screen behind the actor that displays a deep sharp image from the projector. With the advancements in computer effects, however, most productions (that have the computer equipment and software) prefer to create the backdrop in the computer instead of using front or back projection.

SUSPENDED ANIMATION: STOP-MOTION

Stop-motion animation, using clay models, or fabricated characters from molds or household objects is another in-camera effect. Tim Burton opted to direct stop-motion puppets (*The Nightmare Before Christmas*, *FrankenWeenie*) instead of the electronic digital computer generated characters as in *Toy Story*, *The LEGO Movie*, or *Despicable Me*. Stop-motion is even more time-consuming, because small puppet characters have to be designed and then articulated, one frame at a time. Detailed, miniature scenic sets have to be built to scale with the stop-motion puppets. *Gumby and Pokey*, *Shaun the Sheep*, and *Wallace and Gromit* are in the family of this traditional and lovable 3D model animation technique.

Weathering the storm

Weather is considered a special effect on your production because you have to imitate Mother Nature (she doesn't usually storm on command). Many screen-writers don't think twice about starting a scene with, "It was a dark and stormy night." But unless you want to sit and wait for it to really rain, you have to create the storm yourself, and it's not cheap. Same with wind and snow. So unless it's crucial to the scene, leave it out.

TIP

Creating snow or rain outside a window for an indoor scene is a much easier effect to accomplish. Rain is as simple as having someone outside spraying a regular garden hose above the window — the water will fall and look like raindrops against the pane (just don't forget to close the window!). Rain is also easier to see if it's backlit. For snow, you can use various substances like dehydrated potato flakes or laundry detergent. With detergent powder have someone above the window (on a stepladder) sprinkling the dry soap flakes evenly from above. From inside, it looks like snowflakes are falling. Just make sure you don't mix your soap snowflakes with your garden hose rain — you'll have an outdoor bubble bath flooding the neighborhood!

TIP

If your Christmas movie's opening scene needs a warm and cozy shot of a winter home with a Christmas tree sparkling through the window — but you're shooting in the middle of July — here is a way to fool your audience. Get some thin sheets of cotton baton rolls and a garden hose. Lay out the cotton over the grass on the front lawn and a few clumps of cotton on the hedges and tree branches. Spray the cotton with the garden hose to get a more reflective icy looking surface. Wet down the driveway and the street in front so it looks like the snow has melted on the pavement. Winter wonderland in July — that's snow business!

Downsizing Miniatures

Many amazing effects have been achieved in the movies using *miniatures* (which are relatively small and usually built to scale). The film *Independence Day* had miniature cities and buildings, including Washington monuments built so they could be destroyed easily on camera. James Cameron used several miniature versions of the doomed ship in *Titanic*. One model, even though it was called a miniature (or a scale model), was the length of three cars. The establishing shots of the ancient Hogwarts castle in the *Harry Potter* movies was an intricate scale model (about fifty feet across and fourteen feet to the tallest steeple) with meticulous detail down to the weathered stones and the elaborate stained-glass windows. In my film *The Amazing Wizard of Paws*, I used a large ¼-scale working model of a classic steam-engine train for some very believable scenes. Spielberg used miniature sets in *Indiana Jones and the Temple of Doom* during the high speed coal-mining cart chase.

Looking down on miniatures

You need to keep several things in mind when shooting models and miniatures:

>> **Use pinpoint lighting (because you're lighting small objects) when filming indoor miniatures.** For exterior miniatures, such as towns, land-scapes, and roads, build the miniature set outside and take advantage of the real sunlight, as well as the real sky and clouds.

>> **Keep the camera on level with the miniatures, as if you and your camera are to scale with your miniature.** Only shoot higher if you're simulating a shot from a helicopter or tall building.

>> **If you're using miniature vehicles, water, or anything with movement, slow down the action so that the miniature doesn't move unrealistically too fast.** If the miniature is half the size of the real object, you slow the footage down by half. That is, you shoot at 48 frames per second — twice the speed of the normal 24 frames per second (thus, compacting double the frames in the same amount of time, which creates the illusion of slow motion). If your miniature is one-quarter the size of the real thing, slow it down by four times the actual speed — get the idea? By speeding up the frame rate, you slow down the real-time action when it's played back at the regular 24 frames per second. If you're shooting on digital files, you usually control the speed in the post-production phase. See the section "Cranking the camera and speeding slowly" for more on how to manipulate camera speed.

TIP

Keep in mind that the larger in scale your miniature is, the more realistic it will look, and the less chance your audience will think it's a small model. (See Figure 17-3.) This is especially helpful when your model has movement, which appears more real after you apply the appropriate frame rate to slow it down slightly.

Thanks to McCormick-Stillman Railroad Park, Scottsville, AZ.

Foreground Fooling

Figure 17-4 shows a dollhouse incorporated into an actual location with an actor. The actor is standing 30 feet from the camera and slightly to the right of the dollhouse and behind the miniature bicycle. The Victorian house is just 4 feet from the camera, and only 20 inches high. If the actor were to move closer to the camera, you would see the trick — it's only a fancy dollhouse — and the bicycle is a miniature as well.

FIGURE 17-4:
Miniature model house with toy bicycle in foreground.

Actor/model, Raquel Ames

In the movie *Elf* starring Will Ferrell and Ed Asner, director Jon Favreau used forced perspective right in the camera. He had Ed and Will in the foreground and framed the adult actors playing elves behind them so it looked like they were miniature people. He did this by altering the perspective in the design of the sets and by keeping the elves behind Will and Ed in focus.

Forcing the perspective, forcefully

If you stand at the end of a long road and look off into the distance (which I don't recommend, especially if it's a busy highway), the road appears to narrow as it reaches the horizon. With miniatures, you want to create this effect *without* the distance. This concept is called *forced perspective.* If you want to build a miniature road, for example, you cut out a long triangle instead of a long even strip of road. Position the triangle on the ground and put the camera at the widest end of the triangle. The point of the triangle will look like the road is going off into the distance (see Figure 17-5). Spielberg used this perspective trick effectively in *Close Encounters of the Third Kind* for scenes shot of the spaceships swooping down above the constructed runway at Devil's Tower.

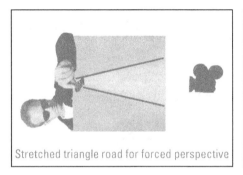
Stretched triangle road for forced perspective

Model, Tim Peyton

FIGURE 17-5: A miniature road designed for forced perspective.

Climbing the walls

In my teenage days, I made a short film called *Superham.* In it I had a scene of a Spider-Man-type character climbing what appeared to be the side of a brick building. The effect cost me all of $13. I bought a plastic sheet pressed with miniature bricks at the local hobby store. To defy the laws of gravity, I turned the miniature brick wall sideways, lining the edge up with the top of a short concrete wall 20 feet behind the miniature wall and had my actor crawl across the top of the short wall in the background. I turned the camera sideways, so it looked like my actor was crawling up the brick wall — and of course the miniature bricks turned sideways closer to the camera helped to complete the illusion. The original *Batman* TV series used this simple technique in every episode in which the caped crusaders used the bat rope to climb to the top of a building (their capes were held up by wires).

TIP

Storyboard your special effects so that the entire production team can see exactly what the effect is. See more on storyboarding in Chapter 9.

Creating Effects Right in the Camera

There are a lot of practical effects you can do right in the camera that don't require expensive or extensive work to create your final effect.

One effect you can do in the camera is to use a *beam splitter,* which is a half-mirrored piece of glass between the camera and your subject. The glass is positioned at a 45-degree angle to reflect an image that's off-camera into the glass that the camera is shooting through. The half-mirror is invisible to the camera except for the image it's reflecting into the glass. This makes your actor appear in the original shot as a transparent ghost. Another effect is keeping the camera on a steady tripod and then shooting your actor in multiple takes in different positions in the same frame. Then, in post-production you can take each different shot of the same actor and make it look like there are multiple versions of him in the same shot — as in my movie *The Amazing Wizard of Paws* where Ozzy magically multiplied. (See Figure 17-6.)

Backward about reverse photography

Reverse photography can be as obvious as somebody having a meal backward (you film your actor normally and then just reverse the footage in post-production) — it can get a hilarious (or gross) response from your audience. Or you can be more subtle and create an effect that doesn't immediately appear as if the footage was reversed.

I was shooting a commercial in which a superhero emerged from a phone booth and, like Superman, leaped up into the sky. It was a simple and easy to do effect. My actor stood on top of the phone booth (remember phone booths?), and the camera only framed to just below the top of the booth. The actor then jumped off the top, entering frame, and then straightened up and walked backward into the phone booth. I simply reversed the footage and it appeared as if he walked out of the phone booth and leapt straight up into the air.

In the opening credits of *Austin Powers: The Spy Who Shagged Me*, Austin Powers emerges from an outdoor swimming pool after a synchronized Busby Berkeley-type water folly and rises up into the air — with his hair and clothes completely dry. This was achieved by lowering him into the water, and then simply reversing the footage.

Double exposure, double exposure

A *double exposure* puts two different pictures or scenes together at the same time and runs them parallel to each other. You create a double exposure on film during post-production in the film lab, or putting one shot on top of another in your time line using a nonlinear editing system and change the transparency of one or both clip layers. The difference between a double exposure and a true blue- or green-screen composite (see the "Turning blue and green" section earlier in this chapter) is that the double exposure causes the person to look transparent like a ghost and not a solid part of the scene that it is double-exposed against.

Cranking the camera and speeding slowly

Undercranking and *overcranking* refer to manipulating the speed of a camera. You can often change speed on a motion-picture film camera by adjusting the camera itself. To change the speed of a digital camcorder, you can speed up the camera using the digital settings to create slow motion. For speeding up the footage to create a comic effect or have cars zipping quickly by, you usually have to change the speed during the post-production phase (unless you do time lapse or use an intervalometer within the camera settings — see more info on this later in this chapter). With these methods you can create interesting effects:

» *Overcranking,* **or speeding up the camera, creates the illusion of slow motion.** The faster the film runs through a film camera, the slower the motion will be. Running the film through the camera quickly gives you more individual frames to play back at regular speed (24 frames per second) — creating the illusion of slow motion. If you set your digital camera to shoot 240 frames per second, then you are slowing your footage down by 10 times when you play it back at 24 frames per second. Overcranking the camera is also a necessity when you're filming miniatures (see the earlier section "Downsizing Miniatures"). Remember that when shooting digital, there is no physical film or tape running through the camera — it's all 0's and 1's — there are no moving parts. Electronically the camcorder's computer is calculating the equation to tell the digital file to create slow motion. Think of it as compacting a lot of action into a small box, and then taking that small box and stretching it with the same information inside, but now it will take longer to play back that visual information which creates the slow motion. The longer you stretch the box, the slower the visual information will become.

» *Undercranking,* **or slowing down the camera, speeds up the action in your scene.** Car chases are often undercranked slightly to make cars appear as if they are traveling dangerously fast, like in the *Fast and the Furious.* *Undercranking* also refers to clicking frame by frame, similar to stop-motion animation (see Chapter 2). Because the frames end up missing some of the actual action, the actor or vehicle on camera appears animated or sped up.

» **Using time-lapse photography captures motion often imperceptible at real-time speeds.** An *intervalometer* is a timer (built in to many digital cameras) that can be set to click a frame at specific intervals, such as every second or every 24 hours. You've seen this effect with flowers blooming, clouds twirling through the sky, and buildings being constructed in a matter of seconds. GoPro is known to capture breathtaking and amazing 2K and 4K time-lapse shots with their new series of HERO cameras.

TECHNICAL STUFF

Speeding up the camera to get slow-motion sounds like a contradiction, but don't be confused. If a film camera is sped up and shoots 120 pictures (frames) a second, the action plays back as slow motion because the film or digital projector plays back at a constant speed of 24 frames per second (or 29.97 frames for some broadcast television). In other words, it takes the projector about six seconds to show the action that took place in one second. Most prosumer and professional digital cameras are capable of capturing amazing slow motion footage, even to the point of seeing the wings of a hummingbird that the human eye can't see in real time (the camera has to capture about 1,600 frames per second to be able to see the wings in slow motion).

Creating effects with lenses and filters

Special lenses and filters that you screw onto your camera or slide into a matte box (see Chapter 10) can alter or create a special element that you couldn't achieve using a normal lens. The difference between a lens and a filter is that a lens changes the size and dimensions of the picture in some way (such as a zoom lens, or distortion with a super-wide-angle lens — see Chapter 10). A filter usually plays with the color, exposure, or glare coming into the camera.

Special-effect filters change colors in unique ways (these are different from the color-correcting filters that I talk about in Chapter 10). For example, if the bottom part of the lens or filter is blue and the top part is yellow, the ground will appear blue and the sky yellow. Tiffen, one of the top developers and manufacturers of camera lens filters, makes a variety of these effects. Check out www.tiffen.com. Here's a list of common special-effect filters and lenses and what they do:

>> **Star:** Makes reflective objects in the picture twinkle

>> **Fog:** Creates a soft fog diffusion effect in the scene

>> **Prism:** Creates multiple images like a kaleidoscope of objects or actors in the frame

>> **Gradual:** Changes the color of the sky or the upper part of the frame

>> **Split diopter lens:** Keeps one side of the frame in focus where an actor might be too far or too close to be in focus with another actor or object. Think of it as a bifocal lens turned sideways for the camera.

TIP

Many third-party software companies make special filter software that emulate a variety of what a physical filter over the camera would do. I prefer to use filter software plug-ins in post-production as opposed to using a physical filter on the camera. You can't remove the filter effect if you use an actual filter over the camera, because then it becomes part of the original footage. BorisFX makes eye-popping effects and filter simulating software called Sapphire Plug-ins. Check out www.borisfx.com. Final-Cut Pro and other editing software programs often come with their own special effects and filter choices. Most of the software effects mentioned work as plug-ins with the various popular editing systems.

Exploding Effects on Fire

Most special effects that look dangerous in a movie are harmless effects created in the mind of the filmmaker. Explosions, fire, and guns, on the other hand, can be very dangerous. A *pyrotechnician* is trained to work with elements that could be extremely dangerous on your set. Creating explosions and fires and using ammunition are some of the skills a pyrotechnician has been trained for.

Never attempt any fire effects or explosions on your own. Always enlist the skills of a qualified pyrotechnician. You're also required to have a firefighter on-set to make sure that everyone remains safe and you are following all safety rules and regulation.

You can add fire later in post-production on your computer by superimposing layers of fire from a stock footage library or effects software plug in. Or with the skills of a licensed pyrotechnician you can actually set a fire in a controlled environment. *Backdraft*, Ron Howard's firefighting film, and Dwayne Johnson's *Skyscraper* used many controlled situations to simulate the danger of fire. These scenes were all supervised by a firefighter on-set along with a skilled pyrotechnician.

TIP

At Halloween time, you see fog machines in almost every novelty and department store — and of course tons to choose from on Amazon. They're small vaporizer-type devices that heat up and expel a harmless smoke-like steam into the air — similar to dry ice but much simpler and safer to use. Fog is great for catching the light and creating a misty and magical look to your scenes. Fog machines cost between $35 and $100, depending on the size of the machine. You can buy fog juice that heats up in the device and turns into fog that can be controlled to shoot out a nozzle in small or large bursts. Great for shooting a foggy night scene or smoking up a bar. Do you remember the flashlight beams cutting through the misty forest in *E.T.?* Fog machines were used to catch the rays of light and enhance the mood of the scene. A similar look was used in the Forbidden Forest in the *Harry Potter* movies.

You can also get a snow-making machine, which looks similar to a fog machine but spews out soap-like flakes to resemble falling snow. I used such a device on my film *Santa Stole Our Dog*. For all the scenes of the actors driving through the snow, I shot in a warehouse looking through the windshield of the car while the snow machine made it appear that the characters were driving through a snowstorm. To sell the effect even more, the windshield wipers were doing their job by keeping the (fake) snow from obstructing the driver's view of the road.

Making Up Your Mind about Makeup Effects

Special effects aren't just limited to illusions that look real only through the camera lens or after the post-production stage. Makeup is make-believe that can walk and talk without the magic of the camera but through the magic of talented makeup artists. Many people think of beauty makeovers when they think of makeup artists. You don't normally think of monsters, alien creatures, and flesh wounds — but the world of the makeup artist is a broad one.

Applying prosthetics

Prosthetics is a term associated with artificial limbs. In the world of special effects makeup, however, *prostheses* are used to create additional limbs, burn victims, and monster effects (often all the sick, gross stuff). Prosthetic pieces, also called *appliances,* are usually made of foam latex, which can move much like human skin and muscles. Makeup effects artist David Miller designed the conehead makeup for Dan Aykroyd and the entire Conehead population in the film *Coneheads.* He also designed Freddy Krueger's makeup for the *Nightmare on Elm Street* films. (Miller was working late one night trying to decide on the look of Freddy Krueger and glanced down at his melted cheese pizza — inspiration hit!) By gluing latex prosthetics in sections over his face and head, Christian Bale was completely unrecognizable as Vice President Dick Cheney in the film *Vice.*

You can also do mechanical makeup effects, like a head-cast made from an actor with features added to a fake head. I made a cameo appearance as a werewolf in one of my short films several years ago. My sister Marlene, a professional makeup artist, and makeup artist Jack Bricker took a cast of my head by pouring plaster over my face, leaving straws in my nostrils so I could breathe (that was the only time in my life that I've ever been plastered). When the plaster dried, they used the mold to design the werewolf head in latex and added hair and an extended muzzle to the *dummy head.* To save time and money, they only made a half-head because the final shot was a profile, and the camera would never see the other side (see Figure 17-7).

Here's looking at scleral lenses

Remember Michael Jackson in *Thriller* with the devilish eyes? Jim Carrey's strange eyes in *The Mask,* and *The Grinch?* What about the White Walkers with the ice-blue eyes in *Game of Thrones?* The apes with the black eyes in Stanley Kubrick's *2001: A Space Odyssey?* The actors all had to wear special contact lenses. These special lenses are called *scleral lenses,* which have funky pupil designs and are fitted to cover the actor's eyes like conventional contact lenses.

Linda Blair wore scleral contact lenses for *The Exorcist* and then again when I revisited her possessed state in my comedy spoof *The Linda Blair Witch Project* (see Figure 17-8), where she finds out she's possessed by famous comedians (did you know that possession is nine-tenths of the law?). You can stream my short on YouTube at www.youtube.com/watch?v=ftqEhTpZtQs.

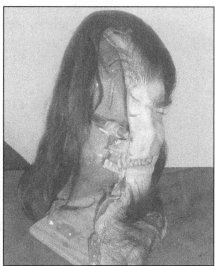

FIGURE 17-7:
Front and profile
shots of a foam
werewolf head.

FIGURE 17-8:
An example of
scleral lenses and
vampire teeth.

Linda Blair (left), Makeup artist, Marlene Stoller (right)

WARNING

Be sure to purchase scleral lenses from an optometrist or from eyewear specialists like Dr. Morton Greenspoon and Dr. Richard Silver (www.provisioncare.com), who have designed and provided special scleral lenses for many Hollywood blockbusters (including *The Grinch* and *Men in Black*). Although specialty stores, especially during Halloween, carry designer effects lenses, you don't know if they're made by a reputable company, and the lenses aren't fitted to your particular eye shape. Not only could they cause discomfort or infection, but worse, damage to your cornea. Always consult an ophthalmologist before putting anything in your eyes!

Take a bite out of this

Another skill of the special-effect makeup artist is designing and creating teeth that fit over the actor's own bite. A mold is taken of the actor's real teeth — very similar to how a dentist takes a mold impression to fit you for a crown or veneers. The artist then sculpts a new set of molars — from ghoulish monster or vampire teeth to rotten buck teeth like Austin Powers. Refer to Figure 17-7 for an example of vampire teeth that fit over the actor's own incisors.

Pulling out your hair with lace hairpieces

Lace hairpieces, including beards and mustaches, are used on almost every movie, and quite often on the main actors. Sean Connery wore a lace hairpiece throughout all his James Bond movies. You've often seen actors that you know are bald in real life sprouting a beautiful head of hair for their latest starring role. Even actors with hair have been known to wear lace pieces when they are becoming a different person on screen, as, for example, Tom Hanks playing Fred Rogers in *A Beautiful Day in the Neighborhood*. Lace hairpieces are created by a specialty makeup and or hair artist. Ron Wolek designed and meticulously punched one hair at a time into a piece of lace netting for Ed Asner's Santa Claus beard in my film *Santa Stole Our Dog*. (See Figure 17-9.) Real hair or yak hair is often used. The weaved hair tied into the netting is then cut and shaped like a real haircut, or trimmed into a beard or mustache (often on a mannequin head so the actor doesn't have to sit there for a long period of time).

FIGURE 17-9: Santa beard and mustache lace piece designed and created by Ron Wolek.

CAPTURING MOTION WITH MOTION CAPTURE

Motion capture (MoCap for short) is a technique that captures a live actor's movements into a computer. The realistic movements can then be transferred to a 3-D computer-generated character of virtually any size and proportion, like the CGI dodo or the snowman with a cold shown here. Small tracking sensors are attached to the actor — like connecting the dots on a stick figure. When the actor moves, the computer tracks movements — an elbow bending, a finger pointing, legs running, or arms punching — in real time. Many studio animated CGI (computer generated image) movies use motion capture (such as *Planet of the Apes,* the Hulk in *Avengers,* and even Spider-Man for certain flying and flighting scenes, to name a few). A company called Reallusion makes a motion capture system that works with its iClone software called Motion Live (www.reallusion.com).

An older technique that's been around since the invention of film is *rotoscoping*. In the old days, animators would laboriously trace an actor's actions off a film or video performance and turn that performance into a series of separate drawings. These drawings would then be photographed frame by frame and the end result would be an animated character with very real human motion. Motion capture using a computer and tracking sensors is the 21st century version of rotoscoping — but it's in real time!

© 1998/2008 Mr. Dodo created by Bryan Michael Stoller / CGI animation by William Sutton/Zandoria Studios; Snowman with a cold in Santa Stole Our Dog, design and CGI animation by Bill Lae

Chapter **18**

Giving Credit and Titles

Credits (a person's name with his or her position) are important to your cast and crew because everyone likes to be recognized for their hard work, and people who work on movies are no exception. Receiving credit on a movie gives your cast and crew members credibility and can help get them their next job working on another production after yours. In this chapter, you discover impressive ways to give credit to everyone who worked on your picture.

Choosing a main title for your film is important, too, just as important as deciding what to name a baby — after all, your film *is* your baby. In this chapter, you see how to create inexpensive titles that can be shot right in the camera, hire a title house or freelancer to design your titles, or even better — design them yourself using any of a myriad of title software plug-ins available that make it inexpensive and easy. You also find out how to prepare a *textless* version of your movie before it's delivered to foreign distributors.

Titling Your Movie

Coming up with a good title for your film is more than just picking a catchy name. The right title can help market your movie to the right audience. (See Figure 18-1.) For the re-release of my movie, *Miss Castaway & the Island Girls*, I changed the title to *Silly Movie 2* because the movie was really silly and the title helped attract the appropriate audience — one that appreciates that type of humor. A film's name also influences what people perceive it to be about. It can be an intriguing title like *Fatal Attraction* or an identifiable title to let the audience know exactly who, or what, the film is about, like *Godzilla*, *John Wick*, *The Lion King*, or *Wonder Woman*.

FIGURE 18-1:
Movie titles: *The Amazing Wizard of Paws* and *Santa Stole Our Dog*.

As you think about the title of your picture, keep these things in mind:

>> **Choose something that sounds intriguing:** *War for Planet of the Apes*, *Guardians of the Galaxy*, and *Back to the Future* are examples of intriguing titles.

>> **Keep it short and easy to pronounce:** *Child's Play*, *Green Book*, and *Get Out*, for example.

>> **Don't reveal too much about the film through its title (except in rare instances where doing so can be intriguing or fun for the audience):** *Batman vs Superman* or *Snakes on a Plane*, which tells you exactly what to expect!

>> **Set the tone or genre of the movie:** *Ghostbusters*, *Shazam!*, and *Sausage Party* (all comedies); *Schindler's List*, *Roma*, and *All the President's Men* (all dramas, although *All the President's Men* could also be a comedy, I guess!)

REMEMBER

A title can't be copywritten, but it's always a good idea to research your title to ensure that it's not the same or similar to another well-known movie title. When your movie is finished, a distributor will request a *title search* be done to make sure there's no other commercial title in release that could be confused with your title. If a title is identical (or very close), a major studio could sic their lawyers on you and pressure you to change the title. That happened with one of my titles: I received a warning letter from a studio — and to avoid costly litigation I changed the title (I probably would have prevailed in court, but I would have had to spend time and expensive legal fees).

Running a List of Names and Positions

From the minute you start thinking of making a movie, start jotting down the name of every person and company involved in your production. Remembering to place a name in a credit roll in the first place is always much easier (and cheaper) than finding out later that you forgot someone and having to deal with the consequences.

Spelling it write

Make sure every name in your opening credits and ending credits is spelled correctly. Many years ago, while attending the American Film Institute (AFI), I made a twenty-minute film project called *Just Joking* starring my comedian friend Howie Mandel (Howie and I were friends before he made it big in Hollywood). When I screened the finished film, Howie pointed out that I spelled his name wrong (I spelled it *Mandle* instead of *Mandel*). It was more of a typo than a case of my not knowing how to spell his name correctly — but for being careless, I felt terrible.

Entitled to a credit

For every favor, product deal, or donation you get, you need to thank people and companies responsible in your film's ending credits. It's cheap to use up a line — it could cost you relationships and friendships if you forget. People and companies like to see their names up on the big screen, and recognizing them in this way shows your appreciation of their contribution to your production (they may contribute to your next one, too!). So credit — don't forget it!

Designing Your Titles and Credits

When you decorate your house or apartment, you pick a style. You should do the same when you design your opening title and credits. Main titles and credits can be presented in many creative styles, limited only by your imagination. Start thinking about a unique style that fits your film.

An appropriately designed main title and credits can convey the feeling of fun with a free-style font, seriousness with a plain unencumbered font, or wild and crazy with letters that look like they want to break free. So make sure the style you choose matches the feel of your movie. If you're filming a murder mystery, for example, you wouldn't want to use cartoon lettering in your opening credits.

Often, an audience doesn't pay too much attention to the fonts of your title and credits, but they have a subliminal effect on the viewer nonetheless. In Michael Jackson's *Thriller,* the title looked like it was scratched in blood — definitely creating a mood. In my film, *Turn of the Blade,* the opening title starts to rotate like the blades on a helicopter. The opening credits to *The Amazing Spider-Man* were caught in an animated web with spiders scurrying about. Next time you go to the movies or watch a video, notice the stylish fonts used in the title and opening credits; you'll be surprised how different and creative they are and often how they keep in the theme of what the movie is about.

Digital Juice makes a line of colorful and effective animated backgrounds, which can add a professional flair to your title and credits. You've probably seen these backgrounds on many TV shows with credits and titles superimposed over them. Instead of setting your title and credits on plain black, you can have them pop and breathe with life, accentuated with lively animated backgrounds. There's an animated background for almost any theme: bubbles, outer space, fire, pulsating colors, which add up to more than thousands of backgrounds to choose from. Digital Juice also includes animated *lower thirds* (for adding names and titles anywhere on the screen), and a vast array of font types to superimpose over your images. Check out www.digitaljuice.com for more details.

You can also contact freelance effects and title artists who can design a unique animated title for your project. Try doing an Internet search for title houses, special effect companies, or freelance title artists that specialize in movie titles. Make sure you are specific in your search or you'll come up with title searches for when you want to buy a house! If a company designs your titles, they usually create storyboard panels illustrating how the titles and credits will look and time out, in the final frames of the finished film.

Designing the style with fonts

You can choose from thousands of different font styles to make up your title and credits. You've probably got a few hundred on your computer right now. Each font has a feeling and sets a mood. One may be perfect for your movie. For example, in my film *Undercover Angel,* my lead character, Harrison, is a struggling book author who still uses an old-fashioned typewriter. I chose the Courier font, which looks like it came from an old typewriter for the opening credits of the film. It worked especially well because the film starts off with Harrison at his typewriter shortly after the opening credits end.

For my movie *Light Years Away,* the opening scene follows a meteorite shooting through space among the stars. As the camera follows the meteorite, the opening title and credits form out of the stars in the sky.

Animating your main title and credits

Animation adds life and character to your opening and ending title and credits. *The Pink Panther* films were popular for their amusing animation credits and helped spawn the *Pink Panther* animated cartoon series. Steven Spielberg used a stylized cartoon opening for his film *Catch Me If You Can, and Spider-Man: Homecoming* used animated images for the ending credits of the movie. Although a full-length animated film is expensive to produce, a few minutes of animation for opening title and credits is usually affordable enough (especially if you use stop-motion, cut-out animation, or animate with flash or animation software — see Chapter 2). Spending your money on animation at the beginning of your picture rather than the ending is better because most people leave as the end credits begin to roll anyway.

TIP

Animation Factory provides a fun angle on presenting your titles and credits. On its website, www.animationfactory.com, you have a choice of 600,000 cycled animations, which can be incorporated into a website announcing your production or used in the opening or ending credits of your movie. The Animation Factory has every themed animated image imaginable. For a small annual fee starting at $59.95, you can access the entire library of animations. It's a really fun site — check it out.

Digitally creating your credits

You can design your title and credits right on your computer. These are called *digital* or *electronic credits.*

Optical credits are done at a title company or film lab that specializes in designing and photographing titles and credits onto film stock. They are then *superimposed optically* (placed over the appropriate scenes by the film lab) over the opening or ending footage of your movie. They can also be printed as white letters on a black background, which is often the way ending roll credits are presented.

END DISTRACTING CREDIT ROLL

I'm not one for having images or scenes, including outtakes, playing parallel to the ending credits roll. It's distracting, and you either have to watch the images playing alongside the credit roll or read the credit roll. You can't do both. A better idea is to do what Marvel does on all their movies. They stop the credit roll and pop up a bonus scene. After the bonus scene ends, the credit roll starts up again until it finishes. The audience usually remains in their seats, because there just might be another bonus scene after the credits end.

It is very rare nowadays that titles and ending credits are done optically, which is more complicated and way, way more expensive than creating them right in a computer digitally. Many title and rolling credit software plug-ins are available to help you easily create animated opening titles and end rolling credits. Some editing programs have them built-in. The software lets you control the font size, the font style, the spacing between the titles and the next line, and the pacing (timing) of your end credit roll. What used to take many hours or days now takes only minutes to create.

When working with a title house or freelance artist finishing your title and end credits, you'll always be sent a sample of the copy to proofread before they start producing your titles and end credits. Be sure to read closely — overlooking the obvious (misspellings and typos) is all too easy as I've pointed out earlier in this chapter.

Crediting without a computer

If you aren't sure how to create your own title and credits, and you can't afford to hire a title company or freelance title artist, you still have hope. Let these ideas spur your own creativity:

>> Go to your stationery or art-supply store and pick up some lettering stencils or vinyl stick-on letters. You can even get three-dimensional letters from an art-supply or toy store.

>> If your story is a beach film, write your title and opening credits in the sand and let the tide come in and wash them away.

>> If it's a college or high school project, write your title and credits on a black-board with chalk or on a dry erase board.

>> If your film involves kids or toys, spell out your title in wooden alphabet building blocks.

I did a stop-motion animated film many years ago that retold the story of the Frog Prince. My ending credits looked like they were at the bottom of a pond that rippled between credits. Here's what I did: I placed my credits on a card and took a clear casserole dish and filled it with water. I shot through the water in the dish with my camera and jiggled the water in between credits. The credits looked like they were under water! You've also probably seen many films use the turning pages of a book for the opening credits — it's easy to do, and it never gets old.

Rolling Your Title and Credits with Software

After your film is completed and you've assembled all the elements for your main title and credits, you need to concentrate on the timing, order, and legibility of those credits.

TIP

If you make your ending credits interesting, you may be able to keep the audience in their seats. Most people get up and leave the theater (or head to the kitchen or bathroom if they're streaming or watching on TV), but you can do some of the following to keep them glued to their seats:

» Have some type of animation or movement to the ending credits.

» Intercut scenes from the film in between the end credits or include an *epilogue* (closure for some of the characters) to your movie which fades in during your end credits, then fades out to let your credits continue.

» Stop the credits to feature funny *bloopers* (flubs or mistakes) from the film (like *Toy Story,* and *Rush Hour* have done). *Evan Almighty* had the cast and crew all doing Steve Carell's dance during the ending credit roll (*Ark Building For Dummies* was featured in the movie!).

» Have an extended ending to your film *after* the credits have finished rolling. Word will get out that there was more to your film, and this will get people to watch until the very end. Marvel is known for doing this — so Marvel fans rarely leave their seats in the theater until after they know the movie is finished, credits and all.

Timing for opening and ending credits

The best way to organize and time your title and credits is to storyboard the opening of your movie (see Chapter 9 for more on storyboarding). This allows you to pace your opening credits to the visuals of your film's opening scenes. If you have your title and credits over black (that is, without scenes from the movie running in the background), you don't have to worry about storyboarding them (but you still want to decide how long each title and credit will be up on the screen).

Titles and credits bookend a film, clearly identifying the beginning and "The End" of a movie. They create a definitive opening, and a closure ending. The opening title and opening credits begin before the film gets into the meat of the story. The ending credits roll when the movie has come to a satisfactory conclusion (at least that's what you hope for!).

Sometimes a movie's opening credits don't start until after a prelude scene that grabs the audience from the first frame of the picture. Some movies don't even have credits until the end of the movie — but this is rare with big studio productions because of filmmaking egos who want you to know who made the movie and their positions right from the beginning.

REMEMBER

Keep in mind, when timing your ending credits, that you don't want them to roll by too fast or too slow. They should be slow enough to read, but not so slow that you put your audience to sleep — or they get bored and leave the theater or living room.

Ordering your title and credits

Just as you have to think about how your title and credits look and when they appear, you also have to think about the order of the credits themselves. Who (or what) appears first, second, and so on? Read on to find out.

Opening credits

The order of opening credits has no real norm, except that usually a big-name star's credit is one of the first to appear (after the distributor logo). The last credit to appear is usually the director's credit. But in between, a myriad of variations exists. Here's one example of a typical opening-credit order:

>> Distributor logo (if you have one)

>> Production company presents

>> The director or production company's possessory credit ("A film by . . .)

>> Title of the film

>> Starring cast

>> Casting by (unless you cast it yourself)

>> Executive producer

>> Producer

>> Co-producer(s)

>> Music by, or Original Score by

>> Costumes designed by (usually reserved for period pieces or wardrobe-heavy films; otherwise saved for the ending credits)

- » Visual effects designed by (if a heavy visual effects film)

- » Production designer (if you even have one)

- » Edited by

- » Director of photography

- » Screenplay by

- » Directed by

REMEMBER

If you're making an independent film, chances are you may be a triple-threat, meaning your credit will read, "Written, Produced, and Directed by. . . ." You might also have cast your movie, built sets and props, scouted locations, and made coffee on-set — but don't put your name in the credits too many times or you'll be shouting that your film is really low budget. Make up some names for some of the positions if you have to!

If you are a triple threat, you may be possessed by the *possessory credit,* which strangely enough has nothing to do with being possessed. (Although I did once direct Linda Blair in a spoof I wrote called *The Linda Blair Witch Project,* which parodied *The Exorcist* and *The Blair Witch Project*.) A possessory credit is a possessive ownership (auteur) credit that usually belongs to the director of the film, such as "A Steven Spielberg Film."

TIP

It is very important for your cast and crew to receive a credit, not only because it will be featured in your movie, but because then their credit is eligible to go up on the entertainment industry's Internet Movie Database (IMDb). This is very important for a person's credibility (pardon the pun). My dog Little Bear, and even my mom, have an IMDb credit and their own page on IMDb. It makes you authentic in the entertainment industry.

Closing credits: The End

The closing credits in a film usually begin with the cast in order of appearance, then a repeat of the opening names and titles, followed by staff and crew names. Next, special effects credits, music and song cues used in the movie, and then special thanks. By the end of the credit roll, there is often a disclaimer about any similarities to names or characters being purely coincidental. And then the end credits usually finish up with ownership of the motion picture and copyright date. And if it's a Marvel movie, you can bet there will be a post-credits scene when the end credit roll is said and done.

Ensuring the safety of your credits

In the old days of analog TVs, *title safety* was an issue. Standard TV sets varied with image size in terms of the edges of a picture. A universal safety zone for standard televisions was established to protect titles and credits from being cut off within the frame. Today, high definition television sets with a 16x9 (widescreen) viewing area generally do not have a cut off area. You should always leave a margin (invisible border) around your titles and credits anyway for aesthetic reasons.

REMEMBER

Make sure your credits are big enough to read if your movie is broadcast on TV or will be streamed on a smartphone or tablet. This was a problem of many of the films I made as a kid. Often, I made the lettering too small. My mom always reminded me to make the lettering legible. To this day I stop to remember her advice — so now my credits are legible on any size screen. Thanks, Mom!

Covering Your Eyes: Stripping Titles for Foreign Textless

Textless opening and ending footage is simply the footage from your movie before you superimpose the title and credits over the picture. When your film goes to the foreign markets, your cast and crew names remain the same, but the names of each position and your main title are translated into another language.

SUBJECT TO SUBTITLES

Subtitles are usually reserved for foreign films coming into the English-language market. The English translation appears in the lower part of the screen (in title safe on a standard TV, or a slight margin at the bottom for HD TV)) as the actors speak in their native tongue. This is similar to turning on the closed-caption feature (not to be confused with subtitles) on your TV, which amounts to English subtitles in English-speaking films so that the hearing impaired can follow the dialogue.

Chances are you're not going to use subtitles in your movie, unless you're doing it for comedy purposes (as in *Austin Powers' Goldmember*), or when your film includes an alien or a person speaking in a foreign tongue among English-speaking characters (like many of the aliens in the various *Star Wars* movies). Most American films are not subtitled overseas; instead the voices are usually replaced by voiceover actors speaking in their own language (see Chapter 19).

After your film is completed, you or the post-production house makes a *textless* copy of your opening and ending credits footage. If you edited your movie on your computer, you create a textless copy of your movie by removing the visual layer that holds your opening and ending credits. When the foreign distributor receives your film, it places the translated title and credits over the picture. Voilà!

5

Finding Distribution for Your Movie

I introduce you to the world of distribution. Distribution includes getting your movie into theaters, into stores on DVD, onto streaming platforms like Amazon and Netflix, as well as airing on TV screens all across the globe. With the right distributor, this is all possible.

I help you negotiate for a fair distribution contract and show you how to self-distribute your movie.

Film festivals are also a great way for distributors and potential buyers to discover you and your film, not to mention great networking opportunities — and this part gives you the information you need.

IN THIS CHAPTER

» **Defining distribution**

» **Finding a distributor**

» **Distributing domestically and overseas**

» **Negotiating for a fair distribution contract**

» **Self-distributing your movie**

Chapter **19**

Distributing Your Movie

D istribution is the final stage of the filmmaking process, and it's definitely the most important one. If it isn't distributed, your movie will sit on a shelf, or remain inside your computer, and no one will ever see it. In this chapter, I explain the secrets of distribution. You find out how media rights for theatrical, streaming, television, and DVD, as well as ancillary rights for merchandising products inspired by your movie, are broken down. You see how a distributor markets a movie and what you can do to help. I also offer invaluable advice on what to look for in a distribution contract and help you discover the secrets of negotiating the best distribution deal for your picture. You also see the advantages of hiring an entertainment attorney who's well versed in distribution contracts.

This chapter also provides information about finding a foreign distributor or sales agents who have relationships with worldwide buyers. I tell you about all the possible markets for your movie, what each territory often pays for an independent film if they're interested. I provide firsthand information about the film markets that can introduce your film to foreign buyers, including Cannes and MIPCOM in France, and the American Film Market in Santa Monica, California. And make sure you check out the lists of the top domestic distributors and foreign distribution sales reps.

Understanding How Distribution Works

Distributing a movie is similar to selling a product. The product needs to get to the customer, and a distributor puts the two together. The world is your potential customer, with global distribution separated into two divisions: domestic and foreign. Including the United States and Canada, more than 65 countries could distribute your movie. Each country, or *territory,* is a potential paying customer. When a territory licenses your movie, it sells it to the various TV, DVD and streaming video services, and possibly theatrical markets within its country — and it has to negotiate a price with your foreign distributor or sales agent to do so.

Many times, securing a distributor before the distributor can see a finished product is difficult. To find a distributor, when you have a finished film, you can send potential distributors a DVD screener (covered later in this chapter) for distribution consideration. Better yet, you can create a private online screener with a special password. Be sure to put a watermark on the image clarifying that it is copyrighted material and that it is an infringement to copy or pirate the movie (the watermark will also be impossible to remove — showing it's for non-commercial screening purposes only).

Because there is more demand for product internationally, you may find it easier to find a foreign distributor (foreign sales rep) first and then find a domestic distributor to cover the United States and Canada (see "Finding a Distributor or Sales Agent," later in this chapter for details). You can also enter your film in the various film festivals domestically and abroad (see Chapter 20), and let the distributors track *you* down. Or you can hold your own screening and premiere your film to invited distributors, film buyers, and film reps.

REMEMBER

When searching for a distributor you will hear the terms *film rep* or *producer's rep, sales agent,* and/or *distributor.* A film/producer's rep represents your film like a real estate broker (*reel*-estate broker) trying to find a domestic or foreign distribution company to license your movie and distribute it. A *distributor* actually distributes your film directly to the movie theaters (if your film gets a theatrical release) or directly to the TV networks or streaming services, or even directly to the consumer if they distribute their own DVD product. Often, domestic distributors handling your film for international sales also call themselves *foreign sales agents* because they're repping your movie to individual distributors in different countries. These individual distributors will license your film and distribute your movie within their own country or territory.

REMEMBER

A film that is distributed overseas usually has to be converted to a system that accommodates the frame rate and scan lines that are compatible with the local broadcasting standards of the specific territory, standards that may be different from those in the United States. A digital system introduced in February 2009 replaces the old broadcast system used in North America. The two main worldwide formats are ATSC (replacing NTSC) and PAL:

- **NTSC** (National Television Standards Committee) has been the standard analog broadcasting format since 1940 in North America, most of South America, and Japan. It is based on 525 lines of resolution and is equivalent to 30 frames (or, more accurately, 29.978 frames) of video per second. This system has been replaced by ATSC, which now accommodates for high definition signals.

- **ATSC** (Advanced Television Systems Committee) replaces the NTSC analog signal for digital signals, effective since February 17, 2009. This broadcast system includes standard and high definition wide-screen images of 16:9 images and up to 1920x1080 pixels. ATSC 3.0 will be able to accommodate 4K content.

- **PAL** (Phase Alternation Line) is the analog television display standard that is the predominant video system used in Europe, Asia, and other parts of the world. PAL transmits 25 frames each second and uses 625 individual scan lines of resolution.

For an NTSC or ATSC video to be viewable overseas, it has to be transferred to PAL format. Your foreign distributor or sales agent usually arranges for the conversion of your movie for sale in the overseas territory. You can also have this done by going to a professional post-production facility.

A third option, *streaming* via the Internet, is a universal format that can play footage on virtually any computer connected to the World Wide Web. Streaming is rapidly replacing physical DVDs, and with Netflix, Hulu, Amazon Prime, Disney+, Apple TV+, and YouTube, audiences are enjoying the convenience and seemingly endless selection of titles via these streaming platforms.

Presenting Your Film to Distributors

Studio distributors are always on the lookout for little gems to distribute, so creating awareness for your movie before and after you shoot it is essential. A film trailer is a great tool to get buyers excited about your movie, and designing a movie poster is the first thing you should think about — even before you start shooting your film.

Posting a poster of your movie

An intriguing poster can excite buyers and raise interest in your movie. You may be thinking, "Why make a poster? I haven't even made my movie yet." But some films are pre-sold by posters that exist way before the film is ever shot. A poster can give your investors (see Chapter 5) or a potential distributor a taste of what's to come.

Adobe PhotoShop and Illustrator, part of the Adobe Create Suite (www.adobe.com), are great software programs that you can use to design a poster. Synthetik (www.synthetik.com) makes a really neat software program called Studio Artist that gives you painting and drawing power. This program is one of my favorites, and it's affordable without a subscription at only $99 for the student and teacher's version (or $199 if you're neither of these).

REMEMBER

When you make a poster before you've started shooting your movie, the credits on the poster are considered *non-contractual*. This means that the people whose names appear in the starring roles and production credits are not officially signed to do the film (but have given you permission to use their names) and could change by the time the movie goes into production. Stating this on the poster protects you and the people whose names appear on the poster from any legal disputes between each other, especially the distributor and/or potential buyers.

After you find a distributor, the company may want to design its own poster (even if it was attracted to your movie because of *your* poster). Your distributor is more savvy to the kind of graphics, colors, and images that appeal to global buyers. Figure 19-1 shows posters from my films *First Dog* and *The Amazing Wizard of Paws*, and a *landscape* format poster for my film *Santa Stole Our Dog*, which was often displayed this way for streaming platforms like Netflix and Amazon Prime video titles.

Picturing the set photographer

Having someone take professional photos on your set while you're shooting your movie is very important. These photos will be invaluable when it comes to marketing your film; they're also a mandatory requirement of any distributor. The distributor needs photos showing stills from your movie for the promotional flyers. It also uses photos to design your main poster. In the worst-case scenario, you can make stills off the original digital footage — but you will still need some high quality posed photos of your actors to design the poster and marketing materials. You don't want your poster to look cheap and unprofessional.

TIP

If you can't afford a professional photographer, you can use a DSLR digital camera — and have someone on your crew with a good eye snap some photos. (Your cinematographer could do this before and after shots.) You can also encourage your crew and actors on-set to take photos with their smartphones and grant you permission to use them if you like them for marketing purposes. Most smartphones today have excellent megapixel quality and will work fine for professional purposes.

FIGURE 19-1:
Posters for *First Dog* and *The Amazing Wizard of Paws*, and a landscape layout poster display for *Santa Stole Our Dog* for Redbox and streaming platforms.

SEEING STARS

If you can get a name actor in your film, even in a small part, your movie will get more attention and help you get financing or a distributor (depending on the actor you get). Casting directors can usually use their relationships with agents, managers, and talent to help you land some stars. Casting Yasmine Bleeth and James Earl Jones helped get my film *Undercover Angel* off the ground. Having Academy Award-nominee Eric Roberts, Christopher Knight (Peter Brady), Hal Linden, and Barry Van Dyke in my film *Light Years Away* added credibility to the project. Iconic actor Ed Asner played Santa Claus in my movie *Santa Stole Our Dog*, which assisted in getting Universal Pictures Home Entertainment interested in distributing my movie. And having Dan Aykroyd as the voice of Dexter the computer in my film *The Random Factor* helped the film find distribution internationally.

Pulling your audience in with a trailer

After you find a distributor and have completed your movie, the distributor will want to create a professional movie *trailer,* which packs the exciting moments from your movie into a sizzling commercial. Sometimes a filmmaker will shoot a trailer to try to interest an investor in putting up money to make the actual movie. A trailer usually runs one to three minutes in length and features highlights from the movie that will spark the interest of buyers. It's also a great idea to post your trailer on www.youtube.com and start a worldwide buzz for your film! Next time you're at your favorite cineplex, study all the "Coming Attractions" trailers before the main feature.

Premiering your movie

Showing your movie on the big screen in front of a captive audience is a good way to influence potential distributors (as long as the audience's reaction is positive!). If you live in or near Los Angeles or New York, set up a premiere for domestic and foreign distributors, theatrical distributors, Streaming companies like Netflix and Amazon, TV stations, and DVD home entertainment companies. If you live outside L.A. or New York, you may want to venture there for the big premiere. The main costs associated with setting up a premiere include rental of a theater and printing and mailing invitations.

TIP

I prefer being old-fashioned and mailing my invitations. People take mailed invitations more seriously than emailed invitations. Would you email your wedding invitations? To me, premiering one of my movies is a lifetime event — I'm introducing my new baby to the world. As for printers, I use UPrinting in Los Angeles — if you're local, you can pick up your order, and if you're not, you can have them ship it anywhere in the contiguous United States. They have done all my printing — from movie posters to my movie premiere invitations — and they've never disappointed. Check them out at www.uprinting.com — and tell them I sent you!

If you can't bring buyers to your movie, you have to bring your movie to the buyers. You can get professional-quality dubs of a feature-length film on DVD for less than 40 cents a disc, plus the DVD box and artwork. Now that DVD copies have come down in price, you can send a DVD that has better picture resolution and CD-quality sound (and that requires less postage than an archaic VHS tape). If you want great service and competitive prices, then Disc Makers is the place to go (www.discmakers.com). But better than the expense and inconvenience of sending out DVDs — is to create an online private screener. The screener can be viewed immediately after the buyer clicks a private link which should also have a secret password. Very few buyers today even bother watching DVDs. Streaming your movie is more convenient and it can be viewed from anywhere on a smartphone, tablet, or computer — and the quality will be much higher than a DVD copy.

WARNING

Before you send screening copies of your movie, whether it's a DVD copy or a private link to stream online — superimpose a visual disclaimer across the bottom of the picture that says something like "Screening Copy Only — not for Internet or broadcast" (if you're using editing software, you can do it yourself). This disclaimer, similar to a watermark on a confidential paper document, prevents thieves from stealing your movie and selling it to television or the World Wide Web — there's no way to get rid of the visual warning unless they cut off that part of the picture that has the disclaimer.

Distributing Your Film Domestically

Domestic distribution is the licensing of your movie to media outlets in the United States and Canada. Domestic usually encompasses Canada as well as the United States because television broadcasts spill over the border, and satellite can be picked up in both the United States and Canada. TV, streaming, DVD, and satellite are part of the media rights for which a distributor negotiates. Many websites between Canada and the U.S. are easily accessible so there could be a spillover with streaming platforms as well.

Domestic distribution can account for 50 percent of your film's profits, the other 50 percent coming from foreign profits. If your movie is picked up by a major motion-picture distributor in the United States for theatrical release, you could receive an advance of $500,000 or more, plus a share of the profits (which is negotiable and varies depending on the distributor, anywhere from 20 to 40 percent). The distributor usually deducts what it paid in an advance from any profits owed to you. Miramax paid $5 million for the independent film *Swingers*, produced on a budget of only $250,000. This was the catalyst that launched Jon Favreau's career, as he went on to direct *Iron Man 1 and 2*, *Zathura: A Space Adventure*, and the CGI version of *The Lion King*.

DVD, TV, and streaming rights with a major studio distributor can pay an advance of around $300,000, depending on the material and whether any recognizable names appear in the movie. In addition to an advance, you would also have profit participation as well. For broadcast, you can get anywhere from $10,000 to $500,000 for a television licensing fee, depending on whether it airs on a major network or an independent TV channel. Then there is syndication, which your movie could be licensed to independent TV stations all around the country.

CLOSING IN ON CLOSED-CAPTIONS

Be prepared to have a closed caption file made of your movie. Closed captioning is a service that originated for the deaf and hard of hearing so they too could enjoy visual entertainment like everyone else. Closed captions are a requirement when delivering a movie for distribution. This includes television, streaming platforms, YouTube, Amazon, and Netflix, and even for DVDs. On most TV programs you will see the letters *CC* or a box enveloping the *CC*'s. Also, most DVD's will feature the closed-caption icon somewhere on the DVD case. There are many services that will prepare a transcript of your movie along with a closed caption file that will match the dialogue of your picture. Such companies that perform this service are Rev (www.rev.com) and Video Caption Corporation (www.vicaps.com). There are even editing programs like FCPX that allow you to generate your own closed-captions within the program.

YouTube has made your closed-captioning task much easier — and for free! You can either type in your closed-captions yourself (through your YouTube account channel) or you can turn on speech recognition and it will automatically generate captions from the dialogue it hears while your movie is playing in real time (don't expect it to be perfect and get every word right, but it will be pretty close — especially if your dialogue is mixed correctly). YouTube will also allow you to upload an existing closed-caption file, or let you manually type in captions as you watch your movie. The company I recommend to do your closed-captions is Rev (www.rev.com). Others can charge up to $7 a minute, but Rev only charges $1 a minute and they are one of the largest. They're known for their excellent service and turnaround time. Rev also guarantees that their captions will be acceptable to most streaming platforms, including YouTube, Hulu, iTunes, and Amazon (and Amazon is very strict on their closed-captioning requirements).

Domestic studio distributors may give you a *negative pickup agreement* for your movie. A negative pickup guarantees that the distributor will buy your film when you deliver the final product. Raising the money is easier when a studio distributor gives you a negative pickup offer in writing. You can then approach investors and show them the negative pickup agreement from the studio insuring that the movie will have distribution when you deliver it. Sometimes you can take the studio's negative pickup deal (in writing) to the bank or a lender and get a loan based on the studio agreeing to pick up the picture when it's completed. There are also companies dedicated to financing films that have a negative pick up letter, such as Film Finances, Inc. (www.filmfinances.com).

REMEMBER

Keep in mind that with the influx of streaming platforms, Netflix, Amazon, and even Apple are becoming major production studios that will be producing and looking for content. Netflix spends several billions of dollars a year just to keep their subscribers happy with high value entertainment and star names. Amazon and Apple are following suit.

Minding media rights

When you sign with a distributor, the distributor negotiates *media rights* for your movie in each country (also referred to as a *territory*). These rights determine in which of the following outlets your movie can be seen in the specific territory and how much is paid for the licensing rights to each medium:

>> **Theatrical:** For theatrical screenings to audiences.

>> **Home entertainment:** On DVDs, including Blu-ray discs. This includes any royalties you will see from the sales.

>> **Pay-per-view:** For broadcast viewing on a pay-per-view basis. Includes Video on Demand (VOD), which lets you watch it exactly when you want to watch it. Also, includes royalties deal.

>> **Pay television:** For broadcast on pay television that has paid subscribers (such as HBO or Showtime) and usually has no commercials.

>> **Satellite:** For TV satellite markets within a territory (broadcast at the same time that pay TV starts).

>> **Cable television:** For broadcast to basic cable television subscribers.

>> **Free television:** For broadcast on television networks like NBC, ABC, CBS, and FOX. This can also include syndication TV rights.

>> **Closed circuit:** For limited exposure in hotels, airplanes, and cruise ships.

>> **Internet:** For streaming or downloading off the Internet via streaming services like Netflix or Amazon Prime, with the choice to the consumer of streaming (renting), or buying the movie (which could include downloading the movie in a QuickTime file, or the movie being available online indefinitely to the consumer for purchasing it).

A *window* is the period of time during which a movie is available for each media right. For example, a theatrical release usually goes to DVD after a window of four months; DVD usually has a window of 30 days before Internet streaming or pay TV can broadcast it. Some TV broadcasters negotiate for an extended window of up to a year or two, depending on what they pay for the licensing of the picture. Each buyer needs to abide by the window so as to not infringe on another buyer's window in a different medium.

When a movie is licensed for a particular medium and has a defined window, the distributor may request a *holdback,* meaning that your movie cannot be shown on any other media until the negotiable period of time has lapsed on the previous window.

Steamlining your movie

Streaming rights could be a big part of your movie's revenue. Streaming platforms like Netflix, Hulu, Amazon, Vimeo, and Apple have popped up over the years, adding to the growing population of product available for immediate enjoyment.

IMAX-IMUM

The world's largest film format originating from Ontario, Canada, called IMAX, is a projection system that distributes movies that were either shot on or transferred to 70mm, 15 frame perforated stock for large image projection. Today, IMAX has converted most of their projection systems to digital and now project movies shot on their new 65mm 4K 3D cameras. Arri also makes a large format camera for IMAX projection: the Alexa 65mm digital camera. The standard projected image is about 5 stories high by 72 feet wide (or 7 stories wide) — obviously requiring a special theater to accommodate the format (there's close to 300 IMAX theaters worldwide). IMAX is best known for its documentaries and travelogue large format movies but also is becoming popular for projecting studio features either digitally remastered or actually shot with the IMAX or Alexa 65mm digital cameras for the IMAX experience. Some of the features projected in IMAX include such blockbusters as *Ant Man & the Wasp, Fantastic Beasts: The Crimes of Grindelwald, Jurassic World: Fallen Kingdom, Rogue One: A Star Wars Story,* and *Avengers: Infinity War,* to name a few.

REMEMBER

Netflix (www.netflix.com) offers a service to rent the latest movies on DVD by mail (as opposed to movie titles that have been out for a while that are available to stream immediately). You make your selection on their Web site after browsing through movie titles — and in a day or so your selection will arrive in the mail. After you watch the DVD, you just return it via the mail. Around three million people still use the DVD service, but word has it that Netflix will discontinue the DVD service by mail around 2022. Netflix is producing a lot of its own movies now, which are available on their platform as soon as they are announced.

Anticipating ancillary rights

Ancillary rights bring in additional income derived from other sources, such as a soundtrack, novelization, comic books, toys, or any type of merchandise inspired by your movie. *Star Wars* figurines, *Harry Potter* books and games (check out my book, *Harry Potter: Imagining Hogwarts* on Amazon — sorry for the plug!), and toys and action figures (like Iron Man and Spider-Man) are all part of this merchandising bonanza. You can find *premiums* (inexpensive toys and gadgets) in cereal boxes and kids' meals at fast-food restaurants as cross-promotion for many of these films. Additional ancillary rights can include a sequel to your movie, a spin-off television series, or even a stage play (like Disney's stage adaptation of *The Lion King* and *Aladdin*).

Successful ancillary merchandising on an independent film is much more difficult without the backing of a major studio. However, my independent film *Undercover Angel* had a character named Mister Dodo in the film, and later used again in my movie *Santa Stole Our Dog,* which created a following and led to the marketing of Dodo dolls and books on Amazon.

LASER LIGHT BLUE

Blu-ray, a DVD disc high definition format, won the format wars many years ago and beat out the competing medium called DVD HD. The Blu-ray name is derived from the laser blue light that reads and can write onto the disc. A single-layer Blu-ray disc (the same dimensions as a standard DVD) can hold up to 50 megabytes of high definition footage, as opposed to the limited 4.7 megs on a traditional DVD disc. The good news for all your standard DVDs — they play just fine (and look even better) in a Blu-ray HD player! Blu-rays, along with DVDs, are becoming less popular now — as the preferred and more convenient way of watching movies is through streaming. The quality is also better and higher resolution than what you would ever get compressing your movie onto a DVD. Some studios even include a digital file link when you buy the physical DVD or Blu-ray so you can download or stream the movie on your computer, phone, or tablet without needing the physical disc. This is starting to become the norm.

Distributing Your Film around the World

Foreign distribution is the licensing of your movie to theatrical, Internet, TV, and DVD buyers overseas in the global market. Your foreign distributor (or sales agent) represents your film to more than 65 countries (also known as *territories*). Each country has individual buyers who license film rights for their territories. (*Note:* Some territories group together multiple countries. Check with your foreign distributor for details.)

Foreign sales can account for 50 percent of all worldwide sales (with domestic representing the other 50 percent). Europe accounts for up to 70 percent of all foreign sales. Finding a foreign distributor or sales agent is much the same as finding a domestic distributor — you send a protected DVD screener, or preferably a private screening link of your film (with a visual watermark on the picture) to the various foreign distributors or foreign sales agent (see "The best foreign distributors (also called foreign sales agents)" later in this chapter) or search the Internet for top foreign distributors and the acquisition person's name.

TIP

With regards to international streaming rights, there are *geo-filtering* laws (also known as *geo blocking*) to protect Internet streaming platforms from spilling over into other countries and interfering with separate rights.

Selling your film at the super markets

When you secure a foreign distributor, that distributor is likely to take your film to a market to connect with potential licensors. Three popular international film markets allow foreign distributors to showcase their library of films for licensing to the global market. These markets are a necessity for foreign distributors to attend, although films are sold between markets as well:

>> **The American Film Market (AFM)** takes place the first week of November in Santa Monica at the Loews Hotel facing the famous Santa Monica pier and the Pacific Ocean. Producers, distributors, buyers, sellers, actors, and filmmakers flock to the beachfront hotel for eight days of dealing and networking. More than 300 exhibitors set up offices in suites at the hotel. Local theaters screen selected movies so that buyers can view the distributors' new products.

>> **The Cannes Film Market** takes place in mid-May for approximately 12 days on the French Riviera, running simultaneously with the Cannes Film Festival (see Chapter 20). The festival is a competition of films, and the market is a film-selling convention. Buyers, distributors, and filmmakers enjoy the festive European culture along with distributor parties on rooftops and luxury cruise boats.

> **MIPCOM,** another popular overseas market, is held in mid-October for four days in Cannes and concentrates on TV series and movies for international television markets. Your foreign distributor could get additional TV sales for your movie by taking it to this market. MIP-TV is put on by the same organization and takes place in April in Cannes, France, as well.

Your foreign distributor or sales agent may agree to pay your way to one or more of the markets in exchange for getting the rights to distribute your film overseas, and will usually deduct your traveling expenses from your film's profits. But hey, wouldn't it be fun to go to France to represent your movie?

DIGITAL CINEMA PACKAGE FOR THEATRICAL RELEASE

Probably 90 percent of all theaters today have been retrofitted to project digital feature films, having put away their bulky and now-archaic 35mm film platters and projectors. Today, DCP has replaced 35mm projectors in all multiplex theaters.

DCP stands for *digital cinema package*. It's a digital process of converting your movie to the proper frame rate, picture image, and audio settings that will guarantee your movie will look exactly as you planned it to look when projected in a theater. No second-guessing by the projectionist is necessary, because the DCP tells the projector what audio channels are designated for your 5.1 or 7.1 surround sound, the calibration for the proper picture projection so the image is not too dark or too bright, and projects the film in the proper screen ratio (16x9, 2:35:1, or 1:78), as you intended it.

You can also have the DCP encrypted so it requires a key code to unlock to accommodate an exact screening schedule. A KDM (key delivery message) key is generated that lets the projectionist and the digital projector know what day and what time the drive will unlock to allow the movie to be projected. Of course, this also greatly protects the movie from being pirated.

You can also have an unlocked DCP generated so you don't have to deal with locking and unlocking it for screenings. If your movie is being distributed to theaters, it should definitely have a key code. It is possible to make your own DCP, but it can be complicated and you'll need the proper software. Having a DCP generated from your master can start at $600 and cost as much as $2,500, depending on where you have it done. But this is much cheaper than it used to be, when you had the major expense of shipping heavy film reels in metal cans to all the theaters (sometimes as many as 3,000 prints). A DCP fits on a lightweight portable external hard drive — and in the not-too-distant future, movies will probably be beamed to the theaters using the Internet or some private protected fiber optics service.

Your distributor may also want to set up some screening times for film buyers to see your film in a nearby theater during the market. Your film can either be projected from a Blu-ray disc or a DCP (digital cinema package).

TIP

In the old days, you would have to provide a 35mm print to screen at the market, and also have expensive 35mm prints made if your film was picked up for a theatrical release. Nowadays, digital has made delivery of your movie so much simpler and so much more affordable. Now you only have to convert your movie to a digital format contained on a DCP (digital cinema package). This is a hard drive with proprietary encryption that you can provide dates and times that the file of your movie will unlock for its scheduled screenings.

Negotiating: How much for your film?

Your foreign distributor (or sales agent) makes separate and exclusive deals with each country for all media rights or combinations thereof to your film. As with domestic media rights, each media right is for a certain window of time so as not to infringe on another market's window. Buyers pay a heftier price if your film has a theatrical release before DVD, Internet, and television.

Usually, filmmakers give foreign distributors (or sales agents) all foreign rights, including all ancillary markets, so the distributor can enter into agreements for, theatrical, TV, DVD, and Internet streaming rights overseas. Domestic works differently because the filmmaker has more control in distribution at home and can negotiate individual deals for theatrical, TV, Internet, and DVD, which would be difficult to track on foreign sales.

REMEMBER

Each country pays a different licensing fee for your movie, negotiated by your foreign distributor or sales agent. The fee depends on the size of the country and other factors, such as these:

>> **The state of the global economy.** Is the world in good economic state, or dealing with difficult financial times?

>> **The genre of your movie.** Action and horror, which translate well visually overseas, tend to bring in higher prices than comedies and family fare. Or is there an oversaturation of your genre (too many titles in that genre)?

>> **Whether any name stars or recognizable talent appear in your movie.** Name stars add credibility to your film, which can make the difference in getting a sale and also fetching higher licensing fees.

>> **The production values of your movie.** Does it look like it was made on a higher budget than it actually was?

>> **What's popular at the time at the world box office.** Is science-fiction popular because a major sci-fi movie is doing well at the box-office? Next week it could be fantasy or crime, depending on the success of major studio releases (everyone likes to follow in the trail of a successful genre).

Table 19-1 shows the low and high rates paid by a selection of foreign territories for television, streaming, and DVD rights. It gives examples of prices that have been paid for independent films with the production values that look like a $1 to $2 million film. As you can see, the numbers really add up. Theatrical rights could pay significantly higher numbers. Note that foreign distribution companies usually deal in U.S. dollars when selling overseas.

TABLE 19-1 **Prices Paid by Foreign Buyers for a Low-Budget Movie for TV, Internet, and DVD Rights (Excluding Theatrical Rights)**

Territory	For a Film That Looks Like a $1 to 2 Million Budget
France	$25,000 to $75,000
Germany	$10,000 to $60,000
Italy	$10,000 to $40,000
U.K.	$15,000 to $50,000
Japan	$15,000 to $50,000
Mexico	$15,000 to $60,000
Poland	$5,000 to $20,000
Turkey	$10,000 to $30,000

PRE-SELLING YOUR MOVIE

Pre-selling is when a distributor sells rights to your movie to foreign buyers even before the film is produced (see Chapter 5). The distributor takes *advances* (down payments of at least 20 percent), which are presented to the bank or to investors to confirm that your film has buyers waiting to license it after it's completed. Doing pre-sales is much more difficult than it used to be, unless the movie has some major stars attached to it.

Speaking their language

After your film is sold to a foreign territory, it's dubbed in the language of the country that purchased it. The filmmaker has prepared a music-and-effects (M&E) track (see Chapter 16) that allows the language of the foreign country to be dubbed while retaining the original music and sound-effects tracks. The foreign buyer or territory that licenses your movie incurs the cost of translation and dubbing and performs the work in its country.

TECHNICAL STUFF

A separate language dub may not have to be done in each and every country. If your film is sold to France and dubbed in French, your distributor can use that same French version to sell to French-speaking portions of Canada. If you sell to Spain, your distributor will inform the buyers for Mexico that a Spanish version is available for licensing.

The English-language dialogue isn't the only thing that has to go when dubbing a film; the English words that visually appear in the film have to be removed as well. When your film goes to another country, you must provide the distributor with a *textless* version with the title and all credits removed. The receiving country translates your film's title, as well as all production credits (of course, the crew and actors' names remain unchanged), into its language. See Chapter 18 for information about credits and titles.

Finding a Distributor or Sales Agent

Finding a distributor or sales agent can be easy if you've made a very commercial movie or difficult if your film can't seem to find an audience. The first thing to do is get a list of distributors (do a thorough search online) and make an introductory call to the acquisition department to see if they may be interested in screening your movie. If there is some initial interest, send a DVD screener, or link to your online screener with a password of your film along with a letter, or email, stating that you spoke with the acquisition department on the phone and thanking the distributor in advance for their consideration.

Another way to get a distributor or sales agent interested in your movie is to submit to film festivals. If your film is accepted to screen at a major film festival, like the Sundance Film Festival or Toronto Film Fest, then you have a very good chance of having a distributor discover your movie. If your film doesn't get accepted or discovered at a film festival, there are other ways to find a distributor:

>> **The American Film Market:** The American Film Market (AFM) has been going strong since the early eighties. It takes place annually in Santa Monica, California, usually the first week of November, and it runs for eight days. If you

buy an *attendee badge*, you gain entry to the market and can network with distributors and foreign sales agents from all over the world and make some excellent contacts. Your badge can also get you into certain seminars and parties by the beachfront hotel. If you want to meet distributors, this is the place to be! Check out www.americanfilmmarket.com.

>> **Producer's representative:** A *producer's rep,* also called a *sales rep* or *sales agent,* is an individual or a company, similar to a manager or agent, which helps you find a distributor (though many distributors also call themselves sales agents when repping your film to other territories — the term is often interchangeable). Producer's reps have relationships with various distributors and attend all the major film markets. They can also advise you on distribution contracts and help negotiate the best deal. Bruder Releasing (www.bruderreleasing.com) is a producer's rep and a distributor for over thirty-eight years who has represented some of my films for domestic television. Tell Marc Bruder I sent you!

>> **Other filmmakers:** Other filmmakers who have films in distribution may be able to provide you with an introduction to their distributors.

>> **Trade papers:** *The Hollywood Reporter* and *Variety* put out annual foreign-film market issues and global distributor listings.

>> **Distribution directories online:** The Hollywood Creative Directory use to put out excellent reference directories, including one on distributors. Unfortunately, the directories are no longer compiled — but you can find virtually the same information online — you just have to do your homework.

See also the lists of the top ten domestic and foreign distributors later in this section.

If a distributor or sales agent is interested in your movie, always ask for referrals. Talk to other filmmakers whose films the distributor represents. This lets you know if the distributor is reliable and transparent in paying their filmmakers. Over the years, I've dealt with some fly-by-night distributors that are here one day and gone the next.

The best domestic distributors

The following are the top 11 domestic studios that distribute movies in the United States and Canada (I've included streaming services because they are becoming their own studios that produce product):

>> **Netflix:** 5808 Sunset Blvd., Los Angeles, CA 90028; www.netflix.com

>> **Amazon Video:** Seattle phone: 888-280-4331; www.videodirect.amazon.com

FOUR-WALLING HAS A CEILING

Four-walling refers to distributing your film yourself without the aid of a professional distributor. I don't recommend this route because it's time-consuming and expensive. You have to pay for your own DCP (digital cinema package) hard drives, place ads in newspapers and magazines (which is not cheap), and make your own posters. You also have to contact the individual theater owners who rent out their facilities to independent films. Usually, only art houses and small theater chains will consider a film that's not represented by a major distributor. In this case, the filmmaker pays the theater a rental fee. In return, the filmmaker gets the total admission fee paid by the theater patrons but the theater owner gets to keep the popcorn and soda receipts!

>> **Columbia Pictures:** 10202 W. Washington Blvd., Culver City, CA 90232; phone: 310-244-4000; www.sonypictures.com

>> **Lionsgate Films:** 2700 Colorado Ave., Santa Monica, CA 90401; phone: 310-449-9200; www.lionsgate.com

>> **Paramount Pictures:** 5555 Melrose Ave., Los Angeles, CA 90038; phone: 323-956-5000; www.paramount.com

>> **Sony Pictures Entertainment:** 10202 W. Washington Blvd., Culver City, CA 90232; phone: 310-244-4000; www.sonypictures.com

>> **Twentieth Century Fox:** 10201 W. Pico Blvd., Los Angeles, CA 90035; phone: 310-369-1000; www.fox.com (Fox was bought by Disney and is now a subsidiary of the mouse house)

>> **Universal Studios:** 100 Universal City Plaza, Universal City, CA 91608; phone: 818-777-1000; www.universalstudios.com

>> **Warner Bros.:** 4000 Warner Blvd., Burbank, CA 91522; phone: 818-954-6000; www.warnerbros.com

>> **The Walt Disney Company:** 55 S. Buena Vista St., Burbank, CA 91521; phone: 818-560-1000; www.disney.com

>> **Redbox** (a division of Coinstar): 1 Tower Lane, Ste. 900, Oakbrook Terrace, IL 60181; www.redbox.com (one of the last major retailers for DVD rentals and sales in the U.S. via their iconic red box kiosks dotting the country)

PUT YOUR MOVIE DIRECTLY ON AMAZON WITH AMAZON DIRECT

Through Amazon, there is a platform called Amazon Video Direct. Now you can officially distribute your movie for streaming or downloading on Amazon, one of the largest retail suppliers in the world. Head over to Amazon Video Direct at `www.videodirect.amazon.com`. Sign up with your Amazon password, or create a new account and follow the instructions. You will be instructed to upload your movie, along with poster artwork that fits their size requirements, and include a closed caption file (see sidebar elsewhere in this chapter on closed captions). You then have options to choose how much you want to charge for streaming (rental of your movie) or download to own.

If you've met all technical requirements — in just a short time, your movie will be available live to millions of potential customers. Your movie will be in great company among major studio productions on the same Amazon platform.

Then it's up to you to promote your movie on social media to get audiences to know about your movie. Send a link to your Facebook, Twitter, and Instagram followers so they can easily click to follow the purchase or rent link to your movie on Amazon.

The best foreign distributors (also called foreign sales agents)

The following are the top ten companies that distribute films to overseas foreign markets. I have worked with some of these companies in the past, and have had meetings with most on this list. Foreign territories usually license DVD, television, Internet, and theatrical rights. Direct all your inquiries to the acquisition department or the acquisition manager:

>> **Spotlight Pictures:** 6671 Sunset Blvd., #1591, Hollywood, CA 90028; phone: 323-871-2551; `www.spotlight-pictures.com`

>> **Crystal Sky Worldwide Sales:** 10203 Santa Monica Blvd., Los Angeles, CA 90067; phone: 310-843-0223; `www.crystalsky.com`

>> **Epic Pictures:** 6725 Sunset Blvd., Ste.330, Hollywood, CA 90028; phone: 323-207-4170; `www.epic-pictures.com`

>> **Film Artists Network:** Canoga Park, CA 91305; phone: 818-528-5938; `www.filmartistsnetwork.com`

>> **Motion Picture Corporation of America:** 10635 Santa Monica Blvd., Ste.180, Los Angeles, CA 90025; phone: 310-319-9500; www.mpcafilm.com

>> **Morgan Creek:** 11601 Wilshire Blvd., Ste.675, Los Angeles, CA 90025; phone: 310-432-4848; www.morgancreek.com

>> **Leomark Studios:** 7113 Bianca Ave., Lake Balboa, CA 91406; email: info@leomarkstudios.com; www.leomarkstudios.com

>> **Fabrication Films:** 1968 S. Coast Hwy. 250, Laguna Beach, CA 92651; phone 323-874-2655; www.fabricationfilms.com

>> **Nu Image — Millennium Films:** 6423 Wilshire Blvd., Los Angeles, CA 90048; phone: 310-388-6900; www.millennium-media.net

>> **Marvista:** 10877 Wilshire Blvd., 10th flr., Los Angeles, CA 90024; phone: 424-274-3000; www.marvista.net

WARNING

Although setting up your own domestic distribution by dealing with individual TV networks, home entertainment (DVD), streaming platforms, and theatrical studios is possible (but it's a lot of work), I don't recommend this approach for foreign distribution. To get your movie distributed successfully overseas, you need a qualified and competent foreign distributor or sales agent who can track your film's sales, speak the languages, and benefit from the relationships with the foreign buyers that they deal with on a regular basis. There are also complicated tax and delivery requirements that are a major headache for an independent filmmaker and should be left up to the expertise of a foreign representative.

Demystifying Distribution Contracts

After you settle on a distributor, you must sign a contract. Distribution contracts can be long, detailed, and confusing. When you get to this stage, I suggest that you contact an entertainment attorney or someone versed in distribution contracts. You don't want to lose your movie and profits to a distributor because you didn't understand the distribution agreement. The following are some of the things a distribution contract addresses:

>> **Grant of rights:** What media rights is the domestic distributor taking — theatrical, TV, home entertainment (that includes streaming and DVD rights)? A foreign distributor representing your film overseas usually takes all rights.

>> **Term:** For how long does the distributor have the right to distribute your film? It can be up to 15 years. If the distributor doesn't fulfill a certain amount of net sales in a certain period of time, you, the filmmaker, should have the option to cancel the agreement (in writing, of course).

Whatever deal you strike with a distributor, decide on a minimum dollar amount that it has to reach in net sales (meaning the dollars that you pocket). If the distributor doesn't reach that number in two years from the date of signing, then all distribution rights revert back to you, and you can find another distributor. I usually use a number like $200,000 to $500,000. If you don't reach that, it's time to move on. The distributor will also be more inclined to be honest with you on how many sales they've made if they want to continue distributing your picture.

>> **Territory:** Is it for the whole world or just certain territories? Usually with a foreign distributor it's all territories except the United States and Canada, which is usually taken by a domestic distributor.

>> **Delivery requirements:** What picture elements do you need to provide? A digital video copy? A hard drive containing all your files? Do all their territories take widescreen format, or will you have to do *pan and scan*. Do you have publicity photos, artwork, actor and crew agreements, and an accurate credit list ready to hand over to your new distributor?

Pan and scan is required when a particular country hasn't switched to high definition and still uses the old TV format and 4:3 (square) image TV's. The widescreen image of your movie then has to be "pan and scanned" for each shot to accommodate the smaller TV screen without cutting off important picture elements.

>> **Accounting terms:** You need to have access to the distributor's books regarding the collection of sales on your movie. How often do you have access to those books? How much notice do you have to give them?

>> **Gross and net dollars:** Look for the definition of *gross receipts* and *net receipts* (after agreed-upon expenses are paid) that will be split between the distributor and you, the filmmaker. You can find further definitions of *gross* and *net* later in this chapter.

>> **Statement terms:** Does the distributor have an obligation to provide you with producer's statements of any and all sales on your picture? Usually, the distributor provides quarterly statements the first two years, and annually thereafter, but this is negotiable. Do you get to see third-party agreements (who your distributor licensed your movie to)?

>> **Payment terms:** When is the distributor obligated to pay you your share of the profits from your picture? It's usually after defined expenses (marketing and distributor's fees). Determine the allocation of gross receipts — what's paid out and when. Also if an *advance* is paid (upfront money to acquire the rights to distribute your film) the distributor considers this an expense and will reimburse themselves from sales of your picture.

>> **Marketing expenses:** This category includes digital files, tapes, DVD screeners, and hard drives, along with advertising costs, film-market expenses, the costs of making a movie trailer, and so on. Put a cap on marketing expenses so that your distributor can't spend beyond that point — otherwise you may never see a profit. Marketing and advertising costs are usually between $50,000 and $100,000 on an independent film.

>> **Proof of copyright:** The distributor wants to ensure that you are the original owner of the property (the script and completed movie should each have their own separate copyright registration). It's always a good idea to copyright your screenplay and movie because it gives you special legal rights that you otherwise would not have. If someone steals your idea or infringes on your rights, the courts slap statutory penalties (damages) and fines that you would not be otherwise entitled to if you didn't file and obtain a legal copyright from the United States Copyright Office. You can file a copyright for your screenplay and completed movie at www.copyright.gov and click on the copyright registration portal.

TIP

Try to have AVOD (advertising video on demand) excluded from YouTube and any other free streaming platforms if your distributor is considering putting your movie free online with commercials. Otherwise, this will kill most of your other potential sales, including DVD, paid streaming, network TV, and syndication. This happened to me on one of my pictures, as AVOD does not bring in very much revenue from YouTube, even if you have millions of views (like my movie did). You'll thank me in the future for this special tip!

REMEMBER

In perpetuity is a term that's used in distribution contracts. It means "forever," ensuring that the distributor has the rights to your movie forever — unless you put a term on it. Agreeing to a limited term, such as ten years with a renewal clause, is to your advantage. Rarely does a distributor get rights in perpetuity unless they do a buyout and pay you an appropriate amount to own your movie outright.

Insuring for errors and omissions

A distributor can purchase *errors and omissions insurance* (E&O) after it decides to distribute your film. E&O protects you and the distributor if you are sued by any third party if someone says that you stole his idea, slandered him in the movie, or used something of his in your picture without permission. A distributer usually also requests a *title search* done by an attorney before purchasing E&O insurance. Even though you can't copyright a title, the distributor wants to know if other movies are out there with similar or competing titles that could cause confusion or concern.

Usually, a distributor makes sure that no such liabilities exist in your film before it takes it on. If it has concerns, it'll ask you to cut out the offending or questionable material. A distributor usually pays the cost of E&O (see Chapter 4), which can run around $8,000 and up, and then deducts it from your profits.

Accounting for creative bookkeeping

Bookkeeping and accounting is another reason why you need to have an attorney review the distribution agreement for your movie. Distributors can be very creative in their accounting, and your movie could end up never seeing a profit in your pocket — no matter how many sales your distributor makes. Expenses have to be clearly defined in your distribution contract. A distributor can charge excess overhead costs and other hidden charges if you aren't careful.

When you receive a contract from a potential distributor or sales agent, it will contain definitions of *gross* and *net.* Your attorney must look over these definitions carefully. *Gross* is all the monies that come in on your film; *net* is what's left after your distributor takes its expenses. Make sure that those expenses are clearly defined. A distributor's expenses consist of:

>> **Distribution fee:** For a foreign distributor, 20 percent to 30 percent is standard off the top of all gross sales. With a domestic distributor, the fee could be an advance, such as $300,000 paid up front to you to acquire distribution rights to your film, with royalties paid on a percentage of the sales (this is negotiable). Or the distributor may want a *complete buyout* (a flat fee paid with no royalties and the distributor ends up owning your movie).

>> **Market expenses:** For foreign distributors, these expenses include overseas film-market costs; for domestic distributors, they include film markets such as the annual American Film Market.

>> **Promotional flyers (also called *one-sheets* or *sell-sheets*):** For handing out to buyers (also includes design and printing costs).

>> **Posters:** To hang up at the film markets (design and printing costs).

>> **Trade ads:** To create buyer awareness of your movie (design and advertising costs).

>> **Movie trailer:** To help sell your movie to buyers (creative and editing costs).

>> **Screeners:** DVD encrypted screeners of your film provided to potential buyers upon request. Nowadays, many distributors prefer to use online screeners with a private password and watermark.

>> **Travel:** For you to attend an overseas market with your foreign distributor. This can include costs for film market badges as well.

REMEMBER

Always put a cap on expenses. Clearly define the amount of expenses the distributor can deduct against the sales on your movie. After the defined expenses are recouped (including the distribution fee), you'll begin to share in the profits.

TIP

Often a domestic distributor also wants to represent your movie for foreign distribution as well — in other words, the distributor wants all worldwide rights. I try to avoid this unless we do two separate distribution agreements: one for domestic and a completely separate one for foreign. The reason for this is that if you give a distributor all worldwide rights to your film, they can group domestic and foreign expenses together — it's called *cross-collateralization*.

When a distributor lumps all expenses together, you see less profits. If the film doesn't do well foreign, but does well domestically, the distributor can still deduct foreign expenses out of your domestic profits. Sometimes, I even go with two different distributors: one for just foreign, and another distributor just to cover North America. This way cross-collateralization of expenses between foreign and domestic is not possible.

Chapter **20**

Exploring and Entering Film Festivals

Y ou've finally completed your movie, and you can't wait to win some awards for all your hard work. Film festivals are the perfect place to get your film noticed and perhaps gain some recognition for it. This chapter provides firsthand information about entering and (hopefully) winning film festivals, along with how to choose the best festival and the right category for your film. I also give you some hints about getting a discount on the festival entry fee or even getting the fee waived.

Being accepted at a festival such as the Sundance Film Festival is almost as good as winning. (It *is* a nomination.) An award or acceptance at a prestigious festival can give you and your movie credibility. In this chapter, you find a list of the top ten festivals where you can enter your film and compete for award recognition.

Film festivals are also a great place to network and even commiserate with fellow filmmakers on the trials and tribulations of getting your picture completed. If you attend the festival in person, you have a chance to talk with agents, distributors, and other people you wouldn't normally have a chance to hang out with informally in Hollywood or elsewhere.

Demystifying Film Festivals

A film festival is a festival to send your film for possible acceptance among other films. It's a place to compete, be judged, and either place, win, or not win. A film festival is also a spot to meet new friends, watch movies that may never make the mainstream market, and make some business contacts that could help further your career.

Film festivals are springing up like weeds all over the world. With so many out there, you're bound to find at least one that will screen your film, regardless of how good or bad it is. Any recognition from a film festival is better than no recognition at all.

Most film festivals are run by committees consisting of the festival director and the organizers, volunteers, and judges. Often, festivals hire judges who are skilled industry craftspeople and can recognize the talents of their peers. Some of the higher-profile festivals involve well-known actors, producers, and directors as judges. These judges are familiar with the process of filmmaking and look for expertise in story structure, direction, acting, editing, and the picture as a whole as well.

Along with the excitement of watching your movie with an audience and gauging the reaction, networking is a very important part of attending a film festival. You never know what new friends or business contacts you're going to meet. After all, you'll be around your peers — people who love film as much as you do.

REMEMBER

Because most filmmakers now make their movies with digital camcorders and DSRL cameras, most film festivals accept finished productions on DVD, Blu-ray, or DCPs — which are screened using digital video projectors — as opposed to 16mm and 35mm film projection.

Film festivals are often endorsed by the state or city in which they're held, such as the Palm Springs Film Festival and the Santa Barbara Film Festival. The festival promotes tourism and revenues for the city. Some festivals are run by nonprofit organizations.

Film festival recognition adds to your credibility as a filmmaker. If you win just one film festival, you're officially known as "an award-winning filmmaker."

Judging the difference between a film festival and a film market

Many up-and-coming filmmakers get confused by the difference between a film festival and a film market. A *film festival* is a competition of films vying for recognition in the form of awards and acknowledgment. The visibility that filmmakers get and the networking can open up the possibilities for finding a distributor, if they don't already have one.

A *film market* is a business convention that showcases movies for sale to buyers looking for film product all over the world. At a film market, the films already have representation with distributors or sales reps who are soliciting the films to domestic and international buyers for the TV, DVD, Internet, and theatrical outlets. The Cannes Film Festival has a film market that parallels the festival but is a separate entity.

REMEMBER

The American Film Market in Santa Monica, California, the Cannes Film Market in France, MIPCOM, and MIPTV (also in France) are the four main worldwide film *markets.* See Chapter 19 for more information about film markets.

WHAT'S A *LAUREL*?

A *laurel* is that fancy icon sprouting leaves on branches that encompasses your award selection. The laurel wreath comes from Greek mythology as a symbol of triumph. The wreaths were often awarded to strong victors in athletic competitions. When you think of laurel wreaths, you might picture the Roman Caesar wearing a laurel wreath as part of his trademark. You will often see laurels on movie posters and marketing materials for films that have garnered film festival awards or nominations. A laurel can envelop a *Winning* announcement, or even an *Official Selection*. As opposed to winning, an official selection into a film festival is also quite an achievement and deserves a laurel as well.

Screening the benefits of entering film festivals

Besides being a great place to check out what other independent filmmakers are doing, a film festival serves two main purposes: showcasing films and helping filmmakers find potential distributors for their films. Also keep in mind these other benefits to entering and attending film festivals as you decide whether your movie is good enough to enter:

>> **They give you the opportunity to network with other filmmakers.** You can meet your peers and share stories and misadventures.

>> **They provide a forum in which you can meet business contacts.** Agents, attorneys, distributors, and studio executives are much more approachable in a festival environment. A great place to exchange business cards.

>> **They give out cash and prizes.** I don't know anyone who's ever complained about winning cash or prizes. Prizes from festivals are often film related, such as free post-production services, camera and editing equipment, film books (maybe *Filmmaking For Dummies*?) and magazines.

>> **They give out statuettes and certificate awards.** Being able to display an award or any type of accolade for your hard work is always nice. An award also gives you and your film credibility. Awards can be anything from a cash prize, an award certificate, and even a beautiful statuette.

>> **They offer panels and seminars that you can learn from.** Many festivals have credible filmmakers and entertainment-industry guests who offer invaluable insights and answer questions.

>> **They can help generate publicity for your movie.** Your movie could get written up in the local paper of the festival or even get a review (hopefully a good one) from one of the major trade papers like *The Hollywood Reporter* or *Variety*. Local news and entertainment shows may interview you on camera and ask you about your film. Many of these interviews on video or print then end up on the World Wide Web — so your story goes international!

>> **Festival parties are fun.** People (especially agents and distributors) are often more relaxed and approachable after a few drinks and some good music. Just don't drink too much and make a fool of yourself by dancing on the tables. You want your *film* to be judged — not *you!*

REMEMBER

Don't be intimidated by film festivals. Your movie may be the little gem a particular festival is looking for. Anyone can enter a film festival as long as you pay the entry fee and submit your film under the festival's rules. Anyone can win, too!

Entering and Winning Secrets

The secret to entering film festivals is what I call *entry etiquette.* Winning is beyond your control, but following the basic rules I describe in this section brings you closer to that win.

REMEMBER

Don't take it personally if your movie doesn't make it into a festival. With many festivals receiving thousands of submissions annually, a film can easily be overlooked.

Sending a work-in-progress — Don't!

Even though some festivals accept works-in-progress, you're just donating your entry fee to the festival when your movie doesn't get selected because it isn't finished. I've made this mistake before and want to warn you to avoid it. Wait until your movie is completed — including music and sound mix — before you submit it for consideration. Many filmmakers eager to make the deadline for the big festivals like Sundance and Toronto end up sending a work-in-progress. But the festival selection committee rarely gives an uncompleted film the benefit of the doubt. The unfinished film is viewed alongside completed films and usually loses out. Submitting a work-in-progress wastes your time and money — and the festival's time as well.

AND THE WINNING FILM IS ABOUT . . . *NOTHING*!

I'm not going to say which festival did this, but several years ago, I entered one of my movies in a major film festival and paid the hefty entry fee. After a few months, I received a form letter with my returned DVD thanking me for submitting — that my film was well done, but didn't make the cut. While staring at my returned DVD, I realized there was no ring or shading on the underside of the disc, which is usually noticeable on a ripped DVD. I popped it in my DVD player and realized that I had accidentally sent a blank DVD to the festival. So, the judges at the film festival didn't even look at it to realize I accidentally submitted a blank DVD. Now, wouldn't it be really funny if I had won!

Entering the right festivals for your film

Your film is in the can, or in the digital realm, and you can't wait to send it out and start collecting invitations to all the great film festivals. But wait: You have to choose carefully which festival is best to enter. You can start by going to Film Freeway (www.filmfreeway.com) for up-to-the-minute information about film festivals, including entry details and deadlines. Also, going to a film festival's website enables you to get updated information, including entry rules and regulations. Note that most film festival websites have the extension .org, *not* .com; many festivals are nonprofit organizations. Film Freeway has become the norm for submitting to virtually any film festival in the world (more on this later in the chapter).

So how do you decide which festival is right for your movie? Think about your intended audience. If your movie is a mainstream piece that *Star Wars* or *Avengers* audiences would love, it isn't exactly Sundance Film Festival fare; Sundance often looks for offbeat or controversial films. If your film's about an escaped convict who kidnaps grandmothers, it isn't going to be accepted at a children's film festival — unless it's a comedy, and the heroes are an odd gang of misfits. But don't enter just one festival — that's like putting all your eggs in one basket. Instead, choose wisely and be selective, with good insight, how many and which festivals (and categories within) seem appropriate for your film.

The following is a list of ten top film festivals, in order of popularity, to consider for your film. The list is a compilation of my favorites, including first-film and independent film-friendly festivals and a family festival dedicated to those rare independent family-produced films.

>> **The Sundance Film Festival** takes place in Park City, Utah, in January, with an entry deadline in early October. This is the festival of festivals, established by actor Robert Redford and named after one of his favorite classic films, *Butch Cassidy and the Sundance Kid.* (That's why he's often still referred to as the *Kid*.) Sundance has become one of the toughest festivals to get a film accepted at. The festival is overloaded with submissions, and a film has to have a sophistication that Sundance audiences and judges have become accustomed to. The festival favors independent films. If your film gets accepted for screening, that's almost as good as winning — being accepted carries a lot of merit. But it's a tough one, so don't rely on Sundance to be your film's festival premiere. For information, go to www.sundance.org/festival.

>> **The Toronto International Film Festival** takes place in Toronto, Ontario, Canada, in September, with an entry deadline in April/May. This festival has been around since 1976 and is considered the second most popular among the elite film festivals, after Sundance. Films are judged on artistic values and subject matter, similar to the Sundance Film Festival. Independent films are

especially welcomed. Like Sundance, this festival is also difficult to get into and has become a lot more commercial over the years with a lot of major studios and movie stars premiering their new movies. Go to www.tiff.net or phone 416-599-8433.

» **Telluride Film Festival** takes place in August/September in the mountain village of Telluride, Colorado, with an entry deadline in April/July. The festival is for real movie lovers and accepts all types of films as well as experimental, first-film, and artsy styles. A lot of gems have been discovered at Telluride. Go to www.telluridefilmfestival.org or phone 510-665-9494.

» **WorldFest Houston** is in April, with an entry deadline in February. Like many of the other festivals, it accepts digitally finished films transferred to Blu-ray or DCPs for best quality projection. The festival accepts a wide array of styles, from films with wide commercial appeal to experimental short films, and welcomes family-friendly films as well. This is one of the world's oldest film festivals (since 1961). Even Steven Spielberg won an award in his early career at WorldFest — as did George Lucas, the Coen Brothers, Oliver Stone, and Robert Rodriguez. This is one of my favorite festivals, run by J. Hunter Todd with Kathleen Haney. They truly respect and love the independent filmmaker. It's also a really fun festival to attend with lots of things to do, including a boating excursion. For information, go to www.worldfest.org or phone 713-965-9955.

» **Cannes Film Festival** takes place in May in the breathtaking city of Cannes, France, with an entry deadline in March. The Cannes Film Festival is in the elite company of Sundance and Toronto. It carries a different sophistication and is run with the international elegance of a European gala event. The festival accepts higher-profile films, especially with an international flair. Go to www.festival-cannes.com or email festival@festival-cannes.com.

» **Sedona International Film Festival** is another one of my favorite festivals, which takes place in the magical and breathtaking elevations of Arizona surrounded by the colossal red rocks of Sedona. (See Figure 20-1.) The festival, which runs for nine days every February, welcomes all kinds of films and filmmakers. Festival director Patrick Schweiss is one of my favorite festival directors. If your film is selected for the festival, Patrick will welcome you with open arms, possibly provide you with free accommodations during your stay, and will be almost as excited about your film being in the festival as you are! The festival accepts all genres, including a special award category for Best Family Film. Check out www.sedonafilmfestival.com or phone 928-282-1177.

» **Burbank International Film Festival** takes place in September, in Burbank, California (just a few miles from Warner Bros. studios), with an entry deadline in April. The festival accepts most styles of films, especially independent films and films from new and up-and-coming filmmakers. The festival runs for five days and includes seminars with industry professionals and celebrities. Go to www.burbankfilmfest.org or phone 818-601-2082.

Actress onscreen, Erica Howard

» **Slamdance Film Festival** takes place in January, with an entry deadline in October. Slamdance was created in 1994 to catch the spillover of films that don't get accepted into Sundance. It's very much a festival for independent filmmakers and first-film entrants who find themselves left out in the cold — even though they have a film that an audience would appreciate and enjoy. Go to www.slamdance.com or phone 323-466-1786.

» **Heartland Film Festival** takes place in October in Indianapolis, Indiana, and is also known as a very family-friendly festival. So if your film is family-oriented, this is one of the best festivals to submit to! Go to www.heartlandfilm.org/festival.

» **Dances with Films** takes place in July, in Los Angeles, California, with an entry deadline in April/May. Also known as the "Festival of the Unknowns," this festival boasts that it features films with no-name directors, actors, and producers. It was originally established to get away from the politics of other film festivals. It's very first-film friendly and welcomes independent films with great stories. Go to www.danceswithfilms.com or phone 323-850-2929.

FAB-ULOUS RECOGNITION

The Film Advisory Board (FAB) is an organization dedicated to recognizing quality films for children and family. FAB has acknowledged many studio pictures, including *E.T.: The Extra-Terrestrial* on its reissue. Films do not compete against each other; rather they are recognized on their own merits and, if worthy of a FAB award, receive recognition. There is no deadline date — films are looked at year-round. You can find more information about The Film Advisory Board at www.filmadvisoryboard.org.

The Telly Awards, founded in 1980, are similar to FAB in that entries do not compete against each other. TV commercials, films, and TV programs are judged on individual merit and receive an award if the judges feel that the film or program has a high standard of excellence. All genres are accepted as long as they have not been broadcast on a major network. For more information about the Tellys, check out www.tellyawards.com.

TIP

The microphone and audio company Røde has its own film festival. The competition, called My Røde Reel, accepts short film entries that used Røde microphones for their production audio. Røde offers over a million dollars in prizes. The requirements state that your film can be up to 3 minutes long, that you shoot a behind-the-scenes video showing the actual production being shot, that you feature your Røde product or products in your behind-the-scenes footage, and finally, that you upload it to the Røde website. So head over and check out www.Rode.com/MyRodeReel for dates and details — sounds good!

REMEMBER

When deciding which festivals to enter, keep in mind deadlines and entry fees are subject to change, so always visit the festival's website or call ahead. Questions are usually answered quickly via email. You should also find updated info on most festivals on the Film Freeway website as well.

Choosing the appropriate genre and category

After you've selected the right film festival, you have the dilemma of entering in the correct genre and category (explained in detail in Chapter 2). If you choose incorrectly, you could blow your movie's chances of winning or placing. Some festivals allow you to enter several genres for this reason — very helpful if you can't decide exactly which genre your movie fits into. Is it a comedy, drama, science-fiction, or fantasy? A combination of several genres? If you don't know your film's genre, who does?

Usually, the judging committee won't correct your mistake if you enter under the wrong category. It has too many entries to weed through. If you're undecided, call the festival and ask its opinion. You can also screen your movie for friends and ask what category they feel your film falls into.

Along with knowing the genre your movie falls under, you have to choose the correct category, which is usually one of the following:

>> **Animation:** Utilizing traditional drawings, stop motion (like *Gumby and Pokey* or *Coraline*), or digital computer-generated images (like *Toy Story* or *Frozen*).

>> **Commercial:** A 30-second to 1-minute commercial whose purpose is to sell a product or idea.

>> **Documentary:** A behind-the-scenes nonfiction (sometimes controversial) production that makes a statement and features the real side of a person or event.

>> **First feature:** Your first attempt at a feature-length film (at least 90 minutes) with a cohesive story.

>> **Independent film (low-budget):** A feature-film length production produced with limited funds and independent of a major studio or distributor.

>> **Public Service Announcement (PSA):** A 30-second to 1-minute commercial making a statement about health issues, environmental issues, or any subject matter that promotes a better society.

>> **Short film:** Usually under 30 minutes. Encapsulates a complete story with developed characters within a shorter running time.

>> **TV movie:** Usually slotted within a two-hour time period on a TV network. Produced specifically for the small screen (TV) keeping in mind the TV censors with regard to subject material.

>> **TV program:** Usually runs within a one-hour time slot. Can be a variety program (such as *America's Got Talent*), a reality show (like *Keeping Up with the Kardashians* — or is it *Putting Up with the Kardashians?*), or a one-hour drama show.

TIP

Some festivals accept screenplay submissions as well. So if you have an unproduced screenplay that you're proud of, submit it to the appropriate festival. I entered my original screenplay *Undercover Angel* in the Santa Clarita International Film Festival (which became the International Family Film Festival), and it received an award certificate. I then put the award logo on the screenplay to show that it was an award-winning script, which gave the screenplay credibility and raised interest in the project. (The film was produced and released successfully a year later!) A few years later, I submitted my screenplay *First Dog* to WorldFest in Houston, and it too won a screenplay award — which was a catalyst in getting that film produced as well.

Writing a great synopsis of your movie

Just like when you had a carefully prepared pitch to sell your movie idea to an investor or distributor (Chapter 3), you need to pitch an intriguing synopsis of your movie that will convince the festival screeners to consider your film for their festival. If you write a boring synopsis, they will anticipate a boring film.

Picture perfect: Selecting the best photos from your film

Photos from your movie are an important marketing tool. Film festivals request still photos from your movie to use in their brochures and marketing materials — should your film be accepted. A picture always draws the reader's attention to an article and helps the reader to understand and remember the material more than with no photograph.

Make sure that you have photos taken on the set. Submit photos that best represent your movie, such as an interesting confrontation between your actors, or something that causes an emotion in the viewer. If you have any name stars, then make sure they're in the photos.

REMEMBER

When you send photos from your film to a film festival, be sure to label each photo with the name of your movie. Identify the scene and the actors in the photo with a caption. If the festival people decide to publish the photo in their publicity ads or festival program, they need to have this information clearly marked. Most festivals accept digital photos through email, or the festival can download the photos from Film Freeway's entry site if you're a member and uploaded your publicity photos there.

Submitting the best format securely

Only a few years ago, if you completed your movie on analog or digital videotape (as opposed to cutting on film for release in theaters), you were out of luck when it came to having a festival show your movie. If a festival accepted your movie for screening, you had to provide a 16mm or 35mm film print. Many independent filmmakers were knocked out of the game because their finished projects were on tape or digital files only. You could always transfer your finished video product to motion picture film, but that process was lengthy and expensive and the picture quality would suffer from magnifying grain and imperfections, depending on the quality of the original footage.

Now that digital filmmaking has come into its own, all film festivals have video projectors that can project virtually any form of video such as digital files, DVD, and Blu-ray. The bigger festivals also have the capacity to project your film if you provide an external hard drive in the form of a DCP (digital cinema package). Independent filmmakers can now receive equal consideration regardless of whether their project is shot and finished on an inexpensive digital DSRL camera or a professional $100,000 digital cinema camera.

REMEMBER

Blu-ray or a DCP is the favored format when using a video projector. A Blu-ray can be excellent picture quality if it's authored and burned properly. Burning your projects onto DVDs or Blu-ray with most computers is easy and inexpensive. A popular software application that burns DVDs and Blu-ray discs easily is Toast by Roxio. It also lets you author your disc with customized menus. You can do lots of other things with the Toast software, like convert formats and even encrypt files. Check out Toast at www.roxio.com.

Entering onto the Film Freeway

The traditional way of entering a film festival consists of filling out an entry form and mailing it in with your film submission (usually in the form of a DVD screener or, more acceptable, a private online screener) along with your entry fee and supporting materials (still photos, synopsis, and so on). A unique company, Film Freeway, has simplified the film festival submission process for the filmmaker.

TIP

Film Freeway (www.filmfreeway.com) is a unique service that creates a direct link between the filmmaker and the film-festival circuit by allowing you to submit your film entry online to thousands of film festivals of your choice worldwide and hassle-free. Under its online private screener service, Film Freeway even gives you the option to upload a copy of your movie that can be accessed by the film festivals you choose. You can also provide a Vimeo link, if you have your film on Vimeo. Create a password so only the festival with your private password can view your film. Online film submission is especially invaluable when you're submitting to more than one festival. Most film festivals accept, and encourage, filmmakers to use Film Freeway. It has become the traditional (and most convenient) way to enter film festivals.

Film Freeway collects all the necessary information from you online and then inputs it into the entry forms of all the festivals you want to enter. Your information is customized to each festival's distinct entry form. This saves you from entering the information every time on individual entry forms for each festival you want to enter.

Film Freeway enables you to do a vast search on the site to find the most suitable festival for your movie, enter multiple festivals, upload scanned publicity photos from your movie, and track your entry submissions. Using Film Freeway is free; you only pay each festival entry fee and the cost of shipping a DVD screener of your film (if you don't upload your movie with a private link).

TIP

Film Freeway is also working on a service to provide filmmakers the ability to make their own DCP (digital cinema package). This is huge! Sign up for a free account at Film Freeway at www.filmfreeway.com and it will notify you with updates on its DCP news as well as keep you up to date on film festival dates and schedules.

Getting an entry-fee discount

Pretty much every film festival in the United States charges an entry or submission fee, which can range from $20 to $200. Then, if you win, some festivals charge you extra to purchase an award statuette or certificate! Some film festivals offer entry discounts to students and independent filmmakers. Calling and asking about available discounts is a good idea. Festivals know that most independent filmmakers are tight on funds, so many will consider a discount on your entry if you ask — especially if you submit early.

TIP

Many festivals reward you with an entry discount if you submit your movie early. It's an incentive to filmmakers to not wait until the last minute. The festival judges need lots of time to sort through and review thousands of films submitted each year. The discount is usually mentioned on the entry forms or festival website and through Film Freeway's site when you're researching which festivals you're thinking of entering.

SEALING YOUR FILM WITH AN AWARD

Award seals are *seals of approval* from various organizations. One such establishment is the Dove Foundation. There is usually no competition to be eligible for a seal — you just have to be approved and found to be within the guidelines of the organization's rules to receive its seal of approval. Many of my movies have received the Dove seal because they satisfied the rules of being wholesome family entertainment. Same with the Parents Television Council seal. Other organizations that award seals to the appropriate films include the Film Advisory Board (FAB) and KIDS FIRST! (from the Coalition for Quality Children's Media — whose judges consist of adults and children).

6

The Part of Tens

You find helpful tips, secrets, and priceless advice that can save you a lot of time and trouble and help make your movie a success.

You're given tips for discovering new talent, ways to avoid Murphy's Law, and ideas for publicizing your film to gain recognition and maybe even attract a distributor.

You learn some great tips if you want to shoot your production entirely on your smartphone.

Chapter 21

Ten Tips for Discovering New Talent

D iscovering new talent can be a fun position to be in. You could be the catalyst that launches someone's acting career. Marilyn Monroe, Sandra Bullock, Dustin Hoffman, and Meryl Streep were all discovered — and you can bet that someone is taking the credit for discovering them. This chapter shows you how to root out unknown talent.

Studios often conduct casting calls, looking for that special someone to play a leading role. Daniel Radcliffe was discovered after an extensive worldwide search for the perfect Harry Potter. Emily Mae Young, the little girl featured in the Welch's Juice commercials, had never starred in a feature film until my mother saw her on the commercials. I hired Emily for my film *Undercover Angel,* and she went on to win several best-actor awards (which weighed more than she did!). After shooting my film, she was called in for auditions with big-time directors, including Ron Howard and Martin Scorsese.

Streaming Independent Films

Watch independent films of actors whose performances you admire. You can easily find their films on Netflix, Amazon, or many other streaming services. If the actor is a member of the Screen Actors Guild — AFTRA (SAG/AFTRA), the actor's union that represents over 160,000 performers, you can call the guild at 858-724-2387 for the actor's representatives (usually the agent or manager). If you're a member of IMDbPro, you can often find contact info for the actor which could include agent, manager, attorney, or publicist. IMDbPro stands for *Internet Movie Database,* which lists pretty much every actor, crew, and cast member who has ever worked on a film. Check it out at `https://pro.imdb.com`.

TIP

One way to track down an actor is to first get the actor's correct name and spelling from the film's credits, and then try searching on the Internet. Many actors nowadays have their own personal websites and can be found by typing in their name with the .com extension or by locating them with an Internet search engine like Yahoo! or Google. Many actors also have Facebook pages, Twitter accounts, and Instagram presences. You may even find them on Linkedin and message them from there.

Visiting Local Theater

No matter what city you're in, you can go to the local stage show and discover great talent. Just make sure the actor is able to tone his acting performance down for your film because stage actors tend to *project* bigger (speak loud and over-enunciate so the theater audience can hear them) than trained film and television actors do. One of the many reasons actors do stage plays is to attract film-industry people (someone like you) who may hire them to act in a movie.

Auditing Acting Schools and Showcases

Almost every city or small town has an acting school or at least a drama department at the local schools or colleges. If you're in a big city like Los Angeles, New York, or Toronto, you'll have no problem finding talent through the many private acting schools and seminars for actors put on by seasoned acting coaches. Even Jeff Goldblum conducted his own acting course in Los Angeles.

Showcases are different from stage plays in that they *showcases* actors' talents specifically for industry people, such as casting directors, directors, producers, or independent filmmakers like yourself. The performances are usually short monologues by an individual actor, or two actors performing a dramatic scene. Go down and see a showcase at a local theater (almost every city has one) — you're bound to find some natural talent. The magazine *Backstage* (`www.backstage.com`)

lists showcases and actors' events. Or check with local stage theaters and even acting schools in your area, where they often post upcoming showcases and performances.

Many actors also showcase their work from scenes they did in acting class on the World Wide Web by uploading samples of their work onto www.youtube.com or www.vimeo.com.

Talking to Agents and Managers

Agents and managers have done the hard work for you by finding and representing talented actors, many of whom may be new to television or film. I've worked with agents and managers who are eager to get their new discoveries out working, gaining experience, and getting performances on-line to showcase their talents.

Accessing Actors Access

Run by Breakdown Services, Actors Access is a full online talent base that is updated daily. You can do a search there for the type of actor you're looking for and immediately reference the actor's resume and possibly a demo reel online. You need to meet the requirements to sign up, and you must be able to prove that you are a filmmaker casting for a legitimate movie. I've discovered many of my actors through Actors Access. Also, check out www.mandy.com for a talent base of over 200,000 actors to choose from.

Schmoozing at Film Festivals and Markets

Film festivals are often attended by actors whose films are being showcased (see Chapter 20). This is an excellent avenue to find new talent eager to do their next project. Film markets also attract actors and (see Chapter 19) offer an informal environment to catch people relaxed and in a schmoozing mood.

REMEMBER

Many actors attend the various film markets and festivals for the sole purpose of meeting filmmakers who can use them in their next films. This could be a win-win situation for you both!

Partying at Parties

Who doesn't like a good party? Parties are a great place to find actors, or those who want to be actors. A good friend of mine, Jeff Gund, started The Info List (www.infolist.com), which has become a successful networking site for film-makers and actors. You need to sign up for his mailing list (it's free). If you sign up to the website, you can put up ads looking for talent or crew, and Jeff will send out an email blast for you. You'll also get invitations to his Hollywood soirees, which often take place at the famous Skybar on Sunset Boulevard. Even if you don't live in Los Angeles, you might consider a trip just for one of Jeff's Info List parties. There's always a Who's Who of Hollywood celebrities there, including working producers and actors — an excellent place to network! I've been a guest at many of Info List's private parties.

Walking Down the Street

I'm not talking literally finding someone "on the street," unless you hit them with your car or literally bump into them on the sidewalk. But you can often find actors in common everyday places. In Los Angeles and New York, coffee shops are places where actors congregate, often working on their resumes, studying their next scripts, or meeting with producers. Again, if you live in Los Angeles or New York, you're bound to run into famous people dining in restaurants or shopping pretty much anywhere. Even Jennifer Garner and Britney Spears have been spotted shopping at Target!

I found my leading lady for my film *Undercover Angel* while dining in a local neighborhood restaurant. I found a purse at my table and a few minutes later saw a woman looking around like she'd lost something. It turned out this was her purse — and she turned out to be Yasmine Bleeth (of *Baywatch* and *Nash Bridges*). I sent my script to her agent explaining how we met, and the rest is history: She starred in my film!

Holding Talent Contests

Clubs, theaters, and TV programs sometimes hold talent contests. Find out where these contests are being held and go down to meet people waiting in line. If you have a comedy club in your town, go down on amateur night, and you're sure to discover some great comedians. That's how Steve Martin, Jim Carrey, and Howie Mandel were discovered (I put Howie Mandel in his first film *Just Joking* when I was a director student at The American Film Institute in the early eighties).

Casting Your Family

Maybe your star is right in your own family. I put my mom in my film *Undercover Angel* as the landlady (besides, if I didn't, I was afraid she'd send me to my room). She did such a great job I hired her again to play the cleaning lady in my movie *Light Years Away,* and then again for the role of Mrs. Claus in my movie *Santa Stole Our Dog.* (See Figure 21-1.) How about your brother, sister, or dog? I cast my dog, Little Bear, to star in my feature film, *First Dog,* where he plays the canine companion to the president of the United States. From the success of that film, Little Bear went on to star in several more successful movies and became one of the oldest canine actors working in Hollywood. He was even featured in a commercial I directed that ran on Super Bowl Sunday.

Maybe *you* have that star quality — so why not cast yourself? Director Kevin Smith cast himself in his films *Clerks, Dogma, Chasing Amy,* and *Jay and Silent Bob Strike Back.* Jon Favreau cast himself in *Swingers,* which he wrote and co-produced, and in *Iron Man* and *Chef,* which he directed. Mel Brooks starred in a lot of the films he produced and directed, like *Young Frankenstein, Blazing Saddles,* and *High Anxiety.* Plus, if you star in your own movie, you can give yourself top billing!

FIGURE 21-1:
Mom Mrs. Claus (the author's mother) playing Mrs. Claus in *Santa Stole Our Dog.*

Chapter 22

Ten Ways to Get Publicity for Your Movie

You made a movie and now you want people to know about it. Some people think publicity is to stroke a filmmaker's ego, but the real purpose is to get your name and film out there — to create awareness through repetition. When you see a commercial for a soft drink, suddenly you're thirsty. You see a pizza commercial and consider ordering one. In this same way, you want to create awareness for your movie so that distributors and audiences will flock to it. Publicity can also give you credibility as a filmmaker and get you more work. It's amazing how people accept you when they see your name in print.

REMEMBER

Generate publicity only when the timing is right. Usually the best time is when you've scheduled a *screening* (projecting your movie in a theater), whether it's for a general audience or one specifically for entertainment industry guests, such as distributors and TV buyers, including home-entertainment that encompasses DVD and streaming services.

Uploading a Press Release Online

A *press release* is a one-page announcement of a publicity event for your movie that you can email to your local newspapers, TV stations and online news outlets, and also calendar event sites. Use a clever heading to catch a reporter's attention. The release should also have the words "For Immediate Release, Please" (it never hurts to be polite) so they know it's timely and important. It should state what, where, when, and why. This way, your press release for a screening or other publicity stunt allows the press and the rest of the population to show up at the proper time and place. You can also find online Press Release services that for a small fee will distribute your announcement to news services — of which some will hopefully pick up the information on your press release and pop up on different news websites. Two of these sites are www.NewsWire.com and www.PRweb.com.

Getting a Review from Movie Critics

When you're planning a screening of your film, contact local movie critics in your town and invite them to the show. Also invite online movie websites like Film Threat (www.filmthreat.com) or MovieWeb (www.movieweb.com) to review your movie and send them a private screener via an online link or a physical DVD.

TIP

If you can't afford a screening, you can also mail DVD screeners to the local critics, or a private link with password to view your film on YouTube or Vimeo (with a protective watermark) and ask them if they'd consider reviewing your film (see the following section). I've had favorable reviews of my films on www.movieweb.com and other sites. If you get a great quote from one of the reviews, you can use it on your DVD box cover, posters, or newspaper advertisements for your film. As a courtesy you may want to ask permission to use a particular quote.

Mailing Out DVD Screeners or Linking to a Secure Online Screener

After you've completed your movie, you need to either make DVD screeners or create a private online screener with a secured link (with password) to distributors, potential TV buyers, and DVD and streaming companies. Even if you plan a screening, you still need to make DVDs and/or an online screener available because many distributors or buyers won't attend but will ask for a viewing copy instead. Important — Don't offer to send a DVD or online link until they let you know they can't attend and actually request to view the film.

Attending Film Festivals

Enter festivals to start creating awareness of your film. If your film is selected or wins at a festival, you can then contact your local newspapers and TV news programs and notify them of the status of your film at the festival.

Here's a crazy idea: Organize your own film festival. Enter your film (don't let anyone else enter) and award yourself first prize for best film. Then send a press release online and to newspapers and local TV news. Even if people find out it's your own private film festival, it still makes for a funny news story.

Emailing and Setting Up a Website

Set up a website for your film. My favorite website for creating websites is Wix. com. It's very user friendly and you don't have to know any code to create your site. They offer you templates you can customize, and also have tutorials that guide you easily through the process. You can also hire a professional to set up your site but that's going to cost money. A website can be a promotional site letting people know the details of your movie (storyline, cast, fun details, movie trailer, and so on). You can direct distributors to your site if they're considering picking your movie up for distribution. If you set up the website before you start production on your film, the site can provide information for potential investors and also for actors you're considering. For an example, check out the website for two of my films that I created for free with Wix.com: www.firstdogfilm.com and www.AmazingWizardofPaws.com. It's also a good idea to put your trailer up on YouTube (www.youtube.com) and Vimeo (www.vimeo.com) and email everyone you can with a link. In addition you should link your YouTube or Vimeo trailer to also appear on the website you created for your movie.

REMEMBER

You can also send email messages to a select group of people or let your Facebook friends, and Twitter and Instagram followers know about your new movie and any publicity events you're planning. Send emails to potential distributors, studio acquisition people, including DVD distribution companies, streaming services, and TV network executives. Be sure to target your mailing list — you don't want to be considered a *spammer* (someone who solicits over the Internet to people who don't request mailings from them).

Being Social by Using Social Media

Social media is one of the most powerful forms of advertising these days. Whether you use Facebook, Twitter, Instagram, or any of a host of other popular social media platforms, you need to spread the word. If you're not good at social media, find someone who is. Chances are you can find a high school student who knows more about social media than most grown-ups. Social media is part of growing up now, and even young kids know how to navigate the Internet better than most adults!

Promoting your movie on certain Internet radio stations, a film blog, or even on an interview uploaded to YouTube is a great way to create exposure.

Designing T-Shirts and Other Premiums

Promotional products, called *premiums* or *giveaways,* such as buttons, T-shirts, coffee mugs, pens, key chains, and hats with your film's logo, create great publicity for your movie. (People rarely throw away something that has any type of value to it.) You can give these away at shopping malls, at your premiere screening, or at film markets and film festivals. Most cities have promotional product and apparel companies (and tons online); I've used ButtonWorks (www.buttonworks.com) for colorful buttons to give out at screenings and film festivals. (See Figure 22-1.) Two other great companies I've worked with that do promotional products are Best of Signs (www.bestofsigns.com) and UPrinting (www.uprinting.com).

FIGURE 22-1:
Buttons from
ButtonWorks.

For my film *Undercover Angel*, I created Mister Dodo stuffed dolls and sent one out with each DVD screener of the film. I even wrote a children's book to help promote the movie. The book is available in Kindle format on Amazon.com (under *Mister Dodo's First Adventure*).

Planning a Publicity Stunt

A *publicity stunt* is anything that draws attention to you or your movie. Choose a publicity stunt that isn't dangerous or illegal (you don't want to get arrested — that's the wrong kind of publicity!). A costumed character giving out flyers or delivering a DVD copy of your movie to a studio executive or distributor is okay (unless security throws you out!). Sending a singing telegram with a DVD of your movie to a potential distributor might work, too.

A more expensive publicity stunt is having a prop plane fly a banner advertising your movie. A cheaper way to go is to hire some models or actors to give out flyers on your film or sell tickets to a screening.

When I was a teenager, I shot a film when the circus came to town and wanted to create some publicity for the screening. My friend Gary Bosloy volunteered to dress up in a gorilla suit and run around the neighborhood. Someone called the local radio and TV stations and reported that a gorilla was loose, and everyone assumed it escaped from the circus that was in town. I then called into the radio stations and local news programs and told them it was a publicity stunt to promote our movie. This stunt got us free publicity! Today, I wouldn't recommend this idea, though. Too many people own guns!

Organizing a Screening Party or Charity Event

If you can afford to rent a screening room or theater, consider setting up a premiere to introduce your movie to an audience. The audience should consist of potential buyers for your film, including distributors, TV, and home-entertainment acquisition people (DVD and streaming).

Your screening can also be a charity event where all proceeds go to a specific charity, like a children's hospital or a retirement home. If it's a charitable event, the theater may not charge you to use the theater. A charity screening creates positive exposure for your movie and helps a good cause at the same time. You might even get written up in the local newspaper.

Placing an Ad in Print or on Social Media

Consider placing an ad in your local newspaper to announce a screening of your film. If you want to see the response to your movie with a paying audience, this is a way to go. However, advertising in a newspaper costs considerable money, so you may only want to run a small ad so you have a better chance of making a profit on your screening. You can also try placing an ad on Facebook as well — and, of course, advertise your screening for free through your Twitter and Instagram accounts.

Chapter **23**

Ten Ways to Avoid Murphy's Law

"Everything that can go wrong will go wrong." Welcome to Murphy's Law — the curse of any project. But you don't have to be a victim of Murphy's Law if you plan ahead. If you anticipate disruptions and know how to problem-solve, you'll be prepared to handle Murphy or even keep him away.

In regards to planning, my dad use to say, "You can't go right doing wrong, you can't go wrong doing right." I always have a plan A and a plan B and even a plan C. Brad Pitt even named his production company Plan B Entertainment. Think through all the possibilities that could hold up your production and then plan for them. It's like puppy-proofing your house — you have to think of everything the puppy could get into and lock those things out of reach. Every time I forget to take my lunch off my desk, the dog always remembers. Avoiding Murphy's Law is like buying insurance. Ensure your production by planning ahead for those things that could go wrong.

Testing Camera and Sound

Before you begin shooting your movie, test the camera. If you're shooting with film stock, shoot some test footage and send it to the lab to check for scratches and steadiness of picture and to make sure you don't have fogging on the film from a light leak in the camera. Testing your camera is really easy if you're shooting with a digital camcorder. Just record some footage and then play it back to make sure the image looks okay and the sound is working.

TIP

Make a checklist of all the items and equipment you'll need, along with any important reminders (like giving your friend Noah a credit for letting you shoot in his house for a week). You can start the list way ahead of schedule and continue to add things until the day of shooting. Don't rely on your memory — no matter how good you may be at remembering things, you'll always end up forgetting something or someone. It's like going to the grocery store. You make a grocery list so you know exactly what you need and don't end up forgetting something.

Scouting Locations for Noise

Planes, trains, and automobiles — not good news for your sound takes. Make sure the location is quiet enough to record sound on your shoot. If you're shooting a scene that's supposed to be taking place on the shores of a desert island, you don't want to find out the first day of shooting that you're in the fly-zone of a major airport. The roar of planes taking off and coming in every few minutes can make it extremely difficult to get a clean audio take (see Chapter 12). Same with train tracks. If you must shoot near train tracks, find out the train schedules so you can be forewarned when recording dialogue — and *never* shoot *on* train tracks, even if you know the train's schedule!

Forecasting a Weather App

If you have an outdoor shoot scheduled, be sure to download a weather app to your phone. If torrential rain is predicted, you'll know to plan for your indoor cover set ahead of time. (A *cover set* is an indoor scene that you're prepared to shoot in the event that your outdoor scenes are rained out.)

Backing Up Locations and Actors

Take nothing for granted. You could lose a location because of the owner changing his or her mind, charging you more than what was agreed upon, or for disturbing the neighborhood. If you don't have a backup arranged, you could waste a lot of time trying to find a new location. This has happened to me more than twice.

Have a backup for actors, too. In Los Angeles, I've had my share of flaky actors who were late or forgot to show up on-set. I've had to hire crew members as actors at the last minute when one of the main actors didn't show up.

Using a Stunt Double

Don't take a chance with your actors. Always use a stunt double for any type of action that could potentially endanger your actor. Even if a stunt seems pretty simple, you don't want your lead actor spraining an ankle and hobbling around the rest of the shoot like Tom Cruise did on his movie *Mission: Impossible – Fallout* when he jumped from one building ledge to another. Other than Tom Cruise and Jackie Chan, very few actors in Hollywood do their own dangerous stunts. Jackie Chan has broken almost every bone in his body in the process!

Standing by with First-Aid Kit or Medic On-Set

Be prepared for injuries — whether a simple knee bruise, a cut finger, or something more serious — by having a first-aid kit on-set. Even better, have a medic on-set if you can afford one (especially if your film has stunts or pyrotechnics). And always make sure you have the phone number and directions to the nearest hospital.

Anticipating That Cellphones and Internet Don't Work Everywhere

Check out your locations beforehand to make sure that cellphones and Internet access work in the area. If it's a remote area and you don't pick up a signal (unless you have satellite service), make sure you have access to a land phone and have Wi-Fi Internet access. You always need communication to and from the location.

Mapping Out Directions with a Link

Either have maps drawn up and distributed or send a mapped out link with directions to cast and crew so no one can say he or she didn't know where the location was. Everyone has a GPS app on their smartphone or an actual GPS (global positioning system) device in their car — so no one can use the excuse that they couldn't find the location.

REMEMBER

Some people are visual and can read maps just fine; others are better at following written or spoken directions. Most map apps have a *turn by turn* voice that speaks and announces street names, and maybe even allows you to select GPS Mary with the cute English accent! You can also email or text these preset maps to cast and crew.

Providing Plenty of Parking

You don't want your cast and crew driving around the block for 20 minutes on the first day of your shoot looking for a place to park. Plan ahead and find a parking lot that your team can use while at this location. If everyone has to park a distance from the set location, arrange to have a mini-van shuttle everyone from the parking lot to the set.

Securing Security Overnight

Pay a few extra dollars to have someone stay with the equipment at your location if you're shooting there the next day. Maybe someone on your crew, like a production assistant, would be willing to sleep on a couch or in a tent. Don't ever leave your equipment like your lights and camera in an unlocked vehicle. (Try not to leave them in a vehicle, period!) Someone will be sure to steal something if it's left unattended — Murphy's Law, you know. I've even had a trampoline, a green screen, a clapboard, lights, and a director's chair stolen off my sets. If the location has Wi-Fi, buy a Wyze camera for $20 and monitor your set for any intruders. The Wyze camera alerts you if there's movement and offers two-way voice communication. The picture quality is amazing — better than many $200 surveillance cameras. I've got four of them and absolutely love them. Go to www.wyze.com and check 'em out. (See Figure 23-1.)

FIGURE 23-1:
WyzeCam.

Powering Up ahead of Time

Here's a bonus tip to guard against Murphy's Law. When you scout your locations, make sure they have places to plug in your lights and equipment. Otherwise, you'll need to budget for a generator to run all your electrical devices. Even if you are running your camera and lights on rechargeable batteries, you still will need power to recharge them.

REMEMBER

Even if the location has power, the location owner may request that you bring your own power and not tap into theirs.

Chapter **24**

Ten Tips for Shooting on Your Smartphone

Today's smartphones are so sophisticated, and the technology so advanced, you can shoot a professional looking short movie, or even a full-length feature on your smartphone. Your phone probably shoots 4K broadcast quality images — something that many older expensive video cameras can't even do.

Some of the advantages to shooting with your smartphone include:

>> You just point and shoot.

>> You don't have to fuss with bulky movie lenses.

>> No manual F or T stops to deal with.

>> No depth of field or focus headaches.

>> No exposure issues.

>> No need to lug around a heavy, bulky camera.

>> Your phone is always with you — ready to capture that million-to-one encounter or shoot that on-the-spot great idea.

Shooting in Landscape

The first thing you have to remember is you're shooting a movie, not a photo, not a selfie, and not something you're just going to post to Facebook or Instagram. So, you now have to remember to turn your smartphone sideways. This is called *land-scape mode*. The normal way you're use to holding your phone is *profile mode*. Note that landscape mode resembles the dimensions of your 16x9 TV. Note also that when you watch YouTube videos or feature films on your smartphone, you turn it sideways for the image to fill the whole screen. If you don't shoot your movie in landscape mode, you'll have black bars on each side of the image, and your movie will not fill the entire screen. So, landscape, don't profile!

TIP

Always make sure your smartphone is charged and ready to go. Shooting video on your phone drains the battery faster than talking or listening to music on your phone.

Take Off with Airplane Mode

You're moving in for the perfect shot, the actors embrace, and you're capturing a priceless moment — *and* then your perfect shot is interrupted by your *phone ringing* — your camera is ringing! *"Cut! Hello? Hi mom, I'm busy, shooting my movie."* It's happened to me.

Go into your phone settings and put your phone on *airplane mode*. All the functions of your phone will work except your shoot won't be interrupted by another phone call or annoying text. You want your smartphone to be a 100-percent dedicated camera for your shoot, not a communications device.

Steady as She Goes

Your smartphone is already a sophisticated movie camera. Most smartphones have a built-in stabilizer to ensure steadier shots. Often, you can handhold your smartphone for many of your shots, especially moving or following shots.

Steady as a Rock

For steady tripod shots, you can get special adapters for your phone that have a tripod mount, so you can attach the phone to a tripod for rock-solid shots or for smooth panning ones. You'll find plenty of smartphone tripod adapters on Amazon for as low as $5.

Shooting Format and Resolution

Before you start shooting with your smartphone, you need to go into your camera video settings. You will have a choice of resolution quality. Usually the options are 720, 1080 (2K), and 4K. I'm sure that 6K and up will soon be available for your phone. I recommend shooting on 720 or 2K because the quality is awesome and both resolutions are broadcast quality. If you shoot in 4K, you will very quickly eat up a lot of storage space on your phone. In the video settings, you should also have the choice of shooting at 30 frames per second or 24 frames per second. Choose 24fps for a more film-like look. A great smartphone app called Filmic Pro will add even more professional shooting options to your already advanced smartphone.

Saving Your Movie Files

Depending on your smartphone's built-in storage capacity — or if your smartphone has a removable SD memory card — you will have to constantly offload (transfer) your shots to an external hard drive or your computer. If you don't, your phone's memory will soon fill up and you will have no more room to shoot anything.

Some smartphones connect to your computer via USB and allow you to download your footage this way. An iPhone allows you to wirelessly download your footage from your phone using AirDrop. This allows you to easily and effortlessly download your footage, which then you can erase (trash) off your phone and continue shooting. There's also a great (free) app called Simple Transfer, which is absolutely one of my favorite apps. It lets you view all your phone's photos and movies on your computer desktop, and you can choose which shots you want to download from your phone to your computer in one batch — so you don't have to transfer one shot at a time. I absolutely love this app so much it's on my phone's main Home screen.

Many smartphones are now synced up with the cloud, so, chances are, your smartphone footage will automatically download to your computer if both are talking to the cloud.

WARNING

I can't emphasize this warning enough. If your phone is talking to the cloud and your footage is automatically downloaded to your computer, be absolutely sure to move those shots (digital video files) to a separate folder *outside your camera roll.* If you don't, they will all get erased in the cloud when you erase them off your phone. They will also get erased off your computer and any other device that also talks to the cloud. This is one major flaw of syncing with the cloud — most people think they can trash stuff on their phone to free up memory because it was transferred to their computer and lives in the cloud, but in reality, your computer is talking to the cloud and unless you transfer it out of your camera roll into a folder on your desktop, you'll lose everything.

REMEMBER

All your movie files will be saved to your camera roll in your phone and filed under Videos. But move your movie shots out of the camera roll into a special folder that isn't mirroring your camera roll in the cloud.

Miniature Camera Equipment

The great thing about your movie camera being your smartphone is that everything is light and portable. Your phone is also small enough to mount on a car dashboard or adhere to the car window (on the inside) for great single shots of your driver and passenger or a nice two shot from inside the windshield. Or, turn your phone around so it's looking out your windshield for a nice POV (point-of-view) shot of the road.

TIP

Use a selfie-stick as your camera crane for high shots or low to the ground shots. (See Figure 24-1.) Cut a slot out of a paper cup to make a tripod to hold your phone — this also works great as a dolly, too — and just slide the cup along a desk top or the floor. Try furniture sliders to slide your smartphone along carpets or hardwood floors for smooth dolly shots.

If you want professional-looking dolly shots, check out Dyno Trek. It's a miniature, motorized dolly system (also called a *slider system*) built just for smartphones. It comes with tracks that magnetically hook together for flawless, smooth movement. You can dolly in and out and side to side, or turn the track vertically and get dolly-up and dolly-down shots. You can program the speed of the dolly and even set it up to move in sync with your smartphone for time-lapse shots or stop-motion animation. The kit is lightweight and portable and comes in a sturdy carry case. You can find the Trek at www.dynoequipment.com.

FIGURE 24-1:
A selfie stick
used as a camera
crane for the
Smartphone
high and
low shots.

Model: Honey Bear

TIP

If you have an older smartphone that you put away after you bought the latest and greatest upgrade, it may be time to dust it off. Even though cellular service isn't activated on your old phone, all its camera functions should be working fine. It's really an iPod without cellular service. But you still have Wi-Fi!

This old smartphone can be used as your action backup camera (make sure it's not a big deal if this extra phone gets damaged or destroyed). Place it in the middle of a quiet neighborhood street and have your actor in a car drive over and past the camera. Just make sure he knows to keep the smartphone between the tires! Secure this "B" action camera on the outside of your car for some dramatic driving shots. You can even find a car suction cup mounting device for your smartphone on Amazon — or, just use lots of masking tape on the phone to secure it. (I recommend tying the phone down securely — just in case. The wind could catch it and send it flying!)

Throw the phone in the air to a friend to simulate the POV of a ball being tossed back and forth. I recommend doing this on the grass in case one of you misses a catch.

Use Several Smartphones to Capture Your Movie

Pretty much everyone on your crew (even if there's just two of you) has a smartphone, so any one of these could be used as a second or third camera on your shoot. If you have two actors talking, you can save time by having one smartphone on each actor, instead of using one camera to shoot each actor separately. You can also use an extra smartphone for your wide shots, and another for close-ups (just don't get the phones used for close-ups in the wide shot!).

TIP

Apple's iPhone 11 Pro was the catalyst for the creation of a new triple-camera system that allows users to shoot multiple different-size shots at the same time with just one smartphone camera. This iPhone has three different lenses: a telephoto lens, a wide lens, and an ultra-wide lens. Using a revolutionary app developed by Filmic Pro through the App Store, each lens can record its own file — thus creating three different-sized shots at one time. It's like three cameras rolled into one smartphone. It's also invaluable for documentaries and spur-of-the-moment events.

Another ingenious advancement with the Filmic Pro app is the ability to use the iPhone Pro 11 to shoot an interview in which both the interviewer and the interviewee are filmed at the same time. The app records footage from both the front and back camera at the same time and creates two separate digital files. So, you don't have to have two separate cameras to shoot your interview! This unique technology is absolutely a game-changer for the independent filmmaker shooting with an iPhone and the Filmic Pro app!

TIP

For more great tips and a fun book that converts into a smartphone projector with speakers, includes ticket stubs to your premiere, and even has popcorn boxes — check out my book, *Smartphone Movie Maker,* at Amazon and other fine bookstores near you!

Great Sound on Your Smartphone Too!

Not only can your smartphone shoot great, broadcast-quality digital images, but it also gives you pristine digital sound recording. To get the best of this, plug in a professional directional microphone. You don't want to use your built-in smartphone microphone because it only picks up good sound close to the phone, or ambient sound from all around your environment. Some wireless sound options can record sound directly into your smartphone without the hassle of tripping over wires. Røde makes the Wireless GO, which is perfect as a wireless, compact microphone for your smartphone shoot. You can get the Wireless Go microphone system at `www.rode.com`.

Your Smartphone Is an Entire Production Studio

Your smartphone gives you a camera to shoot your movie, and it can give you great sound. But that's not all. You pretty much have an entire production studio in your pocket! You can even write your screenplay on your smartphone with the Final Draft app for under $10. Storyboard on your phone with certain storyboard apps like Blocker by AfterNow (an absolutely amazing 3D app) and Storyboard Animator for free. You can create a shot list on your phone with an app called Shotlist – Movie Shoot Planning. You can also download stock footage and sound effects right to your phone. In post-production, edit your entire movie on smartphone apps like the free iPhone version of iMovie or a myriad of Android editing apps. And, when you've completed your movie, use your phone to upload it directly to YouTube or Vimeo!

Index

N

The Naked Gun (films), 23, 241
National Television Standards Committee (NTSC), 341
Neat Video, 281
needle-drop fee, 299
Neewer, 201–202
negative cutter, 283–284
negative film and faulty stock coverage, 73–74
negative pickup, 52, 347
negatives, developing, 283
negotiating, for distribution, 352–353
net, 361
net dollars, for distribution contracts, 359
Netflix, 349, 355
neutral density filters (ND filters), 185
New Media, 69
night/day, 184–185
Nightmare on Elm Street (films), 321
The Nightmare Before Christmas, Frankenweenie (film), 312
No Film School, 70
noise, 290–291, 392
non-contractual credits, 334, 342
nonlinear editing (NLE), 273, 274–275
non-union actors, 127, 142–143, 144
normal lenses, 177–178
North by Northwest (film), 29
novel adaptation, 42
NTG3 (Rode), 217
Nu Image - Millennium Films (website), 358

O

objective acting, 237
Ocean's Eleven series (film), 22
omni-directional microphones, 218
On the Lot (film), 30
Once Upon a Time in Hollywood (film), 22
180-degree rule, 253
one-sheets, 123, 361
online screeners, 386–387
on-the-set special effects, 307
opening credits, 332–333
optical credits, 329
optical track, 302
opticals, 308

optioning a book, 42
OSMO Pocket camera, 176–177
outdoor shooting, 104
outline, 52
Outline 4D, 50
overacting, 236
overcranking, 317–318

P

pacing, as an editing consideration, 268
Paddington (film), 31
pan and scan, 359
Paramount Pictures (website), 356
parenting actors, 230
Parents Television Council seal, 376
parking, for locations, 394
parties, finding talent at, 382
partnership, 85
pay television licensing rights, 347
paying crew, 124–127
payment terms, for distribution contracts, 359
PayPal, 159
pay-per-view licensing rights, 347
The Peanuts Movie (film), 32
pen names, 54
period piece, 22
permits, 104–105
The Phantom Menace (film), 170
Phase Alternation Line (PAL), 341
photos, selecting for film festivals, 373
Picture Book, 158
picture editor, 121–122
The Pink Panther (films), 329
pinpoint lighting, 313
Pirates of the Caribbean (film), 232
pitch, 53–54
Pitch Perfect (film), 23, 30
PixelFilmStudios (website), 307
Planet of the Apes (film), 248, 324
PlanMagic (website), 78
planning production, 13–14
Platoon (film), 28
plug-ins, 307
points, 125
polarizers, 185

U

V

W

About the Author

Bryan Michael Stoller is an international-award-winning filmmaker who has produced, written, and directed over 100 productions that include short comedy films, half-hour television shows, music videos, commercials, and feature films. Bryan and his films have been featured on *Entertainment Tonight* and *Access Hollywood*, as well as in many newspapers and periodicals, including *The Los Angeles Times*, *The New York Times*, *The Hollywood Reporter*, and *People Magazine*. The first edition of *Filmmaking For Dummies* was featured along with Bryan in interviews on *CNN*, *E! Entertainment*, *NBC Dateline*, *The Today Show*, and an exclusive interview with Katie Couric.

Bryan's film career began at the early age of 10, when he hosted the network series *Film Fun* with his little sister Nancy on *The Canadian Broadcasting Corporation (CBC)*. In 1981, Bryan moved to Los Angeles to attend the prestigious American Film Institute (AFI).

His comedy shorts entitled *Undershorts* appeared on ABC's *Foul-Ups, Bleeps & Blunders* hosted by Don Rickles and Steve Lawrence, and NBC's *TV's Bloopers & Practical Jokes* with Dick Clark and Ed McMahon. Bryan's movie, *First Dog* (starring Bryan's dog, Little Bear) was the number-nine top summer release on Redbox with close to half a million rentals. His feature films, *The Amazing Wizard of Paws* and *Undercover Angel*, together have amassed close to 18 million views on Video on Demand (VOD). Many of Bryan's films have also streamed on Netflix to great reviews. Universal Home Entertainment picked up Bryan's holiday movie, *Santa Stole Our Dog*, which can be streamed on Amazon or found on DVD.

Bryan's work has also appeared on major U.S. networks including NBC, CBS, ABC, HBO, and DirecTV. His top-rated episode of George Romero's *Tales from the Darkside* continues to run as a late-night favorite in syndication. His films have screened at MIFED in Italy, the Cannes Film Festival in France, and the American Film Market in Santa Monica, California. His screenplays and films have acclaimed awards from all over the world.

You can find Bryan's award-winning film *Undercover Angel*, which stars Yasmine Bleeth (*Baywatch*, *Nash Bridges*), Dean Winters (HBO's *OZ*, *30 Rock*, "Mayhem Man" commercials), James Earl Jones, Casey Kasem, and Emily Mae Young (of Welch's juice commercials) on Amazon. The movie has aired on Lifetime, Showtime, Bravo, and in U.S. syndication.

In his 2001 mockumentary *Hollywood Goes to Las Vegas* (winner of the Telly Award), Bryan's dream of meeting actress Sandra Bullock finally came true. The program includes appearances by George Clooney, Nicolas Cage, John Travolta, Chris Rock, Sylvester Stallone, and Academy Award-winner Russell Crowe. In various other productions, Bryan has also directed George Carlin, Howie Mandel, Ed Asner, Barbra Streisand, Drew Barrymore, Jerry Lewis, and Dan Aykroyd. Dolly Parton wrote and recorded four original songs for one of Bryan's film, *First Dog*.

Bryan and his actor dog, Little Bear, have been featured guests at The Hollywood Autograph Show in Los Angeles, where Bryan and Little Bear signed autographs (and paw-tographs) promoting Little Bear's movies that Bryan wrote, produced, and directed. The two signed autographs alongside Dick Van Dyke, Richard Dreyfuss, Henry Winkler, and William Shatner, to name a few.

The second edition of *Filmmaking For Dummies* was included in swag bags in Hollywood at the American Cinemateque Awards honoring Ben Stiller. Many of the attendees took home copies, including Jennifer Aniston, Ben Stiller, Will Ferrell, and many Hollywood studio heads.

Bryan has taught filmmaking seminars for The Learning Annex, as well as the Summer Film Camp for the International Family Film Festival. He also teaches film and screenwriting at various venues, including the Screenwriting Expo and Screen Writers Alliance in Los Angeles, and acting techniques at various industry schools in the Los Angeles area, including Action in Acting, APS, The Casting Break, and the Creative Actor's Alliance, as well as internationally in Canada's capitol for the Ottawa School of Speech and Drama.

For more information on Bryan, check out his official website at: www.BryanMichaelStoller.com.

Author's Acknowledgments

The undertaking of this book has been very much like that of producing a movie. And of course, like the production of a film, this book wouldn't have been possible without all the help and support of such wonderful individuals.

I'd like to thank again Natasha Graf, the acquisitions editor for the first edition of this book, for her kindness and understanding and for believing in me; and Alissa D. Schwipps, my original editor, who made the writing of this book such an enjoyable experience. I'd also like to thank Michael Lewis and Tracy Barr for their help with the second edition. For the third edition, special thanks to Ashley Coffey and Christopher Morris.

Additional thanks goes out to family and friends who were there for support and feedback, including my sister Nancy, and my friends, Gary Bosloy, Russel Molot, Tim Peyton, Darren Ballas, Bruce Greene, Alexander (Sasha) Yurchikov), Peter Emslie, Tina and Alan Fleishman, Noah and Sabrina Golden, Erica Howard, Jon and Lois Calof, Robert Caspari, and Gloria Everett.

And a special thanks to the late Jerry Lewis. It shows that life *is* magical when one of your favorite actors/filmmakers endorses your book!

My Cine-cere thanks to you all.

Bryan Michael Stoller

Studio City, California

Dedication

To my mom, who claims the film credit "Producer of the Director" on all my movies. To my dad (who played the ambassador in my movie *The Random Factor*) — I miss you. And to my dog, Little Bear, who was my muse for 16 years.

Publisher's Acknowledgments

Acquisitions Editor: Ashley Coffey

Project Editor: Christopher Morris

Copy Editor: Christopher Morris

Technical Editor: Tim Peyton

Production Editor: Magesh Elangovan

Proofreader: Debbye Butler

Cover Image: © gerenme/Getty Images

Leverage the power

Dummies is the global leader in the reference category and one of the most trusted and highly regarded brands in the world. No longer just focused on books, customers now have access to the dummies content they need in the format they want. Together we'll craft a solution that engages your customers, stands out from the competition, and helps you meet your goals.

Advertising & Sponsorships

Connect with an engaged audience on a powerful multimedia site, and position your message alongside expert how-to content. Dummies.com is a one-stop shop for free, online information and know-how curated by a team of experts.

- Targeted ads
- Video
- Email Marketing
- Microsites
- Sweepstakes sponsorship

20 MILLION PAGE VIEWS **EVERY SINGLE MONTH**

15 MILLION UNIQUE VISITORS PER MONTH

43% OF ALL VISITORS ACCESS THE SITE **VIA THEIR MOBILE DEVICES**

700,000 NEWSLETTER SUBSCRIPTIONS **TO THE INBOXES OF**

300,000 UNIQUE INDIVIDUALS EVERY WEEK

# of dummies

Custom Publishing

Reach a global audience in any language by creating a solution that will differentiate you from competitors, amplify your message, and encourage customers to make a buying decision.

- Apps
- Books
- eBooks
- Video
- Audio
- Webinars

Brand Licensing & Content

Leverage the strength of the world's most popular reference brand to reach new audiences and channels of distribution.

For more information, visit **dummies.com/biz**

PERSONAL ENRICHMENT

Staying Sharp
9781119187790
USA $26.00
CAN $31.99
UK £19.99

Facebook
9781119179030
USA $21.99
CAN $25.99
UK £16.99

Guitar
9781119293354
USA $24.99
CAN $29.99
UK £17.99

Investing
9781119293347
USA $22.99
CAN $27.99
UK £16.99

Beekeeping
9781119310068
USA $22.99
CAN $27.99
UK £16.99

Digital Photography
9781119235606
USA $24.99
CAN $29.99
UK £17.99

Meditation
9781119251163
USA $24.99
CAN $29.99
UK £17.99

Pregnancy
9781119235491
USA $26.99
CAN $31.99
UK £19.99

Samsung Galaxy S7
9781119279952
USA $24.99
CAN $29.99
UK £17.99

iPhone
9781119283133
USA $24.99
CAN $29.99
UK £17.99

Crocheting
9781119287117
USA $24.99
CAN $29.99
UK £16.99

Nutrition
9781119130246
USA $22.99
CAN $27.99
UK £16.99

PROFESSIONAL DEVELOPMENT

Windows 10
9781119311041
USA $24.99
CAN $29.99
UK £17.99

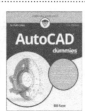
AutoCAD
9781119255796
USA $39.99
CAN $47.99
UK £27.99

Excel 2016
9781119293439
USA $26.99
CAN $31.99
UK £19.99

QuickBooks 2017
9781119281467
USA $26.99
CAN $31.99
UK £19.99

macOS Sierra
9781119280651
USA $29.99
CAN $35.99
UK £21.99

LinkedIn
9781119251132
USA $24.99
CAN $29.99
UK £17.99

Windows 10
9781119310563
USA $34.00
CAN $41.99
UK £24.99

SharePoint 2016
9781119181705
USA $29.99
CAN $35.99
UK £21.99

Fundamental Analysis
9781119263593
USA $26.99
CAN $31.99
UK £19.99

Networking
9781119257769
USA $29.99
CAN $35.99
UK £21.99

Office 2016
9781119293477
USA $26.99
CAN $31.99
UK £19.99

Office 365
9781119265313
USA $24.99
CAN $29.99
UK £17.99

Salesforce.com
9781119239314
USA $29.99
CAN $35.99
UK £21.99

Coding
9781119293323
USA $29.99
CAN $35.99
UK £21.99

dummies.com

dummies
A Wiley Brand

CPSIA information can be obtained
at www.ICGtesting.com
Printed in the USA
BVHW010752240220
573140BV00007B/212